Criminal Law

ASPEN COLLEGE SERIES

Criminal Law
CORE CONCEPTS

G. LARRY MAYS, PHD
Regents Professor Emeritus
Criminal Justice Department
New Mexico State University

JEREMY BALL, JD, PHD
Chair and Associate Professor
Criminal Justice Department
Boise State University

LAURA WOODS FIDELIE, JD, MBA
Associate Professor
Criminal Justice Department
Midwestern State University

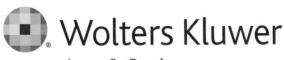
Wolters Kluwer
Law & Business

Published by Wolters Kluwer Law & Business in New York.

Wolters Kluwer Law & Business serves customers worldwide with CCH, Aspen Publishers, and Kluwer Law International products. (www.wolterskluwerlb.com)

To contact Customer Service, e-mail customer.service@wolterskluwer.com, call 1-800-234-1660, fax 1-800-901-9075, or mail correspondence to:

Wolters Kluwer Law & Business
Attn: Order Department
PO Box 990
Frederick, MD 21705

Printed in the United States of America.

1 2 3 4 5 6 7 8 9 0

ISBN 978-1-4548-4127-2

Library of Congress Cataloging-in-Publication Data

Mays, G. Larry, author.
   Criminal law: core concepts / G. Larry Mays, PhD, Regents Professor Emeritus, Criminal Justice Department, New Mexico State University; Jeremy Ball, JD, PhD, Chair and Associate Professor, Criminal Justice Department, Boise State University; Laura Woods Fidelie, JD, MBA, Associate Professor, Criminal Justice Department, Midwestern State University.
     pages cm. — (Aspen college series)
   ISBN 978-1-4548-4127-2
   1. Criminal law — United States. I. Ball, Jeremy A., author. II. Fidelie, Laura Woods, author. III. Title.
   KF9219.M39 2014
   345.73 — dc23
                                                                    2013049243

SUSTAINABLE FORESTRY INITIATIVE

Certified Chain of Custody
At Least 20% Certified Forest Content

www.sfiprogram.org
SFI-01042

   SFI label applies to the text stock

About Wolters Kluwer Law & Business

Wolters Kluwer Law & Business is a leading global provider of intelligent information and digital solutions for legal and business professionals in key specialty areas, and respected educational resources for professors and law students. Wolters Kluwer Law & Business connects legal and business professionals as well as those in the education market with timely, specialized authoritative content and information-enabled solutions to support success through productivity, accuracy and mobility.

Serving customers worldwide, Wolters Kluwer Law & Business products include those under the Aspen Publishers, CCH, Kluwer Law International, Loislaw, ftwilliam.com and MediRegs family of products.

CCH products have been a trusted resource since 1913, and are highly regarded resources for legal, securities, antitrust and trade regulation, government contracting, banking, pension, payroll, employment and labor, and healthcare reimbursement and compliance professionals.

Aspen Publishers products provide essential information to attorneys, business professionals and law students. Written by preeminent authorities, the product line offers analytical and practical information in a range of specialty practice areas from securities law and intellectual property to mergers and acquisitions and pension/benefits. Aspen's trusted legal education resources provide professors and students with high-quality, up-to-date and effective resources for successful instruction and study in all areas of the law.

Kluwer Law International products provide the global business community with reliable international legal information in English. Legal practitioners, corporate counsel and business executives around the world rely on Kluwer Law journals, loose-leafs, books, and electronic products for comprehensive information in many areas of international legal practice.

Loislaw is a comprehensive online legal research product providing legal content to law firm practitioners of various specializations. Loislaw provides attorneys with the ability to quickly and efficiently find the necessary legal information they need, when and where they need it, by facilitating access to primary law as well as state-specific law, records, forms and treatises.

ftwilliam.com offers employee benefits professionals the highest quality plan documents (retirement, welfare and non-qualified) and government forms (5500/PBGC, 1099 and IRS) software at highly competitive prices.

MediRegs products provide integrated health care compliance content and software solutions for professionals in healthcare, higher education and life sciences, including professionals in accounting, law and consulting.

Wolters Kluwer Law & Business, a division of Wolters Kluwer, is headquartered in New York. Wolters Kluwer is a market-leading global information services company focused on professionals.

To Brenda, for her many years of love and support and for buying the lie that this is the last book that I'm ever going to do.

—GLM

To Marcy for her patience and support in everything I do but, in particular, this project. To Jackson for offering moments of distraction and not having a clue about all of this (he's 7), which puts everything into perspective. Love you both!

—JB

To Tony, for his unconditional love and for always supporting me in everything I have ever wanted to pursue. To Guy, my mentor and confidante. Your advice, your listening ear, and our time together are some of my life's best memories.

—LWF

SUMMARY OF CONTENTS

CONTENTS

CHAPTER 9

Inchoate Crimes

CHAPTER 12

Punishment and Sentencing

Why another criminal law book? You might be asking yourself that question and the authors of this book asked themselves the same question. The three of us have many years of experience teaching criminal law to both undergraduate and graduate students. As such, our desire was not to write *another* criminal law book but a *different* one. Therefore, we want to outline the principles that guided us through this process.

First, this book is designed for a one-term undergraduate course in substantive criminal law. The amount of material provided will be sufficient for programs operating on a semester system. Programs operating on shorter terms will still be able to cover all the material in the book but at a slightly accelerated pace.

Second, the book was originally conceived to be a "core" text. That is, our intention was to keep the focus on the foundational and fundamental aspects of the criminal law that are essential for undergraduate student understanding. Some of the early law books used in undergraduate criminal justice programs were law school texts that were heavy on cases and comments and light on structure and general foundational content. These texts were often incomprehensible for undergraduate students. Furthermore, some of the core or essentials books currently available are trimmed-down versions of longer texts by authors who also have more comprehensive books. By contrast, this book was written by design to be an original manuscript focusing on the core elements of criminal law. Based on our collective teaching experience, we determined that it was better for students to know a smaller number of things extremely well than it was for them to learn a large quantity of information only superficially.

Third (and related to our second principle), many of the current undergraduate criminal law books are heavily dependent on court cases. Students are left to wade through a jungle of cases in order to discover the principles of criminal law being discussed. We believe that students continue to struggle with the complex, bewildering, and arcane nature of the criminal law because of the way the subject is presented. Therefore, we were convinced that what was needed was a more student-oriented, user-friendly book that would serve the needs of traditional undergraduate students along with the adult learners who participate in many of the online programs that exist.

More and more, students need the ability to pare down to the detail they need to know without having to read a volume of superfluous material that is simply illustrative, is often incomprehensible to them, and frequently fails to address the core of what they need to learn. This text uses examples and cases to their optimal level without overdoing it. To achieve the student-oriented, user-friendly approach, our goal was to present fewer cases (knowing that professors often will supplement with cases they have used before and are comfortable teaching) to minimize student confusion and maximize student learning.

Fourth, many current criminal law books try to be all things to all people by discussing cases or laws from many different states (again, something we anticipate most instructors will supplement with their own information). For example, some states aggravate a burglary charge if the offense is committed at night while some states do not aggravate the charge. Those professors whose states aggravate the charge can speak about the issue in a supplemental way rather than having students wade through the material on their own, which often results in confusion. As a result, textbooks often become encyclopedic in their presentation, and students are left wondering what all of the complex (and occasionally contradictory) information means. We have chosen to focus our presentation and discussion on the *Model Penal Code*. While not all states have adopted the *Model Penal Code*, many have incorporated significant segments into their most recent criminal law revisions. This allows us to discuss the criminal law from the most fundamental perspective possible and gives students the opportunity to develop a strong foundation of knowledge about core criminal law concepts. This approach also gives individual instructors the ability to bring in their own state examples. However, there are situations where the *Model Penal Code* is silent or where there are newly emerging areas of law (such as cybercrimes) that were not addressed when the *MPC* was drafted. In those cases we have chosen to bring in additional statutes, cases, and other legal materials to address these issues.

Fifth, as the table of contents shows, many of the topics covered are common to all criminal law books (property crimes, homicide, etc.). However, this book has several unique features:

- Chapter 6 covers a broader range of sexual offenses and behaviors than covered in some books.
- Chapter 7, which deals with street crime, is unique to this text. While many books talk about these crimes, none that we are aware of group these offenses into a coherent discussion of the types of offenses most likely to be encountered by agents of the criminal justice system.

- Chapter 8 brings into focus the world of cybercrime, a topic of increasing concern by criminal justice agencies at the local, state, and federal levels.
- The discussion of defenses (Chapters 9 and 10) has been moved to a point later in the text than what is commonly followed. We firmly believe that students should understand substantive offenses before they can fully comprehend the defenses to those crimes
- Chapter 12 on sentencing is also unique to this book. While some texts have limited discussions of sentencing, none of which we are aware devote a full chapter to this very important topic

Finally, our desire from the very beginning of this project has been to present the criminal law in a way that it is interesting and intellectually stimulating for students. We firmly believe that the greatest disservice we can do to students is to bore them with material that we find interesting. Thus, our ultimate guiding principle was to produce an intellectually engaging, yet intellectually accessible book that would help students acquire a real, working understanding of the criminal law.

ACKNOWLEDGMENTS

Anyone who has ever written a book knows that there are many people responsible for the final product (although, ultimately, the authors take the blame for anything that is incorrect). We want to begin by acknowledging the many ways our editor, David Herzig, contributed to this project. His encouragement, suggestions, and unwavering faith in us made this book possible. Next, but certainly no less important, Elizabeth (Betsy) Kenny shepherded us through the minefield of reviews, revisions, and the production process. Her kindness, patience, and good nature were certainly appreciated at times when frustration levels were high. We would also like to acknowledge the comments and suggestions provided by the reviewers. They helped make this a better manuscript. The reviewers for this volume included:

Lisa Clayton, College of Southern Nevada
Mike Hemond, Champlain College
James Kane Record, California University of Pennsylvania
Tricia Martland, Roger Williams University
John Newton, University of Georgia
Susan Ritter, University of Texas–Brownsville
Vidisha Barua Worley, University of North Texas at Dallas
Glenn Zuern, Albany State University

We would like to thank the American Law Institute for permission to reprint the following:

Model Penal Code © 1985 by the American Law Institute. Reproduced with permission. All rights reserved.

Finally, we want to thank the many undergraduate and graduate students who have taken our classes over the years. In many ways they have taught us as much as we have taught them.

G. Larry Mays
Jeremy Ball
Laura Woods Fidelie

Criminal Law

Overview of Criminal Law

CHAPTER 1

LEARNING OBJECTIVES

After reading this chapter you should be able to:

1. Describe the origins and features of the creation of law
2. Distinguish between civil law and criminal law and between substantive and procedural criminal law
3. Explain the theories of punishment
4. Describe the sources of criminal law in the American criminal justice system
5. Analyze different crimes as either *mala in se* or *mala prohibita*
6. Explain the origins and application of the right to privacy
7. Explain the different standards of review for the right of equal protection

INTRODUCTION

What is "law?" Is it a list of dos and don'ts? Is law simply a guideline that we use to adapt our behavior? Where does law originate? What is "criminal" law? What are the basic features of criminal law compared to civil law? Are there limits to the law's expansive authority?

These are the questions this chapter will address. Notice, though, that we did not say "answer" because with law there is rarely a clear answer to any question presented. But, we will address these questions and provide tools for you to answer them.

First, we will examine the question of "what is law?" This inquiry is about law as an overarching concept. As a basis for the rest of this book, it is important to understand what law means in the broadest sense. In order to understand what "law" is, we must explore different perspectives of law and justice, examining the different perspectives of where law originates, what the basic features are, and how the law is utilized.

Second, we will address the question of "what is *criminal* law?" Criminal law is one subset of law in its most expansive form, and it will be distinguished from civil law. This chapter will also address different ways to categorize criminal law—some techniques for categorizing criminal law are more concrete than others. We will also briefly address punishment as a major distinction between criminal law and other types of law.

Third, after discussing the "what is" question, we will explore the sources of criminal law. That is, where can we find criminal law or what factors impact the practice and enforcement of criminal law? Although we leave it to political science to address the process by which laws are made, we will briefly outline the different sources of law.

Finally, we will address particular limits to the authority that criminal law has. Criminal law is not limitless; therefore, based on elements of due process, there are limits to the definitions of criminal law, the application of criminal law, and the punishment prescribed by criminal law.

WHAT IS LAW?

There are essentially three areas of debate in answering the question "what is law": (1) origin of law, (2) relativity of law, and (3) the application features of law. Philosophers, sociologists, and legal scholars have disagreed with where we, as a community, get notions of right versus wrong in the law. Do we receive law from a higher power? Do we receive it from within ourselves as a sense of evolutionary innateness? Do we simply create it as a sociological institution?

Scholars have also disagreed with the universal nature of the law in determining right from wrong. In other words, does law define an absolute right and wrong, or is the law defined relative to the social environment of the community? Some argue that law, as a concept, describes universal rights and wrongs. Even though the law changes, it changes simply because humans are infallible in representing what the law should be. Others argue that the law is relative to the circumstances of the time in an ever-changing moral society.

Finally, scholars disagree on the features of law. Is law a list of dos and don'ts? Is law a social mechanism to mold social cohesion or to create community good? Is the written law merely a written representation of some greater social norm system that is already in place? Further discussion about select scholars is referred to in Box 1.1.

Box 1.1 SELECT PHILOSOPHICAL AND SOCIOLOGICAL PERSPECTIVES ABOUT LAW[1]

Hammurabi, King of Babylon
- Origin of Law—law comes from the Sun God (e.g., **natural law**)
- Relativity of Law—law explains a universal truth
- Features of the Law—first known written code in eighteenth century B.C. (or B.C.E.) (Gaines and Miller 2009); retributive; set of judgments for particular cases

Plato
- Origin of Law—law comes from **theory of forms**, which are immaterial essences that bring forth senses of right from wrong (e.g., natural law)
- Relativity of Law—law explains a universal truth
- Features of the Law—state is virtuous; only the state can regulate behavior; without law, there is chaos and anarchy

Aristotle
- Origin of Law—law is innately defined within the human race (e.g., natural law)
- Relativity of Law—law explains a universal truth
- Features of the Law—law is an egalitarian system in which rulers were even subservient to the law, utilitarian system of justice

St. Thomas Aquinas
- Origin of Law—law is defined by a higher power (e.g., natural law)
- Relativity of Law—law explains a universal truth

Natural Law: principle governing behavior generated from an external force

Theory of Forms: immaterial essences that bring forth senses of right from wrong

---

1. Most of this material is derived from Walsh & Hemmens (2011).

• Features of the Law—utilitarian system of justice, law can be a coercive tool to use for the greater good

Thomas Hobbes
• Origin of Law—law is defined by society through the social contract (e.g., **positive law**)
• Relativity of Law—law explains a relative truth
• Features of the Law—supports legal realism where law is studied as applied; developed the **social contract** where citizens give up a little freedom in exchange for the state protecting them

John Locke
• Origin of Law—law is defined by society through sociological environments
• Relativity of Law—law explains a relative truth
• Features of the Law—human behavior is inherently good and a result of environmental experiences (e.g., blank slates), free and independent from the sovereignty, developed a foundation for the civil liberties we know today

Max Weber
• Origin of Law—law is defined by society through sociological environment
• Relativity of Law—law explains a relative truth
• Features of the Law—developed typology of legal decision making (rational/irrational; formal/substantive); law is different than other rule-following behavior

Emile Durkheim
• Origin of Law—law is defined by society through social interactions
• Relativity of Law—law explains a relative truth
• Features of the Law—law regulates **social solidarity** (e.g., sense of belonging to the community); mechanical solidarity (preindustrialized society where face-to-face interactions created sense of belonging); organic solidarity (industrialized society where specialization created a sense of belonging) (see Durkheim 1997)

Positive Law: principle governing behavior that is defined by society rather than an external force

Social Contract: an agreement between citizens and the state where citizens give up some freedom in exchange for the state protecting them

Social Solidarity: sense of belonging to the community

WHAT IS CRIMINAL LAW?

Criminal law is a subset of the larger concept of "law." There are specific features of criminal law that set it apart from other areas of law—mainly, civil law and regulatory law. It can be best described as having the state's full weight behind it, defining crimes, punishments, and defenses. It is first important to identify the unique differences between criminal law and civil law.

The first difference between criminal law and civil law is that criminal law is a violation against the state whereas civil law is a violation against an individual, corporation, or government agency. As a general rule, the case names are different. In criminal law the case name is the state—or something similar—versus the individual/group; in civil law the case name is the individual/group versus another individual/group.

The form of redress in criminal law is punishment often resulting in the loss of freedom either in terms of incarceration or probation. The redress for civil law is often in the form of financial remedy to compensate the injured party. Although civil lawsuits can include "punitive" damages—similar to fines in criminal law—in most cases the damages provide compensation for injury to person or property.

Punishment

One of the unique characteristics of criminal law is the state's ability to punish the defendant. The ability of the state to restrict the freedom of the guilty party (the defendant) is unmatched in any other type of law. In criminal law, punishment must follow several criteria in order to be valid. The first criterion is that punishment should include a certain amount of discomfort (Bentham 1952). That is, a rational approach to punishment is most effective where punishment's pain will overcome the pleasure in committing the crime. Second, punishment must be prescribed; it must be formally enacted either by statute or administrative guidelines. Third, the administration of punishment must be completed intentionally and not by an accidental occurrence or by chance. It must be *certain* which is related to the prescription of punishment. Finally, punishment must be enacted by the state. American society does *not* support militant behavior and self-redress (Powell 1966). The Fifth and Fourteenth Amendments of the U.S. Constitution protect a citizen's due process rights. Self-redress violates due process; therefore, punishment enacted by the state gives its citizens their due process. Chapter 12 will outline punishment and the variety of reasons for punishment in more detail later.

Categorizing Criminal Law

As we will discuss in Chapter 12, retribution outlines blameworthiness of the offender to determine deservedness of punishment. This is best done through a process of categorizing or grading the severity of crimes. Since criminal law is a substantive law—that is, it defines crimes, punishment, and defenses—the categorization of crimes is mostly driven by statutory language. Given that criminal law is derived from criminal statutes, it is easily tracked via categories and strict organization so that the law can be applied fairly and efficiently. There are many ways we can organize criminal law, but only three patterns are discussed here: (1) felony, misdemeanor, and violation; (2) *mala in se* and *malum prohibitum*; and (3) subject.

One of the most widely used organizational tools in criminal law is the crime's grade—that is, the difference between felony, misdemeanor, and violation. There are significant differences with these labels. For felony offenses the state can sentence the guilty to more than a year of incarceration and, in some cases, death; whereas for misdemeanors the state can sentence someone only to one year or less of incarceration. Violations (e.g., traffic violations) are often merely fineable offenses.

A second way to categorize criminal laws is by the traditional approach of *mala in se* and *mala prohibita* presented by Raffaele Garofalo (see Walsh and Hemmens 2011). Crimes that are **mala in se** offenses are those that are inherently evil. *Mala in se* offenses are those that, across time, place, and cultures, are considered evil, transcending cultural and generational senses of justice. The typical offenses viewed as *mala in se* offenses include homicide and rape.

Mala in Se:
evil in itself or inherently evil/wrongdoing

Crimes that are considered **mala prohibita** are offenses that are *not* inherently evil but have been socially defined as evil or prohibited evil. *Mala prohibita* offenses are defined by communities as wrongful and these can differ between communities. Such offenses are articulated by a community's definition of what is wrong based on their need to preserve justice (Walsh and Hemmens 2011). For example, medical marijuana use is acceptable in certain states (e.g., Alaska, California, District of Columbia, Maine, and Rhode Island) but not in others (e.g., Florida, Idaho, and Texas). Another example of the *mala prohibita* concept is the debate surrounding same-sex marriage. Some states (e.g., Connecticut, Iowa, and New York) have defined same-sex marriage as not wrongful, whereas the majority of states have not accepted such unions.[2] There are many other examples of *mala prohibita* offenses.

Mala Prohibita:
prohibited evil/wrongdoing as defined by the community

---

2. At the time of writing the manuscript of this textbook, two U.S. Supreme Court cases handed down opinions addressing same-sex marriages—one case regarding a federal law and another case regarding a state law. *United States v. Windsor*, 570 U.S. _____ (2013) addressed the Defense of Marriage Act. In part, this law defines marriage as only between a man and a woman and guarantees certain federal benefits and protections of heterosexual marital relationships. The Court decided that each state is to determine to whom to offer marriage licenses. Similarly, the Supreme Court heard *Hollingsworth v. Perry*, 570 U.S. _____ (2013) about a particular state's definition of marriage. However, in this case, a federal

---

Box 1.2   YOU DECIDE: IS CHILD ABUSE *MALA IN SE* OR *MALA PROHIBITA*?

We engage in a discussion about whether particular offenses are *mala in se* or *mala prohibita*. The basic definition of child abuse is intentionally harming a child. Larry and Monique have had a strained relationship since they have moved in together. Oftentimes, they take it out on each other emotionally and it has recently elevated to physical slaps on the face and head. A few years ago they had a son they call Curly because of his curly hair. Recently, in their frustration, they have started hitting Curly in the same manner they have hit each other. The basic definition of child abuse is intentionally harming a child, which is one of the most despised offenses of all criminal law. Is this a *mala in se* offense? Is this activity evil across all times, places, and cultures? Could one define this as merely disciplining one's child? Is the action directed at the spouse a *mala in se* offense? The penal code for Nigeria states that men can beat their wives so long as it does not cause any "grievous harm" (i.e., loss of sight, facial disfiguration, or other life-endangering issues) (Nigeria 1998). Does this mean that spousal abuse may simply be *mala prohibita*?

So, the question is, which offenses are truly *mala in se* offenses and which are *mala prohibita*. You could make the argument that there are no *mala in se* offenses (see Gray 1995). In discussing whether a wrongful act is an "inherent" or a "prohibited" evil, one must turn to whether this act has always been considered wrong or evil at all times, in all communities, or in all cultures. Box 1.2 illustrates the tension between *mala in se* and *mala prohibita*.

A final category tool that can be used is definition by subject; this is the tool we will use for this text. Criminal statutes are usually organized and cataloged by subject, and the first, and arguably most common, category includes personal crimes. This category deals with any offense that involves a physical act against a person. The most notable and most serious of personal crimes is homicide (see Chapter 5). Other acts that fall in this category are sexual offenses, battery/assault, kidnapping, and false imprisonment (see Chapter 6). Robbery (and extortion) is a unique offense because it can be labeled as a personal crime and property crime. We place robbery and extortion in Chapter 4 as property crimes.

The second type of crime by subject is property crime. Although the most interesting category for students is likely to be personal

---

district court had already overruled Proposition 8, which defined a valid marriage as only between a man and a woman. After this finding, state officials did not appeal the case. *Hollingsworth* v. *Perry*, therefore, is about whether citizen supporters have standing to make a claim to the Supreme Court. The Court decided that they did not have standing since the state officials decided not to appeal, which, indirectly, supports the district court's finding that limiting marriage between a man and a woman as unconstitutional.

crimes, property crimes (and street crimes discussed in Chapter 7) compose the majority of cases within the criminal justice system — over 16,000 cases tried in the U.S. District Court alone in 2008 involved property offenses (Bureau of Justice Statistics 2008). However, most of the crimes portrayed in crime dramas on television or in the movies are personal crimes.

The third type of criminal offenses can be classified as street crime (see Chapter 7). In this textbook, we define "street crime" as any offense that is not typically encountered as a property crime (e.g., larceny, robbery) but is also not encountered as a personal crime (e.g., homicide, rape, assault). Street crimes also occur in public rather than in more private settings and are usually "blue collar" offenses committed by the lower to lower-middle classes (Katz 1979). Examples of these crimes are drug offenses, alcohol offenses, prostitution, and low-level gambling.

The fourth type of crime is white collar crime (see Chapter 8), which typically occurs in the corporate world rather than on the streets. Until recently, these crimes did not have a broad awareness by the general public, but recent cases involving Martha Stewart, Enron, and Bernard Madoff have all gained great media attention in negatively impacting American and global economies (Amdur and Oei 2004). White collar crimes include insider trading, embezzlement, and price fixing, and they are often financially motivated (Coleman 1985).

A final type of crime involves offenses committed against the state. For these offenses, the most important aspect is to maintain order and safety. Offenses such as terrorism, espionage, and criminal escape will be discussed in Chapter 8. Sometimes, the state must keep order to retain the freedoms and rights of its citizens and the fair and expeditious administration of justice. These offenses include sedition, obstruction of justice, and contempt of court.

There are several ways to categorize criminal law. A few have been discussed here but certainly these are not the only tools to organize criminal law. Although these tools are intended to illustrate the most typical cases, they are not intended to be an exhaustive list. It is important, now, to address the foundation of American criminal law by outlining its sources.

SOURCES OF CRIMINAL LAW

From a philosophical perspective, we can now better answer the questions "what is law?" and "what is criminal law?" The next question, from a practical standpoint, is "where can one *find* criminal

---

Box 1.3 SOURCES OF LAW

Common Law
- Developed in England
- It started as judge-made law where precedent ruled so that the law was consistently applied across England
- Today, the common law has either been ratified legislatively or used in case law

Legislative Laws
- Constitutions
  - Define government authority and rights of its citizens
- Statutes and Ordinances
  - Define crimes, punishments, and defenses
  - *Model Penal Code*

Case Law
- Judge-made law based on precedent (past rulings)

---

law?" As the study of criminal law is one of the definitions of crimes, punishments, and defenses, it is vital to know where to find these. There are several sources of criminal law: *common law*, legislative laws (constitutions and statutes), and case law. Box 1.3 summarizes these sources of law.

Today, most criminal law is found in statutes (and ordinances). Statutes are constructed either at the state level or at the federal level, whereas ordinances are constructed at the local level (usually, these are cities). In a few cases, constitutions may also outline crimes, punishments, or defenses, but, for the most part, constitutions place limitations on the criminal law rather than offer definitions. However, many of state and federal statutes and constitutions are derived from common law.

Common Law

One of the more important sources of law is the common law. Our American law was derived, at least in part, from the English common law, which was slowly articulated from the spread of the Roman Empire from the sixth century until the mid-twelfth century during King Henry II's reign (Walsh and Hemmens 2011). At that time, there were different rules and traditions in different parts of the English jurisdiction until **common law** was instituted. At this time, the law became "common" to every case under English jurisdiction. Judges started to make decisions on cases by relying on similar cases decided by other judges. The choice to decide a case based on past

Common Law:
a source of law initiated in England to support principles governing behavior that was consistently applied across the country

judicial rulings is referred to as **precedent**. Without any other distinguishing factor, a judge *must* follow the rulings of past decisions in the current case. That is, the doctrine of *stare decisis* (let the decision stand) legally binds judges to follow precedent. There are a few mechanisms in place, however, when a judge can avoid using precedents, including: overruling previous precedents, distinguishing the facts of current case from previous precedent, and legislative action (see Spaeth and Segal 1999).

Precedent: rulings of past decisions governing decisions on current cases

Stare Decisis: binding principle that requires a judge to rule a current case based on precedent

Contrasted with the implementation of common law, which was mostly handed down by word of mouth—only later written down via summary of the law—today common law has been adopted by legislative action or case law. There are definitions of crimes today in criminal statutes that have—at least in part—similar language today as they did during the common law period. For example, elements of common law homicide, rape, burglary, self-defense, and consent defense are found in today's statutes. Some of the details, though, are no longer applied in most state statutes. For example, common law burglary required that the criminal act occur at nighttime. Most states have eliminated this requirement, and for the other states that still include this element, it is a requirement to aggravate the charge to a more serious charge and is no longer a necessary requirement to prove the base crime of burglary.

Legislative Action

When we were forming as a nation, a break from the common law tradition emerged, igniting the power of the federal legislature. Much of today's criminal law is constructed using legislative action. The substantive law—the focus of this textbook—is written in statutes that make up one part of the larger category of legislative action. The other category of legislation—constitutions—identifies the power of the government and the rights of its citizens. Much of procedural law—not the focus of this textbook—is developed in the case law, which is outlined later.

The first legislative action that offers a source of criminal law is state and federal statutes. As we will discuss in Chapter 2, each crime is defined by a common structure called **elements** arranged by state or federal jurisdictions. The *United States Code* is a unique set of statutes that focuses on matters of federal concern such as the safety of our government leaders, interstate drug crimes, and matters of anticompetitive practices in commercial businesses. It is important to note, though, that the vast number of criminal cases in the United States arise within *state* criminal justice systems. Because different states have different interests and political environments, definitions

Elements: points that must be proven in order to establish that a person has committed a crime

of crimes, punishments, and defenses can be very different; however, there are basic similarities among the states. First, all states' criminal codes include the most serious crimes such as murder, rape, burglary, and larceny. Second, most states allow for the most common defenses in their code such as insanity, self-defense, and duress. Finally, most state criminal codes offer imprisonment (and some use the death penalty) for the most serious criminal offenses.

Since states have different needs and political environments, there are some key differences in their criminal codes as well. First, the construction of the elements required for a particular crime can be different between different state jurisdictions. For example, New Hampshire defines a class A felony burglary as the unlawful entrance occurring *at night* (NH LXII, 635:1), whereas Indiana does not include a nighttime requirement in any of the classes of burglary offenses (Indiana Code 35-43-2-1).

Second, the requirements for proving a particular defense may be different between states. Thus, what a defendant must prove in an affirmative defense might be different based on the location and political environment of a particular state. Finally, the selection of the type and length of punishment associated with a particular crime can be different between state jurisdictions. Sometimes, as we will discuss in Chapter 12, the system of punishment can be different; some states rely on a more indeterminate system of punishment where judges have greater latitude in determining the sentence, while other states rely on a more determinate system of punishment where judicial discretion is significantly limited (Spohn 2009). Additionally, some states allow a guilty defendant to be sentenced to death, whereas other states do not. Thirty-two states and the federal government offer the death penalty as their most severe punishment (Death Penalty Information Center n.d.).

Since state jurisdictions differ in the definitions of crimes, defenses, and punishments, in this text we will focus primarily on the *Model Penal Code* (*MPC*) published by the American Law Institute. "The American Law Institute is the leading independent organization in the United States producing scholarly work to clarify, modernize, and otherwise improve the law" (American Law Institute 2011). In 1962, the American Law Institute created a criminal code that was to be used as a basis for jurisdictions to develop their own criminal statutes. Over 40 different states now use the *MPC* to influence their own criminal statutes that codify—in part—the common law traditions of criminal acts. Since this textbook is not limited to a certain geographical locale and has a national audience, discussing one state's definition will likely leave out 49 other states. Therefore, by using the *MPC* as a starting point, students will know how to proceed in learning about their particular state's own definition. Nevertheless, there will be times that we must avoid reliance on the *MPC* due to developments of legal standards after the creation of the *MPC*, but the *Code* is a good place to start.

Local ordinances are a second legislative action that is similar to state and federal statutes; although similar in form and authority, the ranges of severity are different. Local ordinances—usually at the city level—focus more on local concerns. For example, a particular area may have higher amounts of gang-related activity; therefore, a municipality might draft specific ordinances to address gang-related activity that is not as prevalent in other areas. Or, a city might enforce rights-of-way for bicyclists or enforce an antinoise ordinance.

A final legislative action that usually defines government authority or structure or limits governmental authority is referred to as a constitution. The U.S. Constitution articulates the powers and authorities of the branches of government in its Articles but outlines individual civil liberties in its Amendments. These civil liberties are important for criminal law because they place limits on the extent to which the state can define and enforce criminal laws.

State constitutions operate similarly to the federal Constitution with some minor differences. First, state constitutions are more inclined to offer more definitions of crimes, punishments, and defenses. For example, the only crime articulated in the federal Constitution is treason. Second, the level to which state constitutions protect individual civil liberties can be more expansive. For example, 13 states and the District of Columbia have, as of 2013, expanded marriage laws to same-sex couples even though this liberty is not secured by the U.S. Constitution (National Conference of State Legislatures n.d.).[3] Additionally, state constitutions typically are not as difficult to amend as the U.S. Constitution. Finally, victims are much more likely to have their own civil liberties defined in state constitutions compared to the federal Constitution.

Case Law

A final source of criminal law is case law; these are rulings in appellate cases addressing a particular issue asserted by one party or the other. Although most of the substantive criminal law is generated from legislative action—mostly in state criminal statutes—case law is used to interpret either the language or the meaning of these statutes or the violations of civil liberties these statutes present. The previously defined common law traditions of *precedence* and *stare decisis* are often applied in case law today.

---

3. Again, the list of states may expand based on the recent Supreme Court decisions listed in footnote 2.

In order to understand the case law presented in this textbook, there are a few operations to note here. The cases we present are abridged and, therefore, do not include the entire majority opinion. Most of the cases presented in this textbook also do not include concurring or dissenting opinions. Generally speaking case law is written from cases that have been appealed; case law is *not* generated from trial transcripts.

The first operation to understand is that, for case law to be created, one party must assert that a violation of a legal standard had occurred and that the specific appellate court believes this potential violation to be significant enough to hear the arguments. Second, case law follows a certain level of authority and the topmost authority is held as the legal standard for that particular issue. If a case is appealed to the U.S. Supreme Court, the Court holds the topmost authority and, therefore, its decision is held as the legal standard for that particular issue. Finally, it is most important when you read case law that you understand the types of written opinions given—opinions are simply written statements of the court's ruling. The **majority opinion** is the ruling decided by the majority members of the appellate court, and it addresses the issue that was claimed. The **concurring opinion** is the legal opinion of the justices who agree with the majority opinion but disagree with the legal reasoning used. The **dissenting opinion** is the legal opinion of the justices who disagree with the ultimate ruling of the majority opinion. Both the concurring opinions and dissenting opinions are informative but are not used as precedent upon which other cases can rely. Box 1.4 outlines the relevant parts of a legal opinion.

Majority Opinion: an appellate court legal opinion based on the ruling of the majority members

Concurring Opinion: the legal opinion by appellate court justices who agree with the majority opinion but disagree with the legal reasoning used

Dissenting Opinion: the legal opinion of the justices who disagree with the holding of the majority opinion

---

Box 1.4 PARTS OF A LEGAL OPINION

- Fact Summary—summary of the most pertinent facts for the issue asserted
- Issue—the question asserted by one making the appeal and additional questions by the justices of the appellate court
- Judgment—the history of decisions of the lower courts from trial until the present appellate court
  - Affirm—current court agrees with lower court's ruling
  - Overrule—current court disagrees with lower court's ruling and rules accordingly
  - Remands—current court disagrees with lower court's ruling but sends it back for the lower court to decide
- Holding—the court's answer(s) to the question(s) presented
- Rationale—the logic and reasoning upon which the answer(s) were decided

Given that the criminal law has multiple sources, it can be confusing that there are other sources of criminal law, which are actually sources of *limitations* of criminal law. The next section identifies these limitations that are typically generated from the U.S. Constitution, common law, and case law. The next section will explore the history and rules associated with these limitations.

CONSTITUTIONAL LIMITATIONS TO CRIMINAL LAW

Criminal law is the codification of the state's authority to provide its citizens order and safety. Criminal law defines behavior that is unacceptable, what the punishment should be for unacceptable behavior, and what behaviors are excused or justified to avoid criminal liability. The question is, at what point does the state's authority end? At what point do the citizens' rights override the state's authority to pursue order and safety? For this reason, the courts have defined constitutional limits to the state's authority that are outlined here. Keep in mind, these limits are only related to the substantive criminal law. There are more limits related to procedural law that are not included here.

Principle of Legality

The **principle of legality** suggests that the state's authority in criminal law is limited to those acts that are already defined as illegal. A corollary to this general principle suggests that only the guilty can be punished. You cannot be punished by the state without the law already defining a punishment. Therefore, the principle of legality limits law enforcement since the law has to define the kinds of violations to enforce and the kinds of punishments to enact. The principle of legality is the foundation upon which other constitutional limits are based.

Through the Fifth Amendment to the U.S. Constitution and later incorporated to the states through the Fourteenth Amendment, citizens are granted **due process** of the law, which is at the core of the principle of legality. You might ask, "What is a good definition of due process?" The best definition is that due process is the process that is due to every citizen. Another way of describing due process is general fairness to all citizens that is owed to them in response to the assertion of the state's authority. In order for the principle of legality to be effective, one must have due process protected.

The U.S. Constitution mentions a few limitations on criminal law that specifically illustrates the principle of legality. In Article I, Section

Principle of Legality: provides that no one can be sanctioned with a criminal punishment unless there is a law that prohibits the conduct at the time that the actions took place

Due Process: individual liberty that gives citizens the process that is due to them

9, the U.S. Constitution says "No . . . ex post facto Law shall be passed." An *ex post facto* **law** is a law that is enforced retroactively. On Day 1, a citizen does a particular behavior that is not against the law on that day, but on Day 5 the state defines that behavior as illegal and prosecutes the citizen for the Day 1 behavior on Day 5, enforcing the law retroactively. This kind of process is specifically forbidden in Article 1, Section 9 of the U.S. Constitution.

Ex Post Facto Law: principle governing behavior that is enforced retroactively

There is one exception to the constitutional limitation of the state's use of *ex post facto* laws. If a law *benefits* citizens — that is, does not restrict behavior — then the state can retroactively enforce the law. For example, any economic stimulus laws that give tax credits or rebates for taxes already paid would be considered an *ex post facto* law. Certainly, no one is going to turn down money from the government if the state offers it merely because it violates a constitutional limitation on *ex post facto* laws.

One component of the principle of legality is to define laws clearly and understandably to the general public. A legal doctrine called "void for vagueness" is a constitutional limitation that illustrates this concept. The **void for vagueness doctrine** suggests that if a law is so loosely defined that "a person of ordinary intelligence" does not know what behaviors violate the law, then the law violates the individual's due process rights [see *State v. Holcombe*, 187 S.W.3d 496 (Tex. Crim. App. 2006)]. As a reminder, due process requires that citizens receive the process that is due to them and that they are treated with overall fairness. One component of this right is that citizens know which behaviors are illegal and which are not. Without knowing which actions are against the law, it is nearly impossible to give citizens the process that is due to them.

Void for Vagueness Doctrine: principle that voids a law that violates due process because it is so loosely defined that "a person of ordinary intelligence" does not know what behaviors violate the law

In order to evaluate whether a law should be voided for constitutional vagueness, one can apply the void for vagueness test. In this test, there are two questions. First, does the law fail to give adequate notice of what actions are prohibited (i.e., "fair notice")? The State must notify citizens about prohibited acts in a reasonable amount of time. Second, does the law invite arbitrary enforcement (i.e., "arbitrary application")? In other words, do the enforcement agents have an understanding of the law in a way where they can provide consistent enforcement of the law? However, caution should be noted because the void for vagueness doctrine does not restrict the authority of law enforcement in using reasonable discretion in making decisions. On the one hand, this doctrine applies to citizens who comply with the legal restrictions on their behavior; on the other hand, this doctrine applies to agents who enforce these legal restrictions. Box 1.5 articulates the specific prongs of the void for vagueness test.

Box 1.5   VOID FOR VAGUENESS TEST

A law violates due process if it:

- does not give adequate notice to citizens about what is criminal AND
- provides law enforcement the opportunity to apply the law arbitrarily

An example might help to illustrate the void for vagueness doctrine. James—a 47-year-old medical technician—likes to dance. While waiting in line for his vanilla latte at the local coffee house drive thru, he hears the car behind him playing the latest pop hit on the radio. He likes it so much that he starts to dance wildly. A recent law prohibits citizens from all behaviors that are "silly." The question, though, is does "silly" give citizens the due process they deserve? First, does it give fair notice about what behaviors are illegal? Does an ordinary, reasonably minded citizen know which behaviors are "silly" and against the law? Is dancing wildly to latest pop hit silly or not? Would James's age be a factor to contribute to his silliness? Second, do law enforcement officers know what "silly" means in accordance with enforcing the law? Or, does the law invite a law enforcement officer to attribute his or her own standards of what actions are prohibited? What one officer believes to be silly maybe different than another. Maybe the officer would never think to dance to a popular song in public like that. Because these two prongs of the test have been met, the "silly" law is voided for vagueness and is deemed to have violated James's right to due process and, therefore, it is unconstitutional.

Another limitation is the void for overbreadth doctrine. This doctrine is related to the principle of legality in that citizens must know what behavior is unlawful or not and preserves activities that are protected by the Bill of Rights and the sense of due process. The void for overbreadth doctrine suggests that if a law restricts a citizen's expression of a fundamental civil liberty, then the law is unconstitutional. The one exception relies on the state's overriding interest in limiting such behavior; if the state has a legitimate state interest, then it may limit citizens' behaviors that otherwise may be protected. For example, citizens have freedom of speech protected by the Bill of Rights in the U.S. Constitution, but this freedom can be limited if the expression threatens someone's life. More of these exceptions will be discussed in the next section addressing civil liberties as a limitation placed on criminal law.

Individual Liberties

Right to Free Expression

Key individual civil liberties are guaranteed by the U.S. Constitution and many state constitutions. These rights are balanced against the government's interest in keeping order and protecting its citizens from harm. Therefore, civil liberties play an important role in providing limitations to criminal law.

The first relevant civil liberty is citizens' First Amendment right to free expression through speech, petition, press, religion, and assembly. This freedom of "expression" is a freedom to "political" expression and cannot be limited without a legitimate state interest. In other words, the state *can* limit "commercial" speech. For example, the federal Food and Drug Administration (FDA) requires certain language on food and over-the-counter drugs that are sold. For example, all soda that is sold from a vendor is required to include items like caloric, ingredient, and nutritional information on its label. In this instance, the state *can* restrict certain language because it is "commercial" expression rather than "political" expression. Additionally, the state can restrict speech that is harmful to others, such as threatening speech or hate speech.

There are times where the right to free speech, though, can be limited, such as:

- Fighting words
- Obscenity
- Clear and present danger expression

First, political speech that is considered "fighting words" is not protected. Any political speech that is likely to provoke a violent response in other citizens is not protected by the First Amendment. Some would regard speech that spreads hate and is offensive to fit this exception; however, not all offensive speech is considered "fighting words." Even though the *Snyder* case, as outlined in Box 1.6, is a civil case—not criminal—it illustrates this struggle.

Box 1.6 THE RIGHT TO FREE SPEECH — EVEN IF OFFENSIVE

Snyder v. Phelps
131 S. Ct. 1207 (2011)

Chief Justice ROBERTS delivered the opinion of the Court.

A jury held members of the Westboro Baptist Church liable for millions of dollars in damages for picketing near a soldier's funeral service. The picket signs reflected the church's view that the United States is overly tolerant of sin and that God kills

American soldiers as punishment. The question presented is whether the First Amendment shields the church members from tort liability for their speech in this case.

On the day of the memorial service, the Westboro congregation members picketed on public land adjacent to public streets near . . . Matthew Snyder's funeral. The Westboro picketers carried signs that were largely the same at all three locations. They stated, for instance: "God Hates the USA/Thank God for 9/11," "America is Doomed," "Don't Pray for the USA," "Thank God for IEDs," "Thank God for Dead Soldiers," . . .

The church had notified the authorities in advance of its intent to picket at the time of the funeral, and the picketers complied with police instructions in staging their demonstration. The picketing took place within a 10- by 25-foot plot of public land adjacent to a public street, behind a temporary fence. . . . The Westboro picketers displayed their signs for about 30 minutes before the funeral began and sang hymns and recited Bible verses. None of the picketers entered church property or went to the cemetery. They did not yell or use profanity, and there was no violence associated with the picketing. . . .

In the Court of Appeals, Westboro's primary argument was that the church was entitled to judgment as a matter of law because the First Amendment fully protected Westboro's speech. The Court of Appeals agreed. . . .

Whether the First Amendment prohibits holding Westboro liable for its speech in this case turns largely on whether that speech is of public or private concern, as determined by all the circumstances of the case. . . . [R]estricting speech on purely private matters does not implicate the same constitutional concerns as limiting speech on matters of public interest: "[T]here is

no threat to the free and robust debate of public issues; there is no potential interference with a meaningful dialogue of ideas"; and the "threat of liability" does not pose the risk of "a reaction of self-censorship" on matters of public import (*Dun & Bradstreet*, 472 U.S. 749 at 760).

The "content" of Westboro's signs plainly relates to broad issues of interest to society at large, rather than matters of "purely private concern" (*Dun & Bradstreet*, 472 U.S. 749 at 759). . . . While these messages (i.e., the placards) may fall short of refined social or political commentary, the issues they highlight—the political and moral conduct of the United States and its citizens, the fate of our Nation, homosexuality in the military, and scandals involving the Catholic clergy—are matters of public import. The signs certainly convey Westboro's position on those issues, in a manner designed, unlike the private speech in *Dun & Bradstreet*, to reach as broad a public audience as possible. And even if a few of the signs—such as "You're Going to Hell" and "God Hates You"—were viewed as containing messages related to Matthew Snyder or the Snyders specifically, that would not change the fact that the overall thrust and dominant theme of Westboro's demonstration spoke to broader public issues.

Simply put, the church members had the right to be where they were. Westboro alerted local authorities to its funeral protest and fully complied with police guidance on where the picketing could be staged. The picketing was conducted under police supervision some 1,000 feet from the church, out of the sight of those at the church. The protest was not unruly; there was no shouting, profanity, or violence.

Given that Westboro's speech was at a public place on a matter of public concern, that speech is entitled to "special protection" under the First Amendment. Such speech cannot be restricted simply because it is upsetting or arouses contempt. "If there is a bedrock principle underlying the First Amendment, it is that the government may not prohibit the expression of an idea simply because society finds the idea itself offensive or disagreeable." (*Texas v. Johnson*, 491 U.S. 397 at 414).

The judgment of the United States Court of Appeals for the Fourth Circuit is affirmed.

---

1. Should right to free speech outweigh the peace one expects at a military funeral? Would it matter if it were a military funeral or not?
2. What kinds of restrictions were placed on the protest? Why were these restrictions put into place?
3. What is hate speech and why is the kind of speech in this case not hate speech?

The Westboro case signifies that public speech that offends individuals does not necessarily lead to its restriction. In this case, the political expression used was not fighting words; it also was not deemed as obscene even though offensive (which is the second limitation to the right of free expression). However, obscene expressions have been noted and restricted. But, what is obscene? How does one know a particular expression is obscene? As Justice Potter Stewart proclaimed in *Jacobellis v. Ohio*, 378 U.S. 184 (1964), "I know it when I see it." There have been many legal standards created in order to provide some context in determining whether a particular expression is obscene or not, and it is important to understand the historical development of such standards.

First, the *Hicklin* test [see *Regina v. Hicklin*, LR 3 QB 36 (1868)] suggests that if part of some literary material "depraves and corrupts those whose minds are open to such immoral influences and into whose hands a publication of this sort might fall," then the entire material is obscene and unlawful (n.p.). A second standard is the "dominant effect test." In *United States v. One Book Called "Ulysses" by James Joyce*, 72 F.2d 705 (2d Cir. 1934), the Supreme Court ruled that the isolated passage test in *Hicklin* was not appropriate; therefore, the Court applied the dominant effect test, which rules that the dominant effect of the material must be obscene for the entire material to be obscene.

The Supreme Court in *Roth v. United States*, 354 U.S. 476 (1957) initiated the current legal standard in determining obscenity that is now referred as the "tripartite test" [finalized in *Miller v. California*, 413 U.S. 15 (1973)]. In *Roth*, the Supreme Court

---

Box 1.7   TESTS OF OBSCENITY

- *Hicklin* test
  - If any part of the material is considered obscene, then the whole material is obscene
- Dominant Effect test
  - If the dominant effect of the material is considered obscene, then the whole material is obscene
- Tripartite test
  - If a reasonable person applying contemporary community standards would find the material
    - appeals to a morbid interest in sex AND
    - offensively portrays sexual conduct
  - lacks serious literary, artistic, political, and/or scientific value

---

established that if a reasonable person applying community standards would think that the dominant effect of the material—as a whole—had a tendency to excite lustful thoughts and its only appeal is to a shameful or morbid interest in sex, then the material was deemed obscene. The Supreme Court in *Miller* further developed the tripartite test (what we would identify as the "tripartite plus test") to include an assessment that the material must also lack serious literary, artistic, political, and scientific value. This tripartite test extends the standard beyond "I know it when I see it." Box 1.7 summarizes the tests of obscenity.

Another exception to right to free expression is when speech presents a "clear and present danger" to citizens' safety. In this exception, public safety is of paramount interest for the state to restrict political speech that, ordinarily, would be protected by the First Amendment. The most well-known example is yelling "Fire!" in a crowded movie theater when, in fact, there is no fire. The point with this example is that the expression of this speech creates a clear and present danger to the safety of the moviegoers.

Right to Privacy

Another individual liberty that is pertinent to criminal law is the right to privacy. Although citizens' right to privacy is more relevant to procedural criminal law than substantive criminal law, we will outline it here in terms of the type of conduct that has been defined as criminal in violation of the right to privacy. First, it is important to understand the constitutional foundations of the right to privacy. The right to privacy, which is likely recognized by all to be one of our most fundamental rights in the United States, is *not* specifically stated or enumerated in the U.S. Constitution or the Bill of Rights or other Amendments.

The Supreme Court did rule, though, that the right to privacy is implied in several constitutional Amendments [*Griswold v. Connecticut*, 381 U.S. 479 (1965)]. The right to privacy can find its origin in the Bill of Rights—more specifically, the First, Third, Fourth, and Ninth Amendments. The right to privacy has often been termed as the "right to be left alone." The First Amendment suggests that citizen can express themselves and should be left alone by the government. The Third Amendment finds that housing soldiers in private residences is a violation, and the government should leave citizens alone. The Fourth Amendment claims that citizens have the right against unreasonable searches and seizures, and the government should leave them alone. The Ninth Amendment concludes that even though a right is not enumerated in the Constitution or its Amendments, it does not mean that the right does not exist. Therefore, the right to privacy is very much alive even though it is not absolute.

There have been some prominent cases that have displayed legal discussion on the right to privacy. In *Griswold v. Connecticut*, the Supreme Court first enumerated rights to privacy in a very specific way—a married couple has a right to privacy to use contraception because the marital bed is sacred to marriage. Enforcement of such a law would invade the privacy rights afforded to married couples. The Supreme Court has also explored the right to privacy for non-married couples. Unlike the contraception law in *Griswold*, the law addressed in *Bowers v. Hardwick*, 478 U.S. 186 (1986) was a sodomy law. The Supreme Court decided that there was no fundamental right to privacy extending to private, consensual sexual activity among homosexuals. Seventeen years later, though, the Court in *Lawrence v. Texas* ruled on a similar issue as outlined in Box 1.8.

Box 1.8   THE RIGHT TO PRIVACY FOR HOMOSEXUAL COUPLES?

Lawrence v. Texas
539 U.S. 558 (2003)

Mr. Justice KENNEDY delivered the opinion of the Court.

In Houston, Texas, officers of the Harris County Police Department were dispatched to a private residence in response to a reported weapons disturbance. They entered an apartment where one of the petitioners, John Geddes Lawrence, resided. The officers observed Lawrence and another man, Tyron Garner, engaging in a sexual act.

The two petitioners were arrested and charged and convicted before a Justice of the Peace.

The complainants described their crime as "deviate sexual intercourse, namely anal sex, with a member of same sex (man)."

The facts in (*Bowers v. Hardwick*) had some similarities to the instant case. One difference between the two cases is that the Georgia statute prohibited the conduct whether or not the participants were of the same sex, while the Texas statute applies only to participants of the same sex. Hardwick was not prosecuted, but he brought an action in federal court to declare the state statute invalid (whereas the current defendant *was* prosecuted).

The laws involved in *Bowers* and here are statutes that purport to do no more than prohibit a particular sexual act. Their penalties and purposes, though, have more far-reaching consequences, touching upon the most private human conduct, sexual behavior, and in the most private of places, the home. The statutes do seek to control a personal relationship that, whether or not entitled to formal recognition in the law, is within the liberty of persons to choose without being punished as criminals.

This, as a general rule, should counsel against attempts by the State, or a court, to define the meaning of the relationship or to set its boundaries absent injury to a person or abuse of an institution the law protects. It suffices for us to acknowledge that adults may choose to enter upon this relationship in the confines of their homes and their own private lives and still retain their dignity as free persons. When sexuality finds overt expression in intimate conduct with another person, the conduct can be but one element in a personal bond that is more enduring. The liberty protected by the Constitution allows homosexual persons the right to make this choice.

At the outset it should be noted that there is no longstanding history in this country of laws directed at homosexual conduct as a distinct matter. Beginning in colonial times there were prohibitions of sodomy derived from the English criminal laws passed in the first instance by the Reformation Parliament of 1533. The English prohibition was understood to include relations between men and women as well as relations between men and men. Nineteenth-century commentators similarly read American sodomy as criminalizing certain relations between men and women and between men and men. Thus early American sodomy laws were not directed at homosexuals as such but instead sought to prohibit nonprocreative sexual activity more generally.

In *Bowers* the Court referred to the fact that before 1961 all 50 States had outlawed sodomy, and that at the time of the Court's decision 24 States and the District of Columbia had sodomy laws. In our own constitutional system the deficiencies in *Bowers* became even more apparent in the years following its announcement. The 25 States with laws prohibiting the relevant conduct referenced in the *Bowers* decision are reduced now to 13, of which 4 enforce their laws only against homosexual conduct. In those States where sodomy is still proscribed, whether for same-sex or heterosexual conduct, there is a pattern of nonenforcement with respect to consenting adults acting in private. The State of Texas admitted in 1994 that as of that date it had not prosecuted anyone under those circumstances. Persons in a homosexual relationship may seek autonomy for (personal dignity and autonomy), just as heterosexual persons do. The decision in *Bowers* would deny them this right.

The right the petitioners seek in this case has been accepted as an integral part of human freedom in many other countries. There has been no showing that in this country the governmental interest in circumscribing personal choice is somehow more legitimate or urgent. *Bowers* was not correct when it was decided, and it is not correct today. It ought not to remain binding precedent. *Bowers v. Hardwick* should be and now is overruled.

The present case does not involve minors. It does not involve persons who might be injured or coerced or who are situated in relationships where consent might not easily be refused. It does not involve public conduct or prostitution. The case does involve two adults who, with full and mutual consent from each other, engaged in sexual practices common to a homosexual lifestyle. The petitioners are entitled to respect for their private lives. The State cannot demean their existence or control their destiny by making their private sexual conduct a crime. Their right to liberty under the Due Process Clause gives them the full right to engage in their conduct without intervention of the government. The Texas statute furthers no legitimate state interest which can justify its intrusion into the personal and private life of the individual.

The judgment of the Court of Appeals for the Texas Fourteenth District is reversed, and the case is remanded for further proceedings not inconsistent with this opinion.

---

1. What is the original rationale in limiting these kinds of sexual acts? Are other sexual acts still restricted and, if so, for what reasons?
2. As a "maturing society," have we become more free and accepting or too provocative and less tasteful?
3. Is the next step same-sex marriage? Why or why not?

Right to Equal Protection[4]

Another area of civil liberties protection against the State is the Fourteenth Amendment equal protection clause, which says ". . . nor (shall any state) deny to any person within its jurisdiction the equal protection of the laws." This clause does not give citizens the right to equal *treatment*; it simply says that citizens are afforded equal *protection* of the laws in each state. Citizens are free from state control unless the government has a legitimate reason, for the sake of the community, to control its citizens' behaviors. "The equal protection clause has been interpreted to preclude states from making unequal, arbitrary distinctions between (different classes of) people" (Walsh and Hemmens 2011:74).

---

4. As mentioned in footnote 2, a recent case (*Hollingsworth v. Perry*) includes an equal protection challenge for sexual orientation and marriage. This case is also an interesting one for those interested in states' rights and standing to make a claim in an appellate court.

There are times where the state may want to distinguish certain groups of citizens from others. For example, alcohol possession is distinguished by age. Those who are under 21 years of age are not allowed to possess alcohol, whereas those who are 21 years or older are. This distinction is unequal treatment based on age, but there is a state interest in making such a distinction. Another example involves sentencing laws where convicted defendants who have more prior convictions can receive longer or more severe sentences than those with fewer prior convictions. Again, the distinction on prior convictions is based on a legitimate reason for doing so. But, is there a distinction that would violate this equal protection right? And, if there is, what is the process to determine which distinctions are inappropriate?

The process by which the courts rule whether a law violates the equal protection clause of the Fourteenth Amendment is called the **standard of review**. The standard of review is a method by which the courts evaluate the kinds of groups of citizens that the law distinguishes and the level of scrutiny through which the state should assess their reasons for making these distinctions. Walsh and Hemmens (2011) outline the levels of assessment (called scrutiny), which is summarized in Box 1.9.

The highest level of scrutiny—**strict scrutiny**—is applied to laws that address fundamental rights such as privacy, voting, and freedom of speech. The state must have a compelling reason to show that this distinction is necessary to protect the greater community. For example, citizens are afforded a right to free speech. However, this does not grant citizens the right to direct hate speech at others with the intention to incite violence (i.e., fighting words). The state has a

Standard of Review: process by which the courts rule whether a law violates the equal protection clause of the Fourteenth Amendment of the U.S. Constitution

Strict Scrutiny: the highest level of scrutiny under an equal protection claim that is applied to those laws that address fundamental rights and/or suspect class

---

Box 1.9   STANDARDS OF REVIEW FOR THE RIGHT TO EQUAL PROTECTION (SEE WALSH AND HEMMENS 2011)

- Strict Scrutiny
  - For laws that address fundamental rights and are applied to suspect classes (i.e., race, national origin, religion)
  - Requires compelling state interest to make such distinctions
- Intermediate Scrutiny
  - For laws that are applied to quasi-suspect classes (i.e., gender and legitimacy)
  - Requires substantial state interest to make such distinctions
- Rational Basis Scrutiny
  - For laws that apply distinctions other than those listed above
  - Requires rational basis to make such distinctions

compelling reason to restrict this sort of behavior even if, theoretically, the behavior is protected by the First Amendment.

Strict scrutiny has also been established for cases where certain groups of people are distinguished from other groups, known as the **suspect class**, including race, religion, and national origin (Walsh and Hemmens 2011). If a law or system of practices makes such distinctions, then the state must show a compelling reason to make those distinctions. For example, the Supreme Court addressed equal protection in the trial of Joe Hale, an African American, in McCracken County in Kentucky. Hale was tried and convicted of murder by an all-white jury. On appeal, the Supreme Court noted that a long-standing tradition of selecting white jury members, even though a great number of potential African-American jurors were not selected, violated Hale's right to equal protection of the law. In the end, the Court found that states had no compelling reason to make a racial distinction in the selection of juror members for a criminal trial.

Simply finding a pattern of disparate treatment, though, does not always yield an equal protection violation. The defendant in *McCleskey v. Kemp*, 481 U.S. 279 (1987) claimed an equal protection violation in his death sentence because of his race. In fact, there was landmark research that supported his claim in that Baldus and his associates (1983) found a pattern of racial discrimination in the death sentencing in Georgia. However, the Supreme Court rejected the claims saying that a pattern of discrimination in sentencing behavior does not violate equal protection.

A second level of scrutiny is identified as **intermediate scrutiny**, which is reserved for the **quasi-suspect class** of individuals (i.e., gender and legitimacy). The state must show that the law is substantially related to an important reason for the distinction. If a law or system of practices distinguishes men from women, for example, the law or system of practice must be substantially related to the important reason for this distinction. Again, the selection of potential jury members in a criminal trial illustrates this unique setting in *Taylor v. Louisiana*, 419 U.S. 522 (1975). Taylor was found guilty of aggravated kidnapping and claimed that equal protection was violated because women were systematically excluded from jury service. In this case, women were required to submit a written declaration outlining their interest and desire to be subject to jury service. The Court in *Taylor* found that the defendant was not granted the equal protection of the law because of this systematic exclusion of female jurors. Interestingly enough, the defendant was male.

The final level of scrutiny is **rational basis**, which applies to all distinctions that are not fundamental rights, suspect class, or quasi-suspect class. In this category of scrutiny, the one challenging the law must show that a law is not rationally related to the state's purpose in

Suspect Class:
group of individuals upon which a law distinguishes where strict scrutiny is used to test whether the right of equal protection of the law is applied

Intermediate Scrutiny:
the second highest level of scrutiny under an equal protection claim that is applied to those laws that address quasi-suspect class

Quasi-Suspect Class:
group of individuals upon which a law distinguishes where intermediate scrutiny is used to test whether the right of equal protection of the law is applied

Rational Basis:
the lowest level of scrutiny under an equal protection claim that is applied to any law that does not address fundamental rights, suspect class, or quasi-suspect class

making such a distinction. The two examples we addressed before (minor in possession and sentencing laws using prior record) can apply here. For example, the state has a rational reason to keep its community safe when considering alcohol possession among minors and sentencing laws for repeat offenders. Therefore, even though some believe the equal protection clause supports equal *treatment*, we have noted here that it is equal *protection* of the law and the state has different levels of scrutiny it must pass based on the purpose of such distinctions.

Right Against Cruel and Unusual Punishment

A final limitation to state control in criminal law is the Eighth Amendment's protection against cruel and unusual punishment. Although the majority of the cruel and unusual punishment claims have involved the death penalty, some constitutional attacks regarding one's right against cruel and unusual punishment have addressed habitual offender laws and life penalties. The Eighth Amendment protection against cruel and unusual punishment will be discussed in more detail in Chapter 12 on punishment and sentencing.

SUMMARY

The law is constructed in a way to protect society from harm caused by individuals who violate it according to a social contract where individuals give up a bit of freedom in exchange for the state's protection. What happens, though, when this protection enters into one's private life? Does the law cover private actions that may include potentially harmful activities? Or, is there a right to privacy in one's bedroom? Does the law distinguish between the private lives of heterosexual couples versus homosexual couples?

Criminal law is distinguished from civil law as a result of the full thrust of the state behind it. The considerations of the origins and makeup of "law" have been debated. Some take a natural law approach, while others take a more practical and/or social approach. The purposes and rationales for laws also have gained multiple perspectives. Although it is important to understand how law was born within these perspectives, this book is more concerned with addressing the criminal law's legal practicalities.

Substantive criminal law can be found mostly in state and federal statutes—laws created by legislative bodies. Even before American law was created, common law was developed in England to generate a consistent ruling system between judges in different locales. The American system of justice adopted much of the common law, which has been integrated into our constitutions, statutes, and court rulings. The criminal law has several different ways of categorizing criminal offenses such as *mala in se* versus *mala prohibita*, felony or misdemeanor versus infraction, and by subject.

Finally, the state's authority is powerful. However, even the state is limited in the development of the criminal law. There are two essential categories of constitutional limits. First, the principle of legality suggests that the state must define what is criminal prior to enforcing that law. Laws must be clear (void for vagueness doctrine) and must avoid infringing on fundamental rights (overbreadth doctrine). The second category of constitutional limits is individual freedom. There are a number of individual liberties—right to free speech, right to privacy, equal protection, and right against cruel and unusual punishment—that address the substantive criminal law. The criminal law, and how it is applied, must avoid violating these individual civil liberties. The rest of the textbook outlines the more specific components of the criminal law in defining crimes, defenses, and punishments.

KEY TERMS

common law
concurring opinion
dissenting opinion
due process
elements
ex post facto law
intermediate scrutiny
majority opinion
mala in se
mala prohibita
natural law

positive law
precedent
principle of legality
quasi-suspect class
rational basis
social contract
social solidarity
standard of review
stare decisis
strict scrutiny
suspect class
theory of forms
void for vagueness doctrine

CRITICAL THINKING QUESTIONS

1. Although a standardized rule like precedence is helpful, are there potential problems with it? In other words, what if the standardized rule takes legal reasoning to an unreasonable end? How can we avoid this unreasonable end?

2. The U.S. Supreme Court's function is to interpret the law. Some have argued that it has "created" public policy. Do they "create" public policy—a legislative function—or do

they "interpret" law to encompass a social agenda?

3. What is the difference between substantive due process and procedural due process?

4. Are there *any mala in se* offenses? If we conclude that rape or child and/or spousal abuse are *mala prohibita* offenses, then is homicide even *mala in se*? One basic definition of homicide can be the intentional, unjustified killing of another. Is this *mala in se*, considered evil during all times,

places, and cultures? What about suicide bombers or wrongful executions?

5. Are all laws clear? Are there laws that are vague? Are these laws unconstitutionally vague?

6. Are there times of serious and severe criminal activity that *ex post facto* laws *should* be in place? Is there ever a situation to determine that the *ex post facto* law prohibition is outdated?

7. Should privacy outweigh the state's interest? If so, when and to what extent? If a person is known to have committed a crime but a right to privacy is shielding enforcement efforts, does your perspective change? If the state has an interest in reducing domestic violence and they decide that going into homes that are randomly selected without a warrant, does your perspective change?

SUGGESTED READINGS

Ball, T. & Dagger, R. (2006). *Ideals and Ideologies: A Reader* (6th ed.). New York: Pearson. Ball and Dagger give additional philosophical perspectives of law and justice that are not offered in this chapter's short summary of the different perspectives of law. Some of the readings, though, go beyond the scope of this discussion.

Rauch, J. (2004). *Gay Marriage: Why It Is Good for Gays, Good for Straights, and Good for America*. New York: Henry Holt. Rauch addresses same-sex marriage through the lens of a journalist. It is a good discussion of the economic and social impact of allowing for same-sex marriage and a good start to an equal protection discussion for the social characteristic of sexual orientation. This book is a good contrast to Stanton and Maier's book on the same subject with a different perspective offered here in the suggested readings.

Stanton, G.T. & Maier, B. (2004). *Marriage on Trial: The Case Against Same-Sex Marriage and Parenting*. Downers Grove, IL: Intervarsity Press. Stanton and Maier give an accounting from a psychologist's and an academic researcher's perspective through the lens of a Christian-based moral perspective about the right to marry. Again, it is a good discussion of equal protection for those of different sexual orientations. This book is a contrast to Rauch's book on the same subject with a different perspective offered here in the suggested readings.

Sutton, J.R. (2001). *Law/Society: Origins, Interactions, and Change*. Thousand Oaks, CA: Pine Forge Press. Sutton gives an accounting of law and justice with a slightly different perspective. He suggests that it is not law *and* justice but, rather, law/society. In other words, law and society are not independent of each other. It speaks to the progress of law and society and when action is taken via law and justice. It also speaks to the law as a profession and how changes have also occurred in the practice of law.

REFERENCES

American Law Institute (2011). http://www.ali.org/index.cfm?fuseaction=about.overview.

Amdur, M. & Oei, L. (2004). "Conviction Has Martha in a Pickle." *Daily Variety*, March 8.

Baldus, D.C., Pulaski, C. & Woodworth, G. (1983). "Comparative Review of Death Sentences: An Empirical Study of the Georgia Experience." *Journal of Criminal Law and Criminology* 74:661-753.

Bentham, J. (1952). *An Introduction to the Principles of Morals and Legislation*. New York: Harper & Row.

Bergen, R.K. (1999). "Marital Rape." Applied Research Forum: National Electronic Network on Violence Against Women. March.

Bowers v. Hardwick, 478 U.S. 186 (1986).

Bureau of Justice Statistics (2008). *Federal Justice Statistics, 2008—Statistical Tables.*

Coleman, J.W. (1985). *The Criminal Elite: The Sociology of White-Collar Crime.* New York: St. Martin's Press.

Death Penalty Information Center (n.d.). "States With and Without the Death Penalty." http://www.deathpenaltyinfo.org/states-and-without-death-penalty.

Durkheim, E. (1997). *Division of Labor in Society* (L.A. Coser, trans.). New York: Free Press. (Original work published 1893).

Gaines, L.K. & Miller, R.L. (2009). *Criminal Justice in Action* (5th ed.). Belmont, CA: Cengage.

Gray, R.L. (1995). "Eliminating the (Absurd) Distinction Between *Malum in Se* and *Malum Prohibitum* Crimes." *Washington University Law Quarterly* 73:1369-1398.

Griswold v. Connecticut, 381 U.S. 479 (1965).

Hollingsworth v. Perry, 570 U.S. _____ (2013).

Jacobellis v. Ohio, 378 U.S. 184 (1964).

Katz, J. (1979). "Legality and Equality: Plea Bargaining in the Prosecution of White-Collar and Common Crimes." *Law and Society Review* 13:431-459.

Lawrence v. Texas, 539 U.S. 558 (2003).

McCleskey v. Kemp, 481 U.S. 279 (1987).

Miller v. California, 413 U.S. 15 (1973).

National Conference of State Legislatures (n.d.). "Defining Marriage: Defense of Marriage Acts and Same-Sex Marriage Laws." http://www.ncsl.org/issues-research/human-services/same-sex-marriage-overview.aspx#1.

Nigeria (1998). *Women's International Network News* 24:12.

Powell, E.H. (1966). "Crime as a Function of Anomie." *Journal of Criminal Law, Criminology and Police Science* 57:161-171.

Regina v. Hicklin, LR 3 QB 36 (1868).

Roth v. United States, 354 U.S. 476 (1957).

Snyder v. Phelps, 131 S. Ct. 1207 (2011).

Spaeth, H.J. & Segal, J.A. (1999). *Majority Rule or Minority Will: Adherence to Precedent on the U.S. Supreme Court.* New York: Cambridge University Press.

Spohn, C. (2009). *How Do Judges Decide? The Search for Fairness and Justice in Punishment* (2d ed.). Los Angeles: Sage.

State v. Holcombe, 187 S.W.3d 496 (Tex. Crim. App. 2006).

Taylor v. Louisiana, 419 U.S. 522 (1975).

United States v. One Book Called "Ulysses" by James Joyce, 72 F.2d 705 (2d Cir. 1934).

United States v. Windsor, 570 U.S. _____ (2013).

Walsh, A. & Hemmens, C. (2011). *Law, Justice, and Society: A Sociolegal Introduction.* New York: Oxford University Press.

General Principles of Liability

LEARNING OBJECTIVES

After reading this chapter you should be able to:

1. Define and explain the significance of *actus reus*
2. Define the *Model Penal Code*'s four mental states that constitute a criminal *mens rea*
3. Describe the nature of strict liability offenses
4. Define the point at which *actus reus* and *mens rea* converge
5. Describe the nature of "but for" causation
6. Distinguish result crimes from conduct crimes

INTRODUCTION

In criminal law, several questions arise before making an arrest and prosecuting a person for a crime. In order to perform these functions properly, we need to know what was done, by whom, and the extent to which someone should be held criminally liable for his or her actions. Some of these issues were discussed in Chapter 1. Here, we will consider the factors surrounding criminal liability and the required elements that must be proven in order to establish that a person has committed a crime. Our primary focus will be on five general elements of criminal liability: the wrongful act (*actus reus*); the guilty mind (*mens rea*); the point at which *actus reus* and *mens rea* intersect (concurrence); causation; and result.

As always, several terms will be presented and defined throughout our discussion. Each of these terms is important in establishing both the existence of criminal liability, as well as the degree to which a person is criminally responsible for his or her actions.

ACTUS REUS

One of the primary elements that the state must prove beyond a reasonable doubt is that the defendant performed an act that was forbidden by the law. This is known as the **actus reus**, which is simply a wrongful act that is prohibited by a criminal statute. The *actus reus* has been defined as "the action that must be proved for criminal liability," or simply "the legally wrongful act" (Sheppard 2012:75). All crimes have some type of criminal action as part of their legal definition. Section 1.13(9) of the *Model Penal Code* (*MPC*) specifies three components of *actus reus*: **conduct**, the wrongful act that is committed; **attendant circumstances**, factors that further describe the prohibited act such as possessing a firearm during the commission of a burglary; and **results**, the social harm that is caused by the conduct (American Law Institute 1985:18). This third component is not to be confused with the "result element" to be discussed later. We will explain all three of these components further in this chapter.

Actus Reus:
Latin phrase meaning the wrongful act that is part of a crime

Conduct:
the wrongful act associated with a crime

Attendant Circumstances:
statutory language that provides further elaboration of a prohibited criminal act

Results:
in criminal law, the social harm that is caused by someone's conduct

Physical Acts

As indicated by the previous definitions, in most instances the law is concerned with regulating physical acts, and as Section 1.13(2) of the *MPC* explains, an act involves bodily movement (American Law Institute 1985:18). Typically, these are affirmative actions taken by a person who is attempting to commit a crime. However, we should also note that there are situations where a failure to act may constitute an *actus reus*. Failure to act may be a crime in situations where the law imposes a legal duty upon a person to act (see, for example, Romohr 2006). In those situations, a failure to act (an *omission* rather than a *commission*) can constitute a crime. We will examine a number of these circumstances later in this chapter.

Voluntary Act

One of the first components that the state must establish in proving *actus reus* is that the person committed a **voluntary act**. While this may seem like an obvious point, it is important to recognize that some behaviors do not result from voluntary choices. In criminal law, we require that any person who is charged with a crime must have acted through a deliberate choice and the resulting act caused a social harm. The *MPC* (American Law Institute 1985:19) does not specifically explain the meaning of a voluntary act, but it does articulate that there are at least four types of behaviors that *do not* constitute voluntary acts:

Voluntary Act:
action that is a conscious choice

(1) reflexes or convulsions (these are involuntary muscular movements);
(2) bodily movements that occur when a person is unconscious or asleep;
(3) actions taken during the process of hypnosis or as a result of a hypnotic suggestion; and
(4) any bodily movement that is not the result of a conscious or habitual effort or determined by a person.

Based on these exceptions, an example can illustrate the difference between a voluntary act and an involuntary act. Joan is a student at Central High School. One day she has an epileptic seizure in the school cafeteria. When Mary runs to her aid, Joan strikes her with her fist as her arms are flailing about. This blow knocks Mary backward and she strikes her head, which causes a concussion. Is this a crime? Should Joan be charged with battery? A reasonable person would conclude that, due to her seizure, Joan certainly was not responsible for her physical actions at that point and that she should not be charged with a crime. From a legal standpoint, this action was involuntary and, therefore, did not fulfill the *actus reus* element of battery.

By contrast, what if Joan was not epileptic, and she struck Mary in the face with her fist as a result of Mary making insulting remarks about the way Joan was dressed? Now has a crime been committed? Can we say that Joan acted voluntarily or willfully? Again, a reasonable person would conclude that this was a voluntary act and that

Joan has committed some criminal offense. And, from a legal stand-point, this action was voluntary and, therefore, *did* fulfill the *actus reus* element of battery.

In the first example, what if Joan is fully aware of her medical condition? While she drives a car, she has a seizure that causes her to be involved in an accident. In all likelihood she would be held responsible for any damages that might result. Why? We will return to this point later in the chapter when we discuss recklessness and negligence.

Deeds, Not Thoughts

The second consideration is that the law is intended to punish deeds, not thoughts. Therefore, you can think about doing anything you desire, even though these thoughts might be utterly repulsive and perhaps associated with heinous acts (such as robbing your neighbor or choking your professor). However, merely thinking about these activities does not cause harm to anyone. Therefore, the law has no reason to regulate your thoughts. Until you take some steps to act on those thoughts, no crime has occurred.

Acts, Not Statuses

Third, as we will see in Chapter 7 in the discussion of street crimes, the law is intended to punish people's acts, not their statuses, which means that while it is illegal to sell drugs or to be drunk in public [see, for example, *Powell v. Texas*, 392 U.S. 514 (1968)], it is not illegal to be poor, unemployed, a drug addict, or homeless (Charles 2009). While being an alcoholic or drug addict may be socially undesirable and lead to a person committing criminal acts (such as public drunkenness or drug possession), only the actions are considered wrongful and only the actions (not statuses) are subject to the criminal law's regulation.

Poverty, unemployment, and drug dependency are *statuses* not *acts*. In the past, there have been efforts to criminalize statuses such as these, but the courts generally find such regulations unconstitutional for violating the legality principle by being overly vague (Schulz 2002; Vago 2009). It is important that these regulations make a distinction between statuses and actions that may result from statuses. For example, Box 2.1 contains a summary of the U.S. Supreme Court case of *Robinson v. California*, 370 U.S. 660 (1962), in which California attempted to criminalize the status of being a narcotics addict.

Box 2.1   IS IT CRIMINAL TO BE ADDICTED?

Robinson v. California
370 U.S. 660 (1962)

The State of California had enacted a law that made it a crime for a person to "be addicted to the use of narcotics." Robinson was arrested and charged under this statute when two Los Angeles police officers observed scars and marks on his arms that indicated that he had been using narcotics. After his conviction in the Municipal Court of Los Angeles, Robinson began an appeal that eventually took his case to the U.S. Supreme Court. The following is an excerpt from the Court's majority opinion overturning Robinson's conviction.

The broad power of a State to regulate the narcotic drugs traffic within its borders is not here in issue. The right to exercise this power is so manifest in the interest of the public health and welfare, that it is unnecessary to enter upon a discussion of it beyond saying that it is too firmly established to be successfully called in question.

Such regulation could take a variety of valid forms. A State might impose criminal sanctions against the unauthorized manufacture, prescription, sale, purchase, or possession of narcotics within its borders. In the interest of discouraging the violation of such laws, or in the interest of the general health or welfare of its inhabitants, a State might establish a program of compulsory treatment for those addicted to narcotics. Such a program of treatment might require periods of involuntary confinement. And penal sanctions might be imposed for failure to comply with established compulsory treatment procedures. Or a State might choose to attack the evils of narcotics traffic on broader fronts also—through public health education or by efforts to ameliorate the economic and social conditions under which those evils might be thought to flourish. In short, the range of valid choice which a State might make in this area is undoubtedly a wide one. Upon that premise we turn to the California law in issue here.

It would be possible to construe the statute under which the appellant was convicted as one which is operative only upon proof of the actual use of narcotics within the State's jurisdiction. But the California courts have not so construed this law. Although there was evidence in the present case that the appellant had used narcotics in Los Angeles, the jury was instructed that they could convict him even if they disbelieved that evidence. The appellant could be convicted if they found simply that the appellant's "status" or "chronic condition" was that of being "addicted to the use of narcotics."

This statute, therefore, is not one which punishes a person for the use of narcotics, for their purchase, sale or possession, or for antisocial or disorderly behavior resulting from their administration. It is not a law which even purports to provide or require medical treatment. Rather, we deal with a statute which makes the "status" of narcotic addiction a criminal offense, for which the offender may be prosecuted.

It is unlikely that any State at this moment in history would attempt to make it a criminal offense for a person to be mentally ill, or a leper, or to be afflicted with a venereal disease. A State might determine that the general health and welfare require that the victims of these and other human afflictions be dealt with by compulsory treatment, involving quarantine, confinement, or sequestration. But, in the light of contemporary human knowledge, a law which made a criminal offense of such a disease would doubtless be universally thought to be an infliction of cruel and unusual punishment in violation of the Eight and Fourteenth Amendments.

We cannot but consider the statute before us as of the same category. In this Court counsel for the State recognized that narcotic addiction is an illness. We hold that a state law which imprisons a person thus afflicted as a criminal, even though he has never touched any narcotic drug within the State or been guilty of any irregular behavior there, inflicts a cruel and unusual punishment in violation of the Fourteenth Amendment. To be sure, imprisonment for ninety days is not a punishment which is either cruel or unusual. But . . . [e]ven one day in prison would be a cruel and unusual punishment for the "crime" of having a common cold.

1. Was the California law dealing with narcotics addiction overly vague, overly broad, or both?
2. Would most police officers be qualified to testify that someone was a narcotics addict?
3. If the law had been revised, could there have been modifications that would have made it constitutional? Explain.

Omissions

Sometimes, not acting is a criminal act. In other words, an omission or failure to act can result in criminal liability. Generally speaking, in the United States under common law principles, or what is often called the **bystander rule**, there is no duty to act or rescue a person in peril unless such a duty is recognized by law (Groninger 1999; Silver 1985). However, as stated previously, an omission or failure to act may constitute an *actus reus* when someone has a *legal duty* to act. It is important to remember that an omission is "the failure to do something a reasonable person in the place of the person with the duty would do" (Sheppard 2012:1904).

Bystander Rule: no duty to act or rescue a person in peril unless such a duty is recognized by law

In effect, there are five areas where the law imposes a legal duty to act. These are:

1. *Duties imposed by special relationships*—most of the areas in which the law requires action are based on special relationships. The most obvious of these relationships is between parents and their children. However, special relationships also may exist between spouses, employees and employers, public transportation providers and passengers, innkeepers and their guests, correctional facilities and the inmates they house, and teachers and students (see Groninger 1999:359-363). Based on this special relationship, a parent, for example, must take reasonable

actions to protect his or her children. If the parent fails to take such actions, then he or she induces criminal liability.

2. ***Duties imposed by statute*** — these are obligations imposed by statute, which may suggest such duties as parents caring for their minor children, drivers involved in traffic accidents not leaving the scene, and taxpayers filing tax returns; some jurisdictions have passed **Good Samaritan statutes** that require a person to aid another person in need or distress (these statutes, while not related to criminal law, often protect citizens from civil liability from actions that may cause injury during their assistance).

3. ***Duties imposed by contracts*** — contractual duties arise out of explicit or implicit contractual obligations, such as those involving the requirement that health care workers (doctors, nurses, and nursing home personnel) provide for their patients' care; daycare workers also have similar contractual obligations to protect and provide for the well-being of the children in their care.

4. ***Duties imposed by status*** — these arise out of certain occupational or professional situations, such as those involving school teachers and their students, police officers and the people they arrest, and lifeguards at pools and beaches; it is also important to note that irrespective of whether statutory obligations exist (covered under category 2 above), parents may be expected to act to protect the lives of their children as a result of status.

5. ***Duties that have been assumed*** — when someone volunteers to care for another who is unable to care for himself or herself (for example, an elderly neighbor or grandparent), that person is obligated to provide care until some other caregiver is engaged (Schubert 2010:103-104). This category of omission is important for those who administer CPR.

In addition to these five areas, there are at least three more factors that must be considered:

1. if there has been a creation of peril; in other words, if someone pushes a nonswimmer into the lake, that person is obligated to rescue someone who is in danger of drowning;

2. if a person has a duty to control the conduct of another person; this might occur in a situation where a wealthy individual owns a yacht, and he or she allows the yacht's captain to operate the boat in an unsafe manner, thereby endangering smaller boats; and

3. if a landowner operates a business, the building in which the business is housed must be outfitted with sufficient fire suppression equipment and clearly marked emergency exits to protect the public (Groninger 1999; Romohr 2006; Silver 1985).

Good Samaritan Statutes: laws that require a person to aid another person in need or distress

Unlike the bystander rule where it is generally presumed that people are *not required* to act in most circumstances, each of these situations imposes a legal duty upon a person to act. In such cases, when someone fails to act according to a legal duty, that omission can provide the basis for criminal liability. However, as Section 2.01(3) of the *MPC* notes, omissions cannot be the basis for criminal liability unless:

(1) the law defining the offense specifically provides for the omission; or
(2) there is a duty to act imposed by the law. (American Law Institute 1985:20)

Although we will consider both of these factors more fully later in the chapter, an illustration can shed light on this note in the *MPC*. All states today mandate the reporting of child abuse. If someone knows of or suspects any form of child abuse, state laws require that person to report such knowledge or suspicions to the appropriate authorities (see the federal Child Abuse Prevention and Treatment Act of 1974). Therefore, a statutory duty has been created. Failure to report known or suspected cases constitutes a crime (Singley 1998).

Nevertheless, some individuals do have a legal duty to act in certain circumstances, and their failure to act could result in criminal liability. The circumstances in which a person is legally obligated to act may not equally apply to all people. For instance, if someone trained in medicine (doctor, nurse, or physician's assistant) comes upon a traffic accident in which there has been bodily harm, that person has a legal obligation (perhaps based on statutes) to act. This type of obligation would not typically be imposed on citizens in general who lack medical training. Similarly, parents have obligations to act to save their children from danger and to minimize harm to them. This obligation is not imposed on others outside of the immediate family. Thus, if a child falls into a swimming pool and is drowning, the parents may be legally required to act to rescue the child, while others may not have a legal obligation to do so. Instead, their decision to act would be guided by their own moral sense rather than a legal responsibility.

Possession

The final factor that must be considered regarding the voluntary requirement of *actus reus* is what is known as **possession**. It is clear that having illegal objects (drugs, weapons, etc.) and *doing* something with them may constitute a voluntary criminal act. But what if a person merely possesses such items? Examples of

Possession:
to have some item on one's person or to have it under one's custody or control

possession crimes include minor in possession of alcohol (MIP) or possession of illegal drugs. Also, convicted felons are prohibited from possessing firearms, and virtually all private citizens are prohibited from possessing fully automatic weapons or items such as hand grenades or similar explosive devices. It is also against the law in many jurisdictions to be in possession of burglary tools (see, for example, FindLaw 2011; on firearms, see 26 U.S.C. § 5861).

Section 2.10(4) of the *MPC* (American Law Institute 1985:20) notes that "possession is an act . . . if the possessor knowingly procured or received the thing possessed or was aware of his control thereof for a sufficient period to have been able to terminate his possession." Thus, there are situations in which possession of certain items can fulfill the law's requirement of *actus reus*. In other words, the person possessing the item must either have knowledge of receiving the item or aware that he or she is controlling it for a period of time.

Possession of an illegal item applies to **actual possession**, where the item is physically on one's body, or **constructive possession**, where the item was not in the person's physical possession but nevertheless was under the person's "dominion" or "control" (see Sheppard 2012:2104-2105). To be in constructive possession, someone must know of the item's existence and have the ability to access it. An example of constructive possession is when an individual knowingly has an illegal item in his vehicle or home. While that person is away from these locations, he is not in actual possession of the item because it is not physically located on him. However, he is in constructive possession because these items are under his dominion and control.

Actual Possession: to be in physical possession of some item; to have something on one's person

Constructive Possession: to not have an item on one's person, but have dominion or control over the item

A third type of possession is **joint possession**. Joint possession exists when several people maintain access and control over common spaces. For example, four college students rent a four-bedroom house, and they each have their own private bedroom. However, in a raid on the house the police find a kilo of marijuana in the living room, over which each student has common access and control. In this situation, all of the students could be charged with possession of marijuana, perhaps with intent to distribute.

Joint Possession: exists when several people maintain access and control over common spaces

However, it important to note that possession might be used as a defense in cases in which the individual asserts **innocent possession**. An example here would be helpful. Helen is cleaning out her grandfather's garage after he passed away. In the process, she finds a box of what appear to be live hand grenades. Such explosives are illegal to possess, and she decides to put them in the bed of her pickup truck to transport them to the proper authorities. On the way to the police station, she is stopped for a traffic offense and the officer observes the box of grenades in the truck. If she is charged with possessing the

Innocent Possession: possession without knowledge of origin

grenades, she could assert that this was an innocent possession because her intent was to surrender the explosives. A similar situation arose in the case of *United States v. Mason*, 233 F.3d 619 (D.C. Cir. 2000), in which Mason, who was a convicted felon, found a firearm hidden in a paper bag near a school. He took possession of the firearm with the intention of turning it over to a police officer he knew. When another officer found him in possession of the weapon, he was charged with the federal offense of being a felon in possession of a firearm. His defense, supported by the Court of Appeals for the District of Columbia Circuit, was that this was an innocent possession and that he did not intend to keep the weapon (see Anderson 2011).

Throughout this book as we discuss the elements of various substantive crimes, the question of what constitutes *actus reus* and voluntary action will be a part of every discussion. This component of each offense serves as a foundation for the next item that we will examine: *mens rea* or criminal intent.

MENS REA

In addition to proving beyond a reasonable doubt that a person committed a wrongful act, in most instances the state will have to prove that the individual acted with criminal intent in order to establish criminal liability which is known as *mens rea* or "evil mind." In criminal law *mens rea* is normally defined as the "guilty mind" or "criminal mind" (Sheppard 2012:1730). The exceptions to proving *mens rea*—absolute or strict liability—will be covered later in the chapter.

State and federal criminal statutes reflecting the common law tradition can contain a wide array of terms and phrases describing criminal intent. Some of these that frequently appear include "willfully," "with malice," "with malice aforethought," "maliciously," "with premeditation," "feloniously," and "unlawfully." As we will see in the culpability section, in order to reduce confusion, the *MPC* has adopted four criminal mindsets that describe a person's degree of criminal intent: (1) purposely, (2) knowingly, (3) recklessly, and (4) negligently. In subsequent sections we will define and examine each of these more extensively.

Before examining these mindsets, we should note that, under the common law, criminal intent was divided into three categories: general intent, specific intent, and transferred intent. These concepts have caused some confusion even among legal scholars (see, for example, Roth 1979), but we attempt to provide clarification in the following sections.

Common Law Culpability

The first category under common law culpability is **general intent**, which is defined as "the intent to carry out a given action. General intent is an intent to do something regardless of any specific intent to cause a consequence of the something done" (Sheppard 2012:1360). In other words, this is the intent to commit an act itself regardless of one's intent to cause a particular result. One example of a general intent crime would be drug possession. Proof that a person had actual or constructive possession over illegal drugs would be sufficient to establish that the individual had the general intent to possess drugs. The state would not have to prove anything beyond that in terms of the person's potential disposition of the drugs.

While general intent is the purpose to perform a particular act, **specific intent** is concerned with the outcome or result. Therefore, we can say that "specific intent is the motivation to commit an act not merely for the act's sake but for the purpose of causing a particular result from the act" (Sheppard 2012:1361). Under common law, the state would have had to prove that some additional harm was intended beyond the general intent to commit a crime. The key in identifying whether a modern law notes a specific intent requirement is the inclusion of the phrase "with intent to . . ."

Consider the crime of robbery. The Federal Bureau of Investigation defines robbery as "the taking or attempting to take anything of value from the care, custody, or control of a person or persons by force or threat of force or violence and/or by putting the victim in fear" (Federal Bureau of Investigation 2011). The presumption is not only that the person took something of value but also that the intent was to deprive permanently the owner of the item. Therefore, the state would have to prove that one person took something of value from another person through the use of force or threat of force and that the intent was to prevent the original owner from ever being able to use or possess it again.

Another example helps to illustrate the difference between general intent and specific intent—the crime of "joyriding." While the definitions may differ slightly between states that have this activity as a crime, the basic notion of joyriding is "the taking of another person's automobile without that person's consent and with no intent to permanently deprive the owner of the vehicle" (Sheppard 2012:891). Thus, if someone took a vehicle without one's permission, drove it around until it ran out of gas, and then abandoned it, they could be charged with joyriding. This crime would be a general intent offense. By contrast, if a car was stolen and the defendant sold it to someone out-of-state, this activity would be auto theft as a specific intent

General Intent:
the intent to commit an act that results in some degree of harm

Specific Intent:
the purpose to perform a particular prohibited act that is concerned with the outcome or result

offense since the objective was not only to take the vehicle but to deprive permanently the owner of the use and possession of the vehicle.

The distinction between general intent and specific intent can be subjective, and states that have adopted the *MPC* have moved away from these distinctions. One of the main reasons for this movement is that an offender's intent is not always known, which requires the prosecution to infer the defendant's mental state from the crime's surrounding circumstances.

One related notion that might confuse matters further is **transferred intent**. At its most basic level, we can say that with transferred intent, the harm that was anticipated is not the harm that was achieved. For instance, in the case of a drive-by shooting, a gang member shoots at a rival gang member intending to kill him but misses and instead kills an innocent bystander. Although the actual victim was not the intended target, with transferred intent the law will consider the bystander's death as if that person was the intended target. In effect, the intent to commit a killing is transferred from one victim to another since the result is the same type of harm as originally intended. Section 2.03(2)(a) of the *MPC* affirms intent when "the actual result differs from that designed or contemplated . . . only in the respect that a different person or different property is injured or affected or that the injury or harm designed or contemplated would have been more serious or more extensive than that caused" (American Law Institute 1985:25).

Transferred Intent:
the purpose to perform a particular prohibited act that is concerned with the outcome or result

Model Penal Code Culpability

When the state attempts to prove *mens rea*, it is trying to establish **culpability** (see Section 2.02 of the *MPC*) or blameworthiness for the defendant's actions (American Law Institute 1985:21). Fletcher (1998:173-174) says that there are two different legal theories concerning the *mens rea* element. First, the culpability-centered approach focuses on the actor and the wrongfulness of his or her behavior. Here, the chief concern is about the harm intended and a general defiance of legal norms. Second, the harm-centered approach is more concerned with the individual crime victim instead of focusing on general notions of harm (i.e., harms to society). Outside of this approach, the discussion of culpability focuses on the state (or society) as the symbolic victim, rather than the individual person upon whom harm was inflicted. See Figure 2.1.

Culpability:
to possess the *mens rea* for a criminal act; blameworthiness

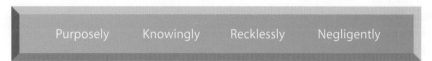

Figure 2.1
Model Penal Code's
Different Degrees of
Culpability

For our purposes, culpability denotes legal responsibility for the commission of a crime. However, unlike the common law categories of general and specific intent, Section 2.02(2) of the *MPC* provides four levels of criminal intent — purpose, knowledge, recklessness, and negligence. Therefore, in order to establish whether and to what degree a person may be criminally responsible, we must consider the degree to which an individual acted.

Purposely

The most serious mental state under the *MPC* is when a defendant acts purposely. The individual must have the "conscious object to engage in conduct of that nature or to cause such a result" (American Law Institute 1985:21). Some states use the terms "deliberately" or "willfully" as substitutes for the *MPC* term of "purposely." The objective with this mental state — whether termed purposely, deliberately, or willfully — is to prove that the person engaged in conduct that was designed to cause a particular outcome.

Knowingly

A less serious mental state under the *MPC* is when a defendant is criminally culpable, demonstrating that the person acted knowingly. Knowledge can be represented in two ways. First, the traditional notion of knowledge is that the accused person is aware of a fact and correctly believes that the fact exists. The second notion of the knowledge mental state is **willful blindness**, where the accused person merely suspects that a fact exists (without actual awareness) and purposely avoids confirming the fact.

Willful Blindness: an attempt to make oneself unaware of some fact or to deliberately avoid confirming a fact

Therefore, to act knowingly means to be aware of (or suspect) one's conduct and the actual or potential results of that conduct. An example might help to illustrate these two concepts of knowledge. Some high school students are standing on a pedestrian overpass, and they decide to drop rocks on the cars passing beneath them. One of the rocks breaks a vehicle's windshield, and the car's owner immediately calls the police who come and arrest all of the students. In such a case, it is apparent that these adolescents knew that they were dropping the rocks and that the rocks had the potential to inflict damage upon passing vehicles.

The case provided in Box 2.2 demonstrates this distinction in which the U.S. Supreme Court has addressed the knowledge mental state. This case addresses knowledge of passengers in an automobile in which drugs were found.

Box 2.2 THE QUESTION OF KNOWLEDGE

Maryland v. Pringle
540 U.S. 366 (2003)

This case addresses the meaning of knowledge of drugs in an automobile that had multiple occupants. The following summary presents the unanimous opinion of the U.S. Supreme Court.

In the early morning hours a passenger car occupied by three men was stopped for speeding by a police officer. The officer, upon searching the car, seized $763 of rolled-up cash from the glove compartment and five glassine baggies of cocaine from between the back-seat armrest and the back seat. After all three men denied ownership of the cocaine and money, the officer arrested each of them. We hold that the officer had probable cause to arrest Pringle — one of the three men.

At 3:16 a.m. on August 7, 1999, a Baltimore County Police officer stopped a car for speeding. There were three occupants in the car: Donte Partlow, the driver and owner, respondent Pringle, the front-seat passenger, and Otis Smith, the back-seat passenger. The officer asked Partlow for his license and registration. When Partlow opened the glove compartment to retrieve the vehicle registration, the officer observed a large amount of rolled-up money.

After a second patrol car arrived, the officer asked Partlow if he had any weapons or narcotics in the vehicle. Partlow indicated that he did not. Partlow then consented to a search of the vehicle. The search yielded $763 from the glove compartment and five glassine baggies containing cocaine from behind the back-seat armrest. When the officer began the search the armrest was in the upright position flat against the rear seat. The officer pulled down the armrest and found the drugs, which had been placed between the armrest and the back seat of the car.

The officer questioned all three men about the ownership of the drugs and money, and told them that if no one admitted to ownership of the drugs he was going to arrest them all. The men offered no information regarding the ownership of the drugs or money. All three were placed under arrest and transported to the police station.

To determine whether an officer had probable cause to arrest an individual, we examine the events leading up to the arrest, and then decide "whether these historical facts, viewed from the standpoint of an objectively reasonable police officer, amount to" probable cause.

In this case, Pringle was one of three men riding in a [car] at 3:16 a.m. There was $763 of rolled-up cash in the glove compartment directly in front of Pringle. Five glassine baggies of cocaine were behind the back-seat armrest and accessible to all three men. Upon questioning, the three men failed to offer any information with respect to the ownership of the cocaine or the money.

We think it an entirely reasonable inference from these facts that any or all three of the occupants had knowledge of, and exercised dominion and control over, the cocaine. Thus a reasonable officer could conclude that there was probable cause to believe Pringle committed the crime of possession of cocaine, either solely or jointly.

Here we think it was reasonable for the officer to infer a common enterprise among the three men. The quantity of drugs and cash in the car indicated the likelihood of drug dealing, an enterprise to which a dealer would be unlikely to admit an innocent person with the potential to furnish evidence against him. We said "[a]ny inference that everyone on the scene of a crime is a party to it must disappear if the Government informer singles out the guilty person." No such singling out occurred in this case; none of the three men provided information with respect to the ownership of the cocaine or money.

We hold that the officer had probable cause to believe that Pringle had committed the crime of possession of a controlled substance. Pringle's arrest therefore did not contravene the Fourth and Fourteenth Amendments.

1. Under most circumstances, would a traffic stop such as the one in the case justify an officer conducting a search of the vehicle? What factors made this search legal?
2. How likely (or unlikely) is it that all of the passengers in the vehicle knew about the presence of the drugs?
3. Given the facts of the case as presented, should or could all of the passengers be charged with possession of drugs? Explain.

Recklessly

Some crimes require that, in order to establish a person's mental state or criminal culpability, the state must prove that the accused person acted recklessly. According to Section 2.02 of the *MPC*, recklessness exists on the culpability seriousness continuum between purposely and knowingly on one end and negligently on the other end (American Law Institute 1985:21).

The issue of reckless conduct will be discussed throughout this text, but here we define recklessness in a more general sense. Recklessness, according to the *MPC*, is any action by which the defendant "consciously disregards a substantial and unjustifiable risk" of harm (American Law Institute 1985:21). This definition includes four important components, each of which will be considered in turn.

First, the defendant must be conscious of the potential risk created. This component helps distinguish recklessness from negligence since negligence does not require the defendant to be aware of the risk he or she creates. Second, the defendant must create a risk by his or her actions. For example, merely driving a car is creating a risk. Whether this risk rises to the level of recklessness is debatable, though. Third, the risk must be substantial; that is, it goes beyond that encountered in normal everyday activities like the example of driving a car. Fourth, the risk must be unjustifiable since not all substantial risks rise to the level of criminal recklessness. For instance, even though an ambulance might travel well over the posted speed limit during an emergency call (creating a substantial risk), this action would not be reckless since it is justified.

When acting recklessly, the defendant chooses to "consciously disregard" a risk that "involves a gross deviation from the standard of conduct that a law-abiding person would observe in the actor's situation" (American Law Institute 1985:21). Thus, recklessness involves an obvious risk of harm of which the actor is aware but chooses to ignore. The case summarized in Box 2.3 provides one illustration of criminally reckless conduct.

Box 2.3   A CASE OF RECKLESSNESS

Young v. State of Indiana
699 N.E.2d 252 (1998)

Young was originally convicted of murder for shooting into a crowd of people standing outside of his house. There was ample evidence to conclude that he was the shooter, but there was a question surrounding the intended target. He appealed his conviction to the Indiana Supreme Court because he claimed that the trial court erred in not giving the jury instructions on reckless homicide which was a lesser included offense. The following presents an abstract of the appellate court opinion.

Reckless homicide is an inherently included lesser offense of murder and thus the . . . only difference between the two crimes is the *mens rea* the State must show to obtain a conviction. The issue in Young's case is thus whether there is a serious evidentiary dispute about whether Young knowingly or recklessly killed Roney when he fired the first shots from the Oldsmobile. We do not consider whether Young "intentionally" killed Roney since the information alleged only that Young "knowingly" killed.

A person engages in conduct knowingly if, when he engages in the conduct, he is aware of a high probability that he is doing so. One engages in conduct recklessly if he or she engages in the conduct in plain, conscious, and unjustifiable disregard of harm that might result and the disregard involves a substantial deviation from acceptable standards of conduct.

The trial court did not make findings regarding whether a serious evidentiary dispute existed on the issue of Young's *mens rea*. Instead, the judge simply stated to the defense counsel that Young was not entitled to lesser included instructions because he had raised an alibi defense. On the other hand, it may be somewhat pertinent in making the central inquiry which remains whether there is a serious evidentiary dispute in regard to the element or elements differentiating the greater offense from the lesser.

The evidence about Young's state of mind at the time he fired the shot that killed Korey Roney is both conflicting and obscure. Several witnesses acknowledged that they knew Raylon from the neighborhood and there had been no problems between Raylon and those who were in the front yard that night, some even stated that Raylon was a friend. Willie Pargo and Glen Underwood testified that Raylon had no reason to be upset with Korey, and that Raylon and Korey had engaged in friendly conversation just a month and a half before the shooting. Raylon's harsh words, "what's up now, punk m f ?", however, could indicate to a jury that Raylon desired to do more than simply scare those on the front lawn. Eyewitness testimony, indeed the testimony of those who were in the line of fire, disputes this inference however. No witness stated that he thought Raylon was actually aiming his gun at any specific person. Daniel Hampton, only seven feet away from Raylon at the time of the first shots, could not determine whether Young was shooting at anyone in particular or just engaged in wild shooting. Damon Brookins testified; "he was just shootin' . . . dude was pullin' off, you know." Though shooting in the direction of numerous people only twenty feet away is obviously "reckless" behavior no matter whether one is in a set or moving position, whether Raylon's acts are sufficient to show he was aware of a high probability that his act would kill is less certain.

While it is Raylon's mental state when he fired the shot which actually killed Korey that would determine whether he committed murder or reckless homicide, a jury might glean inferences from the larger pattern of shots fired to determine this specific *mens rea*. Of the estimated six shots fired, one bullet hit Korey in the back of the head and was discovered on the ground near where Korey lay after being hit, another was discovered rather far away in a wall of the home next door. These neighbors described their home as being "shot up" at the same time the above events occurred. A crime scene specialist was unable to say whether the recovered bullets were fired at random targets or specifically aimed. Also possibly relevant is the fact that Raylon returned and fired four more shots though all except Korey were inside the home. Korey was prone on the ground during this time but was not shot again.

A jury considering these facts could well have found Raylon was acting recklessly but not knowingly when he fired the shot that killed Korey. Firing a handgun towards a group of people only twenty feet away is certainly an act committed in "plain, conscious, and unjustifiable disregard" of the harm that might result, and a "substantial deviation from acceptable standards of conduct," but given the specific facts of this case, a jury might reasonably decide that such behavior did not reflect a knowing killing.

It is the jury's prerogative to decide such questions of fact. We conclude that the evidence before this jury represented a genuinely disputed matter and that it was error to refuse the instruction. Young is entitled to a new trial.

---

1. Given the facts of this case, how can we distinguish between murder and reckless homicide?
2. What factor or factors seem to differentiate the possible crimes?
3. Is it reasonable to infer that someone who fires several shots into a crowd intends to kill someone (although not a specific person)?

Negligently

Finally, proof of culpability can depend on establishing that a person acted negligently. Quite often there is disagreement about the types of actions that constitute negligence. In the end, given that we are dealing with what people are thinking, it may be difficult to distinguish between recklessness and negligence.

Nevertheless, we can say that people act negligently when they *should* be aware of a risk that is facing them or when they fail to perceive a risk and then act without considering the risk. Negligence is unlike recklessness in that the actor may not be aware of the potential risk, or simply may not comprehend the true magnitude of the risk. However, negligence is like recklessness in that it "involves a gross deviation from the standard of care that a reasonable person would observe in the actor's situation" (American Law Institute 1985:22). The standard of the "reasonable person" or a "reasonably prudent person" is the one that is applied in many criminal law situations. The case presented in Box 2.4 provides one situation in which negligence is an important factor in the defendant's behavior.

Box 2.4   A CASE OF CRIMINAL NEGLIGENCE

California v. Sargent
19 Cal. 4th 1206 (1999)

Sargent was charged with felony child abuse as a result of shaking and dropping his infant son. The question before the California Supreme Court was whether criminal negligence had to be proved in order to secure a conviction or whether proof of general criminal intent was sufficient. The section below summarizes the appellate rulings in this case.

A jury found defendant, who had inflicted injuries on his infant son, guilty of felony child abuse for direct infliction of unjustifiable physical pain and mental suffering under circumstances or conditions likely to produce great bodily harm or death. The Court of Appeal, Third Dist. concluded that criminal negligence must be demonstrated to convict a defendant of infliction of unjustifiable physical pain or mental suffering, and that the evidence did not support the inference that defendant had been criminally negligent. The Court of Appeal modified the judgment to a misdemeanor, and remanded to the trial court for resentencing.

The Supreme Court reversed the judgment of the Court of Appeal and remanded the matter for further proceedings. The court held that the Court of Appeal erred in concluding that criminal negligence was the required *mens rea* for felony child abuse. The statute's language is most readily interpreted as requiring general criminal intent. That is, the statute describes a particular act, without reference to intent to do a further act or achieve a future consequence. Also, the language of the statute is similar to statutes defining other general intent crimes, including proscribing corporal punishment or child beating, assault, and assault with a deadly weapon. Thus, when the conduct involves the direct infliction of unjustifiable physical pain or mental suffering on a child, the defendant must have a *mens rea* of general criminal intent to commit the proscribed act. The scienter for felony and misdemeanor child abuse is the same, whether the infliction of the unjustifiable physical pain or mental suffering was under circumstances or conditions likely to produce great bodily harm or death, and its presence is a question for the trier of fact. If so, the crime is punishable as a felony. If not, it is punishable solely as a misdemeanor.

1. Does a certain degree of harm distinguish recklessness from negligence?
2. Does the age of the victim and/or the ability to defend one's self play a role in cases such as this?
3. How can we differentiate criminal negligence from general criminal intent?

Proof of *Mens Rea*

In the following chapters, we will address both the *actus reus* and the *mens rea* necessary to establish that a crime has occurred. Of these two elements, it is typically easier to prove that there has been a wrongful act. By contrast, establishing *mens rea* may be challenging in many criminal cases. As we have already mentioned, the difficulty results from trying to prove what the accused was thinking at the time of the offense. In the absence of a confession specifically outlining what the defendant was thinking, the decision makers in the case (judges and juries) are left to depend on what are called **inferences** and **presumptions**.

An inference is "a conclusion drawn by a reader from a text or an observer from circumstances," and an inferential fact involves "a fact that is established indirectly and is found by the finder of fact by inference from the evidence that supports some other finding of fact" (Sheppard 2012:1305, 1033). Therefore, if we know that someone pointed a loaded rifle at another individual and pulled the trigger, we can infer from this action that the first person wanted to shoot the second person.

Presumptions are associated with inferences, and they help us establish what an offender's intentions may have been. It is important to remember that a presumption is not the same as evidence. Nevertheless, a presumption is "a finding of fact derived from evidence that would not otherwise be sufficient to demonstrate the finding conclusively, but which reaches a threshold of sufficiency to be accepted as a fact" (Sheppard 2012:2146). In criminal law, one of the most

Inference:
a method of reasoning in which a fact that is to be established is deduced as a logical consequence from other facts that might have been proven or admitted

Presumption:
an assumption that a fact exists as a result of other known or proven facts

basic presumptions is that people intend the natural and logical consequences of their actions. Therefore, we can presume that when a person shoots another person, the intention was to cause either great bodily harm or death.

In the absence of direct evidence such as a confession, juries are left to piece together the available evidence surrounding a crime in an effort to form a complete picture from all of the puzzle pieces known as **circumstantial evidence**. In many criminal cases it is all judges and juries have on which to base their decisions.

Circumstantial Evidence: Information and testimony that permit conclusions that indirectly establish the existence or nonexistence of a fact or event that the party seeks to prove

ABSOLUTE LIABILITY

As previously mentioned, the state bears the burden of proving *mens rea* beyond a reasonable doubt in virtually every case. However, there are offenses in which proof of intent is either not required or greatly diminished. These are the so-called absolute or strict liability offenses. This concept emerged in the mid-1800s in England and was originally applied to offenses such as statutory rape and adultery (Johnson 1953; Wasserstrom 1960).

It should be apparent by now that there are many complicated concepts in criminal law, and the subject of absolute liability is certainly among these. The *MPC* includes **absolute liability** as one of the general principles of liability. However, in the commentary on this principle, it says that strict liability may only apply if the legislature has explicitly provided for it in a statute, and then only in cases of "violations" or the least serious misdemeanors (American Law Institute 1985:28-29). The *MPC* commentary on this section speaks of the more familiar concept of **strict liability**, and in this section (and elsewhere as well) we will use the more common label of strict liability.

Absolute Liability: a rule of criminal responsibility that allows for the conviction of an otherwise innocent person without proof of *mens rea*

Strict Liability: a rule of criminal responsibility that allows for the conviction of an otherwise innocent person without proof of *mens rea*

We have already noted several times that in the criminal law the state must establish *mens rea* (the guilty mind or criminal intent), but in the area of strict liability offenses, this requirement is altered. In criminal law terminology, strict liability involves "an offense for which there is no *mens rea* requirement, and thus it may be committed by accident" (Sheppard 2012:1625). There are two categories of offenses—public welfare and non-public welfare—under which most of the strict liability violations occur.

Public Welfare Crimes

Public welfare offenses largely fit into the category of *mala prohibita* crimes (see Chapter 1) in that they are not considered inherently evil, but they can still result in social harm. As such, statutes have been passed criminalizing these activities in order to prevent these harms to society. Over the years, public welfare offenses have included: "(1) illegal sales or transport of intoxicating liquor; (2) sales of impure or adulterated food; (3) sales of misbranded articles; (4) violations of anti-narcotics acts; (5) criminal nuisances; (6) violations of traffic regulations; (7) violations of motor-vehicle laws; and (8) violations of general police regulations, passed for safety health or well being of the community" (Carpenter 2003:330). When these activities occur, courts allow convictions without explicit proof of *mens rea*, and there are at least five reasons for minimizing the *mens rea* requirement in such cases:

(1) these types of violations have no common law basis;
(2) there may be a focus on collective guilt rather than individual liability given the potential for public harm by these violations;
(3) the statutory standards are reasonable;
(4) the penalties are relatively minor and, in most instances, entail only fines; and
(5) convictions often do little to damage violators' reputations. (Dressler 2009:147)

Violations that have no basis in common law include what we might call modern-day offenses. These would include crimes not imagined under the common law such as traffic offenses (speeding, running a red light, and reckless driving).

The offenses that focus on collective guilt deal with issues such as environmental regulations (smokestack emissions or illegal dumping, for example). These actions have the potential to create public harm, and they are often committed by companies rather than individuals.

Some examples of reasonable statutory standards include the prohibition against selling adulterated food or drugs and the whole range of requirements relating to traffic safety (such as speed limits and setting the minimum age for licensed drivers) (Carpenter 2003). These are issues that would have broad public support for their reasonableness and the desirability of such regulations.

The fourth reason—relatively minor penalties—is somewhat connected to the first reason. For instance, in most cases of motor vehicle moving violations, only fines may be imposed and there is no potential for jail time. Therefore, given the relatively nonserious nature of such punishments, the law is willing to treat these offenses as strict liability crimes and to permit a lower standard for proof of *mens rea*.

Finally, when offenses such as environmental violations are committed by corporations, there is virtually no personal or social stigma attached to these crimes. It is unlikely that people would be looked down upon by others or publicly scorned for committing these offenses. Thus, one of the key principles of the criminal law in regards to punishment (the attachment of a stigma) seems to be diminished or totally absent.

Non-Public Welfare Crimes

The most commonly cited example of a non-public welfare, strict liability crime is **statutory rape** (Carpenter 2003). A simple definition of statutory rape is "Sexual conduct with a person who has not reached the statutory age of consent" (Sheppard 2012:2302).

Statutory Rape: the sexual penetration — whether wanted or unwanted — of a person who is under a specified legal age

Every state statutorily defines the age at which a person is able to give consent to have sex, and the **age of consent** is based on the notion that individuals below a certain age are not capable of fully appreciating the consequences of their actions. Therefore, the law must protect minor children from themselves and other people who are older than they are who might take advantage of them. In situations involving statutory rape, even though both parties agree to have sex and even if one person believes that the other is above the age of consent, the law considers the older party criminally culpable for the acts based on strict liability. Even though the party who believed that the other person was able to give consent had no criminal intent, or *mens rea*, the law recognized a need to protect minors from this type of conduct. State laws traditionally provided for different ages of consent for males and females, but these distinctions have been eliminated. However, many states still provide for a difference in age between the "victim" and offender. Box 2.5 provides an illustration of the dilemma potentially posed by strict liability offenses like statutory rape, and Table 2.1 provides the legal age of consent for all 50 states.

Age of Consent: the statutory age at which a person can legally consent to engage in sexual behavior

---

Box 2.5   YOU DECIDE: CHILD'S PLAY OR SEX CRIME?

Two neighborhood children — a girl who is 17 and a boy who is 14 — are caught in the act of mutual oral sex by one of the children's parents. The age of consent for the state is 16. Thus, while the activity is consensual, the law holds that one party (the girl) is an offender and the other party (the boy) is a victim since he is not old enough to give consent. Should the girl be charged with a delinquent act (statutory rape)? If so is, is it reasonable that the state require her to register as a sex offender (perhaps for life)?

Table 2.1	LEGAL AGE OF CONSENT BY STATE						
STATE	AGE	STATE	AGE	STATE	AGE	STATE	AGE
Alabama	16	Indiana	16	Nebraska	16	South Carolina	16
Alaska	16	Iowa	16	Nevada	16	South Dakota	16
Arizona	18	Kansas	16	New Hampshire	16	Tennessee	18
Arkansas	16	Kentucky	16	New Jersey	16	Texas	17
California	18	Louisiana	17	New Mexico	16	Utah	18
Colorado	17	Maine	16	New York	17	Vermont	16
Connecticut	16	Maryland	16	North Carolina	16	Virginia	18
Delaware	18	Massachusetts	16	North Dakota	18	Washington	16
Florida	18	Michigan	16	Ohio	16	West Virginia	16
Georgia	16	Minnesota	16	Oklahoma	16	Wisconsin	18
Hawaii	16	Mississippi	16	Oregon	18	Wyoming	18
Idaho	18	Missouri	17	Pennsylvania	16		
Illinois	17	Montana	16	Rhode Island	16		

Source: FindTheData (2012).

One of the dilemmas that arises in this area is that "all states, as well as the *Model Penal Code*, deny to a defendant charged with a strict liability offense [such as statutory rape] the defense of mistake, yet at the same time, allow most other affirmative defenses" (Bergelson 2011:55). Bergelson uses the example of the two main characters in Vladimir Nabokov's (1955) novel *Lolita* as an illustration of the inability to use mistake as a defense for a strict liability crime. She concludes from her legal analysis "that a person who commits a strict liability offense pursuant to a reasonable mistake deserves punishment even less than the person who commits the same crime under duress." Therefore, she proposes "a revision of the current law and adoption of an across-the-board rule that would make the defense of a reasonable mistake available in any criminal prosecution" (Bergelson 2011:55).

While strict liability is an established legal principle, it is one about which there is some controversy. Given that one of the fundamental criminal law tenets is that the state must prove *mens rea* beyond a reasonable doubt, strict liability offenses set that requirement aside for certain behaviors and make it a crime to have committed the wrongful act (*actus reus*) irrespective of the person's intent. While the U.S. Supreme Court has not spoken conclusively on the issue of strict liability, in a series of recent cases the Court has declared that the issue of the level of proof relative to *mens rea* (presumably including strict liability cases) is a decision left to legislatures rather than to courts [see, for example, *Dixon v. United States*, 548 U.S. 1 (2006) and *Clark v. Arizona*, 548 U.S. 735 (2006)].

CONCURRENCE

Once the state has established the *actus reus* and *mens rea*, further proof is required that these two elements have intersected. This element is most often labeled as **concurrence**. Essentially, in order to be held criminally liable, a person must commit the criminal *actus reus* at the same time as the *mens rea*. As Fletcher (1998:121) notes, in criminal law concurrence is "the required union of act and intent."

Concurrence in criminal law is important since a wrongful act can occur in the absence of criminal intent. In those situations, a crime has technically not taken place—except for strict liability offenses. For instance, there are at least two situations that can illustrate wrongful acts without the presence of *mens rea*. The first of these situations involves a mistake of fact. This circumstance will be dealt with at greater length in Chapter 10 on justification defenses, but a brief illustration is useful. Suppose that Robert has a leather jacket that he has owned for some time and he wears it to dinner at a local restaurant. He hangs his jacket near the door and when he gets ready to leave he reaches for a leather jacket and wears it home. When he arrives home he discovers that the jacket he took was much newer and more expensive than his. Has he committed a crime? Not at this point. While he has committed a wrongful act (taking something that was not his), he did so mistakenly. However, if he decides to keep the jacket, given that it is newer and nicer, he has committed larceny. The issue of criminal liability here rests on whether there is an intent to permanently keep the jacket.

A second example involves what is known as the **innocent instrumentality rule**. This legal concept will be addressed more fully in Chapter 3, but this notion is also relevant to our discussion of concurrence since it involves a wrongful act in the absence of criminal intent. Section 2.06(2) of the *MPC* specifies that "a person is legally accountable for the conduct of another person when (a) acting with the kind of culpability that is sufficient for the commission of the offense, he causes an *innocent or irresponsible person* to engage in such conduct" [emphasis added] (American Law Institute 1985:29). This section's commentary adds that someone is accountable for a crime "when the actor causes an innocent or irresponsible person to engage in the conduct, acting with the kind of culpability that would be sufficient were he committing the offense himself" (American Law Institute 1985:31).

In the case of an innocent instrumentality, one person (for example, an adult) causes another person (such as a minor child) to commit a crime on behalf of the instigating party. Again, an illustration will prove useful. Shannon decides that it is too expensive to buy the daily newspaper so occasionally she gets up early and has her four-year-old son go next door to get the newspaper out of the neighbor's driveway. While the child has engaged in a wrongful act, the law would say that

Concurrence: principle of criminal liability that a person must have a criminal *mens rea* at the same time that they perform a criminal *actus reus*

Innocent Instrumentality Rule: the use by one person of another person who is otherwise not blameworthy to commit a wrongful act

this is a case of an innocent instrumentality and would hold the mother (not the child) criminally liable. Both of the examples given here demonstrate that there must be concurrence between the *actus reus* and *mens rea* to establish that a particular person has committed a crime.

CAUSATION

For result crimes, the state must prove — in addition to *actus reus*, *mens rea*, and concurrence — causation and result. An additional requirement that the state must prove in order to establish that there is criminal liability is that a relationship exists between the conduct and the result — that is, cause. Section 2.03 of the *MPC* notes that "(1) conduct is the cause of a result when: (a) it is an antecedent but for which the result in question would not have occurred; and (b) the relationship between the conduct and result satisfies any additional causal requirements imposed by the Code or by the law defining the offense" (American Law Institute 1985:25).

The *antecedent* requirement is when the conduct exists in time before the "result" (or outcome). In the social sciences we speak of cause-and-effect relationships; in criminal law we have a similar situation with conduct and result. In trying to establish liability, it is accurate to say that the result would not have occurred without the conduct. Legal scholars divide causation into two parts: **actual cause** and **proximate cause**. In the following sections we further discuss these two parts in addition to other peripheral cause issues.

Actual Cause

In order to establish criminal liability for result crimes, the state must establish that the defendant's conduct was the actual cause of the result that was prohibited by law. This also may be called the **factual cause**, and it involves any cause "that leads as a matter of fact to a given result" (Sheppard 2012:368).

When reading appellate court cases, the Latin phrase **sine qua non** may appear; this phrase means "but for," and it is used to explain a cause-and-result relationship. For example, B (the result) would not have occurred *but for* the occurrence of A (the conduct). Thus, the "but for" test is used to eliminate some of the other potential causes of a particular result. The question to be asked is "but for the action, would the result have occurred?" If the answer is "no," then the state proves actual cause. If the answer is "yes," then the state has failed to prove actual cause. However, we should emphasize that while proof of actual causation is necessary, it is

Actual Cause:
the conduct that created a result that was prohibited by law

Proximate Cause:
adding the element of actual cause to the necessary *mens rea* to establish that a crime has been committed and that we have a specific suspect

Factual Cause:
the conduct that created a result that was prohibited by law

Sine Qua Non:
Latin meaning "but for"; a concept in criminal law that says that one action could not have occurred but for the occurrence of another action

not fully sufficient, as there are other potential factors that must be considered.

In some circumstances, it is more appropriate to apply the **substantial factor test**. This test is utilized in situations where there may be two potential causes. An example is helpful to illustrate the situation where the substantial factor test would be needed. Victor dies at the hands of Al and Betty. If Al shoots Victor in the head and Betty shoots Victor in the chest, both at close range and at the same time, the "but for" test may prove to be inadequate. Applying the "but for" test, we would ask the question "but for Al's actions, would Victor have died (the result)?" The answer would be yes. We can also ask the question "but for Betty's actions, would Victor have died?" Again, the answer would be yes. Thus, neither would be *the* cause of death which, obviously, would not make sense. In such cases, therefore, the substantial factor test must be used. Is Al a substantial factor in Victor's death? Is Betty a substantial factor in Victor's death? If so, then both Al and Betty would be the actual cause of Victor's death.

In some situations, judges and juries will have to decide whether something occurred between the initial action and the result that was totally out of the accused individual's control. Factors that break the causal chain are called **independent causes** or **intervening causes**, and they are unrelated to any actions taken by the person accused of the crime (see Sheppard 2012:370). If we consider the example of the hunting trip in Box 2.6, we can see the elements that might establish that there was an intervening cause. Bill fires a shot at Tom, and Tom collapses. Bill then places Tom in his pickup truck and races to the nearest hospital, but on the way to the hospital Bill's truck is hit by another vehicle and Tom dies from the injuries he suffers in the accident. Was Bill responsible for Tom's death? Since Bill was not ultimately responsible for Tom's death as his fatal injuries came from the traffic accident, this means that the accident was an independent, intervening cause in Tom's death.

A typical example of an intervening cause addresses medical malpractice. One might argue that errors in medical treatment may be the independent, intervening cause of death instead of the original injury inflicted. What the courts have said about inadequate medical treatment is that it may be common, but it is only an intervening cause when it can be demonstrated that the medical treatment provided was *grossly negligent* [see *People v. Saavedra-Rodriguez*, 971 P.2d 223 (1998)].

Proximate Cause

In addition to consideration of actual cause, the state also must establish proximate cause. Proximate cause can also be called

Substantial Factor Test:
in situations where there may be two or more potential causes of some harm the courts will employ this test to determine which of the causes was more likely to have contributed to the result

Independent Causes/ Intervening Causes:
any factors that break the chain between the initial cause and the result

> **Box 2.6   YOU DECIDE: CRIME, ACCIDENT, OR SOMETHING ELSE?**
>
> Bill and Tom are long-time hunting partners. On one of their hunting trips, Bill thinks it would be funny to fire a shot in Tom's direction, but without the intention of actually striking him. Bill fires the shot, but he scares Tom so badly that Tom has a heart attack. Could Bill be charged with a crime? Should he be? Could the state maintain Bill legally and actually caused Tom's death?

legal cause. The U.S. Supreme Court has noted that proximate cause is "any cause which, in natural or probable sequence, produced the injury complained of" [*CSX Transportation v. McBride*, 564 U.S. _____ (2011)]. However, Allen (2012:110) warns that "proximate cause is not a question of science or legal knowledge, but a matter of policy considerations." Therefore, in Allen's view, "proximate cause is a particularly extreme example of doctrine that limps along despite near universal consensus that it cannot determine legal outcomes" (77).

Proximate cause can be selected in a multistep process. First, we can ask the question: Was the result *directly* connected to the act? If it was, then we can stop at that point, and proximate cause has been established. Second, if the result was only *indirectly* connected to the act, then we ask the question: Was the result reasonably foreseeable? If the result was reasonably foreseeable, then once again proximate cause has been established. If it was not reasonably foreseeable, then proximate cause has not been established. Box 2.6 provides an example that should be helpful in illustrating this concept.

Legal Cause: adding the element of actual cause to the necessary *mens rea* to establish that a crime has been committed and that we have a specific suspect

RESULT

At this point, it is important to remember that in order to bring a criminal charge and to secure a conviction for a *result crime*, the state must establish that the individual acted voluntarily; that the person acted purposely, knowingly, recklessly, or negligently; that there is a connection between the act and the mental state; and that there is a demonstrable causal link between the conduct and the outcome or the result. The result is independently proven from the physical act. For example, in homicide cases (discussed in Chapter 5) there must be proof that someone actually died, and, therefore, this means the homicide is a result crime rather than a conduct crime. If the crime is theft (discussed in Chapter 4), then the act proven is the taking and carrying away of another's property. The state does not need to prove the result, since the property was taken and the *actus reus* element establishes that fact. Homicide is a result crime — requiring the proof that the person died as a result of the accused's actions — whereas theft is a conduct crime — proof of the act of taking property is, itself, enough to prove criminal liability. If any of these elements are missing, it is much more difficult for the state to prove to a jury that a crime occurred.

SUMMARY

In this chapter we have considered several key elements that are required to establish criminal liability. For example, when charging someone with a crime the state will have to establish that the person committed an act prohibited by criminal law (*actus reus*). The evidence will have to include that there was some physical act or that there was a failure to act in a situation where the law creates a duty to act. Thoughts and statuses are not punishable under the criminal law, but possession of certain items can be considered a criminal act.

Beyond establishing that there was a physical act, the state must prove that the accused person acted voluntarily. In most instances this is not a problem, but there are situations where people may do something that does not fall into the category of voluntary or willful behavior, which can eliminate their liability.

In addition to voluntary action, the state must establish that a person had the mental state necessary to commit a crime, which creates further evidence that the individual is blameworthy for the deed. When describing someone's mental state, statutes typically specify that a person is culpable for a criminal act if he or she acted purposely, knowingly, recklessly, or negligently. Obviously, these terms relate to a particular state of mind, and that may not be readily apparent in all situations.

While virtually all criminal statutes require proof of *mens rea*, the area of absolute (or strict) liability provides a unique point in criminal law. In most situations the state must explicitly establish *mens rea* as a part of proof beyond a reasonable doubt. However, in a limited number of circumstances the state must only prove the act occurred without proof of one's mental state. In effect, intent is inferred from the action.

Concurrence involves the point at which the *actus reus* and *mens rea* intersect, and when these two elements are joined, a crime is said to have occurred. It is important for the law to prove concurrence because, as we have seen in this chapter, it is possible for a wrongful act to have happened without there being criminal intent and for criminal intent to exist without there having been a wrongful act.

Given the difficulty of establishing an individual's state of mind, the law turns to the notion of conduct and result. In other words, did the person act in such a way as to produce a certain result? Is there a direct connection between the conduct and the result, or is the connection indirect?

KEY TERMS

absolute liability
actual cause
actual possession
actus reus
age of consent
attendant circumstances
bystander rule
circumstantial evidence
concurrence
conduct
constructive possession
culpability
factual cause
general intent
Good Samaritan statutes
independent causes

inference
innocent instrumentality rule
innocent possession
intervening causes
joint possession
legal cause
possession
presumption
proximate cause
results
sine qua non
specific intent
statutory rape
strict liability
substantial factor test
transferred intent
voluntary act
willful blindness

CRITICAL THINKING QUESTIONS

1. What do we really mean in saying the law is designed to punish deeds not thoughts? Don't wrongful thoughts precede wrongful deeds? At what point do we start to consider punishment based on what people have been thinking? (Hint: We'll come back to this issue in Chapter 9 when we discuss inchoate crimes.)
2. In the chapter we emphasized that *actus reus* is based on physical acts. Are there situations in which physical acts have not occurred but there has been a crime? Explain your answer.
3. When is a failure to act considered an action? Why do some people have a legal duty to act in situations where others do not? Is it reasonable to expect a parent who cannot swim to jump into the water to save a drowning child?
4. Are the concepts of recklessness and negligence easy to distinguish? What separates the two? Which is considered the more serious under criminal law, and why?
5. What do we mean by the notion of concurrence? Is this a crucial element in the state's case to prove a crime? Why or why not?
6. Distinguish general intent from specific intent. Are these notions viable in criminal law today or have they outlived whatever utility they may have had? How does the *MPC* treat these concepts?

7. What do we mean by actual cause and proximate cause? Again, are these easily distinguishable?
8. Can inadequate medical care serve as an independent, intervening cause? How could we determine whether the original injuries suffered or inadequate medical care actually caused someone's death?

9. We suggested that there are two categories of offenses that fit under the absolute (or strict) liability definition. What are the two categories and what would place an offense in one versus the other? Does one category encompass more serious public harms than the other? If so, which, and what justifies your answer?

SUGGESTED READINGS

Dressler, J. (2009). *Understanding Criminal Law* (5th ed.). Newark, NJ: Matthew Bender/LexisNexis. Dressler's book is one frequently cited throughout the present text. It is designed to introduce law school students to criminal law. Most of the sections are easily understood by undergraduate students, but some parts are especially complex. If you can find a copy of this book (or an older edition) in a used book store it is a worthy addition to your personal reference library.

Eisenstein, J. & Jacob, H. (1977). *Felony Justice: An Organizational Analysis of Criminal Courts*. Boston: Little, Brown. This is a classic in the fields of criminal justice and political science. However, given its publication date you may have to do some looking to find a copy. The authors introduce the concept of "the courtroom work group" and they examine the way felony cases are processed in Baltimore, Chicago, and Detroit. This book clearly illustrates how the law on the books can differ substantially from the law in action.

Fletcher, G.P. (1998). *Basic Concepts of Criminal Law*. New York: Oxford University Press. Fletcher's book is unique in that it is not a standard criminal law text. Instead, it was written to introduce law faculty members from Russia and other previously Communist countries to criminal law concepts from the United States. As he says in his acknowledgments, "I wanted to write a book that would introduce Russian law students to Western ways of thinking about criminal law" (vii). Therefore, he deals with the law in a much more abstract and theoretical way. This book provides a different perspective than that to which most students would traditionally be exposed.

REFERENCES

Allen, J. (2012). "The Persistence of Proximate Cause: How Legal Doctrine Thrives on Skepticism." *Denver University Law Review* 90:77-129.

American Law Institute (1985). *Model Penal Code: Complete Statutory Text*. Philadelphia, PA.

Anderson, J.O., Jr. (2011). "What 'Mens Rea Dilemma'?" *New England Journal on Criminal and Civil Confinement* 37:371-394.

Bergelson, V. (2011). "A Fair Punishment for Humbert Humbert: Strict Liability and Affirmative Defenses." *New Criminal Law Review* 14(1):55-77.

California v. Sargent, 19 Cal. 4th 1206 (1999).

Carpenter, C.L. (2003). "On Statutory Rape, Strict Liability, and the Public Welfare Offense Model." *American University Law Review* 53(2):313-404.

Charles, J.M. (2009). "'America's Lost Cause': The Unconstitutionality of Criminalizing Our Country's Homeless Population." *Boston University Public Interest Law Journal* 18:315-348.

Child Abuse Prevention and Treatment Act, 42 U.S.C. 5101 et seq. (1974).

Clark v. Arizona, 548 U.S. 735 (2006).

CSX Transportation v. McBride, 564 U.S. ___ (2011).

Dixon v. United States, 548 U.S. 1 (2006).

Dressler, J. (2009). *Understanding Criminal Law* (5th ed.). Newark, NJ: Matthew Bender/LexisNexis.

Federal Bureau of Investigation (2011). "Crime in the United States, 2011." http://www.fbi.gov/about-us/cjis/ucr/crime-in-the-u.s./2011/crime-in-the-u.s.2011/violent-crime/robberymain.

FindLaw (2011). "Drug Possession." http://criminal.findlaw.com/crimes/a-z/drug_possession.html.

FindTheData (2012). http://age-of-consent.findthedata.org.

Fletcher, G.P. (1998). *Basic Concepts of Criminal Law*. New York: Oxford University Press.

Groninger, J.L. (1999). "No Duty to Rescue: Can Americans Really Leave a Victim Lying in the Street? What Is Left of the American Rule, and Will It Survive Unabated?" *Pepperdine Law Review* 26:353-377.

Johnson, C.D. (1953). "Note: Strict Liability Crimes." *Nebraska Law Review* 33:462-467.

Maryland v. Pringle, 540 U.S. 366 (2003).

Nabokov, V. (1955). *Lolita*. New York: Random House.

People v. Saavedra-Rodriguez, 971 P.2d 223 (1998).

Powell v. Texas, 392 U.S. 514 (1968).

Robinson v. California, 370 U.S. 660 (1962).

Romohr, P.W. (2006). "A Right/Duty Perspective on the Legal and Philosophical Foundations of the No-Duty-to-Rescue Rule." *Duke Law Journal* 55(5):1025-1057.

Roth, W. (1979). "General vs. Specific Intent: A Time for Terminological Understanding in California." *Pepperdine Law Review* 7:67-84.

Schubert, F.A. (2010). *Criminal Law: The Basics* (2d ed.). Austin, TX: Wolters Kluwer.

Schulz, D.M. (2002). "Vagrancy." In *Encyclopedia of Crime and Punishment*, edited by David Levinson, 1653-1657. Thousand Oaks, CA: Sage.

Sheppard, S.M., general editor (2012). *Bouvier Law Dictionary*. New York: Wolters Kluwer Law & Business.

Silver, J. (1985). "The Duty to Rescue: A Reexamination and Proposal." *William and Mary Law Review* 26:423-447.

Singley, S.J. (1998). "Failure to Report Suspected Child Abuse: Civil Liability of Mandated Reporters." *Journal of Juvenile Law* 19:236-271.

United States v. Mason, 233 F.3d 619 (D.C. Cir. 2000).

Vago, S. (2009). *Law and Society* (9th ed.). Upper Saddle River, NJ: Prentice Hall/Pearson.

Wasserstrom, R.A. (1960). "Strict Liability in the Criminal Law." *Stanford Law Review* 12(4):731-745.

Young v. State of Indiana, 699 N.E.2d 252 (1998).

Parties to Crime

LEARNING OBJECTIVES

After reading this chapter you should be able to:

1. Distinguish the different degrees of individual involvement in crimes
2. Define the term complicity
3. Explain the differences between principals and accessories
4. Describe the nature of crime by innocent instrumentality
5. Describe the differences between the common law and the *Model Penal Code* in defining complicity
6. Define and explain vicarious liability

INTRODUCTION

In some criminal transactions, one individual is responsible for committing the crime. In other instances, multiple parties are involved. For those cases in which several people are involved, the court must decide who was actually responsible for committing the crime, what level or degree of participation each party had in the crime, and to what extent other individuals participated in or facilitated the crime. When more than one defendant is involved in a criminal trial, a common strategy is for each one to place some or all of the blame on his or her codefendant(s) in order to minimize their own level of culpability. The conclusion about who is truly responsible for criminal activity is crucial in deciding whether a person should be charged with a particular crime, whether the person should be convicted, and what the appropriate punishment is for their involvement in the crime.

As a general rule, the criminal law is designed to punish those individuals who have actually committed wrongful acts. However, as we will see in some of the following sections, there are some situations in which one person can be held responsible for actions committed by another person. In this chapter we will unravel some of the most confounding concepts in criminal law: those surrounding the roles played by different parties who may be involved in the commission of a crime to numerous degrees and on many different levels.

PERPETRATORS

As we discussed in Chapter 1, in order to hold a person responsible for the commission of a crime, the state will have to establish that the person committed a criminal act (*actus reus*) and that the individual had a criminal mindset (*mens rea*) at the time the act was committed. As we discussed in the previous chapter, other relevant circumstances may have to be addressed. However, even after a suspect has been identified, the issue of who played what role in a criminal act may continue to raise questions and create uncertainty. The situation becomes much more complicated when several individuals have participated in committing a crime, and each may have had a different degree of involvement. In the sections that follow, we address some of the major distinctions that arise under the criminal law for individuals who have participated in the commission of a crime in various ways and with varying degrees of involvement and culpability.

The most common designation for people who have committed crimes is **perpetrators**. A perpetrator is a "person or entity who executes or carries out a criminal act" (Sheppard 2012:2021). The Bureau of Justice Statistics (1981:154) adds that a perpetrator is "the chief actor in the commission of a crime, that is, the person who directly commits the criminal act." Perpetrators may also be called culprits or suspects. Throughout this book we will be concerned with criminal perpetrators and how the state is able to identify, prosecute, and punish them for their criminal acts.

ACCOMPLICES

When we use the label of perpetrator, there is no distinction between the primary parties who actually committed the crime and secondary parties who may have assisted with or contributed in some material way to the commission of the crime. However, it is important to recognize that the law provides for the punishment of both the people who actually commit crimes, as well as those who assist with the commission of crimes. In regards to punishment, the law often makes distinctions based upon a person's level of participation, as well as the timing of this involvement. Those people who help with or provide some form of assistance in the commission of a crime are generally known as **accomplices** or **accessories** to crimes.

In simplest terms, an accomplice "assists another person in performing a criminal act" (Sheppard 2012:50) and, similarly, an accessory is a person "who provides aid, information, or inducement of a crime" (Sheppard 2012:50, 46). One way that a person can act as an accessory is through the process of being an **aider or abettor**. An aider or abettor is "an accomplice who solicits or knowingly assists another person to commit a crime" (Bureau of Justice Statistics 1981:153). This means that anyone who is called an "aider, abettor, solicitor, accessory before [during, or after] the fact" or something similar is, in fact, an accomplice (Bureau of Justice Statistics 1981:153). These names and descriptions cover numerous levels of criminal involvement and a wide range of activities that may contribute to a crime being committed. For our purposes in this chapter, all of these terms may be used somewhat interchangeably. We will consider several of these categories as we continue through the remainder of this chapter.

An example of an accomplice is someone who provides a handgun that is used in a homicide or someone who drives a getaway car used in an armed robbery. Accomplices are people who assist others in some material way that results in the commission of an offense.

Perpetrators:
a general term for people who commit crimes

Accomplices/Accessories:
people who assist in the commission of a crime in some material way

Aider or Abettor:
any person who knowingly assists another person in the commission of a crime

Later we will see that those who function as accomplices may also be punished for the underlying crime ultimately committed, as well as for other reasonably foreseeable offenses.

It is important to note at this point that the terms "perpetrators" and "accomplices" may be used in very general, nontechnical ways to describe people who commit crimes. However, in most criminal statutes, more precise terms are used to identify the people who are responsible for committing crimes. Therefore, we now turn to a discussion of the broad notion of complicity. We will follow this by examining the common law categories of principals and accessories as these apply to both felonies and misdemeanors.

COMPLICITY

In its simplest terms, **complicity** (or **accomplice liability**) is the legal theory "by which an accomplice is effectively treated as if the accomplice is the principal" (Sheppard 2012:1616). In effect, it is the legal view that one person can be held criminally liable for the actions of another person or persons. It is important to remember that in most instances the criminal law only holds people liable who perform the actions that are classified as crimes. However, some people may participate as accomplices or accessories, and these individuals provide some type of assistance that facilitates the crime, even though they may not actually commit the final act. Nevertheless, those who act in this capacity contribute in a material way to the commission of a crime and the law considers them to have acted wrongfully as well. In fact, many legal standards suggest that, for the most part, accomplices are equally liable and should receive the same punishment as those who were the primary actors.

Complicity/Accomplice Liability: to be associated with or to be an accomplice in a criminal act

Under the concept of complicity, a person can be held criminally liable for the actions undertaken or accomplished by others and in which they were involved in some way. This is known as **derivative liability**, and it means that the accomplice's blameworthiness is attached to the acts committed by the perpetrator or principal. The result is that accomplices can be convicted of any offenses that the principal may have committed as a result of or benefitting from the help or aid of the accomplice (Dressler 2008). Consider the example provided in Box 3.1.

Derivative Liability: to be held criminally liable for the acts of another as a result of acting as an accomplice

In the following sections we examine the ways in which the common law distinguished between the deeds of primary actors and secondary actors in the commission of crimes. As you will see, these distinctions traditionally had significant implications for the potential punishment of the various parties.

Box 3.1   YOU DECIDE: EQUALLY GUILTY OR NOT?

Robert is a financially struggling college student who decides to rob a convenience store for some money. He persuades his roommate, Phillip, to drive him to a convenience store across town where they don't know anyone so that the two of them are less likely to be recognized. Robert is not armed, but he tells the store clerk that he has a weapon. The clerk produces a handgun and the two struggle over it. The handgun goes off, killing the clerk, and Robert leaves with a handful of cash. As Robert and Phillip are returning to their apartment, the police apprehend them as a result of a description of the getaway car.

Since the convenience store clerk was killed in the commission of a robbery, both Robert and Phillip can be charged with a variety of offenses including the shooting of the clerk. Even though Phillip stayed in the car during the robbery, he can be charged for the same crimes as Robert. In this case, the district attorney's office may distinguish between one person being the actual perpetrator of the crime and the other being a criminal accomplice in terms of the charges, although the punishments may be the same.

Many people, including those who could be chosen to sit on a jury, might think it is manifestly unjust to charge Phillip with the store clerk's death since all he did was drive the car to the place where the death occurred. Nevertheless, the law may view him as contributing in a material way to the robbery and subsequent shooting, which would make him equally culpable. He was associated with and contributed to Robert's actions, so under the legal principle of complicity he is as much to blame for the clerk's death as Robert is.

Should both Robert and Phillip be charged equally for the outcome? Has Phillip actually facilitated a crime? Did he really contribute to the death of the store clerk?

COMMON LAW

Throughout this book, the focus is on the definition and description of criminal laws provided by the *Model Penal Code* (*MPC*). Nevertheless, it is also important to consider the common law for at least two major reasons. First, the common law predates the *MPC*. Thus, examining the common law gives us an historical context for much of the statutory criminal law development in the United States. Second, there are instances in which the *MPC* and the common law are substantially in agreement. In these areas, the drafters of the *MPC* seemed to feel that the common law tradition had contemporary viability. However, there are several situations in which the *MPC* departs from the common law. Some of these areas attempt to provide clarity and to remove some of the ambiguity inherent in the long common law tradition of the United States. Therefore, in the following sections we will describe the common law's approach to designating the parties to crime. Later in the chapter, this will be contrasted with the approach taken by the *MPC*.

Principals

In the previous sections we discussed the concepts of perpetrators and accomplices; however, under the common law a different set of labels was used. For instance, those perpetrators who are directly involved in the commission of a crime are considered **principals**. A principal is "the actor who causes the violation of the criminal law, as opposed to an accessory who merely assists the principal" (Sheppard 2012:2160). In one of the classic definitions, Perkins (1941:581) says that "(a)ccording to the ancient analysis only the actual perpetrator of the felonious deed was a principal." Using contemporary terminology employed by laypersons, we could say that a principal is the person who actually carried out the crime or someone who accompanied the primary actor and who was physically present and willing and able to assist when the crime was committed. These are the individuals who will be subject to the full penalty of the law for their actions.

Principals:
the individuals who are primarily responsible for the commission of a crime

Principals in the First Degree

In jurisdictions that follow the common law, there traditionally was a distinction between those individuals classified as principals in the first degree and those who were considered principals in the second degree. When these distinctions existed, a **principal in the first degree** was the person who actually committed the wrongful act (*actus reus*) himself or herself. This is equivalent to the term *perpetrator* that we discussed earlier in the chapter. The exception to this general rule is when the person utilizes an innocent instrumentality. An innocent instrumentality (or innocent agent) is described as a person who does not have the *mens rea* to commit a particular crime, but who is persuaded in some way by another person to commit the offense.

Principal in the First Degree:
an individual primarily responsible for the commission of a crime

Under the **innocent instrumentality rule**, the principal employs either a nonhuman agent or a person who cannot be held criminally responsible to carry out the offense. Common examples of this are using your dog (a nonhuman agent) to steal your neighbor's newspaper out of his driveway or using a minor child (a nonculpable human agent) to steal roses out of the neighbor's flower bed. However, it is important to note that some offenses—such as perjury—can only be committed by principals and not through the assistance of others (see American Law Institute 1985:175-176).

Innocent Instrumentality Rule:
the use by one person of another person who is otherwise not blameworthy to commit a wrongful act

As is generally true in criminal law, the state bears the burden of proving beyond a reasonable doubt that the principal in the first degree committed the *actus reus* and that this person possessed the *mens rea* necessary for the criminal act.

Principals in the Second Degree

In contrast to a principal in the first degree, a **principal in the second degree** is a person who assists in the commission of the crime and who is actually or constructively present when the crime is committed (see Heyman 2010:395). To be constructively present, a person must be physically present at the crime scene or in close enough proximity to assist if called upon by the principal in the first degree.

To illustrate the role of a principal in the second degree, consider the examples of an individual who drives a getaway car from a convenience store robbery or a person who serves as a lookout for someone who commits a burglary. It is important to recognize, however, that not all jurisdictions would classify these individuals as principals in the second degree. Some might simply classify them as principals (without distinguishing the degree of involvement), and others might consider them accomplices or accessories.

Principal in the Second Degree:
anyone who assists in the commission of the crime and who is actually or constructively present when the crime is committed

Accessories

The various participants in a criminal offense can be compared to the actors in a motion picture where characters may be considered leading or supporting actors. At the beginning of the chapter we defined and discussed the notion of accomplices, and it is important to recognize that the terms *accomplices* and *accessories* may be used interchangeably both in this book and within the criminal law itself. Therefore, just as there may be different degrees of principals, accessories also may participate in different ways. Accessories most commonly assist with a crime before or after the fact. The law may distinguish the degrees of participation, or it may treat all accessories the same.

Accessories Before the Fact

Under English common law, practically all crimes were felonies, and nearly all felonies called for the death penalty. Therefore, in order to reduce the law's potentially harsh treatment for those who assisted in the commission of crimes (but who did not carry out the crimes themselves), two categories of accessories were created (see, for example, Tate 1962). The first group of individuals includes those who function as **accessories before the fact**. Accessories before the fact are people who provide some type of assistance (aiding, abetting, or encouraging) that results in a crime being committed at a later time. Participation by accessories before the fact, or prior to a crime taking place, serves to facilitate the commission of the crime.

In some ways this makes accessories before the fact similar to principals in the second degree. However, unlike principals in the second degree, accessories before the fact are not physically or constructively present at the time the crime is committed. Instead, they take part in

Accessories Before the Fact:
people who assist those who are in the process of committing a crime before the actual crime has been completed

some separate activity that makes the commission of a crime possible later on. For example, a person who provides a vehicle or a handgun to be used in an armed robbery, or someone who is the "mastermind" behind a crime, but who is not present when the crime is committed, could be considered an accessory before the fact (see Heyman 2010). These activities also may be included under statutes that prohibit "criminal facilitation" (American Law Institute 1985:31).

Accessories After the Fact

In addition to accessories before the fact, people may also participate in criminal activities as **accessories after the fact**. Accessories after the fact do not engage in the planning or commission of the crime but they provide assistance to the principal offender(s) after the crime has been committed. This could include helping the principals avoid detection or apprehension or by providing them with food and shelter while they attempt to escape arrest and trial. Some jurisdictions will charge individuals who act as accessories after the fact under statutes that prohibit "obstruction of justice" (McLaughlin and Nahum 2007; Roadcap 2004), or those related to "hindering an arrest."

> **Accessories After the Fact:** people who assist those who have committed a crime after the crime has been completed

Currently, many jurisdictions have followed the pattern established by the *MPC* (see the discussion later in this chapter) and have merged the categories of principal in the first degree, principal in the second degree, and accessory before the fact. In states following this pattern, people who traditionally would fall within any of these three groups are treated as principals and there is no distinction in their levels of blameworthiness, criminal liability, or punishment (Dressler 2008; Heyman 2010). The case provided in Box 3.2 illustrates the types of distinctions that can occur.

Box 3.2   A CASE OF OBSTRUCTING JUSTICE?

Hoang v. Holder
641 F.3d 1157 (2011)

Trung Thanh Hoang was a native of Vietnam who came to the United States as a refugee in 1994. He was convicted in 2000 of violating a Washington State statute concerning criminal assistance. As a result of his conviction and incarceration his petition for U.S. citizenship was denied and he was ordered to be deported by a United States Immigration judge as having been an aggravated felon under the Immigration and Nationality Act. The question the U.S. Court of Appeals for the Ninth Circuit had to answer was whether and to what extent Hoang was guilty of obstructing justice, thus justifying his denial of petition for citizenship.

The [Immigration and Nationality Act] defines the term "aggravated felony" to include, as relevant here, "an offense related to obstruction of justice" for which the term of imprisonment is at least one year. We are aware that the Third Circuit recently held that the phrase "a crime relating to obstruction of justice" is unambiguous as used in the INA, and thus did not defer to the BIA's interpretation of that term.

The BIA emphasized that:

> Congress did not adopt a generic descriptive phrase such as "obstructing justice" or "obstruct justice," but chose instead a term of art utilized in the United States Code to designate a specific list of crimes. It employed that term in conjunction with other crimes (e.g., perjury and bribery) that also are clearly associated with the affirmative obstruction of a proceeding or investigation. We do not believe that every offense that, by its nature, would tend to "obstruct justice" is an offense that should be properly classified as "obstruction of justice."

We described the actus reus as "either active interference with proceedings of a tribunal or investigation, or action or threat of action against those who would cooperate with the process of justice;" and the mens rea as "specific intent to interfere with the process of justice."

[The Washington statute] states that a person renders criminal assistance if:

> [W]ith intent to prevent, hinder, or delay the apprehension or prosecution of another person he knows has committed a crime or juvenile offense or is being sought by law enforcement officials for the commission of a crime or juvenile offense he:
>
> (1) Harbors or conceals such person; or
> (2) Warns such person of impending discovery or apprehension; or
> (3) Provides such person with money, transportation, disguise, or other means of avoiding discovery or apprehension; or
> (4) Prevents or obstructs, by use of force, deception, or threat, anyone from performing an act that might aid in the discovery or apprehension of such person; or
> (5) Conceals, alters, or destroys any physical evidence that might aid in the discovery or apprehension of such person; or
> (6) Provides such person with a weapon.

By the statute's plain language, rendering criminal assistance in violation of Washington law has three elements. Defendant must (1) have the "intent to prevent, hinder or delay the apprehension or prosecution of another person"; (2) "know the person has committed a crime or juvenile offense or is being sought by law enforcement officials for the commission of a crime or juvenile offense"; and (3) commit one of the statutorily enumerated acts, including, as relevant here, providing transportation to the offender.

The gist of being an accessory after the fact lies essentially in obstructing justice by rendering assistance to hinder or prevent the arrest of the offender after he has committed the crime. Evidence of this offense is most frequently found in acts which harbor, protect and conceal the individual criminal such as by driving him away after he commits a murder. The very definition of the crime also requires that the felony not be in progress when the assistance is rendered because then he who renders assistance would aid in the commission of the offense and be guilty as a principal. That is precisely the situation we have here.

Nothing in the record of conviction establishes that there was an ongoing investigation or tribunal at the time Hoang provided transportation to an individual he knew had committed a crime. Hoang pleaded guilty only to providing transportation to a person he knew had committed a class B felony — the plea agreement does not state whether, at the time Hoang provided transportation, the offender was subject to an ongoing investigation or pending judicial proceeding. Therefore, we hold that Hoang's conviction does not qualify as obstruction of justice under the modified categorical approach.

In sum, Hoang's conviction for a misdemeanor by rendering criminal assistance in violation of [Washington State statutes] lacks the necessary actus reus and is not categorically obstruction of justice. Nothing in the record of Hoang's conviction establishes that he provided assistance to an individual who was subject to a pending judicial proceeding or ongoing police investigation, and so his conviction does not qualify as obstruction of justice under the modified categorical approach.

1. Obstruction of justice seems like a catch-all phrase. Can such a charge present a problem for the legality principle discussed in Chapter 1?
2. Based on the Washington State statutes mentioned in the case, could a person be an accessory after the fact to a crime and not know it?
3. Do the terms principals and accessories really seem to make a difference in the justice system today?

Methods of Treatment Under the Common Law

The distinctions between principals and accessories under the common law were very important for several reasons. The ways in which individuals who were involved in a crime were classified made a great deal of difference in how the cases would be processed, as well as the potential punishments facing the various actors. In this section we examine the common law treatment of both principals and accessories.

First, under the common law accessories could only be tried in the jurisdiction where they had provided assistance to the principals. In most instances this did not present a problem. However, it is possible to envision situations in which the planning of a crime or the procurement of a criminal instrumentality such as weapons or explosives might occur in one state, while the actual crime might take place in another state. This was the case for Timothy McVeigh and his coconspirators in the bombing of the Alfred P. Murrah Building in Oklahoma City in 1995.

Second, under the common law, all parties charged with treason were treated as principals (for a discussion of treason, see Chapter 8 on crimes against the state). While today this offense is practically never charged, it is still considered such a serious threat to the government that all parties involved are held accountable and prosecuted under the most serious standard that is available under the law.

Third, when the crime committed was a misdemeanor, the common law did not distinguish between principals and accessories. All parties were treated equally as principals. Additionally, there was no charge for accessory after the fact in misdemeanor offenses.

Fourth, the common law allowed accessories to be punished for the same crime as principals. The reason for this is the view that when an individual assists another in the commission of a crime, that person demonstrates consent to be held accountable for the other person's actions. Thus, voluntarily assisting someone in committing a crime causes the accessory to forfeit his or her rights to be treated as a separate person from the perpetrator. However, it is important to note that accessories could not be convicted of more serious crimes than the principals. This was because accessories were considered agents of the principals and, ultimately, the principals were considered the most blameworthy parties.

Fifth, as we have noted, accomplice liability is derivative in nature. Therefore, principals had to be tried and convicted before an accomplice could be held criminally responsible for the same crime. Because of this rule, if the principals were acquitted, then accessories could not be convicted later. This treatment also applied in cases where the principal died before standing trial or where the principal fled the jurisdiction or was unavailable for trial for some other reason.

While these factors were important under traditional common law, it is also important to note that for many jurisdictions, the general trend beginning in the middle of the twentieth century was to eliminate these common law distinctions. As we will see in a later section on the *MPC*, many jurisdictions today have merged the three categories of principal in the first degree, principal in the second degree, and accessory before the fact. As a result of this merger, most accomplices are treated in much the same way as those who actually carry out the crime in terms of liability and potential punishment.

ELEMENTS OF THE OFFENSES

The terms "elements of the offense" and *corpus delicti* (literally, the body of the crime) are interchangeable and, as we noted previously, the state bears the burden of proof for crimes including both the wrongful act (*actus reus*) and the guilty mind (*mens rea*). This is true for principals, but it is also true when the state attempts to establish accessory liability.

Accessories and *Actus Reus*

There are a variety of ways in which accessories can provide aid to principals. The first is through physical assistance. As we have indicated, this covers a broad range of activities, and it could include helping plan a crime, as well as providing the instrumentalities for the crime such as burglary tools and related devices, or weapons that are necessary for the crime's completion. Serving as a lookout and driving a getaway car are also examples of physical assistance. Physical help is often associated with the terms of aiding, abetting, or assisting.

A second way that aid can be given by an accessory is through encouragement or what might be termed psychological help. Aside from soliciting someone to commit a crime (a separate offense with which we will deal in Chapter 9), urging someone to undertake and complete a crime are examples of psychological help. This type of assistance may also be described as procuring, encouraging, advising, or soliciting a crime. As we will see in the next section, it may be much easier to prove that a person gave physical help for the completion of a crime than to prove that psychological help was given.

It is important to note that in order to establish the necessary *actus reus*, accessories do not have to actually cause the wrongful act under the typical definition of causation. In fact, when an accomplice is involved in the commission of a crime, the law treats the acts of the principal as if they were the acts of the accomplice. However, there must be proof of some voluntary action on the accomplice's part in order to hold that person criminally responsible for committing a crime (Dressler 1985, 2008).

We will address the *MPC* sections on complicity later in the chapter. However, we need to note that Section 2.06(3) provides the basis for *actus reus* by an accessory. That section states:

> A person is an accomplice of another person in the commission of an offense if:
>
> (a) with the purpose of promoting or facilitating the commission of the offense, he
>
> (i) solicits such other person to commit it, or
>
> (ii) aids or agrees or attempts to aid such other person in planning or committing it, or
>
> (iii) having a legal duty to prevent the commission of the offense, fails to make proper effort so to do; or
>
> (b) his conduct is expressly declared by law to establish his complicity.

Therefore, the *actus reus* requirement is satisfied by one of four conditions: (1) a person solicits someone to commit a crime, (2) the individual aids or agrees in the planning or commission of a crime,

(3) there is a legal obligation to prevent the crime from happening and the individual fails to act to do so, or (4) the law specifically defines the actions of the individual as meeting the definition of complicity (American Law Institute 1985:30). The last condition simply means that the state has to prove that the elements of the crime were committed by the principal as well as also establishing beyond a reasonable doubt that the accomplice played a role in the commission of the crime.

While the *actus reus* requirement can be relatively straightforward, it can be complicated in situations in which a person supplies a legal good that can be used for illegal purposes. For example, consider cold medicines containing pseudoephedrine (a legal drug). This drug is an ingredient that can be used illegally to manufacture methamphetamine (an illegal drug). However, this substance may also be used legally to treat the common cold. Would a person who supplied someone else with a large quantity of such cold medicines be guilty of acting as an accomplice in the process of manufacturing methamphetamine? Is knowledge of such criminal possibilities sufficient to establish that person's complicity in the commission of a crime? The following section supplies some of the answers to these questions.

Accessories and *Mens Rea*

The commentary to Section 2.06(3) of the *MPC* indicates that an accessory must "have the purpose of promoting or facilitating the commission of the offense" (American Law Institute 1985:31). This means that the accessory must have intent to assist the principal in facilitating the commission of the crime. Second, the accessory must also have the mental state that the underlying crime be carried out.

In support of these two elements, Section 2.06 of the *MPC* (with which we will deal later in the chapter) addresses the concept of complicity and it uses terms such as "causes," "promoting or facilitating," and "solicits, aids, agrees, or attempts to aid" (American Law Institute 1985:30-31). While these terms imply actions, they also deal with *mens rea* or intent. The implication from Section 2.06 is that an individual not only has to have the intent to *assist* in the commission of an offense, but also needs to have the minimum culpability associated with the underlying crime.

However, there is an exception to the requirement that an accomplice must have the *mens rea* associated with the underlying offense. This exception falls under the category of "natural and probable consequences." The natural and probable consequences doctrine "predicates guilt on the causal connection between the target offense and crimes that follow," but rather "than focusing on the causal contributions of the accomplice to the crime, the doctrine simply requires a weak nexus between the crimes themselves for liability to attach" (Heyman 2010:399-400; see also Chism 1998; Stark 1998). Thus, even if an accused does not have the requisite *mens rea* for the underlying crime, he or she can be convicted if the crime commission is a "natural and probable consequence" of his or her actions. For example, Paul wants to kill his wife and he asks his friend David to borrow his shotgun to carry out the deed. Even though David does not want Paul to kill his wife, he lends Paul the shotgun anyway. Therefore, if Paul kills his wife with David's shotgun, David could be criminally liable under the notion of "natural and probable consequences," even though he did not possess *mens rea* for the crime. Box 3.3 presents a case illustrating the concept of natural and probable consequences.

Box 3.3 NATURAL AND PROBABLE CONSEQUENCES

State of Tennessee v. Carson
950 S.W.2d 951 (1997)

The Supreme Court of Tennessee wrestled with the issue of "natural and probable consequences" in this case. The opinion provides some of the historical background of this doctrine as well as the state's statutory response. It also demonstrates how one person can be held responsible for the actions of another.

The defendant, Jubal Carson, and two co-defendants, Aaron Gary and Alton Stover, met to discuss robbing "Jim and Dave's TV Repair" store in Knoxville, Tennessee. Carson, who had been in the store before, described the layout of the store to the co-defendants and told them that a large sum of money could be found in a drawer in a back room. Carson gave a handgun to each of the co-defendants and the three men drove to the scene. While Carson waited in the car, Gary and Stover entered the store under the pretense of having repairs made to a portable stereo system.

Once inside the store, the co-defendants held two employees, James Adams and Dave McGaha, at gunpoint and forced them into a room in the rear of the building.

Both employees were searched and $130 was taken from Adams. As they left the store, Gary and Stover were confronted by police officers. To their surprise, neither the car, nor the defendant Carson, was in the parking lot. Gary and Stover fled from the scene on foot, exchanging gunfire with officers. All three men were later found and arrested.

The lightning quick police response to the robbery was apparent later. Carson and his co-defendants did not realize that "Jim and Dave's TV Repair" store was an undercover sting operation run by the Knoxville Police Department. Unbeknownst to them, the co-defendants' actions were monitored by police officers and recorded on video tape located in the store.

The defendant Carson was charged, along with his co-defendants Gary and Stover. The co-defendants pled guilty and testified at trial against the defendant. Carson did not testify; however, he made a statement to police admitting that he drove the co-defendants to the scene but denying that he knew a robbery would occur. He said he believed the co-defendants were going to the store to sell the guns and that he was across the street from the store at a Hardee's restaurant when he heard shots being fired.

The defendant argues on appeal that the evidence was insufficient to sustain the convictions because he lacked the culpable mental state for the offenses committed by Gary and Stover. The State insists that the defendant was criminally responsible for the aggravated robbery, as well as the additional offenses, because they were a natural and probable consequence of the robbery.

In our view, the Sentencing Commission comments clearly indicate the legislative intent that the statutory provisions embrace the common law principles governing aiders and abettors and accessories before the fact. Accordingly, we conclude that the natural and probable consequence rule, which derives from the common law and has been applied in our case law, as well as in the case law of a majority of jurisdictions, is applicable [here].

Applying the foregoing principles to the present case, we have determined that the evidence was sufficient for the jury to find that the defendant aided and assisted in the offense of aggravated robbery, which requires evidence of an intentional theft from the person of another by violence and by placing the victims in fear with the use of a deadly weapon. The defendant planned the robbery, described the layout of the store, supplied weapons, and accompanied the co-defendants to the scene, where he was to wait in the car. The co-defendants entered the store, held the victims at gunpoint, and took money. Accordingly, there was sufficient evidence from which the jury could find that the defendant solicited and aided in the offense with the intent to promote and benefit from its commission.

We conclude that the natural and probable consequence rule which derives from the common law is applicable under [state law], and that the evidence was sufficient to find that the defendant, having directed and aided in the aggravated robbery with the intent to promote or benefit from its commission, was criminally responsible for all of the offenses committed by his co-defendants, to wit: aggravated assault and felony reckless endangerment.

1. Based on this case (and the discussion in the chapter), what do we really mean by the "natural and probable consequences" rule?
2. How do we establish that the actions of one person (or group of people) can implicate another person in a criminal act?
3. What is the main problem associated with a legal rule such as this?

In some instances, accessory *mens rea* may be difficult to establish. In other instances, it can be inferred from the actions undertaken by the accessory and the principal. Regardless of the circumstances, the state will have to prove that the person charged as an accessory acted in some affirmative way and had the requisite mental state to facilitate the crime.

MODEL PENAL CODE

Unlike the common law, Sections 2.06(1) and 2.06(2) of the *MPC* (American Law Institute 1985:29-30) do not make distinctions between principals and accessories before the fact. The relevant parts of the *MPC* provide that:

> (1) A person is guilty of an offense if it is committed by his own conduct or by the conduct of another person for which he is legally accountable, or both.
>
> (2) A person is legally accountable for the conduct of another when:
>
>> (a) acting with the kind of culpability that is sufficient for the commission of an offense, he causes an innocent or irresponsible person to engage in such conduct; or
>>
>> (b) he is made accountable for the conduct of such other person by the Code or by the law defining the offense; or
>>
>> (c) he is an accomplice of such other person in the commission of the offense.

Section 2.06(3) of the *MPC* provides the definition of an accomplice (American Law Institute 1985:30). It says that

> (3) A person is an accomplice of another person in the commission of an offense if:
>
>> (a) with the purpose of promoting or facilitating the commission of the offense, he
>>
>>> (i) solicits such other person to commit it, or
>>>
>>> (ii) aids or agrees or attempts to aid such other person in planning or committing it, or
>>>
>>> (iii) having a legal duty to prevent the commission of the offense, fails to make proper effort to do so, or
>>
>> (b) his conduct is expressly declared by law to establish his complicity.

The *MPC* does not distinguish degrees of criminal liability in the way traditionally provided for under the common law. Therefore, today the states that follow the *MPC* approach have merged the categories of principal in the first degree, principal in the second degree, and accessory before the fact, and all of these actors are treated as possessing the same degree of criminal liability (see Heyman 2010).

At this point we should note that Section 2.06(3) of the *MPC* provides that in order to establish accomplice liability, knowledge that a crime is about to be committed is not sufficient. It requires instead that an accomplice must act with "the purpose of promoting or facilitating" a crime.

Additionally, Section 2.06(6) outlines three limits to accomplice liability, and these three factors can be used as a defense if a person is charged with a crime. In each of these situations a person cannot be considered an accomplice if these circumstances exist, or if the individual holds a certain status.

The three limits to accomplice liability provided by the *MPC* are:

(1) if a person is a victim of a crime, he or she cannot also be an accomplice;

(2) if the person's conduct is "inevitably incident" to the commission of the crime; and

(3) if the individual terminates involvement prior to the commission of the offense. (American Law Institute 1985:30, 32).

For the first limitation, by statute a child under the age of consent cannot be convicted of being an accomplice to statutory rape. The law views children below a certain age as incapable of giving consent to sexual activity. As such, even if they agree to the activity, they are considered victims and not offenders (especially see *In re D.B.* discussed in Chapter 6). Therefore, they cannot be both victims and offenders.

In the second situation, a person who procures the services of a prostitute is not considered an accomplice to prostitution. The solicitation of an individual for the purpose of sexual favors is an inevitable incident to the commission of the crime of prostitution. This means that by definition an individual who solicits another for the purposes of prostitution has already committed a separate offense ("patronizing prostitutes") and is therefore a principal in that offense and not an accessory to prostitution [see *MPC* Section 251.2(5)].

Finally, a person would not be an accomplice if he or she renounced the intended criminal purpose and terminated commission of the offense (such as by providing a timely warning to law enforcement officials). The defense of renunciation can apply in a number of circumstances (see Chapter 9 on criminal conspiracies), and it must involve more than just a change of mind or having the criminal enterprise interrupted by law enforcement actions.

In regard to the category of accessory after the fact, Section 242.3 of the *MPC* (American Law Institute 1985:183) does provide for the offense of "hindering apprehension or arrest." This exists when a person:

(1) harbors or conceals [an]other; or

(2) provides or aids in providing a weapon, transportation, disguise or other means of avoiding apprehension or effecting escape; or

(3) conceals or destroys evidence of the crime, or tampers with a witness, informant, document or other source of information, regardless of its admissibility in evidence; or

(4) warns [an]other of impending discovery or apprehension except that this paragraph does not apply to a warning given in connection with an effort to bring another into compliance with law; or

(5) volunteers false information to a law enforcement officer.

The commentary accompanying this section adds that "This offense covers the common law category of accessory after the fact but breaks decisively with the traditional concept that the accessory's liability derives from that of his principal" (American Law Institute 1985:181). As a result of this approach, most states retain some type of statutory prohibition relating to persons who function as accessories after the fact, and this is consistent with the *MPC*'s provisions on hindering apprehension or arrest.

Throughout this chapter we have discussed various forms of possible involvement in criminal activity. However, beyond the broad notion of criminal complicity that we have discussed, there is another legal doctrine by which the criminal acts of one person can be imputed to another individual or group of individuals. In the following section we consider the concept of vicarious criminal responsibility or liability, by which one person or group of people can be held culpable for the actions of another person or group of people.

VICARIOUS LIABILITY

Vicarious criminal liability essentially is the offense of relationship. The concept of vicarious liability can arise in several different situations. For example, the owner of an establishment that serves alcohol could be held criminally liable if a bartender served drinks to an intoxicated person who then drove a car that became involved in a fatal accident.

Vicarious criminal liability involves situations where one person is responsible for the criminal actions of another person or group of people (see Sheppard 2012:1626). In these situations, someone else has committed the wrongful act, but an individual not involved in planning or executing the crime is also held responsible (Kreit 2008). Quite often these situations occur when someone serving in a management position within a corporation is criminally charged for the actions of his or her subordinates. The bases for such responsibility are a "failure to foresee" or a "lack of diligence" on the part of managers in preventing the wrongful deed. The case of *United States v. Park*, 421 U.S. 658 (1978) (Box 3.5) illustrates the principle of vicarious criminal liability. There are also cases of noncorporate vicarious liability, and the following sections will examine both of these categories of criminal misconduct.

Vicarious Criminal Liability: to be held responsible or blameworthy for the criminal acts of another

Corporate Criminal Liability

In terms of the law, a corporation is an "artificial person" or a "quasi-artificial person" that has a "legal personality that is created by

Box 3.4 THE FORD PINTO CASE

In the 1970s the Ford Motor Company produced a compact car called the Pinto. After a few years of production, it became apparent that there was a design flaw with the Pinto; specifically, the gas tank was located very near the rear bumper. Therefore, when one of these cars was hit in the rear by another vehicle the gas tank frequently ruptured, and the bursting gas tank along with sparks from the crash occasionally resulted in flaming gasoline being sent into the car's passenger compartment.

After several deaths were reported from these types of accidents, a number of civil suits were filed against Ford, including *Grimshaw v. Ford Motor Co.*, 119 CA 3d 757 (1981) in which a jury entered a multi-million dollar award for civil damages against Ford. Following this case, the district attorney in Elkhart, Indiana filed criminal charges against the company for reckless homicide resulting from the deaths of three teenagers that occurred in a rear-end collision involving a Pinto [*State of Indiana v. Ford Motor Co.*, Cause no. 11-431 (1980)]. This approach to dealing with corporate criminal conduct was considered novel at the time, and Ford was eventually acquitted of the reckless homicide charges. While it is difficult to know the reasons for the acquittal, some have suggested that the criminal standard of proof (beyond a reasonable doubt) made it much more difficult to establish culpability than if the case had been brought as a civil wrongful death suit, which would have been decided on the basis of the preponderance of the evidence. Nevertheless, the Ford Pinto case changed the way in which the criminal law was applied to corporate criminality and the actions of businesses (see Becker, Jipson, and Bruce 2002; Benson and Cullen 1998; Cullen, Maakestad, and Cavender 1987; Strobel 1980).

One of the problems with the criminal case against Ford was how to determine who should be held criminally liable. Were all of the company's individual officers or agents responsible? Did liability extend only to those who were directly involved in the Pinto's defective design? How does the law hold a corporation—that itself is a legal entity or "person"—criminally responsible? A corporation can be fined, but a corporation cannot be placed in prison. Also, some of the evidence introduced at trial questioned whether the company's officers had full knowledge of the Pinto's design flaw. If they did, did they continue on their course of action despite this knowledge? Did they act negligently? Did they act recklessly?

***

The Ford Pinto case provides one example of the difficulty in establishing liability for corporate criminal conduct (see also Brown 2004). By contrast, the situation involving Houston, Texas-based Enron Corporation at the end of 2001 provides a slightly different example. While Enron itself was not found guilty of wrongdoing as a corporation, at least 15 corporate officers—including Kenneth Lay (chairman), Jeffrey Skilling (chief executive officer), Andrew Fastow (chief financial officer), Ben Gilsan (treasurer), and Kenneth Rice (chairman of EBS, Enron's Internet broadband service)—were charged with numerous federal fraud and racketeering charges. Some of these individuals were convicted at trial and others pleaded guilty. As a result, some of them forfeited personal property that was acquired through their illegal corporate dealings, and a few were actually sentenced to serve federal prison time (see Jickling and Janov 2003; *Washington Post* 2004).

Therefore, while establishing liability for criminal conduct associated with corporation may be very difficult, the Enron case demonstrates that in situations involving corporate officers and agents it is not impossible. Box 3.5 provides another example of a corporate officer who was found guilty of criminal vicarious liability.

1. If we compare corporate crime with conventional crime, which is likely to be most damaging? Why?
2. Do we know how much corporate crime exists in the United States? Why or why not?
3. Do crimes committed by corporations often go undetected or unreported?

individuals according to law, often receiving a charter . . . from a government" (Sheppard 2012:2028). Although we will discuss corporate crime at much greater length in Chapter 8, it is important at this point to deal with the issue of determining liability when criminal acts are perpetrated by corporations, their officers, and agents. Historically, under English law, corporations could not be held criminally liable. However, individually their officers and agents could be. As Boxes 3.4 and 3.5 show, now all of that has changed, and in certain situations corporations along with their officers and agents can be held criminally liable (see Kreit 2008).

Corporate crime can be defined as "those illegal activities that are committed in the furtherance of business operations but that are not the central purpose of the business" (Vago 2009:242). As Vago (2009:243) notes, in most instances administrative regulations and civil laws are typically the mechanisms used to deal with corporate crime rather than criminal prosecutions. Nevertheless, as Boxes 3.4 and 3.5 demonstrate, at least since the 1970s we have witnessed the criminal law being applied to some of the activities of large corporations.

The major dilemma when it comes to assigning criminal blame in corporate criminality results from the different actors who may play a role in the criminal conduct. It is possible to describe this situation as a **diffusion of responsibility** (see, for example, Calvi and Coleman 2008). What this means is that many actors may be involved in a decision or action, and it may be difficult to assign blame to any one person (or even to a specific group). Box 3.4 provides an illustration of conduct that might involve criminal liability.

Diffusion of Responsibility: when different actors play a role in the criminal conduct

Box 3.5   A CASE OF VICARIOUS LIABILITY

United States v. Park

421 U.S. 658 (1978)

In this case the U.S. Supreme Court dealt with the issue of the interstate sale of food potentially contaminated with rodent waste.

Acme Markets, Inc., is a national retail food chain with approximately 36,000 employees, 874 retail outlets, 12 general warehouses, and four special warehouses. Its headquarters, including the office of the president, respondent Park, who is chief executive officer of the corporation, are located in Philadelphia, Pa. In a five-count information filed in the United States District Court for the District of Maryland, the Government charged Acme and respondent with violations of the Federal Food, Drug, and Cosmetic Act. Each count of the information alleged that the defendants had received food that had been shipped in interstate commerce and that, while the food was being held for sale in Acme's Baltimore warehouse following shipment in interstate commerce, they caused it to be held in a building accessible to rodents and to be exposed to contamination by rodents.

Respondent was the only defense witness. He testified that, although all of Acme's employees were in a sense under his general direction, the company had an "organizational structure for responsibilities for certain functions" according to which different phases of its operation were "assigned to individuals who, in turn, have staff and departments under them." He identified those individuals responsible for sanitation, and related that upon receipt of the January 1972 FDA letter, he had conferred with the vice president for legal affairs, who informed him that the Baltimore division vice president "was investigating the situation immediately and would be taking corrective action and would be preparing a summary of the corrective action to reply to the letter."

At the close of the evidence, respondent's renewed motion for a judgment of acquittal was denied. The jury found respondent guilty on all counts of the information, and he was subsequently sentenced to pay a fine of $50 on each count.

The Court of Appeals reversed the conviction and remanded for a new trial. That court viewed the Government as arguing "that the conviction may be predicated solely upon a showing that . . . [respondent] was the President of the offending corporation," and it stated that as "a general proposition, some act of commission or omission is an essential element of every crime." The Court of Appeals concluded that the trial judge's instructions "might well have left the jury with the erroneous impression that Park could be found guilty in the absence of 'wrongful action' on his part," and that proof of this element was required by due process.

The question presented by the Government's petition for certiorari in *United States v. Dotterweich*, and the focus of this Court's opinion, was whether "the manager of a corporation, as well as the corporation itself, may be prosecuted under the Federal Food, Drug, and Cosmetic Act of 1938 for the introduction of misbranded and adulterated articles into interstate commerce." The Court recognized that, because the Act dispenses with the need to prove "consciousness of wrongdoing," it may result in hardship even as applied to those who share "responsibility in the business process resulting in" a violation. It regarded as "too treacherous" an attempt "to define or even to indicate by way of illustration the class of employees which stands in such a responsible relation."

[T]he Court has reaffirmed the proposition that "the public interest in the purity of its food is so great as to warrant the imposition of the highest standard of care on distributors." In order to make "distributors of food the strictest censors of their merchandise," the Act punishes "neglect where the law requires care, or inaction where it imposes a duty." "The accused, if he does not will the violation, usually is in a position to prevent it with no more care than society might reasonably expect and no more exertion than it might reasonably exact from one who assumed his responsibilities." Similarly, in cases decided after *Dotterweich*, the Courts of Appeals have recognized that those corporate agents vested with the responsibility, and power commensurate with that responsibility, to devise whatever measures are necessary to ensure compliance with the Act bear a "responsible relationship" to, or have a "responsible share" in, violations.

The duty imposed by Congress on responsible corporate agents is one that requires the highest standard of foresight and vigilance, but the Act, in its criminal aspect, does not require that which is objectively impossible. Congress has seen fit to enforce the accountability of responsible corporate agents dealing with products which may affect the health of consumers by penal sanctions cast in rigorous terms, and the obligation of the courts is to give them effect so long as they do not violate the Constitution.

We conclude that, viewed as a whole and in the context of the trial, the charge [to the jury] was not misleading and contained an adequate statement of the law to guide the jury's determination. Finally, we note that there was no request for an instruction that the Government was required to prove beyond a reasonable doubt that respondent was not without the power or capacity to affect the conditions which founded the charges in the information.

Respondent testified in his defense that he had employed a system in which he relied upon his subordinates, and that he was ultimately responsible for this system. He testified further that he had found these subordinates to be "dependable" and had "great confidence" in them. By this and other testimony respondent evidently sought to persuade the jury that he had no choice but to delegate duties to those in whom he reposed confidence, that he had no reason to suspect his subordinates were failing to insure compliance with the Act, and that, once violations were unearthed, acting through those subordinates he did everything possible to correct them.

Although we need not decide whether this testimony would have entitled respondent to an instruction as to his lack of power, had he requested it, the testimony clearly created the "need" for rebuttal evidence. That evidence was not offered to show that respondent had a propensity to commit criminal acts, or that the crime charged had been committed; its purpose was to demonstrate that respondent was on notice that he could not rely on his system of delegation to subordinates to prevent or correct insanitary conditions at Acme's warehouses, and that he must have been aware of the deficiencies of this system before the Baltimore violations were discovered. The evidence was therefore relevant since it served to rebut respondent's defense that he had justifiably relied upon subordinates to handle sanitation matters.

---

1. Does the legal concept of a corporation give more or less protection to company officers and agents?
2. Can a manager ever simply plead that he or she did not know a situation existed?
3. How can the government go about proving what an individual knew and when he or she knew it?

Noncorporate Criminal Liability

In addition to corporate criminal liability, there are numerous possible illustrations of noncorporate criminal liability. Some of these are covered under the general topics that we have already discussed in this chapter, such as individuals who function in various capacities as accessories. Additionally, in Chapter 9 we will discuss conspiracies and how they relate to the liability for the conduct of others. However, for this section we have chosen to focus on one specific issue: the liability of parents for the illegal actions of their children.

This area of the law is fascinating because it raises the question of when, where, and how the criminal justice system can or should intrude into the life of the family (see Collins, Leib, and Markel 2008). In most situations the state gives wide latitude to parents and the ways in which they interact with their own children. However, increasingly states are holding parents responsible for actions committed by their children.

As Collins, Leib, and Markel note, "most states have laws specifically prohibiting any adults from endangering the welfare of a minor or contributing to the delinquency of minors through specific affirmative actions that can be viewed as proximate causes of the child's wrongdoing, such as knowingly providing guns or alcohol to them" (Collins, Leib, and Markel 2008:1340). Laws such as these focus on affirmative actions by parents and guardians. However, many of the current state statutes are likely to hold parents criminally responsible for omissions under a general theory of "failure to supervise" (Collins, Leib, and Markel 2008:1339).

In addition to criminal liability, a number of states currently impose civil liability on parents when their children commit acts such as vandalism that result in the destruction of public or private property. However, there can also be criminal liability for parents as a result of their children's delinquent conduct. Today, all states, and several municipalities, have developed statutes that link parental responsibility with delinquent behavior (Matthiesen, Wickert, and Lehrer 2012; see also Mays and Winfree 2012:200). In addition to the children being charged with delinquency, the parents may be charged with contributing to the dependency or delinquency of a minor. They may also be charged with violation of specific parental responsibility laws (see Brank and Lane 2008; Sanborn 1996; Schmidt 1998).

The result of this movement is that states now may impose sanctions upon the parents of wayward children. These sanctions can include requirements to participate in court-ordered probation treatment along with their child. There also is the possibility of fines and incarceration (Collins, Leib, and Markel 2008). This means that while the parents may not have committed a criminal offense themselves, they still can be held legally accountable for their children's misconduct.

SUMMARY

The criminal law makes distinctions both in the elements of offenses and in the prescribed punishments based upon the degree of a person's involvement. As we have seen in this chapter, crimes may be committed by only one person, and in those cases the person who commits the crime is called the perpetrator. In some jurisdictions, this individual also may be labeled a principal in the first degree or a principal in the second degree. However, much of the criminal activity that takes place involves groups of perpetrators. Some of them are responsible for the planning and commission of the crime, while others serve as accomplices who provide some form of aid or assistance. Typically, the law designates accomplices to criminal acts as accessories who may participate in some material way before, during, or after the crime is committed. When arrests are made, the accessories to a crime are usually punished for their involvement, but they may receive a lesser punishment than the principals who have committed the crime.

In recent years the common law distinctions between various categories of principals and accessories often have been repealed by state statutes, and now most states treat principals and accessories much the same. This is consistent with the way that the *MPC* classifies the various participants in criminal activity.

We have noted that the law is designed to punish individuals and groups who are responsible for inflicting social harm. In most instances people are only held liable for the acts they personally perform. However, under the notion of vicarious liability individuals can be prosecuted for, and convicted of, acts accomplished by others.

Finally, over the past three decades one of the areas that has presented difficulty for the criminal law has been that of vicarious criminal liability involving corporate criminal conduct. The Ford Pinto case along with financial misconduct cases such as the insider trading charges against Martha Stewart and the Enron scandal have demonstrated how difficult it is to hold corporations liable for criminal conduct carried out by their officers and agents. However, after the Enron case, Congress passed the Sarbanes-Oxley Act of 2002. This law "created a new oversight body for corporate auditors, imposed new disclosure requirements on corporations, including a mandate that CEOs personally certify the accuracy of their firms' public financial reports, and increased criminal penalties for a number of offenses related to securities fraud" (Jickling and Janov 2003:2). This means that the federal government has shown an increasing resolve for dealing both civilly and criminally with corporate misconduct.

In addition to corporate criminal liability, there can also be criminal liability in noncorporate settings. One such situation is when parents are held criminally liable for their delinquent children's acts. In the name of "parental responsibility," states are increasingly holding parents both civilly and criminally responsible for their children's misconduct.

KEY TERMS

accessories
accessories after the fact
accessories before the fact
accomplice liability
accomplices
aider or abettor
complicity

derivative liability
diffusion of responsibility
innocent instrumentality rule
perpetrators
principal in the first degree
principal in the second degree
principals
vicarious criminal liability

CRITICAL THINKING QUESTIONS

1. Should a getaway car driver be held equally liable with the person who pulled the trigger if there is a killing during a robbery? Explain your answer.
2. Does the law in your state distinguish between principals of various degrees and, if so, how is each defined?
3. What do the statutes in your state say about accessories in terms of defining offenses and prescribing punishment? Are there different degrees of accessory liability?
4. What do we mean by the term complicity? What other legal concepts or principles are related to complicity?
5. Do the common law and the *MPC* agree on the descriptions of parties to crime?

6. What is meant by the notion of vicarious criminal liability? How can someone be held responsible for actions taken by another person?
7. What makes corporate crimes so difficult to prosecute? Should corporations be held criminally liable for their actions (or failures to act)? How can or should we punish corporations and their officers for criminal misdeeds?
8. Should parents be held criminally responsible for the actions of their children given the vicarious liability doctrine? Should this non-corporate liability extend to caretakers who are extended family members? What about to non-family members?

SUGGESTED READINGS

Benson, M.L. & Cullen, F.T. (1998). *Combating Corporate Crime: Local Prosecutors at Work*. Boston, MA: Northeastern University Press. This book focuses on the broad sweep of corporate crime, but it does deal specifically with the Ford Pinto case. The book provides a scholarly treatment of the difficulties associated with local prosecutors trying to take on multination corporations that are accused of corporate criminality. It is a follow-up to Cullen, Maakestad, and Cavender's (1987) *Corporate Crime Under Attack*.

Cullen, F.T., Maakestad, W. & Cavender, G. (1987). *Corporate Crime Under Attack: The Ford Pinto Case and Beyond*. Cincinnati, OH: Anderson. This book has become something of a classic in the field of criminology for its examination of "upper world" crime. Cullen and his colleagues address several issues that surround the world of corporate crime and how law enforcement authorities and academics struggle to understand (and deal with) this complex legal phenomenon.

Strobel, L.P. (1980). *Reckless Homicide? Ford's Pinto Trial*. South Bend, IN: And Books. Strobel is a Chicago-based journalist who also possesses a master's degree in legal studies. This book provides a fascinating narrative of the events before, during, and after the reckless homicide trial of Ford Motor Company in Elkhart, Indiana.

REFERENCES

American Law Institute (1985). *Model Penal Code: Complete Statutory Text*. Philadelphia, PA.

Becker, P.J., Jipson, A.J. & Bruce, A.S. (2002). "*State of Indiana v. Ford Motor Company* Revisited." *American Journal of Criminal Justice* 26(2):181-202.

Benson, M.L. & Cullen, F.T. (1998). *Combating Corporate Crime: Local Prosecutors at Work*. Boston, MA: Northeastern University Press.

Brank, E.M. & Lane, J. (2008). "Punishing My Parents: Juveniles' Perspectives on Parental Responsibility." *Criminal Justice Policy Review* 19(3):333-348.

Brown, D.K. (2004). "The Problematic and Faintly Promising Dynamics of Corporate Crime Enforcement." *Ohio State Journal of Criminal Law* 1:521-549.

Bureau of Justice Statistics (1981). *Dictionary of Criminal Justice Data Terminology* (2d ed.). Washington, DC: U.S. Department of Justice.

Calvi, J.V. & Coleman, S. (2008). *American Law and Legal Systems* (6th ed.). Upper Saddle River, NJ: Prentice Hall.

Chism, L.R. (1998). "*State v. Carson*: A Misguided Attempt to Retain the Natural and Probable Consequence Doctrine of Accomplice Liability Under the Current Tennessee Code." *University of Memphis Law Review* 29:273-294.

Collins, J.M., Leib, E.J. & Markel, D. (2008). "Punishing Family Status." *Boston University Law Review* 88:1327-1423.

Cullen, F.T., Maakestad, W. & Cavender, G. (1987). *Corporate Crime Under Attack: The*

Ford Pinto Case and Beyond. Cincinnati, OH: Anderson.

Dressler, J. (1985). "Reassessing the Theoretical Underpinnings of Accomplice Liability: New Solutions to an Old Problem." *Hastings Law Journal* 37:91-140.

Dressler, J. (2008). "Reforming Complicity Law: Trivial Assistance as a Lesser Offense?" *Ohio State Journal of Criminal Law* 5:427-448.

Grimshaw v. Ford Motor Co., 119 Cal. App. 3d 757 (1981).

Heyman, M.G. (2010). "The Natural and Probable Consequences Doctrine: A Case Study in Failed Law Reform." *Berkeley Journal of Criminal Law* 15:393-491.

Hoang v. Holder, 641 F.3d 1157 (2011).

Jickling, M. & Janov, P.H. (2003). *Criminal Charges in Corporate Scandals.* Washington, DC: Congressional Research Service, Library of Congress.

Kreit, A. (2008). "Vicarious Criminal Liability and the Constitutional Dimensions of Pinkerton." *American University Law Review* 57(3):585-639.

Mays, G.L. & Winfree, L.T., Jr. (2012). *Juvenile Justice* (3d ed.). New York: Wolters Kluwer Law & Business.

Matthiesen, Wickert & Lehrer, S.C. (2012). "Parental Responsibility Laws in All 50 States." http://www.mwl-law.com/CM/Resources /PARENTAL%20RESPONSIBILITY%20 CHART%20(00033309).pdf.

McLaughlin, J. & Nahum, J.M. (2007). "Obstruction of Justice." *American Criminal Law Review* 44:793-827.

Perkins, R.M. (1941). "Parties to Crime." *University of Pennsylvania Law Review* 89(5):581-623.

Roadcap, S. (2004). "Obstruction of Justice." *American Criminal Law Review* 41:911-945.

Sanborn, H.V. (1996). "Kids' Crimes Can Send Parents to Jail." *ABA Journal* 82:28, 30.

Schmidt, P.W. (1998). "Dangerous Children and the Regulated Family: The Shifting Focus of Parental Responsibility Law." *New York University Law Review* 73(2):667-699.

Sheppard, S.M., general editor (2012). *Bouvier Law Dictionary.* New York: Wolters Kluwer Law & Business.

Stark, L.G. (1998). "The Natural and Probable Consequences Doctrine Is Not a Natural Result for New Mexico — *State v. Carrasco.*" *New Mexico Law Review* 28:505-518.

State of Indiana v. Ford Motor Co., Cause no. 11-431 (1980).

State of Tennessee v. Carson, 950 S.W.2d 951 (1997).

Strobel, L.P. (1980). *Reckless Homicide? Ford's Pinto Trial.* South Bend, IN: And Books.

Tate, J.H., Jr. (1962). "Distinctions Between Accessory Before the Fact and Principal." *Washington and Lee Law Review* 19(1):96-101.

United States v. Park, 421 U.S. 658 (1978).

Vago, S. (2009). *Law and Society* (9th ed.). Upper Saddle River, NJ: Prentice Hall.

Washington Post (2004). "Timeline of Enron's Collapse." September 30. http://www .washingtonpost.com/wp-dyn/articles/A25624-2002Jan10.html.

Property Crimes

LEARNING OBJECTIVES

After reading this chapter you should be able to:

1. Discuss the significance and rationale for criminal laws that protect people's property
2. Explain the logic and implications of addressing theft offenses through consolidated theft statutes
3. Discuss the historical evolution of property crimes to meet the needs of a changing society and to protect the property that people have and will own as society advances
4. Define and explain the criminal acts that constitute the taking of property
5. Define and explain the criminal acts that constitute the destruction of property
6. Define and explain the criminal acts that constitute the invasion of property
7. Characterize and describe the various types of property to which property crimes may be applicable

INTRODUCTION

One of the fundamental tenets of American society is that people are entitled to own and possess the things that they rightfully earn. We believe that a strong work ethic and hours of labor entitle us to any property that is purchased as a result of our efforts. All of this "stuff" that people own and accumulate is known as **property**. Just as people are entitled to possess what they earn, it is also a principle of the American legal system that people who deprive others of what they have honestly earned and worked for should be subjected to some criminal sanction. Punishing people for depriving others of their rightful possession of property is done through laws governing **property crimes**.

> **Property:**
> things that people own and accumulate, and which are protected by property crimes statutes

There are three primary categories of property crimes: taking someone's property, damaging or destroying someone's property, and invading someone's property. Despite their obvious differences, each of the property crime categories has one important thing in common: They interfere with a person's ability to possess and fully enjoy the property to which he or she is entitled.

> **Property Crimes:**
> punish people for depriving others of their rightful possession of property

The regulation and punishment of property crimes has evolved significantly throughout our nation's history. As people's property (and corresponding property interests) have changed and expanded, so too have the laws that regulate and protect that property. Early property crimes were designed primarily to protect property such as livestock, farming equipment, and rudimentary homes. However, times and people's property have changed significantly; this means that the law of property crimes now protects things such as automobiles, airplanes, elaborate homes, electronics, and intellectual property. White collar crime, another significant area in the law of property crimes, is addressed more extensively in Chapter 8. Regardless of these advances in society and people's property interests, one thing remains constant: People do not want to be deprived of what is theirs, and they fully expect the legal system to help protect their property through the enforcement of laws governing property crimes. In Table 4.1, you can observe the prevalence of various types of property crime in the United States, as well as their respective rates of increase or decrease.

TAKING OF PROPERTY

Before we begin a discussion of property crimes, is important to understand the different types of property to which property crimes may apply. **Tangible property** is property that can be seen and touched and that has value in itself. Examples of tangible property

> **Tangible Property:**
> property that can be seen and touched and that has value in itself

Table 4.1	2010 U.S. PROPERTY OFFENSES			
PROPERTY CRIME	**ESTIMATED NUMBER (NATIONWIDE)**	**PERCENTAGE INCREASE/ DECREASE FROM 2009**	**PERCENTAGE INCREASE/ DECREASE FROM 2001**	**NUMBER PER 100,000 INHABITANTS**
Larceny — theft	6,185,867	3% decrease	19.4% decrease	2,003.5
Motor vehicle theft	704,464	7.4% decrease	40% decrease	245.1
Burglary	2,159,878	2% decrease	2% increase	704.9
Arson	52,191	7.6% decrease	Not available	19.6

Source: *Uniform Crime Reports*, Federal Bureau of Investigation (2010).

include currency, household goods, and furnishings. By contrast, **intangible property** is property that has no value in and of itself, but which signifies something of value. Examples of intangible property include stock certificates, property deeds, retirement accounts, bank accounts, and bonds. Each of these items indicates a person's ownership in an investment or other property, as well as the value that exists in their ownership of that property.

Intangible Property: property that has no value in and of itself, but which signifies something of value

When we think of offenses against property, one of the first things that probably comes to mind is one person taking something that another person owns. The taking of someone else's property is called **theft**. The crimes that are considered theft offenses are larceny, embezzlement, obtaining property by false pretenses, extortion, blackmail, fraudulent conversion, and receiving stolen property (American Law Institute 1985:148). It is important to note that theft can occur in the context of both tangible and intangible property when either type of property is wrongfully taken from its rightful owner. One important practical aspect of prosecuting theft cases is that the fact-finder (judge or jury) must determine the value of the property stolen in order to impose an appropriate punishment. The valuation of property is very important as it often makes a significant difference in both the crime classification and the resulting punishment for a particular instance of theft.

Theft: the taking of someone else's property

Larceny

The essence of the crime of **larceny** is someone taking and sneaking away with another person's property. Traditionally, larceny was the most basic form of taking someone else's property. During the period of the common law, larceny was intended to protect the items that people owned at that time and often used in making their living. This

Larceny: taking and sneaking away with someone else's property

generally included such things as livestock, farming tools, and a few basic household items. However, the law is responsive to the needs of an ever-changing society, and the law regarding larceny and other property crimes has evolved significantly throughout time. In today's modern world, people's property includes possessions that would have been unimaginable to earlier societies, such as advanced electronics, automobiles, extensive household items, and intellectual property. As a result, the legal system and the definition of various property crimes has progressed to protect these advancing property interests.

The *Model Penal Code* (*MPC*) deals with larceny and other theft offenses (discussed in subsequent sections) by making a distinction between **movable property** and **immovable property**. Movable property is anything that can be transported, such as books, furniture, and other personal property. Immovable property is that which is fixed or attached to land in such a way that it cannot be easily moved. Examples of immovable property include land, buildings, and other structures. The *MPC* states that "a person is guilty of theft if he unlawfully takes, or exercises unlawful control over, movable property of another with purpose to deprive him thereof" (American Law Institute 1985:149). This means that if Harvey takes Elizabeth's mp3 player with the intent to keep it permanently for himself, he has committed larceny.

The *MPC* also states that for the unlawful taking or disposition of immovable property, "a person is guilty of theft if he unlawfully transfers immovable property of another or any interest therein with purpose to benefit himself or another not entitled thereto" (American Law Institute 1985:149-150). This type of larceny takes place if Aaron unlawfully transferred ownership of Jeff's land to himself in order to make a profit on later selling the land to another person. Box 4.1 outlines the elements of larceny.

Movable Property: property that can be transported, such as books, furniture, and other personal property

Immovable Property: property that is fixed or attached to land in such a way that it cannot be easily moved, such as land, buildings, or other structures

---

Box 4.1 ELEMENTS OF LARCENY (*MPC* — REFERS TO THE OFFENSE AS THEFT)

Actus Reus	*Mens Rea*
• Unlawfully taking or exercising control over another's movable property OR • Unlawfully transferring another's immovable property or any interest in the property	• Intent to permanently deprive the owner of that property

Concurrence

Linking of *actus reus* and *mens rea*

Larceny essentially involves someone else trespassing on the *entitlement* of the rightful possessor or owner of property to hold and make productive use of their property. This is a significant societal issue because people's ability to use their own property in a lawful manner often has a direct correlation to their ability to work, make a living, and contribute to the community and economy. For instance, a plumber cannot fix house pipe systems without his plumbing tools. An attorney will have a difficult time practicing his trade without case files and law books. A farmer cannot grow crops if he does not have access to his land or farming tools. While the common law definition of larceny applied primarily to tangible property, the law has changed as our society has advanced, and theft offenses now apply to intangible property, as well as many types of services. For instance, larceny statutes could be applied to the unlawful taking of a person's intellectual property, electronic files, yard, and utilities services that have already been paid for, or stealing electricity or cable TV services without paying for them.

Larceny is generally punished based upon the amount or the monetary value of the items that were taken without permission from their rightful owner. Obviously, as the value of the items taken increases, larceny charges become more severe and involve longer and more extensive criminal punishments. The monetary amounts at which these divisions may be made for larceny convictions vary among different criminal law jurisdictions.

It is also important to note that when people have been permanently deprived of their property, the person who committed the crime first may be subject to criminal punishment for larceny. However, that person may also be required to make **restitution** (restore the rightful owner to their original position before the property was taken) to the person who was denied the property through the civil law violation of **conversion**.

Restitution:
restoring the rightful owner of property to his or her original position before being wrongfully deprived of the property

Conversion:
civil law violation of unlawfully obtaining another person's property

Embezzlement

Like larceny, embezzlement is also a theft offense and also involves taking other people's property with the intent to permanently deprive them of that property. However, the difference between larceny and embezzlement is that in an instance of embezzlement, the perpetrator has been entrusted with the property and has a legal right to possess it (although not having a legal right to *keep* the property). People commit embezzlement when they take property that they are legally entitled to *possess*, and then **convert** that property for their own use and enjoyment in a way to which they are not legally entitled.

Convert:
keep another person's property by an unlawful possessor for his or her own use and enjoyment

---

Box 4.2 ELEMENTS OF EMBEZZLEMENT

Actus Reus	***Mens Rea***
• Unlawfully taking or exercising control over the property of another with which that person has been entrusted	• Intent to permanently deprive the owner of that property

Concurrence

Linking of *actus reus* and *mens rea*

Embezzlement often takes place in the environment of employment situations. As employees, individuals frequently have the right to possess property in the context of their job. However, their right to possess this property does not give them ownership rights to that property. For instance, it may be part of a store employee's job duties to make a bank deposit of the day's proceeds at the end of the shift. As part of their job, they have the legal right to possess the money while they are transporting it to the bank. However, while on their way to the bank, the employee may decide to keep some of the day's monetary proceeds for himself. At that point, the employee has committed embezzlement because he has taken property with which he has been entrusted (but which he has not been given the right to keep), with the intent to permanently deprive the rightful owner of that property.

Embezzlement is a form of an **abuse of trust crime** and it often takes places in the context of white collar or occupational crime, which is discussed in more detail in Chapter 8. Box 4.2 outlines the elements of embezzlement. The facts required for embezzlement are explored more extensively in *People v. Casas*, which is found in Box 4.3. In this case, you will observe that embezzlement is a crime that can take place throughout all occupations, not just those that are traditionally defined as white collar professions.

Abuse of Trust Crime: crime that takes place when people neglect or improperly perform their job duties

---

Box 4.3 WHAT CONSTITUTES EMBEZZLEMENT?

People v. Casas
184 Cal. App. 4th 1242 (2010)

On January 18, 2008, Clifford B. went to a Ford dealership to purchase a new F-150 truck. Defendant was the salesperson who assisted him in the transaction. Clifford B. was driving a 2004 F-150 truck, which he intended to use as a trade-in. In addition, the purchase agreement called for a down payment of $1,500. At the time of the purchase, Clifford did not have the down payment with him; in such situations, the practice is for the salesman to follow the buyer home to collect the down payment and submit it to the finance officer upon return to the dealership. This is referred to as "chasing" the buyer.

On this occasion, after signing the purchase agreement, Clifford B. drove home in the newly purchased truck, followed by defendant who drove the trade-in vehicle. Normally, salespersons are supposed to drive their own vehicles to "chase" a customer. When they arrived at Clifford's residence, Clifford gave defendant a check in the amount of $1,000 and $500 in cash. However, defendant did not return immediately with the trade-in truck or the down payment.

The next day, January 19, 2008, Clifford B. realized he had left something in the old truck that he had traded in, so he called the dealership to arrange to retrieve the item. An assistant sales manager took the call but the trade-in vehicle was missing, along with the keys to the vehicle. Defendant did not show up at the dealership that day, although he was scheduled to work. The sales manager then reported the vehicle as stolen. On January 21, 2008, defendant showed up at the dealership with the trade-in vehicle and the check from Clifford B., but without any cash. When the police arrived, defendant informed the officer he had driven the truck to numerous locations over the two-day period in search of drugs to purchase. The odometer indicated defendant had driven the trade-in vehicle nearly 400 miles.

Our research revealed cases holding that embezzlement, a form of larceny, has the same theft elements. The offense is committed by every person who (1) takes possession (2) of personal property (3) owned or possessed by another (4) by means of trespass (5) with the intent to steal the property, and (6) carries the property away. The general rule, as stated by the *Davis* court, is that the intent to steal required for larceny is an intent to deprive the owner permanently of possession of the property.

However, there are decisions that have affirmed convictions for embezzlement after noting that an intent to temporarily deprive the owner of the property is sufficient. Some cases have affirmed embezzlement convictions reasoning that the gist of the offense is the appropriation to the defendant's own use of property delivered to him for a specified purpose other than his own enjoyment of it.

It is difficult to reconcile the two lines of cases dealing with contradictory mental states. However, to the extent that the cases are consistent in holding that the gist of the offense of embezzlement is the appropriation to one's own use of property delivered to him for devotion to a specified purpose other than his own enjoyment of it, the necessary mental state may be found to exist whenever a person, for any length of time, uses property entrusted to him or her in a way that significantly interferes with the owner's enjoyment or use of the property.

Here, the owner's use and enjoyment of the trade-in vehicle and monetary deposit for the truck purchase was interfered with significantly by defendant's use of the vehicle to travel approximately 400 miles, over the course of two days, in search of drugs, which were purchased with the cash portion of the down payment. Even if defendant had intended to eventually return both the trade-in vehicle and the money, his appropriation of both, for his own personal use, was significant in duration and incompatible with the owner's enjoyment or use of the property.

Using the definition we have adopted, the proffered evidence was irrelevant, so the exclusion of same by the trial court was not an abuse of discretion. Further, the court's modification of CALCRIM No. 1806, instructing the jury that an intent to temporarily deprive was sufficient to prove the mens rea of the crime of embezzlement was not error. The judgment is affirmed.

1. Is it right to hold a person accountable for embezzlement when he or she intended only to borrow the property, rather than to permanently deprive the owner of the property? Explain your reasoning.
2. What role should the length of time a person keeps property play in determining whether a person intended to deprive a rightful owner of their property? Is there a specific time that should be used to demonstrate this intent?
3. Should people who intend to permanently deprive others of their property be punished more harshly than those who intend only to temporarily deprive them? Explain your reasoning.

False Pretenses (Theft by Deception)

While larceny and embezzlement both deal with a perpetrator taking property without the knowledge or consent of the rightful owner, obtaining property by **false pretenses** involves an individual receiving property wrongfully, but with the knowledge and consent of the person who surrenders the property. However, the person who surrenders the property is operating with an incorrect or mistaken set of facts in giving up the property. Obtaining property by false pretenses is also known as **theft by deception.**

False Pretenses: obtaining the property of another by the use of deception

Under the *MPC*, "a person is guilty of theft if he purposely obtains property of another by deception" (American Law Institute 1985:150). Deceiving another person in order to obtain property may encompass several different types of conduct, including when a person:

Theft by Deception: obtaining the property of another by the use of dishonesty

(a) creates or reinforces a false impression, including false impressions as to law, value, intention, or other state of mind;
(b) prevents another from acquiring information which would affect his judgment of a transaction; or
(c) fails to correct a false impression which the deceiver previously created or reinforced, or which the deceiver knows to be influencing another to whom he stands in a fiduciary or confidential relationship; or
(d) fails to disclose a known lien, adverse claim or other legal impediment to the enjoyment of property which he transfers or

Box 4.4   YOU DECIDE: IS THIS A MATERIAL FACT?

Joe is a delivery driver who has an important package that is to be delivered to Tony Williams. The package contains some valuable electronic devices that Tony has paid for and intends to use in his business. Guy Smith (who is certainly not Tony Williams) wants to acquire the package and its contents, so he makes a fake I.D. card identifying himself as Tony Williams. When Joe attempts to deliver the package, Guy is waiting for him and shows Joe the I.D. card that identifies him as Tony. Joe makes no other inquiries about his identity and willingly gives the package to Guy. Has Guy acquired the package and its contents through misrepresentation of a material fact? Is he guilty of committing theft by false pretenses? Should Joe have any level of responsibility in the fact that Guy received the package that was meant for Tony?

encumbers in consideration for the property obtained, whether such impediment is or is not valid, or is or is not a matter of official record. (American Law Institute 1985:150)

As you can see, there are numerous circumstances under which a person can be guilty of obtaining property by false pretenses. However, the most important aspect of obtaining property by false pretenses is that there must be intentional misstatement or misrepresentation of a **material fact**. In other words, the information that the perpetrator either lies about or fails to disclose must be the reason, in whole or in part, that the person parted with or gave up the property. If the misstated fact does not significantly contribute to the person's willingness to part with the property, then the crime of false pretenses has not taken place. Box 4.4 illustrates the issues presented in determining what constitutes a material fact.

Box 4.5 outlines the elements of obtaining property by false pretenses.

Material Fact:
information that is the reason a person is willing to part with his or her property

Box 4.5   ELEMENTS OF OBTAINING PROPERTY BY FALSE PRETENSES (*MPC* — REFERS TO THE OFFENSE AS THEFT BY DECEPTION)

Actus Reus	*Mens Rea*
• Obtaining the property of another by deception or misrepresentation of a material fact	• Purposely

Concurrence

Linking of *actus reus* and *mens rea*

Receiving, Retaining, or Disposing of Stolen Property

In addition to taking someone else's property, it is also a crime to take possession of property that someone else has stolen. This is known as the crime of **receiving stolen property**. Receiving stolen property is also classified as a theft offense because even though the culprit did not steal the property himself or herself, he or she still has an equal level of criminal culpability by purposely receiving property that he or she knows to be stolen. Under the *MPC*, "a person is guilty of theft if he purposely receives, retains, or disposes of movable property of another knowing that it has been stolen, or believing that it has probably been stolen, unless the property is received, retained, or disposed with purpose to restore it to the owner" (American Law Institute 1985:151). It is important to note that receiving stolen property applies to movable property, so this crime generally takes place in the context of personal property such as electronics, automobiles, and other "stuff."

Under the *MPC*, "'receiving' means acquiring possession, control or title, or lending on the security of the property" (American Law Institute 1985:151). Therefore, a person does not have to gain ownership of the stolen goods in order to have received stolen property. Simply having possession or control of the items is sufficient. Another term that is often associated with receiving stolen property is **fencing**. Fencing stolen property takes places when a person knowingly purchases stolen goods in order to resell them later on for a profit. People involved in fencing make money because they are able to purchase the stolen items for a low price and then sell them to legitimate consumers for market value since the purchasers frequently have no idea that the items they are buying are stolen. Box 4.6 illustrates some of the issues that may arise in a case of someone receiving stolen property; Box 4.7 outlines the elements of receiving stolen property.

Receiving Stolen Property: receiving, retaining, or disposing of property that has been stolen

Fencing: knowingly purchasing stolen goods in order to resell them for a profit

---

Box 4.6   YOU DECIDE: IS PAUL GUILTY OF RECEIVING STOLEN PROPERTY?

Bobby steals a shipment of stereo equipment off of a company truck with the intention of reselling it. However, Bobby is known for his criminal endeavors and the police have been monitoring his activities since the stereo equipment disappeared. He needs a place to store the stereo equipment until the police stop following him and he is able to find a place to sell it at a profit. He asks his friend Paul if he can store the equipment in his home. Paul is extremely hesitant to take possession of stolen goods. After some persuasion from Bobby, Paul agrees to store the stolen equipment, but says that he will only store the goods for 24 hours and will have nothing to do with Bobby's plan to resell it. Is Paul guilty of receiving stolen property when he is only willing to take possession of the goods for a short period of time? Would it make any difference if Paul intended to inform the police as soon as Bobby departs?

Box 4.7   ELEMENTS OF RECEIVING STOLEN PROPERTY (*MPC*)

Actus Reus	*Mens Rea*
• Receiving, retaining, or disposing of movable property that has been stolen	• Purposely

Concurrence
Linking of *actus reus* and *mens rea*

Extortion

Another theft offense is **extortion**, which takes place when a person obtains someone else's property by threatening to harm them in some way unless they surrender their property. Under the *MPC*,

> A person is guilty of theft [by extortion] if he purposely obtains property of another by threatening to:
>
> (1) inflict bodily injury on anyone or commit any other criminal offense;
> (2) accuse anyone of a criminal offense;
> (3) expose any secret tending to subject any person to hatred, contempt or ridicule, or to impair his credit or business repute;
> (4) take or withhold action as an official, or cause an official to take or withhold action;
> (5) bring about or continue a strike, boycott or collective unofficial action, if the property is not demanded or received for the benefit of the group in whose interest the actor purports to act;
> (6) testify or provide information or withhold testimony or information with respect to another's legal claim or defense;
> (7) inflict any other harm which would not benefit the actor.
> (American Law Institute 1985:150-151)

As you can see, the types of threats that may constitute extortion are extremely broad and encompass a significant amount of potential harm or damage. Extortion includes threats of bodily harm; damage to a person's reputation; injury to a person's business, finances, and criminal records; and any other action that would cause detriment to the extortion victim. When people commit extortion, they are threatening to inflict this harm at some point in the future unless the victims comply with a demand to surrender their property. The threats associated with extortion are not immediate and will be carried out at some impending time unless the demands are met. Extortion may also be referred to as **blackmail**. Box 4.8 outlines the elements of extortion.

Extortion: obtaining the property of another through threats of future harm

Blackmail: obtaining the property of another through threats of future harm

---

Box 4.8 ELEMENTS OF EXTORTION (*MPC*)

Actus Reus	*Mens Rea*
• Obtaining property of another by threatening to inflict future harm	• Purposely

Concurrence

Linking of *actus reus* and *mens rea*

Consolidated Theft Statutes

One issue that is encountered with theft crimes is that a single criminal transaction may include several different types of theft. Furthermore, when examining a defendant's actions, it may be difficult to distinguish one type of theft from another. These issues have led many criminal law jurisdictions to adopt **consolidated theft statutes**. The *MPC* also utilizes a consolidated statute in addressing theft offenses (American Law Institute 1985:147).

Consolidated theft statutes operate to proscribe and punish any and all forms of theft within one concise statute. Consolidated theft statutes generally include all of the theft offenses provided for under the common law: larceny, embezzlement, obtaining property by false pretenses, receiving stolen property, and extortion. In a jurisdiction that utilizes a consolidated theft statute, taking any of these actions would result in a person being charged with committing theft. Consolidated theft statutes have been enacted to streamline the legal process and to eliminate fine line distinctions among the theft offenses. This reduces some confusion and simplifies the process of handling theft offenses. However, the core of each theft crime remains the same: wrongfully acquiring another person's property. Consolidated theft statutes allow criminals to be more efficiently convicted and punished for their actions.

Consolidated Theft Statutes: statutes that combine larceny, embezzlement, obtaining property by false pretenses, receiving stolen property, and extortion into a single crime of theft

Robbery

The ultimate goal of the criminal law is to protect human life, and life is given a much higher value than property. Because of the tremendous potential for robbery to result in the loss of or injury to a human life, it is taken more seriously and punished much more severely than a simple theft offense. For this reason, robbery sits at a crossroads between being a crime against property and a crime against people. Beyond merely acquiring someone else's property unlawfully, **robbery** poses significant issues because of its potential to cause

Robbery: taking anything of value from a person by force or threat of force

harm to victims. A person is guilty of robbery when, in the course of committing a theft, he:

(a) inflicts serious bodily injury upon another; or
(b) threatens another with or purposely puts him in fear of immediate serious bodily injury; or
(c) commits or threatens immediately to commit any felony of the first or second degree. (American Law Institute 1985:144-145)

In determining whether a person has committed a robbery, the *MPC* takes into consideration:

(1) any special circumstances or considerations that distinguish this act from general theft;
(2) the time span during which the action(s) in question took place; and
(3) the individual responsibility that the defendant has for the actions that took place.

Special circumstances include such things as either inflicting or threatening to inflict bodily injury upon the victim; placing the victim in fear for his or her safety; and threatening to commit a serious crime (American Law Institute 1985:145). Furthermore, robbery can be distinguished from ordinary theft by the presence or threat of violence, as well as an immediate and serious threat to the victim's safety (American Law Institute 1985:145).

The end result of robbery (taking the property of another) is substantially similar to that which takes place in an ordinary theft case. However, robbery goes beyond theft considerations, and may be punished separately and in addition to any theft that takes place during the course of a robbery. The reason for this is that because robbery involves taking another person's property through the use (or threatened use) of force, it presents the special circumstance of potential harm to a human being. Therefore, policy considerations dictate that a person who commits such an act should be punished for both the theft of property, as well as placing a human life in danger.

Another important point to note about robbery is that the threat that causes someone to part with their property does not have to be a real threat to constitute robbery. For instance, threatening someone with an unloaded gun is considered a legitimate threat for robbery purposes so long as the person who gave up her or his property perceived the threat to be real. This would certainly be the case here, as the person would have no way of knowing whether or not the gun was loaded. They would assume that a person who tried to take their property by pointing a gun at them would only point a loaded gun that could be used to force someone to give up their property. It is

---

Box 4.9   YOU DECIDE: OF WHAT CRIME IS ROSE GUILTY?

Jennifer has just made a large cash withdrawal from the bank when she is approached by Rose. Rose tells Jennifer that she has a gun in her purse and will shoot her if she does not give Rose the cash. Jennifer complies and gives Rose her money. Of what crime is Rose guilty?

Would it make a difference if Rose did not really have a gun in her purse? What if Rose tells Jennifer that if she does not give her the cash, Rose will begin spreading malicious and damaging rumors about Jennifer and her family?

---

also important to note that the use of force must occur at the same time as the surrender of the property. This is consistent with the idea that robbery requires the use of **imminent harm**, or harm that will be inflicted immediately.

Imminent Harm: harm that will be inflicted immediately

There is often some confusion between robbery and extortion. At first glance, they appear quite similar as both crimes involve taking the property of another person through the use of force or harm. However, the type of harm that is threatened is what causes these crimes to be classified differently. As discussed previously, robbery involves the taking of property through the use or threat of imminent harm. However, extortion involves the taking of property through the threat of future harm. Box 4.9 demonstrates the distinctions between robbery and extortion.

Box 4.10 outlines the elements of robbery. In Box 4.11, the case *State v. Shoemake* demonstrates the facts required to prove that a robbery took place within the course of a crime spree that also included automobile theft. This case is an excellent example of the numerous property crimes that may take place within a single criminal transaction, and the importance of the ability to distinguish these crimes from one another.

Box 4.10   ELEMENTS OF ROBBERY (*MPC*)

Actus Reus	*Mens Rea*
• Inflicting serious bodily injury upon another person OR • Threatening another person with serious bodily injury OR • Committing or threatening to commit a felony during the course of committing a theft	• Purposely

Concurrence

Linking of *actus reus* and *mens rea*

Box 4.11   WHAT CONSTITUTES ROBBERY?

State v. Shoemake

618 P.2d 1201 (Kan. 1980)

Sometime during the night of August 21, 1979, a yellow 1972 Ford Torino was stolen from a residence in Kansas City, Missouri. On August 25, 1979, a green 1972 Ford Torino was stolen from a parking lot in Wyandotte County. Around 7:00 p.m. on August 25, John Lucas was seen by an employee of Nigro's Supermarket driving a yellow Torino through the parking lot of the supermarket in Kansas City, Kansas. Shortly thereafter, Lucas was seen sitting in front of the supermarket in a green Torino. Lucas subsequently entered the supermarket, approached the manager, brandished a pistol, and demanded money. The manager delivered money from one cash register to Lucas, who then took money by force from another store cashier at a different cash register. The manager was then forced into the store's office and more money was taken there.

A Kansas City police officer, having received a police dispatch description of both automobiles, attempted to stop a yellow Ford Torino matching the description. The automobile failed to respond to the officer's red light and siren, and a ten-minute, high-speed chase ensued. The chase ended when the yellow Torino collided with some parked cars and became disabled with a flat tire. Defendant Shoemake was the driver of the vehicle. John Lucas was the only passenger. In the car the police found currency, food coupons, receipts, and checks payable to Nigro's on the floorboard on both the driver's and passenger's side. A pistol was found under the driver's seat. In the rear of the car, the police found a slidehammer, an instrument used in automobile body work and frequently used by car thieves to remove

ignitions. An ignition was still attached to the slidehammer. The key to the yellow Torino operated the attached ignition. The green Torino was found two blocks from Nigro's Supermarket with the engine still running. Both cars, when recovered, were without their ignition switches and could be started without keys. Shoemake and Lucas were charged as codefendants on two counts of felony theft involving the yellow and green Ford Torinos and three counts of aggravated robbery of three persons at the Nigro Supermarket. The cases were severed for trial. On November 16, 1979, a jury found defendant Shoemake guilty on all five counts.

Defendant's contention is that there was only one robbery committed at Nigro Supermarket and that the charges and convictions of three separate counts of robbery allowed multiple convictions for a single offense. The amended information in this case charged in substance in Count I that Lucas and Shoemake took property from the person or presence of Frederick Larison by force or threat while armed with a handgun. Count IV charged Lucas and Shoemake with taking property from the person or presence of Lee Trial by force or threat while armed with a handgun. Count V charged the codefendants with taking property from the person or presence of Michael Jones by force or threat while armed with a handgun. The undisputed evidence showed that the robber, Lucas, threatened the manager, Lee Trial, with a handgun and received from him the contents of a cash register and a money depository. The evidence further showed that, after being threatened with a gun, the other cashier, Frederick Larison, delivered to Lucas money from his cash register. The evidence was undisputed that Michael Jones did not have money under his control to deliver to the robber and his only participation was in holding a sack while the property taken from the other employees was placed therein by Lucas to facilitate its transportation. Under these circumstances, we have concluded that the evidence was not sufficient to justify the conviction of defendant Shoemake for aggravated robbery of Michael Jones in a separate count, since no property was forcibly taken from him by Lucas.

Where, in the course of the robbery of a business establishment, several employees are held at gunpoint and compelled by force to deliver to the robber property in the possession or custody of the employee, a separate and distinct aggravated robbery occurs with the taking of property from each victim. In the present case, property was taken from the manager, Lee Trial, and from the cashier, Frederick Larison, both of whom were custodians of store property. The forcible taking of such property from these employees constituted separate and distinct aggravated robberies which could be charged in separate counts. As noted above, no property was actually taken from Michael Jones. There being no property taken from Michael Jones, the defendant could not be charged with a separate and distinct crime of aggravated robbery involving that employee. We have concluded that the conviction of defendant on Count V, charging defendant Shoemake with aggravated robbery of Michael Jones, must be set aside.

1. Should a defendant be able to be convicted of multiple robberies that take place during the acquisition of only one piece of property? Or does this allow multiple prosecutions for the same offense? Explain your reasoning.
2. Is it possible for a person to be guilty of robbery when they use force to take something from another person that they mistakenly believe to be of value? Why or why not?

DESTRUCTION OF PROPERTY

A different type of property crime takes place when people damage or destroy someone else's property. Like the taking of property, the end result of this crime is that the rightful owner of property is deprived of the ability to use and enjoy the property that is rightfully owned.

Arson

Arson is generally considered to be the most severe crime associated with the destruction of property. Like other property crimes, the ultimate goal of criminalizing arson is to protect people from harm. The primary purpose of arson laws is protect homes, where people live and sleep, and where they could be subjected

Arson:
starting a fire or causing an explosion with the purpose of damaging or destroying a building or property

to potential danger or death if someone attempted to burn the structure. Arson is punished quite severely due to the tremendous potential for it to result in either significant harm to people or the loss of human life. As such, arson is punished as a felony under the *MPC*. The *MPC* divides arson into grades based upon the potential that the destruction of property has to endanger human life, the type of property damaged, and the amount of personal responsibility that can be attributed to the defendant (American Law Institute 1985:138).

The *MPC* states that "a person is guilty of arson, a felony in the second degree, if he starts a fire or causes an explosion with the purpose of (a) destroying a building or occupied structure of another; or (b) destroying or damaging a property, whether his own or another's, to collect insurance for such loss" (American Law Institute 1985:140).

Although arson requires that a structure be damaged in some way, there is no requirement that the structure be fully destroyed or burned to the ground. In fact, a very slight amount of damage is sufficient to constitute arson. Many jurisdictions have enacted statutes that allow for smoke damage, water damage from sprinklers, or slight damage from a fire. The logic for allowing such a small amount of damage to trigger conviction and punishment for arson is to serve as a strong deterrent for a crime that has the potential to inflict significant harm upon people.

The definition and punishment of arson has undergone significant revision throughout the evolution of society and the criminal law. Under the common law, a person could only be convicted of arson for setting fire to a dwelling. It is important to note that under the *MPC*, a person is only guilty of arson for setting fire to an occupied structure, which is defined as "any structure, vehicle or place adapted for overnight accommodation of person, or for carrying on business therein, whether or not a person is actually present" (American Law Institute 1985:140). Under the modern law, this has been expanded considerably and may include unoccupied structures as well. Most arson statutes now include setting fire to any type of building or structure. Many statutes even include cars, boats, and other vehicles within their scope. However, most jurisdictions have other types of criminal statutes that encompass the burning of personal property. Box 4.12 outlines the elements of arson. People may also be convicted of arson for setting fire to their own property (usually to make an insurance claim). This issue, which is discussed in the case *Maier v. Allstate Insurance Company* in Box 4.13, is a unique area of the law since property crimes are generally intended to protect property from harm inflicted by outside parties. The *Maier* case involves a situation in which an insurance company attempted to

---

Box 4.12   ELEMENTS OF ARSON (*MPC*)

Actus Reus	*Mens Rea*
Starting a fire for the purpose of	• Purposely
• destroying a building or occupied structure of another OR	
• destroying or damaging a property to collect insurance for the loss	

Concurrence

Linking of *actus reus* and *mens rea*

---

use arson as a defense to a civil law claim demanding that the insurance company pay for the fire loss under the terms of an insurance policy.

Box 4.13   ARE PEOPLE GUILTY OF ARSON FOR SETTING FIRE TO THEIR OWN PROPERTY?

Maier v. Allstate Insurance Company
41 A.D.3d 1098 (N.Y. 2007)

Plaintiff owned a home in the Town of Sand Lake, Rensselaer County that was insured by a homeowners insurance policy issued by defendant. On August 8, 2000, the property was completely destroyed by fire. Plaintiff submitted a proof of loss statement to defendant seeking to recover $240,000 in insurance proceeds. Defendant paid the balance of the mortgage on the property (approximately $92,000), but otherwise denied plaintiff's claim. When plaintiff then commenced this action to compel defendant to cover his loss, defendant asserted the affirmative defense of arson.

Evidence at trial established the following. Previously, plaintiff lived at the Sand Lake residence for half the year and rented in Florida for the other half of the year, but in 2000 he decided to move to Florida to live full time. In the week preceding the fire, plaintiff appeared personally at his insurance agent's office and for the first time in memory of

his agent paid his monthly homeowners insurance premium on time. He also held a moving sale, packed up some of his furniture and personal property in a moving truck, and placed his home for sale with a local realtor at a list price of $120,000. He planned to leave Sand Lake permanently on August 8, 2000 and, after giving keys to his residence to the realtor and posting "For Sale" signs, he locked up and left the property at approximately 4:30 P.M. He then went to the home of friends, where he planned to have dinner prior to departing for Florida. At 5:45 that evening, area fire departments responded to a fire call at plaintiff's residence.

After the fire was extinguished and the cause of the fire was not readily apparent, a Rensselaer County fire investigator was called to inspect the property. The investigator, along with his canine companion trained in the detection of combustibles, arrived at the scene and determined that combustible flammable vapor residue was present in an upstairs hallway as it leads into a bedroom, where a burned-out mattress was located on the floor. A few days later, a private arson investigator hired by defendant conducted another inspection of the property and concluded that the fire had started in the upstairs bedroom and attached hallway and, in his opinion, was the result of a flammable liquid being poured on the floor of the hall and bedroom and then ignited. At the time of the fire, plaintiff was supporting himself and his two minor children on a yearly net income of less than $10,000. His bank accounts showed no significant savings and he owed $2,103 in 2000 property taxes.

Here, the record amply supports Supreme Court's conclusion that clear and convincing evidence existed that the fire was deliberately started. Testimony from the County fire investigator and the arson investigator supports their conclusion that the fire began when an accelerant was poured on the floor of an upstairs hall and bedroom and then ignited. Their unrefuted testimony provided ample support for the court's finding that the fire was not the result of an accident or a natural cause, but due to human intervention. Contrary to plaintiff's contention, the testimony describing the behavior of the canine in detecting the presence of a combustible vapor residue on the property was not equivocal or inconsistent in any

way. Further, the fact that laboratory results performed on the burned-out mattress material came back negative for the presence of an accelerant is not inconsistent with the findings of the fire investigators inasmuch as the private arson investigator testified that negative results were expected because either the accelerant was completely consumed by the fire or washed away in the effort to extinguish the fire.

Further, Supreme Court appropriately considered circumstantial evidence of strong motivation, opportunity and means to establish that plaintiff, despite his denial, committed the arson. Plaintiff testified that he left the property vacant and locked up less than 90 minutes before the fire was reported, and that only he, his oldest son and his realtor had keys to the property. Financial motive was established by the fact that plaintiff would almost certainly have gained more if his home had been lost in a fire than if he had sold it; although the home was listed at plaintiff's urging at $119,900, the realtor originally valued the home at less than $100,000. This, combined with the evidence of plaintiff's precarious financial conditions, the steps that plaintiff had taken in preparation for permanently leaving the area and the evidence of opportunity, constitute sufficient evidence that it was plaintiff who set the fire in order to collect the insurance proceeds.

1. Is it appropriate for courts to consider circumstantial evidence, such as the defendant's motivation and lack of financial means in determining whether he or she purposely burned his or her own property? Might the consideration of such circumstantial evidence ever result in a miscarriage of justice? Explain your reasoning.
2. Should people who set fire to their own property be punished as harshly as those who set fire to the property of others? Why or why not?

Criminal Mischief

The crime of criminal mischief is the result of combining many historical crimes related to the destruction of personal property. While arson is applicable to the destruction of homes and real property, the somewhat lesser charge of criminal mischief applies to the destruction of personal property. The logic for this is that the destruction of homes, structures, and real property, where people work and live, has a greater potential to endanger human life. While still a significant threat and an invasion of people's right to enjoy their property, the destruction of personal property does not have the same potential to result in injury or the loss of life.

Under the *MPC*,

a person is guilty of criminal mischief if he:

(a) damages tangible property of another purposely, recklessly, or by negligence in the employment of fire, explosives, or other dangerous means . . . ;
(b) purposely or recklessly tampers with tangible property of another so as to endanger person or property; or
(c) purposely or reckless causes another to suffer pecuniary loss by deception of threat. (American Law Institute 1985:141)

Criminal mischief is a rather broad crime that covers a significant amount of conduct. It is meant to encompass the burning of personal property (whereas arson applies to real property), as well as other damage to personal property. One type of criminal mischief is **vandalism**, which is damaging or injuring someone's personal property. Criminal mischief includes damage or destruction of personal property that does not fall within the scope of other property crime statutes. Like other property crimes, criminal mischief is graded and punished based upon the monetary amount of the damage done to another person's property. Box 4.14 outlines the elements of criminal mischief.

Vandalism: damaging or injuring someone's personal property

Box 4.14   ELEMENTS OF CRIMINAL MISCHIEF (*MPC*)

Actus Reus	*Mens Rea*
• Damaging another person's tangible property OR • Tampering with another person's tangible property OR • Causing another person to suffer pecuniary loss by deception or threat	• Purposely, recklessly, or negligently

Concurrence

Linking of *actus reus* and *mens rea*

INVASION OF PROPERTY

Just as the law protects property from being taken or damaged, the law also protects a person's property from being unlawfully invaded. The primary invasion of property crimes discussed in this chapter are burglary and criminal trespass.

Burglary

The crime of **burglary** is modeled after the idea that a man's home is his castle and that people are entitled to no greater level of privacy than that which is expected inside their own home. The criminal law is most concerned with protecting the places where people live and dwell. This is where people spend a significant amount of their time, and where they are most likely to be injured if someone invades their property. Although invasion of property crimes have been expanded considerably over time, the law generally affords the greatest protection to a person's home and the area surrounding that home. The area surrounding a person's home (such as residential yards and structures on the residential premises) is known as the **curtilage**.

Under the *MPC*, a person has committed the crime of burglary "if he enters a building or occupied structure . . . with purpose to commit a crime therein, unless the premises are at the time open to the public or the actor is licensed or privileged to enter" (American Law Institute 1985:142). The law of burglary has been expanded significantly over time. Under the common law, burglary consisted of breaking and entering the occupied dwelling of another person in the nighttime with the intent to commit a felony once inside. While burglary still requires the breaking and entering of a building, that building may be a person's dwelling or home, or any other structure. Also, most burglary statutes no longer require the structure to be occupied at the time of the breaking and entering. Burglary statutes have also abandoned the requirement that the crime take place in the night, and burglary may now take place at any time of day. Most jurisdictions have now expanded the common law requirement that the breaking and entering take place with the intent to commit a felony so that now a burglary may take place when there is a breaking and entering with the intent to commit any crime (not necessarily a felony). Box 4.15 illustrates some of the issues that may be present when determining whether an act constitutes burglary.

Burglary requires that there be a breaking and entering of a structure. However, this raises a significant number of issues. For instance, how violent or extensive does the break have to be?

Burglary:
breaking and entering a building or structure with the intent to commit a crime

Curtilage:
the area surrounding a person's home, such as residential yards and structures on residential premises

In most jurisdictions, breaking into a structure may be an **actual breaking** or a **constructive breaking**. An actual breaking involves actions such as breaking glass to enter a window or kicking in a locked door. A constructive breaking includes things such as opening an unlocked door or window. Even though the perpetrator encountered no resistance and did not have to technically "break" anything, these actions still constitute a breaking for purposes of defining burglary. Both actual and constructive breakings involve a person gaining entry to a home without permission, and the law has a strong interest in protecting people from this invasion of their property.

Actual Breaking: actions taken to break into a home or other structure that involve the use of force

Constructive Breaking: actions taken to break into a home or other structure that do not involve the use of force

The breaking and entering requirement also raises questions about how extensive the entry must be. Does the perpetrator have to enter the structure? What about a partial entry? How far does a person have to get into a structure for it to be considered entering? In most jurisdictions, any action that breaks the plane of a structure is sufficient to constitute an entering. For instance, if Kim breaks a window in Wendy's home and reaches only her arm inside to steal Wendy's laptop computer, this is a sufficient entry to constitute a burglary. Also, entering includes not only the entry of a person's physical body, but also extensions of a person's body that they might use to reach into a structure, such as crowbars, poles, or other devices. In the previous example, if Kim breaks a window in Wendy's home and reaches inside with a pole and an attached net in order to capture the computer, this is still considered an entry even though Kim's body may not have broken the plane of the building. Box 4.16 outlines the elements of burglary.

Box 4.16   ELEMENTS OF BURGLARY (*MPC*)

Actus Reus	***Mens Rea***
• Breaking and entering a building or occupied structure	• Intent to commit a crime

Concurrence

Linking of *actus reus* and *mens rea*

Criminal Trespass

There are two primary contexts in which **criminal trespass** may take place: unlawfully *entering* another person's property, and unlawfully *remaining* on another person's property. In regard to buildings and occupied structures, a person is guilty of criminal trespass if "knowing that he is not licensed or privileged to do so, he enters or surreptitiously remains in any building or occupied structure" (American Law Institute 1985:144). Remaining on property when a person's privilege to be on that property has expired is referred to as **surreptitious remaining**. An example of this would be if a customer entered a store during normal business hours to purchase an item sold in the store. At that point in time, the customer is permitted to be in the store for that purpose. However, if the customer hid in the restroom until after the store closed, the customer would no longer be permitted to be in the store because her or his authorization expired or lapsed. Therefore, the customer would have remained in the store surreptitiously and would be guilty of criminal trespass.

Criminal trespass may also take place on open land, or in areas not confined to buildings and structures. Under the *MPC*, a person is guilty of criminal trespass if:

> knowing that he is not licensed or privileged to do so, he enters or remains in any place as to which notice against trespass is given by:
>
> (a) actual communication to the actor; or
> (b) posting in a manner prescribed by law or reasonably likely to come to the attention of intruders; or
> (c) fencing or enclosure manifestly designed to exclude intruders. (American Law Institute 1985:144)

In this instance, a person is guilty of criminal trespass if they have been told by those in authority that they are not permitted to enter an area; if signs have been posted stating that people are not permitted to enter an area; or if some physical barrier has been put up to keep people from entering. Box 4.17 outlines the elements of criminal trespass.

Criminal Trespass: unlawfully entering or remaining on another person's property

Surreptitious Remaining: continuing to stay on property once the privilege to be on that property has expired

---

Box 4.17   ELEMENTS OF CRIMINAL TRESPASS (*MPC*)

Actus Reus	*Mens Rea*
• Unlawfully entering another person's property OR • Unlawfully remaining on another person's property	• Knowing that they do not have license or privilege

Concurrence
Linking of *actus reus* and *mens rea*

SUMMARY

Property crimes include the taking, destruction, and invasion of another person's property. Although there have been significant revisions and developments of property crime statutes, they all reflect the long-held idea that people are entitled to possess and enjoy their own property without interference from others. As the types of property that people own have changed, and as society has evolved, so too have the laws protecting property. Property crimes may extend to both tangible and intangible property.

Larceny, embezzlement, obtaining property by false pretenses, receiving stolen property, and extortion are the major categories of property crimes. These crimes are referred to as theft offenses. In order to clarify the theft offenses and simplify the prosecution of these crimes, many jurisdictions have enacted consolidated theft statutes to include each of these actions within one single statute. Robbery, another crime that involves the taking of property, extends beyond mere theft into the area of crimes against people because it is the taking of property from a person through the use of force or the threat of immediate harm.

The criminal law also protects people from the destruction of their property. The crimes that protect against property destruction are arson and criminal mischief. Arson includes destroying a building or structure belonging to another person, or destroying one's own property in order to collect insurance money. Criminal mischief is a rather broad crime that includes damaging, destroying, or tampering with another person's tangible property.

Finally, one of the most important purposes of the criminal law is to protect people from the invasion of their property. These statutes are derived from the common law notion that a person's home is a particularly special place that is entitled to extra protection from the legal system. It is from this idea that the crime of burglary originated. Burglary is the breaking and entering of a structure with the intent to commit a crime. A lesser offense is criminal trespass, which is unlawfully entering or unlawfully remaining on someone else's property. Each of these crimes combines to form the body of property law that strives to ensure rightful property owners that they will be able to use and enjoy their property without it being unlawfully taken, destroyed, or invaded.

KEY TERMS

abuse of trust crime
actual breaking
arson

blackmail
burglary
consolidated theft statutes
constructive breaking
conversion

convert

criminal trespass

curtilage

extortion

false pretenses

fencing

imminent harm

immovable property

intangible property

larceny

material fact

movable property

property

property crimes

receiving stolen property

restitution

robbery

surreptitious remaining

tangible property

theft

theft by deception

vandalism

CRITICAL THINKING QUESTIONS

1. Why does the legal system put such a significant amount of emphasis on protecting people's property? What is the real purpose of property crimes? Be specific and give examples.
2. You have seen in this chapter how the law has evolved and expanded to accommodate changes in the property that people own. How do you think that property crimes may change in the future to meet the needs of a changing society?
3. How should courts balance the value of human life and the value of property? For instance, should a law enforcement officer be permitted to use deadly force to prevent someone's expensive car from being stolen? Explain your reasoning.
4. What factors should be taken into consideration in determining how property crimes should be punished?
5. In the crime of obtaining property by false pretenses, should the person who gave up the property be subject to any criminal liability? Explain your reasoning.
6. Should the criminal law be most concerned with protecting homes and dwellings, or should all structures receive equal protection? Explain your reasoning.
7. Should people be subjected to equal punishment for arson in destroying their own property as they would for destroying another person's property? Explain your reasoning.

SUGGESTED READINGS

Cromwell, P.F. (2003). *Breaking and Entering: Burglars on Burglary*. Belmont, CA: Wadsworth. In this book, the author conducts a detailed study of the activity of burglars through in-depth interviews. The author addresses the activities that are carried out by burglars and why they conduct this activity, as well as how individuals can protect themselves and their property from burglary. This book addresses such topics as how burglary victims and targets are selected, and what avenues are used to make a profit on stolen goods.

Indermauer, D. (1995). *Violent Property Crime*. New South Wales: Federation Press. In this book, Indermauer explores the reasons that crimes against property often lead to violent crimes against people. This is accomplished by examining numerous instances of property crimes. This book also explores the social issues relating to both property crime and violent crime.

Moore, S.A. (2008). "Nevada's Comprehensive Theft Statute: Consolidation or Confusion?" *Nevada Law Journal* 8:672-697. This article addresses the advantages and disadvantages of addressing the crime of theft in a consolidated theft statute rather than retaining the common law distinctions in the theft offenses. The author discusses the fact that while utilizing a consolidated theft statute should and generally does lead to the simplification of theft offenses, there are certain considerations that need to be addressed before a consolidated theft statute can efficiently and comprehensively address the theft crimes in a jurisdiction.

REFERENCES

American Law Institute (1985). *Model Penal Code: Complete Statutory Text*. Philadelphia, PA.

Federal Bureau of Investigation (2011). "Crime in the United States, 2010." http://www.fbi.gov/about-us/cjis/ucr/crime-in-the-u.s/2010/crime-in-the-u.s.-2010/property-crime.

Maier v. Allstate Insurance Company, 41 A.D.3d 1098 (N.Y. 2007).

People v. Casas, 184 Cal. App. 4th 1242 (Cal. App. 2010).

State v. Shoemake, 618 P.2d 1201 (Kan. 1980).

Homicide

LEARNING OBJECTIVES

After reading this chapter you should be able to:

1. Define criminal homicide
2. List and explain the five elements of homicide
3. Distinguish murder from manslaughter
4. Define the types and degrees of homicide frequently encountered
5. Explain the meaning of felony murder
6. Describe the situations included as "special cases" of homicide

INTRODUCTION

Homicide is probably the crime that causes the greatest degree of fear and concern within the general public, and homicide statutes provide for the most serious sentences for those who violate them. At the upper end, convicted homicide offenders may face the death penalty; in fact, at the end of 2010, 36 states and the federal government had some form of capital punishment (Snell 2011). Adults convicted of homicide may also be imprisoned for life—with or without the possibility of parole—although, in some instances, those convicted of homicide may receive prison terms shorter than life. For individuals who were under the age of 18 at the time of the offense the range of punishments may be somewhat more limited. In *Roper v. Simmons*, 543 U.S. 551 (2005) the U.S. Supreme Court held that the death penalty was unconstitutional for those convicted of homicide before their eighteenth birthday. Furthermore, the use of life without parole for young offenders should be confined to homicide offenses [see, for example, *Graham v. Florida*, 560 U.S. 48 (2010)].

Among the eight *Uniform Crime Reports* Part I Index crimes, homicide is one that occurs with the least frequency. Nevertheless, as Table 5.1 shows, in 2011 the police received 14,612 reports of murders and non-negligent manslaughters in the United States, which was down from the record high of 24,703 in 1991 (Federal Bureau of Investigation 2013). Over the two decades from 1991 to 2011, there have been year-to-year fluctuations in the number of homicides in the United States, but the general trend during this

Table 5.1 HOMICIDE AND NON-NEGLIGENT MANSLAUGHTER IN THE U.S., 1991-2011			
YEAR	**NUMBER REPORTED**	**YEAR**	**NUMBER REPORTED**
1991	24,703	2002	16,229
1992	23,760	2003	16,528
1993	24,526	2004	16,148
1994	23,326	2005	16,740
1995	21,606	2006	17,309
1996	19,645	2007	17,128
1997	18,208	2008	16,465
1998	16,974	2009	15,399
1999	15,522	2010	14,748
2000	15,586	2011	14,612
2001	16,037		

Source: Federal Bureau of Investigation (2013).

period has been downward, with nearly a 60 percent decrease between 1991 and 2011.

In addition, there were 10,832 arrests for murder and non-negligent homicide in 2011 (some of which could have occurred in previous years). Table 5.2 shows the estimated numbers of arrests for murders and non-negligent manslaughters in the United States for the years 2005-2011. As should be apparent from both Tables 5.1 and 5.2, the numbers of homicides in the United States have declined and, as a result, the numbers of arrests for homicides have declined as well.

In this chapter we examine the legal definition of homicide in all its forms, including murder and manslaughter, as well as the elements associated with those offenses. However, before we leave this introduction, it is important to make some brief comments about the issue of motive. Throughout the text, we have discussed the notion of intent and the essential role that it plays in the criminal law. However, in law enforcement investigations, the question of motive is raised early and often. Simply stated, **motive** is the reason someone commits a crime. Sheppard (2012) says that motive "describes the reason a person chooses to commit a crime. The reason, however, is different than a required mental state such as intent or malice" (1788). Therefore, understanding motive is not a crucial element for understanding criminal law. Nevertheless, discovering the motive for any crime—and particularly for homicide—is a crucial piece of the puzzle for law enforcement officers as they begin an investigation. Motive is also important for prosecuting attorneys as they attempt to explain what happened and why to a jury. Even though motive is not a required element for proof in the criminal law, motive is often a part of the state's "theory" of the case upon which the prosecutor can tell the story to the jurors. Therefore, understanding motive

Motive:
the reason someone commits a crime

Table 5.2 ESTIMATED NUMBERS OF ARRESTS FOR MURDER AND NON-NEGLIGENT MANSLAUGHTER, 2005-2011	
YEAR	ESTIMATED NUMBER OF ARRESTS
2005	14,062
2006	13,435
2007	13,480
2008	12,955
2009	12,418
2010	11,201
2011	10,832

Source: Federal Bureau of Investigation (2013).

may provide some insight into why a homicide (or any crime, for that matter) may have occurred.

COMMON LAW MURDER AND MANSLAUGHTER

There are several legal terms used to describe the unlawful killing of another person. Under the common law, there were two crimes to describe such killings: murder and manslaughter. The most serious killing was labeled **murder**, and this offense consisted of the unlawful killing of a human being with **malice aforethought**. Historically, most crimes in England were felonies, and many felonies called for the death penalty, which was certainly true for murders. However, the common law also recognized that some killings resulted from intentional acts that took place without malice aforethought. Therefore, in order to punish these killings with something less severe than execution, the crime of **manslaughter** was created. In its simplest terms, manslaughter was the killing of a human being *without* malice aforethought. Within the context of the common law, there was no system of grading or distinguishing the offenses beyond these two very broad categories.

The words "homicide" and "murder" are often used interchangeably by both actors in the criminal justice system and by members of the general public. However, these terms are not identical in the eyes of the law, and in this chapter we will address the distinctions between these two terms.

Murder:
the most serious form of criminal homicide; taking the life of another human being intentionally, deliberately, and with malice aforethought

Malice Aforethought:
hatred or ill feelings that result in one person killing another after deliberation

Manslaughter:
under both the common law and the *Model Penal Code* the killing another person without the presence of malice aforethought

GENERAL ELEMENTS OF HOMICIDE

The *Model Penal Code* (*MPC*) utilizes the broad category of **criminal homicide** to describe all unlawful killings of another human being. This category includes the criminal offenses of murder, manslaughter, and negligent homicide. Therefore, while all murders are homicides, not all homicides are murders. The definition provided by the *MPC* states that criminal homicide is "purposely, knowingly, recklessly, or negligently caus[ing] the death of another human being" (American Law Institute 1985:120). The five elements associated with homicide—*actus reus*, *mens rea*, concurrence, causation, and result—will each be examined in this section. Furthermore, for the sake of consistency, we use the term criminal homicide (or simply homicide) throughout this chapter to refer to any type of unjustified killing of another person.

Criminal Homicide:
the *Model Penal Code*'s classification for the unlawful killing of another person

Actus Reus

As the *MPC* definition notes, the *actus reus* for homicide is causing the death of another human being. However, at this point we need to ask two questions related to the issue of *actus reus*: (1) when is a person alive? and (2) when is a person dead? In order for a suspect to be charged with homicide, the presumed victim must be alive to begin with. Sometimes this question is raised when the defendant mistakenly believes the person to be alive and attempts to kill that person. If the victim is already dead, then the defendant's actions cannot lead to a charge of homicide, but only attempted homicide (see Chapter 9 for a further discussion of criminal attempt).

Another area of concern with the question "when is a person alive" is a situation in which a pregnant woman's fetus is terminated against her will. The "when does life begin" question may result from statutes that govern abortions, but it may also be raised in circumstances in which a woman is assaulted or killed and an unborn fetus also dies. Prior to the U.S. Supreme Court decision of *Roe v. Wade*, 410 U.S. 113 (1973), many states made it a crime to perform elective abortions. The *MPC*—which was originally drafted in 1962—reflects the legal environment of the criminal law prior to the *Roe v. Wade* decision in 1973. Section 230.3 specifies that:

> A person who purposely and unjustifiably terminates the pregnancy of another otherwise than by a live birth commits a felony of the third degree or, where the pregnancy has continued beyond the twenty-sixth week, a felony of the second degree.

This provision also includes cases where

> A woman whose pregnancy has continued beyond the twenty-sixth week commits a felony of the third degree if she purposely terminates her own pregnancy otherwise than by a live birth, or if she uses instruments, drugs, or violence upon herself for that purpose. (American Law Institute 1985:165)

Roe v. Wade altered the legal landscape in the United States in that it provided a constitutional "right to privacy" between a woman and her physician in electing abortions for medical or nonmedical purposes. States have continued to refine and redefine the circumstances under which women may elect to have abortions, but the parameters are much broader than they were prior to *Roe v. Wade*, and most situations are no longer prohibited by the criminal law.

Nevertheless, there are situations in which pregnant women have been assaulted or killed and the question is raised whether the unborn fetus is a person that is protected by the criminal law. Currently,

38 states have enacted some type of **fetal death statute**, in which the death of a fetus can also be charged as criminal homicide. Some of these statutes specify a certain stage of embryonic development, while others cover fetuses from the point of conception or fertilization (see National Conference of State Legislatures 2013).

The question of "when is a person dead" must also be addressed in relation to determining *actus reus* in a homicide case. This question may seem like a strange one for the criminal law to try to answer since in most criminal homicides the victim dies immediately or soon after the assault. However, given the advances in modern medicine, some people who have sustained very serious injuries may not die right away.

Essentially, there are two ways to measure whether a person is dead. First, death could be marked by the cessation of heart function. However, artificial means can be used to keep blood circulating through the body even after the heart has completely ceased to beat. The second way is through measurement of brain activity. Today, most states consider what might be called "brain death" to be the point at which we can say a person has died. Essentially, brain death is the cessation of brain activity that is necessary to support life, and this is a condition that cannot be reversed by medical treatment or artificial means. While this sounds like a relatively certain condition, at least one medical expert warns that there is not a "global consensus on diagnostic criteria" for this concept (Wijdicks 2001, 2002).

Under the common law, the rule was that a victim of an assault had to die within a year and a day in order for the case to be considered a homicide. At the time the rule emerged it was medically difficult to connect some injuries due to assaults that took place from which the victim died after a considerable amount of time had passed. As a result, the arbitrary time frame of a year and a day was applied since it was assumed that deaths occurring after that point were related to some other cause (see Legal Information Institute 2013). Today, this rule typically plays little to no role in the determination of the connection between the wrongful act and the resulting death, and most states do not have time limitations for causation.

In the case of *Rogers v. Tennessee*, 532 U.S. 451 (2001), the U.S. Supreme Court seemed to give the states a great deal of leeway in eliminating the year and a day rule, even retroactively. Nevertheless, some state court systems continue to apply this common law legal tradition. Box 5.1 presents an abbreviated form of the *Rogers* case.

Fetal Death Statute: law that makes it a form of criminal homicide to cause the death of an unborn fetus

Box 5.1   THE YEAR AND A DAY RULE: DEAD OR ALIVE?

Rogers v. Tennessee
532 U.S. 451 (2001)

In 2001 the U.S. Supreme Court addressed the issue of the common law year and a day rule in relation to the connection between when the harm occurred and when a death resulted. Justice Sandra Day O'Connor wrote the majority opinion in a 5-4 decision.

Following James Bowdery's death 15 months after petitioner stabbed him, petitioner was convicted in Tennessee state court of second degree murder under the State's criminal homicide statute. Although that statute makes no mention of the common law "year and a day rule"—under which no defendant could be convicted of murder unless his victim died within a year and a day of the defendant's act, petitioner argued on appeal that the rule persisted as part of the State's common law and, as such, precluded his conviction. The Tennessee Court of Criminal Appeals disagreed and affirmed the conviction. In affirming, the State Supreme Court abolished the rule, finding that the reasons for recognizing the rule at common law no longer existed.

The Tennessee court's abolition of the year and a day rule was not unexpected and indefensible. Advances in medical and related science have so undermined the rule's usefulness as to render it without question obsolete, and it has been legislatively or judicially abolished in the vast majority of jurisdictions recently to have addressed the issue. Despite petitioner's argument to the contrary, the fact that a vast number of jurisdictions outside Tennessee have abolished the rule is surely relevant to whether its abolition in his case, which involves the continuing viability of a common law rule, can be said to be unexpected and indefensible by reference to the law as it then existed.

Perhaps most importantly, at the time of petitioner's crime the rule had only the most tenuous foothold as part of Tennessee's criminal law. It did not exist as part of the State's statutory criminal code, and while the Tennessee Supreme Court concluded that the rule persisted at common law, it also pointedly observed that the rule had never once served as a ground of decision in any murder prosecution in the State. Indeed, in all the reported Tennessee cases, the rule has been mentioned only three times, and each time in dicta.[1] These cases hardly suggest that the Tennessee court's decision was "unexpected and indefensible" such that it offended the due process principle of fair warning articulated in *Bouie* and its progeny. There is nothing to indicate that abolition of the rule in petitioner's case represented an exercise of the sort of unfair and arbitrary judicial action against which the Due Process Clause aims to protect. Far from a marked and unpredictable departure from prior precedent, the court's decision was a routine exercise of common law decision making that brought the law into conformity with reason and common sense.

---

1. Dicta are individual opinions of judges or justices and they do not express an official opinion or the ruling court on legal matters (see Sheppard 2012).

[Therefore], the Tennessee Supreme Court's retroactive application to petitioner of its decision abolishing the year and a day rule did not deny petitioner due process of law in violation of the Fourteenth Amendment.

---

1. What seems to be the basis for the so-called year and a day rule?
2. Has this rule outlived the reason for its initial existence?
3. How many states still apply the year and a day rule either by statute or by court-implemented common law rule?

Mens Rea

One of the requisite elements in homicide and all criminal cases is *mens rea* or the guilty mind. As a basic definition, the *MPC* states that acting intentionally or with intent means to act purposely (American Law Institute 1985:19). Statutory provisions and many legal scholars also use the terms "purposely" or "with purpose," as well as "willfully" (see American Law Institute 1985:18-19) to describe behavior that is carried out with this intentional mindset. We will not make distinctions among all of these words or terms given the similarity of their meaning. The thrust of each of these terms is that a person acted purposefully, regardless of what the motivation for acting this way might have been. In other words, a person engaged in an action that had an intended purpose or end result.

In addition to intent, two terms that repeatedly occur in any examination of homicide are recklessness and negligence. In fact, the *MPC* includes both of these words in its definition of criminal homicide (American Law Institute 1985:120). In this section we examine both recklessness and negligence, explore the distinctions between the two, and discuss the ways in which these concepts relate to criminal homicides.

Recklessness exists any time a person takes "a substantial and unjustified risk." A person who acts recklessly engages in behaviors in which the average individual (that is, a reasonable person) would not participate. In comparing recklessness with negligence, we can say that recklessness implies a greater degree of culpability or blameworthiness than negligence. In fact, we can say that people act with recklessness when they act rashly or heedlessly in situations in which they are aware of the possible consequences of their actions and persist anyway. This means that people who act recklessly are aware of the potential danger of their actions and choose to continue their course of conduct in spite of the danger they pose or are creating.

Recklessness: to undertake a substantial and unjustified risk about which a person has knowledge

---

Box 5.2   YOU DECIDE: ARE THESE CASES OF RECKLESSNESS?

Alice is a college student who is celebrating her twenty-first birthday with a group of friends. They go to a local restaurant where Alice has several alcoholic beverages over a two-hour period. Susan, one of Alice's sorority sisters, is concerned that Alice has had too much to drink and that she is too impaired to drive. Susan offers to drive Alice back to the sorority house on campus. Alice refuses her offers, and Susan becomes insistent that Alice cannot drive. A major argument then breaks out between the two and Alice storms out of the restaurant and takes off out of the parking lot in her car, driving at a high rate of speed. Alice hits and kills a pedestrian who was walking through the parking lot. Legally, can it be said that Alice acted in a reckless manner? Did she know, or should she have known, of the danger of her actions, but she continued on in spite of the danger? Is Susan liable for causing the agitation that might have led to Alice's actions?

Stephan lives in a community that frequently celebrates holidays such as New Year's Eve by shooting firearms into the air. One year, at the stroke of midnight, Stephan and his two brothers fire handguns and shotguns into the air. Within a few seconds a falling bullet strikes Stephan's 10-year-old nephew in the head, killing him instantly. We might say that this was an unfortunate accident, but could the law consider this to be a homicide because Stephan and his brothers acted in a reckless manner? Would it be foreseeable to a reasonable person that shooting firearms into the air is dangerous and that, given the inevitability of the law of gravity (what goes up must come down), this could result in someone's death? Once it has been determined who fired the shot that killed Stephan's nephew, could authorities file criminal charges for the unfortunate death because of the foreseeable danger of these actions?

Box 5.2 provides two examples of cases that illustrate the concept of recklessness.

In contrast to recklessness, **negligence** is said to exist in any situation where a person's conduct departs from that normally practiced by a reasonable person. It is important to note that negligence is also a civil law concept that can be confused with criminal negligence. However, while these are similar ideas, they have different applications in different areas of law.

Negligence:
acting in a way that deviates from the standard of care that would be exercised by a reasonable or reasonably prudent person

From a criminal law perspective, negligence is an "unreasonable failure to be aware of a risk either through inadvertence or mistake" (Simons 2002:2). We view the negligent person as less culpable or blameworthy than the reckless person. However, the real difference between the two is really an awareness of the risk (recklessness) or lack of awareness of the risk (negligence). This may be a very subtle difference and hinges on the degree of dangerousness and the likelihood of foreseeing the ultimate outcome. Box 5.3 gives two illustrations of deaths that might result from a person's negligence.

> **Box 5.3   YOU DECIDE: ARE THESE CASES OF NEGLIGENCE?**
>
> Veronica's 5-year-old son Chad throws a temper tantrum every time he has to ride in his child safety seat in the back seat of the vehicle. Rather than making a big deal out of this, Veronica has started to let Chad ride in the front seat wearing a regular seatbelt. One day she was involved in a head-on accident with another vehicle and Chad was thrown into the windshield and killed. Is it possible — depending on state statutes dealing with child abuse — that Veronica could be charged with child abuse resulting in death based on her negligent behavior?
>
> Elizabeth is a homeowner in an area that has experienced a very cold winter accompanied by large amounts of snow and ice. For the past three weeks, Elizabeth's front steps have been covered with ice. She has slipped several times while entering her home, but she has not taken any action to remove the ice from her steps. One day, the postman is delivering Elizabeth's mail and he slips on her icy steps. The postman falls on the back of his head causing a major brain hemorrhage, and he dies the next day. Is it possible that Elizabeth could be charged with the postman's death, which occurred as the result of her failure to act? Is this criminal negligence, civil negligence, or both? Could it be recklessness?

Concurrence

The third element associated with the crime of homicide is concurrence. As we mentioned in Chapter 2, concurrence is the point at which the wrongful act (*actus reus*) and the intent (*mens rea*) intersect. There must be a wrongful act — one that is prohibited by law — and it must be joined with criminal intent. If either of these is absent, a crime has not occurred.

Causation

To review briefly the requirements for cause discussed in Chapter 2, there must be a causal link between the mental state of the killer, the wrongful act, and the resulting death. Section 2.03 of the *MPC* says that "Conduct is the cause of a result when: (a) it is an antecedent but for which the result in question would not have occurred; and (b) the relationship between the conduct and the result satisfies any additional causal requirements imposed by the Code or by the law defining the offense" (American Law Institute 1985:25). The requirements for the causation element are: (1) actual (factual) causation and (2) proximate (legal) causation. To prove actual causation, the state must use the "but for" test. In cases where there might be multiple possible causes, we might have to apply the substantial factor test. Both of these were discussed in Chapter 2. To establish

---

Box 5.4   YOU DECIDE: IS THIS A CASE OF HOMICIDE?

James Odom, a married father of three has taken a night job as a convenience store clerk to supplement the income of his financially struggling family. One night a masked gunman comes into the store brandishing a large-caliber handgun. The gunman demands that James open the cash register and give him all of the money inside. During the course of these events James has a heart attack and drops to the floor dead. The gunman assumes that he has fainted and he opens the register himself and empties out all of the cash.

A customer is entering the store as the gunman rushes out and this person gets a license number for the getaway car. When the police and paramedics arrive they find that James has died, but there is no sign of bullet wounds or other trauma. An autopsy confirms that he died of a heart attack. When the gunman is eventually arrested he is charged with armed robbery as well as with murder in the death of James Odom.

Is this a case of murder, or should it be some lesser crime? Would it matter if the medical examiner determined that James had a congenital heart defect and that the stress of the robbery was the factor that contributed to his death?

---

proximate causation of a death, the state has to prove that the result is directly linked to the defendant's actions. Or, if not direct, the state must prove that the result was foreseeable given the defendant's actions. Box 5.4 presents an illustration of the difficulty that can arise when trying to establish the proximate cause of death.

Result

The final element associated with homicide is result, and this element distinguishes homicide from many other types of crimes (such as larceny), which are conduct crimes that do not require any additional resulting harm to be proven. Regardless of the different types of offenses that can fall under the broad category of criminal homicide, the resulting harm—that is, the wrongful death of another person—must be proven. Box 5.5 presents the elements associated with criminal homicide.

TYPES AND DEGREES OF HOMICIDE

As we have mentioned, the *MPC* classifies three different types of criminal homicide: murder, manslaughter, and negligent homicide. In terms of seriousness, the *MPC* classifies them as first, second, and third degree felonies, respectively. Therefore, one of the primary reasons for providing different designations or degrees of homicide is for the purpose of sentencing convicted offenders.

Box 5.5 ELEMENTS OF CRIMINAL HOMICIDE	
Actus Reus	**Mens Rea**
• Killing a live human being	• Intent to cause the death of another human being; recklessness or negligence

Concurrence

The joining of the *actus reus* with the *mens rea* element

Causation	**Result**
• Actual causation AND • Proximate causation	• A wrongful death must have occurred

Pennsylvania seems to have been the first state to distinguish different degrees of murder by statute (see Keedy 1949), and today most states have continued to follow the homicide designations developed by Pennsylvania and set out in common law. Accordingly, these states' statutes provide for classifications of crimes along with different degrees of seriousness that are different from the *MPC*—there are similarities in some states, though, with some variations (American Law Institute 1985:117). While the laws in every state are different, in this section we will present the typical common law designations for homicide that are likely to be encountered within the criminal law.

Much like the *MPC*, most states classify the most serious form of criminal homicide as murder. However, unlike the *MPC*, states that follow the common law tradition typically distinguish at least two forms or degrees of murder: first degree murder and second degree murder.

First Degree Murder

The FBI's *Uniform Crime Report* defines murder as "the willful (non-negligent) killing of one human being by another" (Federal Bureau of Investigation 2013). On its face, this definition is a little vague. The *MPC* provides a more thorough definition and states that murder involves a criminal homicide that is "committed purposely or knowingly" or one that is "committed recklessly under circumstances manifesting extreme indifference to the value of human life" (American Law Institute 1985:120).

First degree murder is frequently defined as the premeditated and deliberate killing of another person. Deliberate killings are those that are "cold-blooded" or carefully considered. Premeditated killings imply that the person who committed the killing has had a sufficient amount of time to formulate a plan for, or thought about, carrying out the homicide. The amount of time necessary to develop the plot may involve days, weeks, or months, or it may evolve within a matter of minutes. The word *deliberate* implies a "quality" of thought, whereas premeditated implies a "quantity" of thought. One can have a deliberate killing without premeditation but cannot have premeditation without deliberation.

First degree murder recognizes that some people who kill do so with purpose, intention, and planning. The assumption is that the killer spent some period of time (varying from situation to situation) considering how to kill the victim and perhaps the best way to carry out the killing in order to avoid detection. Whatever the circumstances, a key consideration under the common law is the presence of "malice aforethought." The requirements of premeditation and deliberateness distinguish first degree murders from other homicides. Additionally, some states base first degree murder charges on the number of victims killed or who the victim of the attack was. Box 5.6 lists the elements that constitute first degree murder.

> **First Degree Murder:** under common law the unlawful killing of another person as a result of malice aforethought; the deliberate or premeditated killing of another person

---

Box 5.6   ELEMENTS OF FIRST DEGREE MURDER

Actus Reus	*Mens Rea*

• Killing a live human being	• Intent to cause the death of another human being
	  • Premeditated AND
	  • Deliberate

Concurrence

The joining of the *actus reus* with the *mens rea* element

Causation	**Result**
• Actual cause AND • Proximate cause	• A wrongful death must have occurred

Second Degree Murder

Second degree murder can present some definitional problems for criminal law students. It is often described as an offense that falls somewhere between first degree murder and manslaughter in terms of the level of seriousness or blameworthiness (Legal Definitions 2011). Sheppard (2012:1795) says that second degree murder is "the crime of intentionally killing another person in circumstances that are less culpable than those of first degree murder" and that it includes homicides that occur "without any premeditation or prior intent to kill." Unlike first degree murder, in states that provide for the offense of second degree murder it is a deliberate, unlawful killing in which the requirement of premeditation is absent.

In the most basic terms, it is any killing other than those defined in statutes as first degree murder, manslaughter, or negligent homicide. In some cases when prosecuting attorneys are uncertain about whether they can prove first degree murder, they may choose second degree murder as the most appropriate charge. A guilty verdict of second degree murder may also be chosen by juries that cannot agree unanimously for a conviction on a first degree murder charge.

In some states (Pennsylvania is one example) felony murders (discussed later in the chapter) are classified as second degree murders. Additionally, a few states provide that homicides that demonstrate a "depraved heart" (sometimes called an abandoned or malignant heart) or "reckless indifference to human life" constitute second degree murders (FindLaw 2013a). See Box 5.7 for the elements that constitute second degree murder.

> **Second Degree Murder:** deliberately taking a human life without malice aforethought; malice is implied rather than express; in common law a crime that exists in terms of seriousness between first degree murder and manslaughter

---

Box 5.7   ELEMENTS OF SECOND DEGREE MURDER

Actus Reus	*Mens Rea*
• Killing a live human being	• Intent to cause the death of another human being • Deliberate • Depraved heart; OR • Reckless indifference to human life

Concurrence

The joining of the *actus reus* with the *mens rea* element

Causation	**Result**
• Actual cause AND • Proximate cause	• A wrongful death must have occurred

Manslaughter

Manslaughter is considered a less serious form of criminal homicide than murder. Manslaughter can be defined as a killing that is either in the "heat of passion" or "committed recklessly" or one that otherwise would be murder but is "committed under the influence of extreme mental or emotional disturbance for which there is reasonable explanation or excuse." The *MPC* prescribes that, unlike murder, manslaughter is classified as a second degree felony (American Law Institute 1985:120). State criminal codes and the *MPC* distinguish manslaughter from other forms of criminal homicide, and most states provide for two different types of manslaughter: voluntary and involuntary.

Voluntary Manslaughter

The crime of **voluntary manslaughter** takes place whenever a person has been killed intentionally, but without malice aforethought. Voluntary manslaughter occurs after one person provokes another, causing the accused to act in a heat of passion, which leads to the use of deadly force. The definition of a heat of passion is somewhat imprecise, but in general terms it "refers to an irresistible emotion that an ordinarily reasonable person would experience under the same facts and circumstances. This idea of an irresistible impulse contrasts with the idea of premeditation present in first degree murder, and a showing of one necessarily negates the other" (FindLaw 2013b). In order for a person to act in a heat of passion, there must not be a cooling-off period between the provocation and the wrongful act. Since the killing was done intentionally, adequate provocation is what allows these cases to be classified as voluntary manslaughter rather than first or second degree murder.

> **Voluntary Manslaughter:** intentional killings absent malice aforethought; deaths resulting from "heat of passion" actions, or in response to adequate provocation

There are many circumstances that can be considered as adequate provocation. For example, adequate provocation may occur when there has been adultery, an assault and battery, under circumstances of mutual combat, and resisting an illegal arrest. The common law view is that the provocative act must be of such a nature that it would overwhelm a reasonable person and cause him or her to act in a manner that he or she would not without the presence of this extreme circumstance.

One important exception to the notion of adequate provocation is the use of words. Almost universally, state legislatures have decided and court rulings have held that the use of words alone—no matter how hateful or intimidating the nature of the communication—is not sufficient provocation for a deadly retaliation. Furthermore, even words plus actions may not provide sufficient provocation unless the action is physically threatening and it warrants a self-defense

Box 5.8   ELEMENTS OF VOLUNTARY MANSLAUGHTER

Actus Reus

- Killing a live human being

Mens Rea

- Intent to cause the death of another human being
  - In the heat of passion;
  - Caused by adequate provocation; AND
  - With no cooling-off period

Concurrence

The joining of the *actus reus* with the *mens rea* element

Causation

- Actual cause AND
- Proximate cause

Result

- A wrongful death must have occurred

Box 5.9   YOU DECIDE: WHICH CRIME IS THIS?

John arrives home from work early one day and discovers his wife Mary in bed with their next-door neighbor, Tom. John opens a desk drawer and pulls out a 9 mm semiautomatic handgun, which he points at Tom. Mary throws herself between the two men just as the handgun fires. She is struck by one bullet in the chest and dies in the ambulance on the way to the hospital.

When the police interview John he truthfully explains the circumstances surrounding the shooting, but he consistently maintains that he only meant to threaten Tom and that he never intended to shoot anyone, let alone Mary.

With what crime should John be charged? Would your answer change if John went on a long walk first?

Which charge would you recommend if you were the lead criminal investigator? What factors did you consider in arriving at your answer?

response. Box 5.8 contains the elements associated with the crime of voluntary manslaughter; Box 5.9 presents a scenario in which you must decide, based on the elements presented, which crime has occurred.

Involuntary Manslaughter

It is important to remember once again that with any case of manslaughter we know that there has been an unlawful killing of another person. We also know that the more serious offense of murder can be distinguished from manslaughter. However, it is very important that we be able to distinguish between the two types of manslaughter (involuntary and voluntary).

In the case of **involuntary manslaughter**, a death must have occurred, and the action that caused that death must have been committed recklessly. Because the *mens rea* here is recklessness, involuntary manslaughter is distinguished from the other types of homicide—first degree and second degree murder and voluntary manslaughter—because it is *not* an intentional killing.

The key to understanding the criminal act of involuntary manslaughter is to recognize that there must be a gross deviation from the standard of care that should be exercised by a reasonable person. Juries sometimes struggle with the notion of the "reasonable person" or "reasonably prudent person." In effect, jurors are being asked to place themselves in the position of the person accused of causing the death and to determine how they would have behaved in an identical situation. This allows jurors to decide how a reasonable person would have acted, and whether the defendant acted in an appropriate manner. Box 5.10 contains a case abstract in which a North Carolina court dealt with the issue of the exact nature of the wrongful death. Box 5.11 contains the essential elements associated with manslaughter.

Involuntary Manslaughter: the unintentional killing of another person as a result of recklessness or criminal negligence

---

Box 5.10   A CASE OF MANSLAUGHTER?

State v. Elmore
736 S.E.2d 568 (2012)

The following case decided by the North Carolina Court of Appeals shows how some charges of homicide may result in convictions and sentences for lesser, included offenses such as involuntary manslaughter.

Matthew Lee Elmore was convicted of two counts of involuntary manslaughter on 29 July 2011. Defendant was sentenced to a term of nineteen to twenty-three months in prison, followed by a consecutive term of nineteen to twenty-three months in prison. This sentence was suspended for thirty-six months of supervised probation.

The evidence at trial tended to show that Defendant was involved in a vehicle collision on 13 June 2009. Defendant was driving a Chevrolet Suburban when he ran a red light and collided with a Chrysler Le Baron Convertible. Both occupants in the Le Baron were killed.

Defendant was indicted on two counts of felony death by motor vehicle on 4 January 2010. A superseding indictment issued 4 April 2010, adding charges for manslaughter, misdemeanor death by motor vehicle, driving while impaired, running a red light, and reckless driving. At the beginning of trial, Defendant made an oral motion to dismiss, arguing that the State was prohibited by statute from prosecuting Defendant for both death by vehicle and manslaughter charges arising out of the same death. The trial court denied Defendant's motion, ruling that the statute in question prevented punishment under both theories, but not prosecution.

After trial, the jury found Defendant not guilty of felony death by vehicle, but guilty of voluntary manslaughter and misdemeanor death by vehicle. The trial court sentenced Defendant based on manslaughter, and arrested judgment in the charges of misdemeanor death by vehicle. Defendant appeals.

1. What do we mean by lesser, included offenses?
2. Is a motor vehicle death a serious form of homicide or not? Does it make a difference whether alcohol is a factor or not?
3. What causes juries to choose the option of a lesser, included offense?

Box 5.11   ELEMENTS OF MANSLAUGHTER

Actus Reus	*Mens Rea*
• Killing a live human being	• Recklessness

Concurrence

The joining of the *actus reus* with the *mens rea* element

Causation	**Result**
• Actual cause AND • Proximate cause	• A wrongful death must have occurred

---

Negligent Homicide

In addition to the traditional common law crimes of murder and manslaughter, the *MPC* includes the crime of **negligent homicide**. A negligent homicide occurs when a person's death results from another person's negligence (rather than intent or recklessness). The *MPC* provides a modest clarification on this point when it explains that

> A person acts negligently with respect to a material element of an offense [in this case homicide] when he should be aware of a substantial and unjustifiable risk that the material element exists or will result from his conduct. The risk must be of such a nature and degree that the actor's failure to perceive it, considering the nature and purpose of his conduct and the circumstances known to him, involves a gross deviation from the standard of care that a reasonable person would observe in the actor's situation. (American Law Institute 1985:121)

Negligent Homicide:
to cause the death of another human being as a result of a negligent act or actions

There are three factors contained in this definition that are worth noting. First, the definition suggests that a person who is charged with negligent homicide should be aware of the risk that he or she is taking in a given situation. Second, the risk that the person is taking is "substantial and unjustifiable." A substantial risk is one that goes beyond the types of actions that people normally engage in as part of their daily lives, and there must be no justification for taking such a risk. Finally, the conduct that the person engages in is considered a deviation from the behavior of a reasonable person.

At one level it is possible to say that negligence is a less blameworthy standard than is recklessness. When people act recklessly they perceive the danger that exists from what they are doing and choose to continue with the behavior despite this risk. In contrast, when people act negligently they do not perceive the risk of harm to themselves or to others. Though they fail to perceive this risk of harm, they should have perceived the risk, and therefore they can be held legally responsible for the resulting harm.

Based on this definition, in most states a driver who is intoxicated or otherwise impaired and causes a traffic accident resulting in a death would be guilty of negligent homicide. This person owed a duty of care to other drivers on the road not to operate a vehicle when impaired. Although there was no intent to injure another person, the driver failed to exercise the required duty of care, and will be held responsible for negligent homicide for any resulting death. We will return to this topic in a later section about vehicular homicide. However, it is important to note here that some jurisdictions may label this type of situation as motor vehicle homicide (or a similar classification). This offense recognizes that while some deaths may not be intentional, they are still deserving of criminal punishment.

In some ways, when involuntary manslaughter is a felony, it is much the same as the *MPC*'s category of negligent homicide (American Law Institute 1985). There are at least two reasons for this comparison. To begin with, the *MPC* defines negligent homicide as a third degree felony. Furthermore, the *Code* specifies that negligent homicide is a criminal homicide that results from negligence (American Law Institute 1985:121). Thus, unlike manslaughter under the *Code* (or voluntary manslaughter under the common law) that results from recklessness, negligent homicide and involuntary manslaughter result from criminal negligence. The *MPC* elements for negligent homicide are provided in Box 5.12.

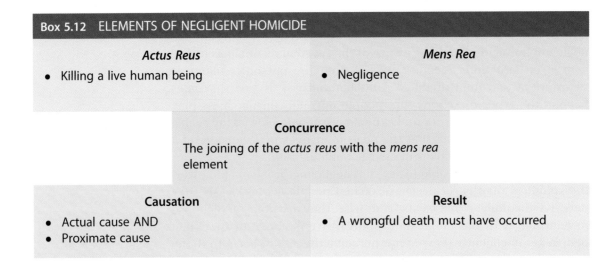

Box 5.12   ELEMENTS OF NEGLIGENT HOMICIDE

Actus Reus	*Mens Rea*
• Killing a live human being	• Negligence

Concurrence

The joining of the *actus reus* with the *mens rea* element

Causation	**Result**
• Actual cause AND • Proximate cause	• A wrongful death must have occurred

HOMICIDE: SPECIAL CASES

There are several circumstances that fall outside of the definitions of homicide (murder, manslaughter, and negligent homicide) that we have previously provided. These are special cases or situations in which the circumstances go beyond our traditional definitions. In this section we consider the cases of felony murder, misdemeanor manslaughter, criminally negligent manslaughter, the use of motor vehicles, suicides, and mercy killings.

Felony Murder

Most jurisdictions in the United States include a statutory provision for killings that occur during the commission of one or more enumerated felonies, although the historical roots of this tradition are somewhat obscure (see Tomkovicz 1994). Furthermore, even though the *MPC* does not specifically include the offense of **felony murder**, it describes situations in which the offender is "engaged or is an accomplice in the commission of, or an attempt to commit, or flight after committing or attempting to commit robbery, rape, deviate sexual intercourse by force or threat of force, arson, burglary, kidnapping, or felonious escape" (American Law Institute 1985:120). We can classify these as felony murders.

Currently, 46 states have established in their homicide statutes that any unintentional death that takes place during the commission of certain other felonies is felony murder, and these can be a type of first degree or second degree murder. The four states that do not

Felony Murder:
the incidental killing of another person during the commission of one of the statutorily specified felonies

recognize the felony murder rule are Hawaii, Kentucky, Michigan, and Ohio (Gramlich 2008).

Felony murders typically occur during the commission of a limited range of felony offenses. These offenses are often described as **inherently dangerous felonies**, and these include crimes such as rape, robbery, carjacking, burglary, or home invasion. Whatever the circumstances surrounding the commission of such crimes, one major factor distinguishes felony murder from other cases of first degree murder: In felony murders, there is an absence of malice aforethought or deliberation (see Finkel and Smith 1993). This means that when a felony murder takes place, the death was incidental to the commission of the underlying crime.

Nevertheless, legislatures assume that even though no death was intended, a person committing certain felonies (especially with weapons such as firearms) may be prepared to act with deadly force if resistance is encountered. So, for example, when an armed robber shoots a convenience store clerk (who may be a complete stranger), this supplants or substitutes for the requirement of deliberation for traditional murder (see Fletcher 1981). It also means that legislatures recognize that when an individual purposely sets out to commit an inherently dangerous felony, that person takes a substantial risk that puts the lives of others in jeopardy. When a death results from the commission of a specified felony (even though the death may have been unintentional), that person's *mens rea* makes him or her culpable to a degree that justifies criminal punishment.

Box 5.13 provides a U.S. Supreme Court case dealing with the issue of felony murder. Justice O'Connor delivered the opinion of the Court in a 5-4 decision in this case that dealt with a prison escape and the murder of a group of people whose car was taken by the escapees and their confederates.

> **Inherently Dangerous Felonies:**
> any one of a group of statutorily defined crimes (such as rape, robbery, or home invasion) that are designed to cause, or that may cause, death or great bodily harm

---

Box 5.13   SHOULD FELONY MURDER QUALIFY FOR THE DEATH PENALTY?

Tison v. Arizona
481 U.S. 137 (1987)

Gary Tison was sentenced to life imprisonment as the result of a prison escape during the course of which he had killed a guard. After he had been in prison a number of years, [his] wife, their three sons Donald, Ricky, and Raymond, Gary's brother Joseph, and other relatives made plans to help Gary Tison escape again. Plans for escape were discussed with Gary Tison, who insisted that his cellmate, Randy Greenawalt, also a convicted murderer, be included in the prison break.

On July 30, 1978, the three Tison brothers entered the Arizona State Prison at Florence carrying a large ice chest filled with guns. The Tisons armed Greenawalt and their father, and the group, brandishing their weapons, locked the prison guards and visitors present in a storage closet. The five men fled the prison grounds.

After leaving the prison, [they] proceeded on to an isolated house. As the group traveled on back roads and secondary highways through the desert, a tire blew out. The group decided to flag down a passing motorist and steal a car. . . . One car passed by without stopping, but a second car, a Mazda occupied by John Lyons, his wife Donnelda, his 2-year-old son Christopher, and his 15-year-old niece, Theresa Tyson, pulled over to render aid.

Raymond recalled being at the Mazda filling the water jug "when we started hearing the shots." In any event, petitioners agree they saw Greenawalt and their father brutally murder their four captives with repeated blasts from their shotguns. Neither made an effort to help the victims, though both later stated they were surprised by the shooting. The Tisons got into the Mazda and drove away, continuing their flight.

Several days later the Tisons and Greenawalt were apprehended after a shootout at a police roadblock. Donald Tison was killed. Gary Tison escaped into the desert where he subsequently died of exposure. Raymond and Ricky Tison and Randy Greenawalt were captured and tried jointly for the crimes associated with the prison break itself and the shootout at the roadblock.

The State individually tried each of the petitioners for capital murder of the four victims as well as for the associated crimes of armed robbery, kidnaping, and car theft. The capital murder charges were based on Arizona felony-murder law providing that a killing occurring during the perpetration of robbery or kidnaping is capital murder, and that each participant in the kidnaping or robbery is legally responsible for the acts of his accomplices. Each of the petitioners was convicted of the four murders under these accomplice liability and felony-murder statutes. [And] the judge sentenced both petitioners to death.

Petitioners argue strenuously that they did not "intend to kill" as that concept has been generally understood in the common law. As petitioners point out, there is no evidence that either Ricky or Raymond Tison took any act which he desired to, or was substantially certain would, cause death. [T]he Arizona Supreme Court attempted to reformulate "intent to kill" as a species of foreseeability.

Participants in violent felonies like armed robberies can frequently "anticipat[e] that lethal force . . . might be used . . . in accomplishing the underlying felony." Indeed, the possibility of bloodshed is inherent in the commission of any violent felony and this possibility is generally foreseeable and foreseen; it is one principal reason that felons arm themselves. The Arizona Supreme Court's attempted reformulation of intent to kill amounts to little more than a restatement of the felony-murder rule itself.

On the other hand . . . Raymond Tison brought an arsenal of lethal weapons into the Arizona State Prison which he then handed over to two convicted murderers, one of whom he knew had killed a prison guard in a previous escape attempt. By his own admission he was prepared to kill in furtherance of the prison break. He performed the crucial role of flagging down a passing car occupied by an innocent family whose fate was then entrusted to the known killers he had previously armed. He robbed these people at their direction and then guarded the victims at gunpoint while they considered what next to do. He stood by and watched the killing, making no effort to assist the victims. Instead, he chose to assist the killers in their continuing criminal endeavors, ending in a gun battle with the police in the final showdown.

Ricky Tison's behavior differs in slight details only. Like Raymond, he intentionally brought the guns into the prison to arm the murderers. He could have foreseen that lethal force might be used, particularly since he knew that his father's previous escape attempt had resulted in murder. He, too, participated fully in the kidnaping and robbery and watched the killing after which he chose to aid those whom he had placed in the position to kill rather than their victims.

These facts not only indicate that the Tison brothers' participation in the crime was anything but minor; they also would support a finding that they both appreciated that their acts were likely to result in the taking of innocent life. The issue raised by this case is whether the Eighth Amendment prohibits the death penalty in the case of the defendant whose participation is major and whose mental state is one of reckless indifference to the value of human life.

A narrow focus on the question of whether or not a given defendant "intended to kill," however, is a highly unsatisfactory means of definitively distinguishing the most culpable and dangerous of murderers. Many who intend to, and do, kill are not criminally liable at all. Other intentional homicides, though criminal, are often felt undeserving of the death penalty—those that are the result of provocation. On the other hand, some nonintentional murderers may be among the most dangerous and inhumane of all—the person who tortures another not caring whether the victim lives or dies, or the robber who shoots someone in the course of the robbery, utterly indifferent to the fact that the desire to rob may have the unintended consequence of

killing the victim as well as taking the victim's property. This reckless indifference to the value of human life may be every bit as shocking to the moral sense as an "intent to kill." Indeed it is for this very reason that the common law and modern criminal codes alike have classified behavior such as occurred in this case along with intentional murders. Similarly, we hold that the reckless disregard for human life implicit in knowingly engaging in criminal activities known to carry a grave risk of death represents a highly culpable mental state, a mental state that may be taken into account in making a capital sentencing judgment when that conduct causes its natural, though also not inevitable, lethal result.

The petitioners' own personal involvement in the crimes was not minor, but rather, as specifically found by the trial court, "substantial." The Tisons' high level of participation in these crimes further implicates them in the resulting deaths. Accordingly, they fall well within the intermediate position which focuses on the defendant's degree of participation in the felony.

We will not attempt to precisely delineate the particular types of conduct and states of mind warranting imposition of the death penalty here. Rather, we simply hold that major participation in the felony committed, combined with reckless indifference to human life, is sufficient to satisfy the *Enmund* culpability requirement. The Arizona courts have clearly found that the former exists; we now vacate the judgments below and remand for determination of the latter in further proceedings not inconsistent with this opinion.

1. What is the fundamental justification for the felony murder rule?
2. Why does it seem that so many states have continued to apply the felony murder rule? What are some of the reasons four states may have chosen not to employ this rule?
3. Is the felony murder rule potentially overly broad in that people only slightly involved in the initial crime might be charged with homicide?

Misdemeanor Manslaughter

Involuntary manslaughter charges may also result when the defendant committed a misdemeanor and an unintentional death resulted from his or her actions. In fact, some states classify this as misdemeanor manslaughter. Therefore, when a death occurs as a result of the commission of a misdemeanor, the defendant can be charged with involuntary manslaughter. Misdemeanor manslaughter is comparable to felony murder in that an unintentional death resulted from the commission of an unlawful act. However, because misdemeanor manslaughter involves an unlawful act that is less extreme or severe, there is no malice implied. Therefore, the act is classified as manslaughter rather than murder.

Criminally Negligent Manslaughter

Involuntary manslaughter charges may also result from an individual causing someone's death through their negligent actions. This is referred to as criminally negligent manslaughter. Recall the previous example in Box 5.3 in which the postman died from an injury he received slipping on Elizabeth's icy steps. In this case, Elizabeth did not intend to cause the postman's death. However, her negligence in failing to remove the ice from her steps set a chain of events into motion that ultimately led to his death. Therefore, Elizabeth's negligence could result in a charge of criminally negligent manslaughter.

Use of Motor Vehicles

The use of motor vehicles in circumstances leading to death presents a special category of criminal offenses. Most of these situations involve driving under the influence of alcohol or other drugs. The specific offenses are either driving while intoxicated (DWI) or driving under the influence of drugs or alcohol (DUI), depending on the laws of each jurisdiction. In this section we will deal with situations involving the use of motor vehicles resulting in deaths from drunken driving.

Drunken or drug-impaired driving has become a major problem in the United States, and in recent years many states have increased their penalties for this offense. The Centers for Disease Control and Prevention (2011) reported that in 2009 there were over 1.4 million arrests for impaired driving in the United States. This probably constitutes only a small fraction of the actual number of incidents. Additionally, there were 10,839 fatalities associated with drunken driving, including 181 children under the age of 14 who had been

Table 5.3 NUMBERS OF DWI FATALITIES IN THE UNITED STATES, 1990-2009			
YEAR	NUMBER	YEAR	NUMBER
1990	22.587	2000	17,380
1991	20,159	2001	17,400
1992	18,290	2002	17,524
1993	17,907	2003	17,013
1994	17,308	2004	16,919
1995	17,732	2005	16,885
1996	17,749	2006	15,829
1997	16,711	2007	15,387
1998	16,673	2008	13,846
1999	16,572	2009	10,839

Source: AlcoholAlert (2011) and Centers for Disease Control and Prevention (2011).

riding in vehicles with impaired drivers. Table 5.3 shows that although the annual amount of DWI fatalities generally has been decreasing over the past two decades, the number of deaths in 2009 is still astonishing when we compare it with the number of murders and non-negligent homicides recorded by the Federal Bureau of Investigation in 2011 (10,832). In effect, for these two years there was nearly the same number of deaths resulting from DWI fatalities as there were total criminal homicides. This makes DWI-related fatalities a source of death that should not be ignored or minimized by the criminal law. In some states the drivers responsible for these deaths are charged with some type of motor vehicle homicide, which may be equivalent to second degree murder or voluntary manslaughter.

Suicide and Assisted Suicide

In the context of this chapter, suicide is another special case. By one definition suicide is "self-homicide" or "the intentional taking of one's own life" (Sheppard 2012:2696). Traditionally, under common law suicide was a felony and people who tried, but were unsuccessful, could be prosecuted for attempted suicide. During the course of the twentieth century more and more states removed suicide as an offense from their criminal codes. Today, neither suicide nor attempted suicide is considered a statutory offense, although these actions could be prosecuted as common law offenses. However, causing another person to commit suicide and aiding, soliciting, or assisting another person to commit suicide can be a crime.

Section 210.5 of the *MPC* treats causing a suicide as criminal homicide. The *Code* says that "A person may be convicted of criminal homicide for causing another to commit suicide only if he purposely causes such suicide by force, duress, or deception" (American Law Institute 1985:121). In terms of aiding or soliciting suicide, the *Code* provides that "A person who purposely aids or solicits another to commit suicide is guilty of a felony of the second degree if his conduct causes such suicide or attempted suicide, and otherwise of a misdemeanor" (American Law Institute 1985:121).

The issue of assisted suicide, and particularly physician-assisted suicide, came to national attention in the 1990s with the case of Dr. Jack Kevorkian, who became known as "Dr. Death." Kevorkian was a Michigan pathologist who believed that individuals had the right to choose when and how they wanted to die. Beginning in 1990 he assisted 130 people who wanted to die, some because they suffered from incurable, terminal illnesses. As a result of these cases, the State of Michigan revoked Kevorkian's medical license and eventually he was prosecuted for his role in one of the cases in which he assisted the suicide. He was convicted of second degree murder and served eight years in prison.

Currently, only three states — Montana, Oregon, and Vermont — allow for assisted suicides by statute. Montana permits the practice as a result of the ruling in the case of *Baxter v. Montana*, _____ P.3d _____ (2009). In all other states it remains a crime for anyone to assist another person in the commission of suicide.

Mercy Killings

Another area of killings that has proven somewhat problematic for the criminal justice system and for society in general includes instances of what may be described as **mercy killings**. These cases frequently involve elderly couples in which one of the spouses suffers from a prolonged and incurable ailment. As an act of "mercy" the healthier spouse kills the ailing partner, for example, by administering a drug overdose or through poisoning, shooting, or suffocating. There is no question, given the statutory definitions of homicide, that this constitutes an unlawful killing. However, a number of questions remain about the extent to which the goals of the justice system are served by convicting an elderly man for killing his elderly wife who was in an advanced degenerative physical or mental state. This area, and the related topic of assisted suicide, is a place where law, ethics, public policy, and morality all seem to clash, and there are no easy answers about the most appropriate ways in which to handle these situations.

As we conclude this chapter, it is important to remember that criminal homicide is a broad umbrella under which different crimes

Mercy Killings: to take the life of another person as a result of that individual being in an advanced state of mental or physical decline

involving the unlawful killing of another person would fit. In cases of unlawful deaths, prosecutors often charge a defendant at the highest possible statutory level for criminal homicide. They do this recognizing that a jury may determine that conviction for a lesser crime is more appropriate. Therefore, an individual charged with murder may end up being convicted of manslaughter (or negligent homicide) once the jury hears the facts of the case and renders its decision.

SUMMARY

Homicide may be the one crime that attracts the greatest degree of public attention. It causes fear in many segments of the population—especially from the elderly, even though they are among the least likely to be victims. Common law tradition has divided homicide into murder and manslaughter, and states have expanded the designations into first degree murder, second degree murder, voluntary manslaughter, and involuntary manslaughter. The *MPC*, by contrast, treats criminal homicide as the overarching offense and then divides that into the crimes of murder, manslaughter, and negligent homicide.

The issues of when life begins and when it ends present ongoing dilemmas for the criminal law. Although the laws criminalizing abortion have been significantly altered in the past three-plus decades, there are still state-level restrictions on when abortions can be performed and for what reasons. Increasingly, states are also adding provisions in their criminal codes addressing the death of unborn fetuses. The end-of-life issue is raised in trying to connect the harms that someone received as a result of an assault with the causation of the person's death. The ability to sustain life artificially makes this a problematic concern for the law.

In considering homicide it is important to be able to distinguish the five key elements—*actus reus*, *mens rea*, concurrence, causation, and result—to fully understand the wrongful act that was committed and the appropriate criminal charge. The nature of these elements helps us to differentiate one crime (or degree of crime) from another, and to guide in the imposition of the appropriate sentence.

Finally, this chapter has defined the offenses of first degree murder, second degree murder, voluntary manslaughter, involuntary manslaughter, and the *MPC* offense of negligent homicide. We have also seen that there can be special cases involving felony murders, misdemeanor manslaughter, deaths resulting from motor vehicle offenses (DWI/DUI), suicide, and mercy killings.

KEY TERMS

criminal homicide
felony murder
fetal death statute
first degree murder
inherently dangerous felonies
involuntary manslaughter
malice aforethought

manslaughter
mercy killings
motive
murder
negligence
negligent homicide
recklessness
second degree murder
voluntary manslaughter

CRITICAL THINKING QUESTIONS

1. Look up the definition of criminal homicide in your state's statutes. Does your state define these offenses by degrees or types, or does it more closely resemble the *MPC*? What are the similarities and differences?

2. Does your state statute on murder include the phrase "malice aforethought" or does it say "premeditation" (or a similar word)? Since this doesn't sound like modern speech, where do you think the notion of "malice aforethought" came from? Can you do a little detective work to try to track down the origin?

3. Is there a separate offense of felony murder in your state? If so, does the statute specify the type of felony that must be committed or does it include a list of specific felonies?

4. Do the terms "intent" and "motive" mean the same thing or not? Is there a distinction provided for in criminal law that does not occur in our everyday speech?

5. Is there an easy way to distinguish recklessness from negligence? Explain the kinds of circumstances that create risks but that are not necessarily the kinds of risks that fall under the categories of recklessness or negligence. In discussing omissions or failures to act, we raised the question about how would you respond to seeing two men beating another man. Recognizing that we are dealing with the issue in the abstract, what would be your first inclination? Would you try to intervene in some way or not? Explain why.

6. Does your state employ the year and a day rule in relation to the time of death in homicides? Is it included in a statute somewhere, or is it merely common law tradition?

7. Is physician-assisted suicide the same as criminal homicide or manslaughter? Does your state have a law that specifically allows (or prohibits) physicians from helping terminally ill people end their own lives?

8. Are abortion laws consistent with fetal death statutes?

SUGGESTED READINGS

Cooper, A. & Smith, E.L. (2011). *Homicide Trends in the United States, 1980-2008.* Washington, DC: Bureau of Justice Statistics, U.S. Department of Justice. This is a government document that is available online from the Bureau of Justice Statistics website or perhaps in the government documents section of your university library. This publication is very important for anyone who is interested in studying the issue of homicide in the United States because it examines victim characteristics such as age, gender, and race; it also describes the relationships between victims and offenders. Two particularly critical topics covered are the numbers of law enforcement officers killed and the clearance rates for homicides in the United States.

Fox, J.A., Levin, J. & Quinet, K. (2012). *The Will to Kill* (4th ed.). Upper Saddle River, NJ: Pearson. The authors of this book examine the legal environment of homicide in the United States. Part of the book's focus relates to the discussion of motive, as the authors set out to explain why people kill. They examine the relationships among victims and offenders, and provide a chapter on violence and killings within the context of the family and other intimate relationships. Additionally, they present statistics on workplace violence, serial killers, rampage killings, hate-motivated homicides, and serial killers.

Moreno, J.D., ed. (1995). *Arguing Euthanasia: The Controversy Over Mercy Killing, Assisted Suicide, and the "Right to Die."* New York: Touchstone. This book presents a series of reprinted articles that deal with issues such as physician-assisted suicides and other life-ending procedures for terminally ill patients. It explores the legal, philosophical, moral, and emotional aspects of life-ending choices.

REFERENCES

AlcoholAlert (2011). "2008 Drunk Driving Statistics." http://www.alcoholalert.com/drunk-driving-statistics-2008.html.

American Law Institute (1985). *Model Penal Code: Complete Statutory Text*. Philadelphia, PA.

Baxter v. Montana, ___ P.3d ___ (2009).

Centers for Disease Control and Prevention (2011). "Impaired Driving: Get the Facts." http://www.cdc.gov/MotorVehicleSafety/Impaired_Driving/impaired-drv_factsheet.html.

Federal Bureau of Investigation (2013). "Crime in the United States, 2011." http://www.fbi.gov/about-us/cjis/ucr/crime-in-the-u.s./2011.

FindLaw (2013a). "Second Degree Murder Overview." http://criminal.findlaw.com/criminal-charges/second-degree-murder-overview.html.

FindLaw (2013b). "Voluntary Manslaughter Overview." http://criminal.findlaw.com/criminal-charges/voluntary-manslaughter-overview.html.

Finkel, N.J. & Smith, S.F. (1993). "Principals and Accessories in Felony-Murder Cases: The Proportionality Principle Reigns Supreme." *Law and Society Review* 27(1):129-156.

Fletcher, G.P. (1981). "Reflections on Felony-Murder." *Southwestern University Law Review* 12(3):413-429.

Graham v. Florida, 560 U.S. 48 (2010).

Gramlich, J. (2008). "Should Murder Accomplices Face Execution?" http://www.stateline.org/live/details/story?contentID=33317.

Keedy, E.R. (1949). "History of the Pennsylvania Statute Creating Degrees of Murder." *University of Pennsylvania Law Review* 97(6):759-777.

Legal Definitions (2011). "Second Degree Murder Law and Legal Definition." http://definitions.uslegal.com/s/second-degree-murder.

Legal Information Institute (2013). "Year and a Day." http://www.law.cornell.edu/wex/year_and_a_day.

National Conference of State Legislatures (2013). "Fetal Homicide Laws." http://www.ncsl.org/issues-research/health/fetal-homicide-laws.aspx.

Roe v. Wade, 410 U.S. 113 (1973).

Rogers v. Tennessee, 532 U.S. 451 (2001).

Roper v. Simmons, 543 U.S. 551 (2005).

Sheppard, S.M., general editor (2012). *Bouvier Law Dictionary*. New York: Wolters Kluwer Law & Business.

Simons, K.W. (2002). "Dimensions of Negligence in Criminal and Tort Law." *Theoretical Inquiries in Law* 3(2):2-58.

Snell, T. (2011). *Capital Punishment, 2010— Statistical Tables*. Washington, DC: Bureau of Justice Statistics, U.S. Department of Justice.

State v. Elmore, 736 S.E.2d 568 (2012).

Tison v. Arizona, 481 U.S. 137 (1987).

Tomkovicz, J.J. (1994). "The Endurance of the Felony-Murder Rule: A Study of the Forces That Shape Our Criminal Law." *Washington and Lee Law Review* 51(4):1429-1480.

Wijdicks, E.F.M. (2001). "The Diagnosis of Brain Death." *New England Journal of Medicine* 344:1215-1221.

Wijdicks, E.F.M. (2002). "Brain Death." *Neurology* 58(1):20-25.

Personal Crimes: Sexual Conduct, Bodily Injury, and Personal Restraint

LEARNING OBJECTIVES

After reading this chapter you should be able to:

1. Compare and contrast common law rape with modern law rape
2. Identify the elements to which the intrinsic/extrinsic force standards and the utmost/reasonable resistance standards apply
3. Identify the difference between the marital rape exception and the marital rape allowance
4. Analyze and apply elements of rape to a set of facts
5. Identify the difference between common law battery and common law assault
6. Analyze the difference between felonious restraint, false imprisonment, and kidnapping

INTRODUCTION

The previous chapter discussed personal crime—where bodily injury is possible—where death was the result. This chapter outlines crimes against the person where death was *not* the result. Unlike homicide, these crimes do not require proof of a result; rather, only the action (with the requisite mental state) needs to be proven. Crimes requiring proof of a result beyond the action itself are classified as result crimes. Crimes that do *not* require proof of a result are called conduct crimes (e.g., theft, assault, and false imprisonment). Therefore, the state must only prove the action along with the mental state required for the crimes in this chapter. Although many of the crimes discussed in this chapter do require a certain amount of injury to aggravate the crime to a higher severity, the base crime does not require the proof of injury.

CRIMINAL SEXUAL CONDUCT

Criminal sexual conduct—or sexual assault—is a broad term that encompasses many activities but should not be classified as a purely sexual matter—especially for the victim. According to the National Center for Victims of Crime, sexual assault is "when any person forces you to participate in a sexual act when you don't want to . . . ." including "touching or penetrating the vagina, mouth, or anus of the victim . . . penis of the victim; or forcing the victim to touch the attacker's vagina, penis, or anus" (National Center for Victims of Crime 2013). We call it criminal "sexual" conduct because the activity usually involves parts of the body that are often sexualized in adults. However, we should note that these offenses are generally not about sex but about power and control (Myers et al. 2006). Even when the offense might be sexual in nature for the defendant, it is usually perverse in nature (McDougall 1972). Therefore, criminal sexual conduct, for the most part, should be characterized as a crime of power and aggression rather than a crime of sex, especially for the victim.

Rape

The most serious crime under the heading of criminal sexual conduct historically has been referred to as **rape**, which is the unwanted sexual penetration of another. In 2006 in the 75 most populous counties in the United States, there were 466 defendants prosecuted for rape, resulting in convictions for 62 percent of these defendants (Cohen and Kyckelhahn 2010). (See Table 6.1.)

Rape: unwanted sexual penetration of another

Table 6.1 ADJUDICATION OUTCOME FOR FELONY DEFENDANTS, BY MOST SERIOUS ARREST CHARGE, 2006

	NUMBER OF DEFENDANTS	CONVICTED			NOT CONVICTED		
		TOTAL %	% FELONY	% MISDEMEAN OR	TOTAL %	% FELONY	% MISDEMEAN OR
All offenses	**51,922**	**68**	**56**	**11**	**24**	**23**	**1**
Violent offenses	**11,303**	**61**	**50**	**11**	**34**	**33**	**1**
Murder	266	81	81	—	18	13	5
Rape	466	62	50	12	34	32	2
Robbery	2,988	71	64	7	25	24	1
Assault	5,582	54	40	14	41	39	2
Other violent	2,001	62	52	11	32	31	1
Property offenses	**15,351**	**70**	**57**	**13**	**22**	**22**	**1**
Burglary	4,132	77	67	10	17	16	1
Larceny/theft	4,722	67	53	14	24	23	1
Motor vehicle theft	1,501	72	65	7	24	23	1
Forgery	1,301	70	55	16	20	19	1
Fraud	1,835	64	49	15	26	26	—
Other property	1,860	69	49	20	26	26	—
Drug offenses	**19,295**	**68**	**59**	**10**	**20**	**20**	**1**
Trafficking	7,574	74	63	11	20	19	1
Other drug	11,720	64	56	8	21	20	—
Public-order offenses	**5,973**	**72**	**60**	**12**	**21**	**21**	**1**
Weapons	1,175	68	59	9	28	26	2
Driving-related	1,642	85	75	10	11	11	—
Other public order	2,557	67	51	16	24	24	—

Source: Adapted from Cohen and Kyckelhahn (2010).

Although traditionally sexual crimes of this sort were narrowly defined as rape, within the last few decades legal scholars have broadened the criminal activity by characterizing it as **sexual assault** (Spohn and Horney 1992). Sexual assault involves not only unwanted intercourse and other penetrations but also uninvited touching and lewd behavior. One of the advances in criminal law is that acts like unwanted groping and petting are now placed in the broader category of criminal sexual conduct. The term sexual assault implies the reality of the action—it is an assault that is unwanted by the victim, and it is a personal violation. For our purposes, we address rape as only the act of sexual penetration.

Sexual Assault: a more expansive term than rape and involves both unwanted sexual penetration but also includes uninvited sexual touching and lewd behavior

History

The crime of rape has evolved over the years into a criminal act that is very different than how it was defined at common law. Since the *Model Penal Code* (*MPC*) was originally written in 1962, the definition of rape is similar to that of traditional references to rape. For this particular crime, the *MPC* will not be used as a basis for outlining the elements of rape and other sex crimes.

At common law, rape was defined as a man's carnal knowledge of a woman who was not his wife using force without consent. To more thoroughly understand common law rape, the definition is broken down as follows:

- the action is carnal knowledge
- the defendant is an adult man
- additional action requires force
- the defendant did not obtain the victim's consent
- the victim is an adult woman
- the victim is not the defendant's wife

It is relevant and important to elaborate further each of these common law requirements to better understand the evolution of the definition of rape.

Carnal knowledge is the sexual penetration of the victim. More specifically, carnal knowledge is the penile to vaginal penetration—the traditional sense of sexual intercourse. At common law, other types of penetration—anal, oral, by object, etc.—did not fulfill this requirement; traditionally, these acts were treated under sodomy laws. Since the requisite act is penile to vaginal penetration, the defendant must be male. Additionally, based on common law definitions of age as a defense, defendants were usually adult males. Similar to the gender requirement for defendants in common law rape, it is equally necessary that the victim be a woman.

Carnal Knowledge: penile to vaginal sexual penetration

During the late nineteenth century, youthful offenders were treated differently, given the advent of the separate juvenile court system in 1899 (see National Research Council and Institute of Medicine 2001). Therefore, juveniles were treated separately for rape or any other criminal act. In fact, more rehabilitative approaches were used, and criminal action was not the predominate approach (Bernard and Kurlychek 2010). Not only must the defendant be male but also an adult.

To establish common law rape, the use of force must be proven. There are two different approaches used in the evolution of rape. The first is the **extrinsic force** approach. Here the state must prove that the defendant used some additional force other than simply the force necessary for the penetration itself. In other words, sexual penetration requires a certain level of force in itself to be completed. Under common law, therefore, the state must prove the use of extra force beyond that which is necessary for the penetration to take place. For example, the defendant might hold the victim down or strike a blow or shove the victim. All of these actions could be classified as extrinsic force. The second approach is **intrinsic force**, which is the approach used today. In this approach, the minimal threshold for the state to prove is the force used in the penetration itself.

Extrinsic Force: force required beyond the force necessary to sexually penetrate

Intrinsic Force: force required for sexual penetration itself

The state must also prove that the victim did not consent to the penetration. Much like the force requirement, common law had a different orientation compared to the current law. At common law, to prove that the victim did not consent required the victim to resist the defendant. There are two approaches that proved that a victim did not consent to the sexual penetration. The first approach is the **utmost resistance** approach. This approach requires the state to prove that the victim used all of the physical faculties at her disposal. Only if the state can prove that she exhausted her efforts in resisting the offender will it be able to prove that she did not consent to the attack. The second method to prove the victim did not consent to the sexual penetration is called the **reasonable resistance** approach. This approach requires the state to prove that the victim reasonably believed that an elevated defense would be futile and would lead to bodily injury. We need to add a special note here, though. The force requirement and the resistance requirement are often confused. The force requirement addresses actions by the defendant in performing the sexual penetration, whereas the resistance requirement addresses the actions by the victim to prove her non-consent to the sexual penetration.

Utmost Resistance: the victim used all of his or her physical faculties to defend against an attack

Reasonable Resistance: the victim used a reasonable amount of his or her physical faculties to defend against an attack

The final requirement is often referred to as the **marital rape exception**. This exception removes criminal liability from a husband for forcing sexual penetration on his wife against her will. If not for the relationship of husband and wife, the act would be rape and subject to criminal prosecution. However, at common law a husband could not

Marital Rape Exception: a husband cannot be charged with a rape for the unwanted sexual penetration of his wife

be charged with the rape of his wife. There are a few reasons for this. First, under common law, women were viewed as property transferred from the father to the husband (Wald 1997). Therefore, the husband had the sole voice in the use of that property. Second, the wife was assumed to give automatic consent to sex at the time of marriage. Finally, the marriage and what happens in the marriage under common law was considered a personal issue and not a matter in which it would be acceptable for the state to intervene.

To date, though, significant changes have been made to common law rape. The most significant movement in how rape (or sexual assault) has been defined occurred during the feminist movement of the 1960s and 1970s (Donat and D'Emilio 1992). First, the unlawful penetration required for sexual assault, today, goes beyond carnal knowledge. Other penetrations are considered unlawful and fit within the definition of sexual assault. For example, penetration by objects or by fingers or other body parts and penetration of the anal and oral cavities are now all considered unlawful penetrations that fit the crime of sexual assault (Donat and D'Emilio 1992). Because of this new broader definition of the illegal act, there are no gender limitations for both the offender and the victim.

As already discussed, the proof of force is still required for sexual assault. However, the standard of force used today is intrinsic force, where the prosecution only must prove that the force necessary for the penetration itself was used. Nevertheless, there are some states that elevate the seriousness of the charge if additional force (or extrinsic force) is used or injury is caused or both.

The proof that the victim did not give his or her consent is the most difficult element to establish in a criminal case. Under the common law, the state had the responsibility to prove that the victim resisted — whether following the utmost resistance standard or the reasonable resistance standard. Otherwise, if the victim did not resist, then the court would conclude that she consented and, therefore, the defendant could not be found guilty of rape. Today, however, there is research that indicates that rape victims may be paralyzed with fear and that they regularly do not fight back (Mui and Murphy 2002). To prove the victim's non-consent is difficult. Although the state is allowed to prosecute more cases because they do not have to prove the victim's resistance, without that resistance, prosecuting a case of sexual assault can come down to one's word against another without clear physical evidence of a non-consensual act. However, there are states (see Nebraska Statute 28-319) where resistance is still required to prove non-consent in certain classes of rape or sexual assault. Box 6.1 includes a case about the proof of non-consent in a sexual assault case.

Box 6.1   FORCE AND CONSENT IN SEXUAL ASSAULT

People v. Bowen
609 N.E.2d 346 (1993)

Although this case presents some resemblance to "he said/she said" components, the ultimate purpose of this case is discussion on what consent is and, relatedly, whether without consent, force is nevertheless proven. To gain consent, is the defendant required to receive an overt affirmation to the sexual activity?

On the weekend of May 4 and 5, 1991, the victim was awakened when she heard someone at her door. It was defendant asking her if he could get to the roof from her bedroom. She responded he could, but she was sleeping and he should go through Becky's room. She heard the door close and thought he had left. She testified defendant had not left but rather got onto her bed and straddled her. He attempted to kiss her, and she tried to get away by moving her head. She tried to push him away, but she could not move him. During this time, she repeatedly said to him "'What are you doing,'" and "'Please get out of my room. Stop.'" She did not recall how loud she was saying this. He then went under her shorts and underwear and inserted his fingers into her vagina. She told him to "'Stop. Please stop'" and repeatedly told him "no.'" She continually tried to push his hand away and eventually did so.

He then pulled her shorts and underwear down and forced his penis inside her vagina. She again told him "no," and "'[she] [did not] want this to happen. This shouldn't happen.'" She did state she did not assist him in taking his clothes off nor did she assist in taking her own shorts off. She also testified she did not scream because she could not believe what was happening, thought she could control the situation, and was scared.

She tried to push him away by the shoulder area, and when this was unsuccessful, she moved her hands down to his waist and tried to push. She was able to push his penis out of her. As she pushed him away, he told her to "jack him off." He pushed her over on her side so they were facing each other and moved his arms around her body and rubbed his penis against her legs. He kept telling her to come closer and not go away. Eventually, she was able to push herself off the bed. When she got out of bed, her shorts and underwear were off, but her shirt was still on.

Defendant offered another version of the alleged incident. He testified after returning to the apartment from the bars he went upstairs to go to the roof. He opened the door and asked the victim what she was doing and why she did not come out on the roof with everybody. The victim told him she was tired and had to study the next day. She started to talk to him more, and he sat down on the bed. He was sitting up by her head, and he reached his arm across the bed and gave her a kiss. He sat back up in bed, and then reached back down and French-kissed her. He stated the victim kissed him back and never said "no."

After they French-kissed again, he got up and shut the door. The victim had taken off the sheet and was lying on her side looking at him. He got back on the bed, and they began French-kissing again. He put his leg on hers, and her hand was rubbing his thigh. He took off his shirt and straddled her. Her legs were between his, and his hands were by her shoulders.

After kissing her stomach, he unbuttoned her shorts, and the victim said in a "very quiet, soft voice * * * '[n]o.'" When she said "no," he stopped and started kissing her again. He thought by saying "no" she meant "[s]low down. You're going too fast. Take your time." He denied she told him to leave or tried to push him away. He kissed her stomach again and tried to take her pants down, but they would not come off because they were tight. At that point, the victim took her pants down to her ankles. Defendant removed them the rest of the way and then removed his. While he took off his pants, the victim spread her legs. He placed his fingers in her vagina, and then tried to place his penis in her vagina. When he started to do this, the victim said "in a soft, quiet voice, '[n]o.'" He testified it was the same type of "no" as when he was trying to take her pants down. He interpreted it as meaning "slow down, you're still going too fast here. Take your time." He stopped and began kissing her again. He moved down to kiss her stomach again and then placed his penis in her vagina. His penis slipped out, and he started to place it back in again when the victim said: "'No, I can't do this.'" This time, he testified she said "no" in a different, stronger voice. He stopped and rolled over on his side. She got up and put some clothes on. As she started to dress, he told her: "Don't put your clothes on. You have a nice looking body.'" He then asked her to "'jack [him] off'" and she told him no and to put his clothes on. After dressing, he put his arms around her and said: "'No problem. No big deal. Maybe I'll see you tomorrow.'"

We first address whether the statutory provisions defining force and consent are unconstitutionally vague. Criminal sexual assault is defined in section 12-13(a)(1) of the Criminal Code of 1961 (Code), which provides in pertinent part:

> "(a) The accused commits criminal sexual assault if he or she:
> (1) commits an act of sexual penetration by the use of force or threat of force."

"Force or threat of force" is defined in section 12-12(d) of the Code as follows:

> "[T]he use of force or violence, or the threat of force or violence, including but not limited to the following situations:
>
> (1) when the accused threatens to use force or violence on the victim or on any other person, and the victim under the circumstances reasonably believed that the accused had the ability to execute that threat; or
> (2) when the accused has overcome the victim by use of superior strength or size, physical restraint or physical confinement."

Section 12-17(a) of the Code provides consent shall be a defense to any charge under section 12-13 through section 12-16 of the Code "where force or threat of force is an element of the offense."

"Consent" is defined as:

> "[A] freely given agreement to the act of sexual penetration or sexual conduct in question. Lack of verbal or physical resistance or submission by the victim resulting from the use of force or threat of force by the accused shall not constitute consent.'

Defendant claims these sections defining "force" and "consent" are unconstitutionally vague because a person of common intelligence could not determine what constitutes "force" and what level of force renders an alleged victim's lack of resistance irrelevant. He further argues, under the broad terms of the statute, various acts in consensual sexual activity could subject a participant to prosecution.

The question of whether the term "force" is unconstitutionally vague was decided by the supreme court in *People v. Haywood* (1987), 515 N.E.2d 45. Specifically, defendants contended the definition of "force or threat of force" did not set forth with specificity the nature of the force required for the commission of criminal sexual assault. The supreme court judged the statute was not vague as to what conduct it proscribed.

Likewise, the definition of "consent" appears sufficiently definite to meet the requirements of due process. The statutory definition of consent makes clear when consent has been given and that lack of verbal or physical resistance resulting from force does not constitute consent. We conclude a person of ordinary intelligence is afforded a reasonable opportunity to understand when consent has been freely given and when lack of resistance is the result of force, as that term is defined.

1. Is a "he said/she said" argument successful in a court of law? If you were a juror in this case, would you rule differently? If you were the defendant, what would *your* argument be?
2. If consent is not given, then does the sexual activity, in itself, fulfill the force requirement?
3. Can a man be sexually assaulted by a woman through sexual intercourse? Explain.

Finally, the marital rape exception has been abolished in every state. Therefore, a man can now be prosecuted for the forced sexual penetration of his wife. The reason for abolishing the marital rape exception is that: (1) women are not viewed as property but as individuals independent of the status of their spouse, and (2) the marriage license does not give individuals permission to demand sexual favors of their spouses (Spohn and Horney 1992). In other words, marriage does not give the husband automatic consent to engage in sexual activity with his wife regardless of whether he garnered consent during that particular engagement. However, based on the evolution of the sexual assault definition, some states have defined a **marital rape allowance** where defendants do not escape criminal liability, but their liability is reduced to a less severe offense because the victim is his or her spouse.

Marital Rape Allowance: charging a husband with a lesser degree of rape for the unwanted sexual penetration of his wife; the mitigated charge is the result of their marital status

Modern Law of Rape
Today, the law of rape has changed significantly, which we will outline here with respect to the parallel components to the common law. More than any other personal crime, rape—or, more broadly, sexual assault—has seen the most revision due to progressive, feminist thought (Spohn and Horney 1992). For our purposes, we will retain the term "rape" so that comparisons can be made.

First, no longer does rape require penile-to-vaginal sexual penetration. It is the penetration of any sexual parts of the body. For example, penetration of the anus with one's penis, fingers, or objects results in a rape. Oral sex also results in a rape charge since the sexual penetration no longer needs to be penile-to-vaginal sexual penetration.

Second, the defendant no longer needs to be an adult man. Youthful offenders can now be charged with rape. Although rarely prosecuted with less than 1 percent of the forcible rape cases, females can now be prosecuted (Federal Bureau of Investigation 2006). Since the definition of sexual penetration has been expanded to other types of penetration, offending is no longer restricted by gender. Similarly, the victim is not required to be an adult woman; men and children can now be classified as rape victims.

Third, the requirement of force has been modified in a number of statutes. The standard that a prosecutor must prove additional force beyond the force necessary to complete the penetration (called "extrinsic force") has been replaced by either the "intrinsic force" standard—that is, only the force necessary to complete the penetration—or allowances for other requirements such as impairment or incompetence. Thus, if the victim is impaired and/or mentally incompetent to give consent, then proof of force would not be necessary. In fact, even though the *MPC* is more akin to the traditional definition of rape, it does address impairment and incompetence in Section 213.1(b)-(d).

A male who has sexual intercourse with a female not his wife is guilty of rape if:

(b) he has substantially impaired her power to appraise or control her conduct . . . ; or
(c) the female is unconscious; or
(d) the female is less than 10 years old. (American Law Institute 1980:132)

Box 6.2 illustrates the quandary when alcohol is present.

Fourth, although both the traditional definition of rape and the modern definition of rape require the victim's non-consent (or, as in the *MPC* references, the offender's compulsion), the different treatment in modern law compared to common law is the procedure used by the prosecutor to prove a lack of consent. Under the common law, a prosecutor must show utmost resistance by the victim in order to demonstrate that she did not consent. Today, although resistance is no longer required as a necessary element, showing physical resistance can bolster the proof of non-consent. Relatedly, several scholars have offered that non-consent is interrelated with force. One cannot reasonably give consent when force is noted [see *People v. Haywood*, 515 N.E.2d 45 (1987)].

Box 6.2   YOU DECIDE: WHO IS THE OFFENDER?

Bob and Lindsey have been dating for four months. Bob is 20 years old and in his second year at State University, while Lindsey is 18 years old and in her first year at State University. They have decided to date exclusively and commit to each other. They have only engaged in foreplay (deep kissing and petting) but have not performed any additional sexual acts. Both are good students and study regularly and engage in social activities on the weekends, occasionally drinking alcohol. Lindsey has had two sexual partners prior to dating Bob, whereas Bob has not had any sexual partners.

For Halloween Bob and Lindsey attend a mutual friend's costume party. Bob dresses as a male stripper, and Lindsey dresses as a "Naughty Nurse Nancy." They are both quite flirtatious before and during the party. They also drink heavily during the two hours they are in attendance. Bob is encouraged by his friends to give Lindsey a lap dance, which Lindsey enjoyed. Both return to Bob's place to make out before Lindsey goes to her residence hall room. Both are extremely intoxicated but neither is blacked out. The passionate kissing progresses to oral sex, which progresses to sexual intercourse. During this time, Lindsey asks Bob if "he's okay" and Bob hesitantly says "yeah, I think so." After sexual intercourse, they both pass out on Bob's bed.

The next morning, Lindsey wakes up and suspects they had sexual intercourse but cannot remember. She immediately regrets having had sex and leaves Bob's place while he is still sleeping. Who, if anyone, is responsible for rape? Is there a lack of consent? If so, why? If not, why not?

The proof of non-consent is often tied with force and resistance. If force is proven, then it is presumed the victim did *not* consent (Fried 2012). However, the defendant cannot use the opportunity to prove consent simply because the victim did not resist. In fact, "passive resistance" was offered as late as the 1990s as a way for the defendant to avoid prosecution for sexual assault. The argument is that if the victim did not engage in active resistance, then victim was presumed to have given consent to the act (Fried 2012). Today, resistance is not needed to prove that the victim did not consent to the sexual activity.

Finally, the marital relationship between the defendant and the victim is irrelevant. Today, women are not viewed as their husbands' property and are viewed as independent citizens with their own rights and privileges. Regardless, since an offender can be male or female and a victim can also be male or female, the marital rape exception—"not his wife"—no longer applies. However, there are some jurisdictions that have a marital rape allowance that mitigates the level of the rape offense (see Bergen 2006).

Oregon provides a modern definition of rape:

A person who has sexual intercourse with another person commits the crime of rape in the first degree if:

(a) The victim is subjected to forcible compulsion by the person;
(b) The victim is under 12 years of age;

Box 6.3   ELEMENTS OF RAPE (MODERN LAW)

Actus Reus	***Mens Rea***
• Sexual penetration AND • By force or threat of force AND • Without consent of another	• Intent/purpose

Concurrence

Linking of *actus reus* and *mens rea*

    (c) The victim is under 16 years of age and is the person's sibling, of the whole or half blood, the person's child or the person's spouse's child; or

    (d) The victim is incapable of consent by reason of mental defect, mental incapacitation or physical helplessness. (Oregon Statutes, Section 163.375)

Section 163.305 of the Oregon Statutes defines "forcible compulsion" as "by (a) physical force; or (b) a threat, express or implied, that places a person in fear of immediate or future death or physical injury to self or another person, or in fear that the person or another person will immediately or in the future be kidnapped." The modern elements of rape are summarized in Box 6.3.

    In most states, there are simple rapes and aggravated rapes. Simple rape is the base charge whereas certain circumstances can increase the seriousness of the charge, thereby increasing the level of punishment to aggravated rape. Circumstances that can aggravate the charge are: injury to the victim, stranger relationship between the offender and the victim, the rape occurred in connection to another crime (usually a felony), the difference in ages of a minor victim and the offender, and whether the offender is armed (see Horney and Spohn 1996).

Other Sexually Invasive Offenses

Since modern law has advanced beyond the traditional definition of rape, there have been other sex offenses identified such as **statutory rape** (see the discussion of age of consent in Chapter 2). Much like the modern law definition of rape, statutory rape requires the physical element of sexual penetration. Unlike the definition of rape, though, statutory rape does not require consent to the sexual penetration by force, threat of force, or deception. In many cases, the parties—including the victim—indicate that the sexual act was consensual (Oberman 2000). However, by law, the victim is not capable of giving

Statutory Rape:
the sexual penetration — whether wanted or unwanted — of a person who is under a specified legal age

consent—the victim is younger than the established age of consent. This offense is intended to protect a group of citizens who are not legally able to give consent. In most jurisdictions, this age is 16 years old, but some states define the age of consent as 17 (e.g., New York) or 18 years old (e.g., Arizona).[1] (See Table 2.1.)

The purpose of the crime of statutory rape is to protect minors from the potential emotional harm of engaging in sexual activity (Oberman 2000). Social norms determine the adult nature of sexual activity, and legislators have articulated penal codes to determine that individuals of a certain age do not have the capability to give consent to such activity. In essence, statutory rape becomes a strict liability crime. That is, statutory rape does *not* require proof of intent to sexually penetration *with force*. Even in circumstances where the minor gave consent to engage in such sexual activity, thereby absolving the offender from criminal liability if the crime were a traditional rape, the offender can still be prosecuted for statutory rape simply because the victim is under the age of consent. The case summarized in Box 6.4 articulates the dilemma of statutory rape when the defendant is also a minor.

Box 6.4 CAN A MINOR COMMIT A STATUTORY RAPE?

In re D.B.
950 N.E.2d 528 (2011)

In this case the Ohio Supreme Court discusses the constitutional viability of a conviction of a statutory rape offender even though the offender, himself, is below the age of consent.

On August 1, 2007, appellee, the state of Ohio, filed a complaint in the Juvenile Division of the Court of Common Pleas of Licking County against D.B., who was then 12 years old, charging him with nine counts of rape . . . arising from conduct occurring between him and an 11-year-old boy, M.G. The complaint also charged D.B. with one count of rape arising from conduct occurring with A.W., also 12 years old.

D.B. filed a motion to dismiss the complaint, alleging that application of R.C. 2907.02(A)(1)(b) in this case violates his federal and state rights to due process and equal protection because the statute is vague and overbroad. A.W. testified that

---

1. A few states, however, have lower ages of consent based on age of defendant. For example, Missouri defines age of consent in statutory rape as 14 years old when the defendant is over the age of 18 but under the age of 21 (Mo. Rev. Stat. Section 566.032).

he had observed D.B. and M.G. engage in anal sex. A.W. testified that D.B. "bribed" M.G. with video games to engage in sexual conduct. Both A.W. and M.G. stated that the sexual conduct was always initiated by D.B. and that D.B. would either bargain with, or use physical force on, M.G. to convince M.G. to engage in sexual conduct.

According to A.W., D.B. and M.G. did not engage in sexual conduct until M.G. himself agreed to the activity. Following the presentation of the defense's case, the court stated that while there was "no question whatsoever" that the sexual acts detailed in the remaining counts took place, it could not find that D.B. used force during any of the acts. The court therefore adjudicated D.B. delinquent.

On appeal to the Fifth District Court of Appeals, D.B. argued that application of R.C. 2907.02(A)(1)(b) violated his federal rights to due process and equal protection, that the juvenile court abused its discretion in adjudicating him delinquent for rape. The court of appeals upheld the constitutionality of R.C. 2907.02(A)(1)(b) as applied and held that the trial court did not abuse its discretion in adjudicating D.B. delinquent for rape for engaging in sexual conduct with an 11-year-old child.

II. Analysis

D.B. asserts that (the finding of delinquency) is unconstitutional as applied to him. In an as-applied challenge, the challenger 'contends that application of the statute in the particular context in which he has acted, or in which he proposes to act, [is] unconstitutional.'

R.C. 2907.02(A)(1)(b) criminalizes what is commonly known as "statutory rape." The statute holds offenders strictly liable for engaging in sexual conduct with children under the age of 13—force is not an element of the offense because a child under the age of 13 is legally presumed to be incapable of consenting to sexual conduct.

D.B. argues that R.C. 2907.02(A)(1)(b) is unconstitutional in two ways. First, he argues that the statute is vague as applied to children under the age of 13 and thus violates his right to due process. Second, he argues that the statute was applied in an arbitrary manner in this case in contravention of his constitutional right to equal protection. This case thus asks whether a child's federal constitutional rights are violated when, as a member of the class protected under R.C. 2907.02(A)(1)(b), he or she is adjudicated delinquent based upon a violation of this statute.

As applied to children under the age of 13 who engage in sexual conduct with other children under the age of 13, R.C. 2907.02(A)(1)(b) is unconstitutionally vague because the statute authorizes and encourages arbitrary and discriminatory enforcement. When an adult engages in sexual conduct with a child under the age of 13, it is clear which party is the offender and which is the victim. But when two children under the age of 13 engage in sexual conduct with each other, each child is both an offender and a victim, and the distinction between those two terms breaks down.

The prosecutor's choice to charge D.B. but not M.G. is the very definition of discriminatory enforcement. D.B. and M.G. engaged in sexual conduct with each other, yet only D.B. was charged. The facts of this case demonstrate that R.C. 2907.02(A)(1)(b) authorizes and encourages arbitrary and discriminatory enforcement when applied to offenders under the age of 13. The statute is thus unconstitutionally vague as applied to this situation.

The plain language of the statute makes it clear that every person who engages in sexual conduct with a child under the age of 13 is strictly liable for statutory rape, and the statute must be enforced equally and without regard to the particular circumstances of an individual's situation. R.C. 2907.02(A)(1)(b) offers no prosecutorial exception to charging an offense when every party involved in the sexual conduct is under the age of 13; conceivably, the principle of equal protection suggests that both parties could be prosecuted as identically situated. Because D.B. and M.G. were both under the age of 13 they were both members of the class protected by the statute, and both could have been charged under the offense. Application of the statute in this case to a single party violates the Equal Protection Clause's mandate that persons similarly circumstanced shall be treated alike.

All three boys allegedly engaged in sexual conduct with a person under the age of 13; however, only D.B. was charged with a violation of R.C. 2907.02(A)(1)(b). This arbitrary enforcement of the statute violates D.B.'s right to equal protection. We accordingly hold that application of the statute in this case violated D.B.'s federal equal protection rights. The statute is unconstitutional as applied to him.

We thus hold that R.C. 2907.02(A)(1)(b) is unconstitutional as applied to a child under the age of 13 who engages in sexual conduct with another child under 13.

Judgment reversed and cause remanded.

---

1. In a maturing society where sex is discussed more openly and is more accepted for younger and younger individuals, should the age of consent be lowered? Why or why not?
2. Given the circumstance that the "offender" had more sexual experiences than the victim which might presume he is more mature, is the result of the case correct?
3. Why is sex the only crime with an age of consent?

The mental element for sexual assault is unique in each jurisdiction. Some require intent to sexually penetrate without consent, much like the modern definition of rape with one minor difference: The lack of consent is automatic given the victim's age. Some require only knowledge of the victim's age prior to the completion of the penetration. To this end, some states allow for a mistake of fact defense. Some of these states use the objective standard (i.e., the mistake was reasonable), whereas other states, such as California, use the subjective standard (i.e., the mistake was honest regardless if it was reasonable or not).

Not all sexual crimes require penetration. A minor, albeit still criminal, sex offense is **sexual contact**. This offense does not rise to the level of penetration but still involves intimate areas of the body. Criminal sexual contact involves activities including unwanted petting and groping of intimate areas of the body such as the groin, breasts, and buttocks. Here, too, there is simple criminal sexual contact and aggravated criminal sexual contact. The distinction is based on duration, severity, and level of injury to the area. With new cell phone technology, sexting is more and more common. Box 6.5 outlines the tension about whether sexting should be a crime or not.

Sexual Contact:
a criminal charge of touching sexual areas of a person's body

Box 6.5   IS SEXTING A CRIME?

What happens when a conversation that starts as merely flirtatious becomes something more? In this age of instant communication with mobile devices, communication can move very quickly from desirable to undesirable to unwanted. When those advances become unwanted, does a crime occur? The term sexting means "self photographing nude body or body parts and sending to others, as well [*sic*] texting obscene words to known persons (in most cases) using mobile phones" (Jaishankar 2009:21). In most cases, sexting is an avenue of child pornography since texting behavior is mostly performed by youths (Jaishankar 2009). Public responses to sexting among youths are gaining legislative and policy ground. City ordinances, school policies, and state legislation are the newest responses to this activity.

But is this behavior, especially among youths, a social harm or merely a different mode of sexual behavior? Fradella and Galeste (2011) suggest that the state may be overreacting by criminalizing ordinary (at least "ordinary" in the era of mobile devices) sexual behavior that, even though it may be determined to be immoral, is socially acceptable. However, is unwanted sexting an extension of criminal sexual contact? Is it a matter of sexual harassment, or is it simply flirtatious communication that, in the end, is not desired? Does it matter the degree and/or frequency of the images and/or comments made? This is a relatively new area of law that will continue to be explored.

ASSAULT

The next set of offenses outlines criminal activity that may cause injury to the victim without the sexual nature of the activity. At common law, assault and battery were two distinct offenses. **Common law battery** was the offensive, unlawful touching of another. **Common law assault** was the attempted or threatened battery. Today, modern law identifies these as the same offense either noted as "assault and battery" or merely "battery" or merely "assault." Since our focus is on the *MPC* definition of this offense, we will use "assault."

> **Common Law Battery:** offensive, unlawful touching of another
>
> **Common Law Assault:** attempted or threatened common law battery

Like many other offenses, there are two levels of culpability under assault: simple and aggravated. Simple assault is the base offense whereas aggravated assault raises culpability based on particular circumstances such as level of injury, disregard for human life, or increased mental state (intent rather than negligence, for example).

Section 211.1(1) of the *MPC* states that a simple assault is:

a person is guilty of assault if he:

(a) Attempts to cause or purposely, knowingly or recklessly cause bodily injury to another; or
(b) Negligently causes bodily injury to another with a deadly weapons; or
(c) Attempts by physical menace to put another in fear of imminent serious bodily injury. (American Law Institute 1985:126)

Box 6.6 outlines the elements of simple assault.

Box 6.6 ELEMENTS OF SIMPLE ASSAULT (*MPC*)

Actus Reus	*Mens Rea*
1. Attempts to cause or cause bodily injury to another OR	1. Intent/purpose, knowledge, reckless OR
2. Cause bodily injury to another with a deadly weapon OR	2. Negligent
3. Threaten serious bodily injury to another by physical menace	3. Intent/purpose

Concurrence

Linking of *actus reus* and *mens rea*

The *MPC*, therefore, defines four activities that can be classified as an assault. The first is causing bodily injury to another. Section 210.0 of the *MPC* says that "'bodily injury' means physical pain, illness or any impairment of physical condition" (American Law Institute 1985:119). A second activity is attempting to cause bodily injury to another. One part of common law assault—that is, attempted battery—has been incorporated under the same offense. The *actus reus* for these two activities is either the attempted causing or the causing of bodily injury to another. The *mens rea* connected to this activity is one of the following: purpose, knowledge, or recklessness. It should be noted, though, that the *mens rea* for this physical act is *not* negligence.

A third activity is causing bodily injury to another with a deadly weapon. Here, there are two necessary distinctions. First, there is no "attempt" language. Therefore, injury *must* be a result. Second, an added circumstance is the use of a deadly weapon. Section 210.0 of the *MPC* suggests that a deadly weapon is "any firearm, or other weapon, device, instrument, material or substance, whether animate or inanimate, which in the manner it is used or is intended to be used is known to be capable of producing death or serious bodily injury" (American Law Institute 1985:119). Another distinction is that the mental state is negligence. Therefore, negligently causing bodily injury with the use of a weapon is a simple assault.

The final activity that can be defined as a simple assault is the attempt "to put another in fear of imminent serious bodily injury" (American Law Institute 1985:126). This statement is similar to the second part of common law assault—threatened battery. Here, though, it is limited to serious bodily injury with the addition of the "attempt by physical menace," which suggests that the person must show a physical act to be interpreted as a threat of serious bodily injury. This statement presumes a difference in that for common law assault only the threat of offensive touching must have occurred. "Serious bodily injury" means bodily injury which creates a substantial risk of death or which causes serious, permanent disfigurement, or protracted loss or impairment of the function of any bodily member or organ" (American Law Institute 1985:119). The threat must be a serious threat and, unlike the common law, conditional threats are acceptable under this provision (American Law Institute 1980). A simple assault in any of these four activities is classified as a misdemeanor unless "committed in a fight or scuffle entered into by mutual consent" (American Law Institute 1985:126). If actions are deemed as entering into a mutual fight, then it is considered to be a petty misdemeanor—one with lesser culpability and punishment. The case in Box 6.7 articulates whether the offensive touching was forcible or not.

Box 6.7   IS IT FORCIBLE BATTERY?

State v. Hearns

961 So. 2d 211 (2007)

This case addresses what constitutes force within the context of a sentencing enhancement under a three strikes law—that is, the defendant was sentenced to life as a career criminal because he was previously convicted of three violent felonies (i.e., three strikes) even though the current offense does not, itself, carry a life sentence. The ultimate question in this case addresses whether one of the previous felonies was a "violent" felony. In this state, "violent" requires proof of use or threat of force in the commission of a prior battery.

In 2000, Respondent, Bill Monroe Hearns, was convicted of unlawful possession of a firearm by a three-time convicted felon. The trial court designated him a violent career criminal and sentenced him to life in prison. One of the qualifying offenses on which the trial court relied in designating Hearns a violent career criminal was a 1985 conviction for a battery on a law enforcement officer (BOLEO).

Respondent then filed a motion for post-conviction relief, arguing that BOLEO should not be considered a qualifying offense for VCC sentencing. The district court reversed, holding that "[b]attery on a law enforcement officer . . . is not *invariably* a qualified offense for VCC sentencing." The district court noted that BOLEO may be committed either through an unwanted touching or by causing bodily harm to a law enforcement officer. Citing our holding in *Perkins v. State*, the court held that BOLEO is a forcible felony only when it involves bodily harm. The court held that for a BOLEO conviction to qualify as a forcible felony under the VCC statute, the State must prove that the defendant caused bodily harm, rather than mere unwanted touching.

In applying the *Perkins* test, we analyze the elements of the battery statute from which BOLEO derives its conduct element. Section 784.03 defines battery as (a) actually and intentionally touching or striking another person against the will of the other; or (b) intentionally causing bodily harm to an individual. Therefore, three separate acts may constitute BOLEO:

1. actually and intentionally *touching* a law enforcement officer against his will;
2. actually and intentionally *striking* a law enforcement officer against his will; or
3. intentionally *causing bodily harm* to a law enforcement officer

Under *Perkins*, for BOLEO to constitute a forcible felony, all three alternatives must involve the use or threat of physical force or violence. If one of the elements does not, then BOLEO can be committed without the use or threat of physical force or violence, and BOLEO would fail the *Perkins* test.

Neither party in this case disputes that intentionally causing bodily harm involves the use or threat of physical force or violence. It is also difficult to argue that intentionally striking a law enforcement officer does not involve the requisite level of physical force or violence contemplated by the forcible felony statute. This leaves intentional touching as the conduct element most likely to fail the *Perkins* test. We must determine whether intentionally touching a law enforcement officer necessarily involves the use or threat of physical force or violence as described in the final clause. If it does not, then BOLEO cannot be a forcible felony.

The State asserts that any intentional touching of a law enforcement officer necessarily involves the use or threat of physical force, "even if only a *de minimis* amount of such force is used." The State argues that "the fact that only a very slight amount of physical force is used to accomplish a touching does not negate the fact that physical force is used." Essentially, the State argues that any physical contact suffices to make BOLEO a forcible felony. The weight of authority contradicts the State's argument.

As Respondent argues, if BOLEO were considered a forcible felony based on its intentional touching element, it could lead to potentially outrageous results. For example, tapping a law enforcement officer on the shoulder without consent would constitute a forcible felony. But such minor infractions are incompatible with the level of force the forcible felony statute contemplates.

Based on the reasoning above, we approve the district court's reversal of Respondent's life sentence because BOLEO is not a forcible felony under section 776.08 and should not have been counted as a qualifying offense for VCC sentence enhancement.

---

1. Why is the status of the victim—in this case a law enforcement officer— an important factor to increase the severity of the underlying offense?
2. If you were the State's attorney, could you provide an alternative argument to the court's decision to identify why "intentionally touching" is a result of "force"?
3. Should "circumstances" be considered outside of what the "elements" require in a statute? If so, why? If not, why not?

An aggravated assault increases culpability, severity, and punishment from that of a simple assault. The circumstances that transform a simple assault into an aggravated assault are: level of injury, mental state, and perception of the value of life. Section 211.1(2) of the *MPC* states that

A person is guilty of aggravated assault if he:

(a) Attempts to cause serious bodily injury to another, or causes such injury purposely, knowingly or recklessly under circumstances manifesting extreme indifference to the value of human life; or

(b) Attempts to cause or purposely or knowingly causes bodily injury to another with a deadly weapon. (American Law Institute 1985:126)

Box 6.8 outlines the elements of aggravated assault.

A simple assault becomes an "aggravated assault" if the accused either attempts to cause serious bodily injury to another or actually causes injury with extreme disregard or indifference to the value of human life. Therefore, under this first provision, the accused will either *attempt* a serious injury (not actually cause serious injury) or cause injury in such a way to demonstrate that he or she had no regard for the other's life. The second provision deals with the use of a deadly weapon. Unlike simple assault where the state only had to prove that the accused negligently attempted to cause injury with the use of a deadly weapon, aggravated assault requires that the state prove that either the accused attempted to cause injury, or purposely or knowingly caused injury with the use of a deadly weapon (American Law Institute 1985).

Given that the modern definition of assault provides a wide range of behaviors that can be criminalized, the question is whether there are other activities that might be perceived as a criminal

---

Box 6.8 ELEMENTS OF AGGRAVATED ASSAULT (*MPC*)

Actus Reus	*Mens Rea*
1. Attempt to cause or cause serious bodily injury to another with extreme disregard to the value of human life OR 2. Attempt to cause or cause bodily injury to another with a deadly weapon	1. Intent/purpose, knowledge, or reckless 2. Intent/purpose or knowledge

Concurrence

Linking of *actus reus* and *mens rea*

assault but, in fact, are not criminal assaults. For example, words alone cannot constitute an assault. For Sections 211.1(1a) and 211.1(1b), the accused must either cause or attempt to cause bodily injury with or without the use of a deadly weapon. In Chapter 9 we will learn that an attempt must require some actions or steps toward the completion of the underlying crime. For Section 211.1(1c), an assault requires action of "physical menace" to communicate a clear threat of bodily injury, and this action cannot merely be spoken. Much like other aggravated offenses, it requires prosecutors to go beyond what is required for the base elements of the underlying crime.

DOMESTIC VIOLENCE

A specific form of personal violence akin to battery and assault is multiple forms of domestic or family violence. **Domestic violence** is aggressive physical, emotional, and/or sexual behavior that is either provoking and/or threatening to another family and/or household member. Violence against women and family violence were largely ignored until recently. "A concerted effort and movement pushed domestic violence from a topic that was previously not discussed, to a visible problem that needed to be addressed" (Foster 2011:143). This movement included passage of the federal Family Violence Prevention and Services Act in 1984, Violence Against Women Act in 1994, and Keeping Children and Families Safe Act of 2003 (Foster 2011).

Domestic Violence: aggressive physical, emotional, and/or sexual behavior that is either provoking and/or threatening to another family or household member

During this surge, victims started to become an important part of the criminal justice system environment. Although victims were always a necessary component of the system since, without a victim, many crimes would not have occurred, the focus in the 1980s was turned from enforcing criminal statutes and punishing the offender to the inclusion of victims' rights in the process. A task force was convened to address the feasibility of amending the Sixth Amendment to the U.S. Constitution to include victims' rights. Given the potential setbacks if failure occurred, the task force suggested that victims' rights should be protected at the state level rather than at the federal level (National Center for Victims of Crime 2012). Therefore, many states responded with their own state constitutional amendments.

Although there are several avenues where victims of family violence are protected (e.g., victims' rights amendments to state constitutions, victim compensation programs, restraining orders), the focus here is on the definition of domestic violence as a crime. Once again, there are several criminal offenses that might fit the term "domestic violence," such as battery and assault, sexual assault, and rape, but we focus on the specific crime of domestic violence. Ordinarily, the focus would be on the *MPC* definition; however, domestic violence crimes did not gain significant attention until after the *MPC* had been authored. Therefore, we will place our attention on a few current state domestic violence laws as examples. Illinois defines domestic battery as the following:

> A person commits domestic battery if he or she knowingly without legal justification by any means:
>
> (1) Causes bodily harm to any family or household member;
> (2) Makes physical contact of any insulting or provoking nature with any family or household member. (720 ILCS 5/12-3.2)

Similarly, West Virginia defines domestic battery as:

> Any person who unlawfully and intentionally makes physical contact of an insulting or provoking nature with his or her family or household member or unlawfully and intentionally causes physical harm to his or her family or household member, is guilty of a misdemeanor. (West Virginia Code, Section 61-2-28)

The crux of the issue, therefore, is a definition of the physical injury or unlawful physical contact with a family or household member. It is the establishment of the status of the victim (i.e., family or household member) to whom legislatures have given particular protection. Box 6.9 outlines the elements of domestic battery.

Here, an "unlawful physical contact" is one that is done in a provoking or insulting manner. The physical contact required illuminates the psychological and emotional control of power in a relationship setting. Domestic or family violence is gaining attention and more research and legal acknowledgment occurs today.

Box 6.9   ELEMENTS OF DOMESTIC BATTERY (MODERN LAW)

Actus Reus	*Mens Rea*
1. Attempts to cause or cause bodily injury to a family and/or household member AND 2. Makes unlawful physical contact of a family and/or household member	1. Intent/purpose OR 2. Knowledge

Concurrence
Linking of *actus reus* and *mens rea*

FALSE IMPRISONMENT

We move from unlawful touching to restraints of freedom in false imprisonment and kidnapping. **False imprisonment** is a crime against a person based on our desire to be free from personal restraint. This crime is not "false imprisonment" in terms of the state's wrongful conviction and "false" imprisonment of a defendant. The concept of false imprisonment, though, is not related to a wrongful conviction. The adjudication process outlines certain steps that protect defendants' rights and administer justice as efficiently and fairly as possible even though sometimes the system gets it wrong.

> **False Imprisonment:** intentional unlawful restraint of freedom of another

The concept of false imprisonment, here, is centered on the notion that someone unlawfully restrains the freedom of another against that person's will. The *MPC* defines two types of these offenses: felonious restraint and false imprisonment. Both are guided by the general principle that unlawful restraint of another is against the law.

Section 212.2 of the *MPC* describes felonious restraint as

A felony of the third degree if he knowingly:

(a) Restrains another unlawfully in circumstances exposing him to risk of serious bodily injury; or

(b) Holds another in a condition of involuntary servitude. (American Law Institute 1985:129)

Box 6.10 outlines the elements of felonious restraint.

Felonious restraint is a third degree felony defining two types of activities that can fulfill the physical element. The first activity is the unlawful restraint of another by presenting a risk of serious bodily injury. One who restrains the liberty of another against that person's will without justification has committed an unlawful restraint. Locking an individual in a basement in order to obtain a bank code or pinning someone against a wall to prepare for a sexual assault can be unlawful restraint. Activities such as law enforcement making a lawful arrest, parents grounding children for disciplinary purposes, and victims

> **Felonious Restraint:** the *MPC*'s version of false imprisonment that also includes involuntary servitude

Box 6.10 ELEMENTS OF FELONIOUS RESTRAINT (*MPC*)	
Actus Reus	***Mens Rea***
1. Unlawful restraint with risk of serious bodily injury OR 2. Unlawful restraint in involuntary servitude	• Knowledge

Concurrence
Linking of *actus reus* and *mens rea*

restraining their victimizers are not unlawful restraints under Section 212.2 because they are justified. The first activity also calls for risk of serious bodily injury. Again, the *MPC* does not require the actual carrying out of the harm but just activity that causes a *risk of harm*.

The second activity under felonious restraint is the special circumstance of involuntary servitude. If the defendant restrains the liberty of another for the purpose of forced labor without pay — that is, involuntary servitude — then it is a third degree felony called felonious restraint. As one example, **human trafficking** is a social injustice that occurs across the entire world. Chuang (2006) defines human trafficking as "the recruitment or transport of persons through some form of fraud, force, or coercion for an exploitative end purpose." Organizations have been created to deal with human trafficking. For instance, Invisible Children has produced documentaries about children in Uganda used as soldiers and victims of a civil war (see http://www.invisiblechildren.com/). They visit college campuses nationwide to share their newest documentary and stories about human trafficking and other atrocities in Africa. Finally, the level of culpability for forcible restraint is knowledge. It is not required that the defendant have purpose to execute these activities but only that he or she is aware that these activities would occur.

Section 212.3 of the *MPC* describes false imprisonment as "a misdemeanor if he knowingly restrains another unlawfully so as to interfere substantially with his liberty" (American Law Institute 1985:129). Under the false imprisonment offense, the physical element is one where the defendant "substantially" restrained the liberty of the victim. A reasonable person standard is used to determine what restraint is "substantial." Minor or temporary restraints are not enough to elevate the behavior to false imprisonment. Physical force or threat of force can usually accomplish this type of restraint. The mental element required by the *MPC* is knowledge, and it does not require intent or purpose. One must simply be aware that he or she is restraining the liberty of the victim. Box 6.11 outlines the elements of false imprisonment.

Human Trafficking: the recruitment or transport of persons through some form of fraud, force, or coercion for an exploitative end purpose

---

Box 6.11   ELEMENTS OF FALSE IMPRISONMENT (*MPC*)

Actus Reus	*Mens Rea*
1. Unlawful restraint AND 2. Substantial interference of liberty of another	• Knowledge

Concurrence

Linking of *actus reus* and *mens rea*

KIDNAPPING

The crime of **kidnapping** is similar to the crime of felonious restraint or false imprisonment in that it requires the defendant to restrain the liberty of the victim. The main difference in kidnapping, however, is the **asportation** requirement. Asportation is the physical movement of someone else. Section 212.1 of the *MPC* describes kidnapping as:

Kidnapping:
taking and carrying away of another against their will

Asportation:
the carrying away or moving requirement for kidnapping

> unlawfully removes another from his place of residence or business, or a substantial distance from the vicinity where he is found, or if he unlawfully confines another for a substantial period in a place of isolation with any of the following purposes:
>
> (a) To hold for ransom or reward, or as a shield or hostage; or
> (b) To facilitate commission of any felony or flight thereafter; or
> (c) To inflict bodily injury on or to terrorize the victim or another; or
> (d) To interfere with the performance of any governmental or political function. (American Law Institute 1985:128-129)

Box 6.12 outlines the elements of kidnapping.

There are two activities that meet the physical element for kidnapping under the *MPC*. The first suggests that the offender must unlawfully remove the victim from either his or her residence or place of employment or remove the victim a "substantial distance" from where

---

Box 6.12 ELEMENTS OF KIDNAPPING (*MPC*)

Actus Reus	*Mens Rea*
1. Use of force, threat of force, or deception AND	• Intent/purpose
2. Removing of another from residence or business or a substantial distance OR	
3. Restrains liberty of another for a substantial period of time in isolation with one of the following:	
a. For ransom/reward or as a shield or hostage	
b. For the commission of felony or flight from a felony	
c. To inflict bodily injury on or to terrorize another	
d. To interfere with governmental or political function	

Concurrence
Linking of *actus reus* and *mens rea*

he or she was found originally. According to Section 212.1, "unlawfully" means the confinement or removal is "accomplished by force, threat or deception" (American Law Institute 1985:129).

Although the restraint of liberty is involved much like that of false imprisonment, it further requires some sort of movement of the victim. The question is how much movement? Is it to a foreign country away from family support (i.e., common law) or to a different city or merely to a different spatial position, whether it is feet or inches? The common law required that the defendant move the victim to a foreign country so that federal jurisdiction (or state jurisdiction for that matter) does not hold any authority over the defendant (American Law Institute 1980). "Expansion of the original concept (of moving or removal) . . . has been the chief development in the law of kidnapping" (American Law Institute 1980:211). The *MPC* is silent on the precise definition of the moving requirement (except for the language of "substantial distance," which is limited to moving in a public place).

The asportation requirement (or "moving" or "removing" requirement of kidnapping) has been debated over the years. Does this element of kidnapping follow the common law rule of removing the victim away from family support to a foreign country away from federal jurisdiction, or does it require something less? Since each state has a different understanding of this requirement, there are no U.S. Supreme Court cases discussing the matter. Therefore, in Box 6.13, we turn to California Supreme Court for an example of the analysis of this requirement.

Box 6.13   ASPORTATION REQUIREMENT

People v. Rayford
884 P.2d 1369 (1995)

At approximately 10:30 on the evening of April 24, 1991, the victim, Elizabeth R., was walking home from a bus stop when she was accosted by defendant as she entered the parking lot of a closed store. He told her to stop and that he had a gun. Defendant took Elizabeth by the arm, and led Elizabeth beyond a block wall at the end of the parking lot. Defendant took Elizabeth to a slender tree behind the wall, located approximately 34 feet from the street. The ground behind the wall was undeveloped, and made up of dirt and rocks. The incident lasted 15 to 20 minutes. Subsequent measurements showed she was moved a distance of approximately 105 feet.

The jury was instructed in relevant part:

"Kidnapping is the unlawful movement by physical force or by any other means of instilling fear, of a person . . . for a substantial distance, where such movement is not merely incidental to the commission of the rape, and where such movement substantially increases the risk of significant physical injuries to such person over and above those to which such person is normally exposed in the commission of the crime of rape itself."

The jury found defendant guilty of simple kidnapping (Cal. Pen. Code, § 207, subd. (a)), and found true the allegation that he had kidnapped the victim with the intent to commit rape pursuant to section 208, subdivision (d) (hereafter § 208(d)). He was sentenced to 17 years in state prison.

(T)he (Court of Appeal) concluded that the 105-foot distance alone was insufficient to constitute movement "Adding a consideration of the boundaries crossed does not convert the movement in this case from a slight movement to a substantial one. [T]he victim here was not moved into an enclosed area out of public view. [She] was taken to a place which was equally visible from the street and equally visible to people on the victim's side of the block wall. The wall only blocked the view from the parking lot side . . . . We therefore find the evidence insufficient to demonstrate asportation." The Court of Appeal reversed the kidnapping conviction, and remanded for resentencing.

We granted the Attorney General's petition for review.

In 1951, section 209 was amended to provide that the "holds or detains" language applied only to kidnapping for ransom or extortion. That remains the law today, and hence kidnapping under section 209(a) has no asportation requirement. However, section 209(b) kidnapping for robbery is committed only where the defendant "kidnaps or carries away" the victim.

In *People v. Chessman* (1951), we upheld the defendant's conviction for kidnapping for the purpose of robbery for which he had received the death penalty. The defendant had forced one victim to walk 22 feet at gunpoint from the car she was in to his car, and there committed "sex crimes." We stated, "It is the fact, not the distance, of forcible removal which constitutes kidnaping in this state."

In *Cotton v. Superior Court* (1961), the AFL-CIO picketed a labor camp which housed certain farm workers. Fighting ensued during which one man was dragged 15 feet. We stated that "the only movements that occurred [here] were those natural in a riot or assault. All 'asportation' would appear to be only incidental to the assault and rioting."

We explained, "involving section 209 and section 207 construe the term 'kidnaping' to mean movements which are not merely incidental to associated crimes.' However, in view of the fact that 'section 209 prescribes increased punishment when the kidnaping is for the purpose of ransom or robbery' violation of section 209 requires *not only* that the asportation be not merely incidental to the associated crime of robbery but also that it 'substantially increase the risk of harm over and above that necessarily present in the crime of robbery itself.'"

In *People v. Bradley* the victim was moved 50 to 60 feet from the open street, and forcibly led around a building to the inside of a separate structure. Applying the section 207 simple kidnapping asportation test, the court then stated, "distance, in and of itself, is not the only factor probative of asportation" under sections 207 and 208(d). "Consideration must be given to the change in surroundings between the point of capture and destination. A distance of 50 feet in the open desert is of far less importance to fulfilling the goal of a sexual perpetrator than 50 feet in the city where characteristics of location change much more quickly. [T]he inherent danger from sexual attack in the secluded dumpster area was considerably more than the public phone area."

(T)he standard of asportation for section 208(d) kidnapping requires that the movement of the victim be for a distance which is more than that which is merely incidental to the commission or attempted commission of rape, oral copulation, sodomy, or rape by instrument, and that this movement substantially increase the risk of harm to the victim over and above that necessarily present in the commission or attempted commission of these crimes.

The jury (found) that defendant moved Elizabeth a "substantial distance" and that this movement "substantially increased" her risk of physical injury "over and above those to which such person is normally exposed in the commission of the crime of rape." Applying the same test, we conclude that the evidence of asportation in this case was sufficient to support the kidnapping conviction.

Here, Elizabeth was forcibly moved 105 feet at night from the parking lot of a closed store to the other side of a wall located at the edge of the lot. She was forced to sit against the wall and beside a small tree, 34 feet from the street. The wall blocked the view of any passersby from the parking lot side, and the tree and the bushes at the end of the wall limited detection of Elizabeth from the street. While the area beyond the wall bordered on a two-lane street, it was undeveloped, and made up of dirt and rocks. Finally, while it was light enough for Elizabeth to observe defendant's actions in this area, and for defendant to be able to see the blood on Elizabeth's underwear, the two were located right next to each other. There is no evidence as to whether they were detectable from the street.

For the reasons set forth above, the judgment of the Court of Appeal is reversed, and the case is remanded to that court for further proceedings consistent with this opinion.

1. Do you believe that the offender and victim were not visible from the street? Does a tree or bush make it private enough to keep the victim from being seen by others?
2. How far does the movement need to be for it to match the asportation standard in this case? Is there a "bright line" (clear distinction) rule on this, or is it a case-by-case decision?
3. If it is a case-by-case decision, what are some additional scenarios where longer distance is required to meet the asportation requirement? Shorter distances?

It is apparent that the meaning of asportation in modern law is not entirely clear. The Supreme Court of California even struggles through the precedent and statutory language of the kidnapping laws. In fact, one of the most transparent statements of the entire *Rayford* case regarding the difficulty in defining asportation is in footnote 9:

As one Court of Appeal subsequently observed: "The increasing complexity of the law marches on. What *Stanworth* and *Brown* seem to teach is this: the test of simple kidnaping *is not* (1) whether the movement is incidental to an underlying crime; (2) whether there is an increase in the risk of harm above that present in an underlying crime; (3) a mathematical formula; or (4) the crossing of arbitrary boundaries. Thus we are left to ponder what the movement *is* in simple kidnaping. We are told it 'is the actual distance of the victim's movements' and they must be substantial in character but, of course, it is not a question of mathematical measurement or crossing of arbitrary boundaries. Thus, we are led in circles." (*People v. Stender* (1975) 47 Cal. App. 3d 413, 422, 121 Cal. Rptr. 334, italics in original.) (*People v. Rayford*, 884 P.2d at 1378)

Under common law, asportation meant the carrying away to a foreign country away from family support and outside of the reach of the jurisdiction of the United States. In California, it requires movement beyond that which is required for the underlying crime and presents substantial risk to the victim. Box 6.14 illustrates the emotional trauma of a recent case of kidnapping.

The second activity that can lead to a kidnapping charge is confining an individual in isolation (no moving or asportation is required) under four circumstances. The first situation is holding someone either for ransom or reward or using that person as a shield or a hostage. The second circumstance is facilitating the commission of a felony or flight. The third involves inflicting bodily injury or terrorizing the victim. A final circumstance is interfering with a governmental or political function. The reading of these two activities suggests one either confines and removes or simply confines with additional circumstances of ransom or hostage, commission of a felony, inflicting injury, or interfering with governmental action for the restraint of the victim to be kidnapping.

Both of these activities must be completed either with force or threat of force or by deception. The force (or threat of force) required does not have to be of serious bodily injury but must be enough to rise

---

Box 6.14   IN THE NEWS: DECADE KIDNAPPING AND RAPE IN CLEVELAND, OHIO

In May of 2013, Ariel Castro was arrested and charged with the kidnapping and raping of three women held for more than a decade in addition to the kidnapping of the daughter he fathered with one of the victims (Gabriel et al. 2013). At the time of their kidnapping, the victims were teenagers and were not released from captivity until well into their 20s. The secret of his kidnapping of these victims was held for a decade while he lived a normal life. His two brothers were also suspects but were not formally charged after interviewing all of the victims (Gabriel et al. 2013). Can you contemplate the fear that the victims had in being held for ten years or more? What is the emotional recovery going to be like? How could he keep this kidnapping and rape so secret for so long without being caught?

to the level of "unlawfulness" (see Section 212.1). One exception to this requirement is when a victim is under the age of 14 or incompetent, which implies some sort of mental impairment and, therefore, has no ability to consent to leave with the defendant.

SUMMARY

Non-homicide personal crimes are among the more devastating crimes since the victim's suffering continues. One might even argue that a few of these non-homicide personal crimes are more serious than homicide since the victim must live with the pain and suffering of victimization. Regardless of this debate, these offenses either include potential for injury or a restraint of liberty without the result of death. But, what if this "injury" is not as serious as one might expect from a personal crime? For example, Cathy merely wants to spread her good cheer to Duane and make his day a happy day by giving him a hug. Little did Cathy know—or expect—Duane saw this as uninvited advance. Is Cathy guilty of a crime or simply guilty of not knowing her personal boundaries?

Obviously, some non-homicide personal crimes are more destructive than others, and, one might argue, the most destructive of these personal crimes are those that are sexually invasive. Today, these crimes are treated under one common term—sexual assault. Sexual assault includes rape but can also include criminal sexual contact. The definition of rape has evolved over the years and has experienced the most significant change among all personal crimes. At common law, the offenders must be adult males and the victims must be female because only penile-to-vaginal sexual penetration was criminal under rape laws. Also, the force required to prove rape was in addition to that necessary to complete the penetration. Common law also required the state to prove that the victim resisted as an indication that she did not consent to the penetration. Finally, common law required the victim to be anyone other than the defendant's wife—known as the marital rape exception.

Today, the law has changed where the elements require (1) sexual penetration (penile-to-vaginal and other types of penetration), (2) of another, (3) without that person's consent, and (4) intent to penetrate. Offenders and victims are no longer gender specific. The force required is that necessary to complete the penetration. Resistance, in most states, is no longer required as proof of the victim's lack of consent. Finally, the marital rape exception has been abolished.

Battery and assault have also experienced a transition from the common law to how these crimes are defined today. Under common law, battery was the unjustified, offensive touching, whereas attempt was the attempted or threatened battery. Today, these crimes are typically merged into the same offense. Now the basic assault offense requires a physical element of (1) attempting to cause or causing bodily injury, (2) causing bodily injury with a deadly weapon, or (3) threatening serious bodily injury. An aggravated assault charge requires that the injury attempted or caused is serious bodily injury with a disregard for the value of human life or with a deadly weapon. Similarly, another offense criminalizes violence given a specific status of victim: a family member. Domestic violence is similar to the crime of assault except that the victim is a family or household member.

The next two crimes examined here describe invasions of one's privacy and freedom rather than a physical attack like sexual assault, assault, and domestic violence. False imprisonment and kidnapping criminalize restricting another's movement and freedom. The main difference is the asportation requirement—that is, moving the person. False imprisonment requires proof that the defendant restrained someone's liberty against her or his will either with the risk of injury or to place the person into involuntary servitude—a byproduct in some situations of human trafficking. Kidnapping, therefore, adds the asportation (moving) requirement. Common law required the victim to be moved to a foreign country out of federal jurisdiction away from the safety of family and friends. Today, the debate continues. We know that it does not necessitate movement to a foreign country, but the requirement is inconsistently applied across jurisdictions, and the U.S. Supreme Court has not entered into the legal discussion.

All of these offenses have lasting effects and can cause trauma and injury that continue for a lifetime. It is important to understand the historical references and reformations of these laws, and it is important to view the progression of these legal definitions.

KEY TERMS

asportation
carnal knowledge
common law assault
common law battery
domestic violence
extrinsic force
false imprisonment
felonious restraint
human trafficking

intrinsic force
kidnapping
marital rape allowance
marital rape exception
rape
reasonable resistance
sexual assault
sexual contact
statutory rape
utmost resistance

CRITICAL THINKING QUESTIONS

1. Some would rank sexual assault as the most serious, and emotionally debilitating, offense that could be committed. Do you agree? Explain. Within the crime of rape, is it more serious to be victimized by a stranger, acquaintance, or spouse/significant other? Explain.

2. In Chapter 1, we learned that citizens have the right to privacy for married couples (see *Griswold v. Connecticut*). Does the elimination of the marital rape exception violate the right to privacy? If not, how can we justify this elimination while still remaining consistent with the precedent created in *Griswold*?

3. In a "maturing" society where talking about sex is more acceptable and men and women are more openly expressing themselves in sexual ways, should the age of consent be lowered? Or, should the law be written in a way to articulate a stronger moral code? That is, should the age of consent be raised?

4. Is it "fair" to hold a minor guilty of statutory rape of his or her significant other just because he or she is above the age of consent and his or her significant other is not? How do you define "fair?"

5. What is the purpose of the asportation requirement in kidnapping? How would *you* define it?

6. Should a noncustodial parent have the right to take his or her own child? Or is this kidnapping? Would your answer be any different if the noncustodial parent honestly believes his or her child is in danger? Reasonably believes? Does it matter if the danger believed is physical or emotional?

SUGGESTED READINGS

Llewellyn, J.R. (2006). *Polygamy's Rape of Rachael Strong*. Scottsdale, AZ: Agreka Books. Llewellyn gives an account of Rachael Strong's experience in a plural marriage society. The intersection of criminal liability and religious freedom are addressed in this biography. Stories of manipulation, violence, and spiritual questioning are at the forefront of this text.

Lynch, G. (2003). "Revising the Model Penal Code: Keeping It Real." *Ohio State Journal of Criminal Law* 1:219-239. This article addresses the need for reform to the *Model Penal Code*. Although the *MPC* is a good starting place for most crimes defined in this text, there are a few offenses that are either outdated (e.g., rape) or not even addressed (e.g., domestic violence). Lynch identifies these areas (and more) where reform is needed for the *MPC* to be an exemplar of criminal codes.

National Center for Victims of Crime website (www.victimsofcrime.org). This website has a multitude of resources about victims, in general, and about domestic and sexual violence, specifically. It not only provides literature of research completed on the topic, but it also provides information about funding, training, and education on the topic.

REFERENCES

American Law Institute (1980). *Model Penal Code and Commentaries, Part II*. Philadelphia, PA.

American Law Institute (1985). *Model Penal Code: Complete Statutory Text*. Philadelphia, PA.

Bergen, R.K. (2006). "Marital Rape: New Research and Directions." VAWnet, a Project of the National Resource Center on Domestic Violence/Pennsylvania Coalition Against Domestic Violence, Harrisburg, PA, February. www.vawnet.org.

Bernard, T.J. & Kurlychek, M.C. (2010). *The Cycle of Juvenile Justice*. New York: Oxford University Press.

Chuang, J.A. (2006). "The United States as Global Sheriff: Using Unilateral Sanctions to Combat Human Trafficking."

Michigan Journal of International Law 27:437-494.

Cohen, T.H. & Kyckelhahn, T. (2010). "Felony Defendants in Large Urban Counties, 2006." Report No. NCJ228944. http://bjs.ojp.usdoj .gov/content/pub/pdf/fdluc06.pdf.

Donat, P.N. & D'Emilio, J. (1992). "A Feminist Redefinition of Rape and Sexual Assault: Historical Foundations and Change." *Journal of Social Issues* 48:9-22.

Federal Bureau of Investigation (2006). *Crime in the United States, 2005: Uniform Crime Reports.* Washington, DC: U.S. Department of Justice, Federal Bureau of Investigation.

Foster, B.P. (2011). "Norms and Costs of Government Domestic Violence Policies: A Critical Review." *Journal of Family and Economic Issues* 32:140-151.

Fradella, H.F. & Galeste, M.A. (2011). "Sexting: The Misguided Penal Social Control of Teenage Sexual Behavior in the Digital Age." *Criminal Law Bulletin* 47(3):438.

Fried, J.M. (2012). "Forcing the Issue: An Analysis of the Various Standards of Forcible Compulsion in Rape." *Pepperdine Law Review* 23:1277-1315.

Gabriel, T., Kovaleski, S.F., Yaccino, S. & Goode, E. (2013). "Cleveland Man Charged with Rape and Kidnapping." *New York Times,* May 8. http://www.nytimes.com/2013/05/09/us/cleveland-kidnapping.html?pagewanted=all.

Horney, J. & Spohn, C. (1996). "The Influence of Blame and Believability Factors on the Processing of Simple Versus Aggravated Rape Cases." *Criminology* 34:135-162.

In re D.B., 950 N.E.2d 528 (2011).

Jaishankar, K. (2009). "Sexting: A New Form of Victimless Crime?" *International Journal of Cyber Criminology* 3:21-25.

McDougall, J. (1972). "Primal Scene and Sexual Perversion." *International Journal of Psychoanalysis* 53:371-384.

Mui, C.L. & Murphy, J.S. (2002). *Gender Struggles: Practical Approaches to Contemporary Feminism.* Lanham, MD: Rowman & Littlefield.

Myers, W.C., Husted, D.S., Safarik, M.E. & O'Toole, M. (2006). "The Motivation Behind Serial Sexual Homicide: Is It Sex, Power, and Control, or Anger?" *Journal of Forensic Sciences* 51:900-907.

National Center for Victims of Crime (2012). *2012 National Crime Victims' Rights Week Resource Guide.*

National Center for Victims of Crime (2013). http://www.victimsofcrime.org/help-for-crime-victims/get-help-bulletins-for-crime-victims/bulletins-for-teens/sexual-assault.

National Research Council and Institute of Medicine (2001). *Juvenile Crime, Juvenile Justice.* Panel on Juvenile Crime: Prevention, Treatment, and Control. Joan McCord, Cathy Spatz Widom & Nancy A. Crowell, eds. Committee on Law and Justice and Board on Children, Youth, and Families. Washington, DC: National Academy Press.

Oberman, M. (2000). "Regulating Consensual Sex with Minors: Defining a Role for Statutory Rape." *Buffalo Law Review* 48:703-784.

People v. Bowen, 609 N.E.2d 346 (1993).

People v. Haywood, 515 N.E.2d 45 (1987).

People v. Rayford, 884 P.2d 1369 (1995).

Spohn, C. & Horney, J. (1992). *Rape Law Reform: A Grassroots Revolution and Its Impact.* New York: Plenum.

State v. Hearns, 961 So. 2d 211 (2007).

Wald, A. (1997). "What's Rightfully Ours: Toward a Property Theory of Rape." *Columbia Journal of Law and Social Problems* 30:459-502.

Street Crimes

LEARNING OBJECTIVES

After reading this chapter you should be able to:

1. Explain the importance of street crimes to the criminal justice system
2. Define "hot spots" and explain their importance as a policing strategy
3. Define victimless or vice-related crimes
4. Discuss the significance of confidential informants to many police operations
5. Define and explain constructive possession
6. Compare and contrast the pros and cons of legalizing or decriminalizing vice crimes

INTRODUCTION

The offenses classified as **street crimes** could have been (and some were) discussed in previous chapters. However, the types of violations that we will discuss in this chapter are among the most commonly encountered offenses by criminal justice system personnel. As a result, these are the criminal violations that make up the caseloads for courts of limited jurisdiction (municipal, magistrate, and similar courts) across the United States (Mays 2012). While not all street crimes occur in the streets, we will see in this chapter that street crimes have several common characteristics.

First, the crimes that often are considered street crimes include many types of drug and alcohol offenses, prostitution, gambling, weapons offenses, strong-arm robbery, pocket-picking, simple assaults, gang-related crimes, and loitering or vagrancy. Second, almost by definition, many of these crimes are committed in public places. This does not mean that they all occur outdoors, since public places can include schools, buses and subways, shopping malls, and bars or restaurants.

Third, while some street crimes are minor felonies, most of them are misdemeanors or even petty misdemeanors. Fourth, street crimes involve victims and offenders who often share similar characteristics. They are frequently members of the same racial or ethnic groups, they may be close in age, and they are generally of the same gender. This can be explained by the concept of **exposure**. Exposure means that people who are in frequent contact are the most likely to victimize and to be victimized by one another.

Fifth, street crimes tend to take place in certain locations. Research has shown that these so-called "high-crime" areas have a disproportionate number of businesses that sell and serve alcohol (see Gray 2010; Gyimah-Brempong 2001; Zhu, Gorman, and Horel 2004). The police call these localities crime **"hot spots"** (Braga, Hureau, and Papachristos 2011), and these areas and the crimes associated with them have been the focus of research—especially aimed at policing policies and practices—for over 20 years (Eck et al. 2005; Sherman 1995; Sherman, Gartin, and Buerger 1989). These areas often disproportionately involve people within the lowest socioeconomic groups as both victims and offenders.

Sixth, individual property-related street crimes usually do not account for large monetary losses. Nevertheless, these offenses create fear and apprehension in communities. For this reason, they are often called "quality-of-life" crimes (Taylor 1999). Seventh, in some locations street crimes are associated with street gangs and other illicit activities. This is especially true for street-level drug

Street Crimes:
any type of criminal activity that occurs in open, public spaces; some of these offenses are felonies, but many are misdemeanors or petty misdemeanors

Exposure:
to come into close contact; with street crimes, the people in closest contact are most likely to be both victims and victimizers

"Hot Spots":
locations that have disproportionately high levels of criminal and other disorderly behavior

sales (Ratcliffe, Taniguchi, and Taylor 2011). Finally, uniformed police officers encounter most of these offenses on a daily basis.

Before ending this introduction it is important to note that street crimes are not just an urban phenomenon in the United States. These offenses occur in cities of all sizes throughout the world. They also take place in suburban and rural areas. We will highlight the ways the different types of street crimes are manifested in different locations throughout the chapter.

In the following sections we address the street crimes listed at the beginning of the chapter that occur in the United States. This list is not exhaustive and there may be other types of street crimes that could be included. However, these are the ones most frequently associated with the notions of street crimes and community disorder (Bernasco and Block 2011; Gray 2010; Santos 2011).

DRUG OFFENSES

The 2011 *Uniform Crime Report* (*UCR*) indicated that there were 1,531,251 arrests in the United States for drug law violations (Federal Bureau of Investigation 2011). This is a significant number of arrests for what are classified as Part 2 offenses. Within the *UCR* there are 21 Part 2 offenses, including prostitution, drug abuse violations, gambling, drunkenness, and driving under the influence. For reporting purposes, the FBI considers these crimes (many of which are misdemeanors) as less serious than the eight Part 1 index offenses.

Within most large cities, in many smaller ones, and in suburban and rural areas, there are public places where drug crimes are transacted on a regular basis. This section will consider the following offenses: sales, distribution, use, and possession.

Sales

Most people associate street-level drug sales with the notion of drug crimes. These sales occur on street corners, in alleyways, in doorways, in public parks, in interstate highway rest areas, and even in parked cars. The transactions are often concealed, but sometimes are publicly visible as well.

Street-level sales typically involve small amounts of drugs exchanged for cash. The most frequently purchased drugs in these transactions are marijuana, crack cocaine, heroin, and, increasingly, methamphetamine. Sometimes other substances such as powder cocaine, phencyclidine (PCP), and prescription drugs may be sold, but the majority of transactions involve the four substances mentioned.

"Crack" or rock cocaine has presented a difficult problem for the criminal law in that while it is not chemically different than powder cocaine, federal drug laws have mandated the same penalty for sale or possession of 1 gram of crack cocaine as for 100 grams of powder cocaine. Box 7.1 provides information on the changes incorporated in the Fair Sentencing Act of 2010 and in the U.S. Supreme Court cases of *Dorsey v. United States* (docket number 11-5683) and *Hill v. United States* (docket number 11-5721). Although these cases primarily deal with the issue of sentencing, they illustrate the potential penalties that can be imposed based on the law and the offense that is charged.

Box 7.1   DOES THE FORM OF THE DRUG MAKE A DIFFERENCE?

Dorsey v. United States
Docket number 11-5683

Hill v. United States
Docket number 11-5721

In 1986, Congress established a tiered system of mandatory five- and ten-year prison sentences for drug-trafficking offenses. Congress was concerned about the proliferation of crack cocaine. To dissuade individuals from using crack, Congress set a 100:1 ratio that treated one gram of crack cocaine as equivalent to 100 grams of powder cocaine for the purposes of mandatory minimum sentencing. Trafficking of five grams or more of crack cocaine imposed a minimum mandatory five-year sentence, and trafficking of fifty grams or more of that substance imposed a minimum mandatory ten-year sentence. In comparison, violators would need to traffic 500 grams of powder cocaine for a mandatory five-year sentence, and five kilograms of the substance for the mandatory ten-year sentence. Additionally, a first time conviction for possession of five grams of crack cocaine triggered a minimum five-year sentence, while the maximum penalty for first time possession of any amount of powder cocaine was one year.

In the 1990s, the public began to question the sentencing disparities between powder and crack cocaine offenses. Critics asserted that the disparities tended to disproportionately impact minorities. In response, in 1994, Congress directed the Sentencing Commission, an agency that establishes sentencing guidelines and policies for the Federal Courts, to prepare a report on the various penalty levels.

Between 1995 and 2007, the Commission released a series of reports recommending amendments to the Sentencing Guidelines to address sentencing anomalies. On August 3, 2010, the President signed the [Fair Sentencing Act] which increased the required amount of crack cocaine for a mandatory five-year sentence from five grams to twenty-eight grams, and from fifty to 280 grams of crack for a mandatory ten-year sentence.

Petitioner Dorsey was arrested and charged with possession of 5.5 grams of crack cocaine with intent to distribute on

August 6, 2008. He pleaded guilty on June 3, 2010. Because Dorsey already had a prior felony drug conviction, the pre-FSA sentencing guidelines required a mandatory minimum 10-year prison term. However, the sentencing occurred on September 20, 2010, after the FSA's enactment; under the FSA guidelines, Dorsey would have to have been in possession of 28 grams of crack cocaine to be eligible for the mandatory minimum 10-year term. He appealed, arguing that the FSA applied retroactively to sentences that were pending at the time it became effective.

Petitioner Hill was found guilty in 2009 of possessing 50 or more grams of crack cocaine with intent to distribute. Like Dorsey, Hill would have received a reduced sentence under the new FSA guidelines.

However, the Seventh Circuit, relying on its prior decision in Dorsey's case, held that the FSA does not apply when the underlying criminal conduct occurred before enactment, even if the sentencing occurred after enactment.

At the time of sentencing for both Dorsey and Hill, as well as during the time when both were appealing their respective sentences, the United States maintained that the FSA did not apply to individuals who committed criminal conduct before the FSA, but were sentenced after the FSA. However, in July 2011, the United States changed its position. The Attorney General issued a memorandum on July 15, 2011 stating that the FSA does not apply to sentences already imposed, but it does apply to all sentencing proceedings occurring on or after August 3, 2010.

Source: Legal Information Institute (2013).

1. What factors would have influenced Congress to impose the 100:1 penalty differential for crack cocaine and powder cocaine?
2. Were there (or could there have been) differentials in the application of the federal drug laws based on race?
3. What kinds of problems are raised by retroactive application of laws?

For street-level dealers, drugs must be easily concealed. The drugs will be sold for small amounts of money (often in the $10 or $20 range) to increase the speed with which transactions can be conducted. Most of these sales are misdemeanors, although if a sufficient quantity is sold in one transaction or if there are multiple sales, the total transaction may be considered a felony.

If a case goes to trial, in order to prove guilt beyond a reasonable doubt, prosecutors must establish that there was an exchange of money, and that the substance sold was illegal. To prove that there were sales, the police often observe transactions from a hidden viewpoint or use undercover officers to make purchases. With undercover purchases, the drugs will be sent to toxicology laboratories for analysis, and laboratory technicians then submit their analytical reports and, if necessary, testify in court [see *Bullcoming v. New Mexico*, 564 U.S. ____ (2011)].

Distributing

Drug distribution links manufacturing or importation to street sales. Distributors are the "middlemen" in the drug business, and distribution efforts may occur in secluded locations as well as houses, apartments, or motel rooms. However, some distributors make regular rounds and contact their street sellers to drop off drugs and collect money. Public sales, however, increase the distributors' visibility and bring their activities to the attention of the police. In making their rounds, they increase their exposure to authorities, as well as the likelihood that they may be apprehended with sizable amounts of drugs and cash. Therefore, while distributing is linked to street sales, most distribution activities fall outside of our definition of street crime.

In Chapter 2 we discussed possession (both actual and constructive) in relation to certain crimes. With drug distribution, simply having a large quantity of drugs in one's possession may be the basis for the state's proof of *actus reus*, and knowledge of the drug's presence will provide a strong presumption of the intent to distribute. Unlike most street sales, drug distribution is a felony in virtually every case. The type of drug and the amount of the drug distributed will determine the seriousness of the charge.

Use

Technically speaking, in the United States, being a drug user is not a crime in and of itself. In fact, the U.S. Supreme Court struck down a California law that made it a crime to be addicted to narcotics in the case of *Robinson v. California*, 370 U.S. 660 (1962) (see Chapter 2). However, for someone to be a drug user, at some point the person must acquire and possess drugs. These activities *are* crimes. Additionally, some users are also drug dealers. Therefore, law enforcement authorities often have a difficult time separating those who are addicted to drugs from those who use and sell them.

Possession

As we mentioned in Chapter 2 and earlier in this chapter, possession fits into a unique place within the criminal law (see American Law Institute 1985:§ 5.06). There are certain items that are **contraband**, meaning they are illegal to possess in and of themselves. Examples of this include possession of burglary tools or possession of firearms by convicted felons. Another example is the possession of illegal drugs.

Contraband:
any item or device that is illegal to possess in and of itself

Therefore, persons who are aware that they are in possession of any amount of marijuana, heroin, cocaine (in any form), hallucinogens (such as LSD or peyote), methamphetamine, or other illegal drugs are breaking the law. Furthermore, as we have noted, the amount of the drug in one's possession, along with packaging and tools for preparation, may result in a more serious charge of "possession with intent to sell or distribute."

Additionally, some jurisdictions also prohibit items considered **drug paraphernalia**. Drug paraphernalia includes anything that helps a person use drugs. These items may be for the obvious use of drugs, or they may be everyday items that have otherwise legitimate purposes. For example, pipes may be used to smoke tobacco, or they may be used to smoke marijuana, hashish, crack, or methamphetamine. Therefore, they are not illegal in and of themselves. However, if police officers find drug residue in a pipe, they may also charge a person with possession of drug paraphernalia. Other items considered drug paraphernalia can include spoons, hypodermic syringes, and elastic tubing for preparing and injecting heroin. Cigarette rolling papers may also be considered drug paraphernalia. While the *Model Penal Code* (*MPC*) does not specifically address this offense, jurisdictions that have laws against possessing drug paraphernalia usually have a list of items that are classified in this category in order to meet the principle of legality and to provide more precise guidance for law enforcement officers. Box 7.2 presents the elements associated with drug crimes.

> **Drug Paraphernalia:** any implement or device that can be used to smoke, ingest, or inject illegal drugs

At the end of the chapter we will discuss the notions of legalization and decriminalization. As should already be apparent to you, these two topics seem especially relevant to the criminal law and the drug-related offenses we have discussed in this section.

Box 7.2   ELEMENTS OF DRUG CRIMES

Actus Reus	*Mens Rea*
• Sale of illegal drugs • Distribution (trafficking) illegal drugs • Possession of illegal drugs • Sale, distribution, or possession of legal drugs by an unauthorized person	• Intent to sell, distribute, or possess illegal drugs; intent to sell, distribute, or possess legal drugs in an unauthorized manner or by an unauthorized person

Concurrence

Linking of *actus reus* and *mens rea*

ALCOHOL-RELATED CRIMES

As is the case with drug crimes, alcohol-related offenses come in a variety of forms and a wide range of severity relative to the way they are treated by the criminal law. For our purposes, we will consider four offenses: public intoxication, illegal manufacturing, drunk driving, and possession by minors. To provide some perspective, in 2011 there were 1,034,866 arrests in the United States for liquor law violations and for intoxication combined (Federal Bureau of Investigation 2011). This means that alcohol-related offenses consume a considerable amount of time and resources for state and local law enforcement agencies, as well as the courts of limited jurisdiction (Mays 2012).

Public Drunkenness

First, public intoxication is an offense with which many local governments have struggled. Sheppard (2012:1391) says that in terms of *actus reus* intoxication is "A state of altered mental or physical ability caused by the consumption of alcohol or chemicals." Much like drug addiction, public intoxication raises the question of whether this behavior should be criminal, or whether this is a public health or mental health issue.

In the past, police officers routinely arrested people who were found to be publicly intoxicated. Most of these individuals had the strong smell of alcohol on them, were staggering or passed out in public places, or were causing a disturbance by their loud and obnoxious behavior. The resulting charge was often public drunkenness, and sometimes that was expanded to drunk and disorderly conduct. It was not uncommon in many large cities to find jail cells full at nights and on weekends with people who had been charged with one or more public intoxication offenses. The same was true of suburban and rural jurisdictions. Some of these individuals were clinically certifiable as alcoholics, and those who were put in jail for public intoxication on a routine basis were labeled "frequent fliers" (Ford 2005). After spending some time in jail, judges would either levy small fines against these individuals or would simply release them with credit for time served.

Police departments know that they can expend a significant amount of resources on processing people for public intoxication. In some jurisdictions, when citizens complain about people who are publicly intoxicated, officers simply pick them up and take them to a location other than jail for detoxification. Nevertheless, every year in this country there are still many arrests for public intoxication and related minor offenses. In the case of *Powell v. Texas*, 392 U.S. 514 (1968), the U.S. Supreme Court ruled in a 5-4 decision that a Texas law prohibiting public intoxication was constitutional. Box 7.3 provides an edited version of the *Powell* case.

Box 7.3   IS PUBLIC DRUNKENNESS A DISEASE OR A CRIME?

Powell v. Texas
392 U.S. 514 (1968)

In this case the Supreme Court noted that the *condition* of being an alcoholic was not being criminalized; rather, it was the *behavior* of appearing in public while intoxicated that was prohibited. Justice Thurgood Marshall announced the decision for a five-member majority.

In late December 1966, appellant was arrested and charged with being found in a state of intoxication in a public place, in violation of Texas Penal Code. [He] was tried, found guilty, and fined $20. He appealed to the County Court at Law where a trial *de novo* was held. His counsel urged that appellant was "afflicted with the disease of chronic alcoholism" and therefore that to punish him criminally for that conduct would be cruel and unusual, in violation of the Eighth and Fourteenth Amendments to the United States Constitution.

The trial judge, sitting without a jury, made certain findings of fact, but ruled as a matter of law that chronic alcoholism was not a defense to the charge. He found appellant guilty, and fined him $50.

Appellant testified concerning the history of his drinking problem. He reviewed his many arrests for drunkenness; testified that he was unable to stop drinking; stated that when he was intoxicated he had no control over his actions and could not remember them later. On cross-examination, appellant admitted that he had had one drink on the morning of the trial and had been able to discontinue drinking.

Despite the comparatively primitive state of our knowledge on the subject, it cannot be denied that the destructive use of alcoholic beverages is one of our principal social and public health problems. The problem is compounded by the fact that a very large percentage of the alcoholics in this country are "invisible"—they possess the means to keep their drinking problems secret, and the traditionally uncharitable attitude of our society toward alcoholics causes many of them to refrain from seeking treatment from any source.

One virtue of the criminal process is, at least, that the duration of penal incarceration typically has some outside statutory limit; this is universally true in the case of petty offenses, such as public drunkenness, where jail terms are quite short on the whole. "Therapeutic civil commitment" lacks this feature; one is typically committed until one is "cured."

Faced with this unpleasant reality, we are unable to assert that the use of the criminal process as a means of dealing with the public aspects of problem drinking can never be defended as rational. But before we condemn the present practice across-the-board, perhaps we ought to be able to point to some clear promise of a better world for these unfortunate people. Unfortunately, no such promise has yet been forthcoming. This Court has never held that anything in the Constitution requires that penal sanctions be designed solely to achieve therapeutic or rehabilitative effects, and it can hardly be said with assurance that incarceration serves such purposes any better for the general run of criminals than it does for public drunks.

Obviously, chronic alcoholics have not been deterred from drinking to excess by the existence of criminal sanctions against public drunkenness. But all those who violate penal laws of any kind are by definition undeterred.

Appellant claims that his conviction on the facts of this case would violate the Cruel and Unusual Punishment Clause of the Eighth Amendment as applied to the States through the Fourteenth Amendment. The primary purpose of that clause has always been considered to be directed at the method or kind of punishment imposed for the violation of criminal statutes; the nature of the conduct made criminal is ordinarily relevant only to the fitness of the punishment imposed.

Appellant, however, seeks to come within the application of the Cruel and Unusual Punishment Clause announced in *Robinson v. California*, 370 U.S. 660 (1962) which involved a state statute making it a crime to "be addicted to the use of narcotics."

On its face the present case does not fall within that holding, since appellant was convicted, not for being a chronic alcoholic, but for being in public while drunk on a particular occasion. The State of Texas has not sought to punish a mere status, as California did in *Robinson;* nor has it attempted to regulate appellant's behavior in the privacy of his own home. Rather, it has imposed a criminal sanction for public behavior which may create substantial health and safety hazards, both for appellant and for members of the general public.

We are unable to conclude that chronic alcoholics in general, and Leroy Powell in particular, suffer from such an irresistible compulsion to drink and to get drunk in public that they are utterly unable to control their performance of either or both of these acts and thus cannot be deterred at all from public intoxication. And in any event this Court has never articulated a general constitutional doctrine of *mens rea*.

If a person in the "condition" of being a chronic alcoholic cannot be criminally punished as a constitutional matter for being drunk in public, it would seem to follow that a person who contends that, in terms of one test, "his unlawful act was the product of mental disease or mental defect," would state an issue of constitutional dimension with regard to his criminal responsibility had he been tried under some different and perhaps lesser standard. It is simply not yet the time to write into the Constitution formulas cast in terms whose meaning, let alone relevance, is not yet clear either to doctors or to lawyers.

1. What should the criminal justice system do to people who are found to be intoxicated in public? Is arrest the appropriate response or, if not, what should be done?
2. Is public drunkenness justifiably a crime, or are we really dealing with a public health issue?
3. Is there a fundamental difference between being addicted to drugs and being publicly drunk? Explain.

Illegal Manufacturing

There are also alcohol-related offenses that are similar to those for other drugs. For example, in this country it is illegal to manufacture most forms of alcohol for sale without a license or permit from the Bureau of Alcohol, Tobacco, Firearms, and Explosives. For much of our nation's history, federal revenue agents (along with state and local law enforcement officers) have tried to track down people who are illegally manufacturing distilled spirits. Department of the Treasury revenue agents often spent their time in the 1930s through the 1970s chasing moonshiners in a number of states, especially in the Southeast. Increases in sugar prices in the 1970s made most moonshine production unprofitable, although it has made a comeback in the past decade or so. The exceptions to the federal licensing requirements include individuals who produce beer and wine for personal consumption, or what is known as home micro-brewing.

Drunk Driving

One of the most significant alcohol-related crimes in the United States is drunk driving. This is considered to be among the most public of the public offenses. Some states classify this violation as driving while intoxicated (DWI) and others consider it driving under the influence (DUI). Whatever the label, the offense is the same and it is a significant legal issue.

In 2011, there were 1,215,077 arrests in the United States for driving under the influence (Federal Bureau of Investigation 2011). In simplest terms this means that one out of every ten arrests made by the police in 2011 was for drunk driving. While these numbers are astonishing, the Centers for Disease Control and Prevention (2013) estimates that there are as many as 112 million cases of alcohol-impaired driving in the United States annually. Furthermore, as we saw in Chapter 5, alcohol-related traffic accidents accounted for a low of 10,800 and a high of 22,500 deaths during the period from 1990 to 2009.

Most states classify drunk driving (if there is not a fatal accident) as a misdemeanor for the first and some of the subsequent arrests. These arrests generally lead to short jail terms of a few days, fines, and suspension or restriction of driving privileges. Eventually, most states consider multiple arrests (for example, starting with the third or fourth) as felonies, and these cases can result in state prison time. Obviously, if there has been an accident with serious injuries or a fatality then more serious charges can be imposed.

Minor in Possession

Finally, there is the ongoing problem of possession and consumption of alcoholic beverages by minors. This offense may be *minor in possession* (MIP), or *minor in consumption* (MIC), which is a slightly different offense. Minor in consumption exists when the state has evidence that the minor has actually consumed alcohol (by being caught in the act or having a discernible blood alcohol content), whereas minor in possession is simply being in control of alcohol.

The charge of minor in possession includes not only persons under 18 years of age (the age of majority for most purposes other than alcohol), but also individuals who are 19 or 20 since they are legally prohibited from possessing or consuming alcohol as well. It is illegal for minors to drink, transport, possess, sell, or be involved in any way with alcoholic beverages. Additionally, the minor does not need to be in actual possession (that is, alcohol on the person or in-hand). The law also prohibits minors from being in **constructive possession**. Constructive possession exists when the individual has some sort of control over the item in question but does not have actual physical possession of the item. For this reason, there have been instances in which minors who were at a party where alcohol is served have been charged with minor in possession because they had access to and potential control over the alcohol (constructive possession).

Since it is illegal for minors to buy alcohol, they often have adults buy it for them, or they turn to outlets that will illegally sell to them. It is important to emphasize that it is also illegal for adults (including parents) to provide minors with alcohol. This can result in the adults being charged with contributing to the delinquency of a minor. See Box 7.4 for the elements that constitute alcohol offenses.

Constructive Possession: to not have an item on one's person, but have dominion or control over the item

---

Box 7.4 ELEMENTS OF ALCOHOL OFFENSES

Actus Reus	*Mens Rea*
• Public intoxication • Manufacturing and/or selling alcoholic beverages without a license • Minor in possession (this includes consumption)	• Intent to use, manufacture, or sell beverage alcohol in a way prohibited by law

Concurrence

Linking of *actus reus* and *mens rea*

PROSTITUTION

Before we discuss prostitution it is important to note that the broad umbrella under which prostitutes are classified is that of sex worker. Sex workers include prostitutes, escorts, massage parlor workers (those who give so-called "full body" massages), bar girls, call girls/boys, pornography models and actors, phone sex operators, individuals who engage in webcam sex and live sex shows, and exotic dancers. In some cases the criminal law provides little or no control over the activities of these individuals (for example, phone sex operators). In other cases there can be outright prohibition (as with prostitution) or general restrictions (for massage parlor employees and exotic dancers). Among these various occupations, prostitution is the one that is most pervasively restricted.

The *MPC* classifies prostitution as a petty misdemeanor and defines the offense as inhabiting a house of prostitution or engaging in "sexual activity as a business" (American Law Institute 1985:197). This definition includes not only engaging in sexual activity as a business, but also inhabiting the premises of a house of prostitution. In its simplest terms, the *actus reus* for prostitution is selling sexual favors for money or in exchange for any goods of value (such as drugs). It is illegal everywhere in the United States except Nevada, where it is permitted locally by county option (Caron 2008).

Prostitution also goes beyond the people engaging in sex as a business. It also includes people who promote prostitution (called **pimps**) as well as the people who solicit the services of prostitutes (called **johns**). Unlike the act of prostitution itself, the *MPC* classifies those people who promote prostitution as third degree felons. The *actus reus* for promoting prostitution can include:

(1) Owning or operating a house of prostitution;
(2) Obtaining people to work in houses of prostitution;
(3) Encouraging people to become or to continue to serve as prostitutes;
(4) Soliciting people to use the services of a prostitute (obtaining johns);
(5) Finding prostitutes for potential clients;
(6) Transporting an individual in order to facilitate prostitution;
(7) Allowing a structure to be used for the purpose of prostitution; and
(8) Receiving any benefit from the services of prostitutes (this is sometimes called living from the services of prostitutes). (American Law Institute 1985:198)

From the *MPC*'s perspective, the assumption is that those who promote or otherwise facilitate prostitution are more criminally

Pimps:
individuals who control one or more prostitutes by arranging for their clients (johns) and taking a percentage of their earnings

Johns:
the people who procure the services of prostitutes

culpable than the prostitutes themselves. They are providing the means by which prostitutes can ply their trade, and they are living off of the earnings of prostitutes. In contrast, the *Code* considers "johns" or the clients of prostitutes to be guilty only of a misdemeanor.

In order to prove that a location is a house of prostitution, the state must establish a pattern of behavior. For example, if there were multiple arrests for prostitution at a certain location, or if the state demonstrates that there were several known prostitutes living or working together, then this could be the basis for charging the owner with operating a house of prostitution. The police can sometimes gather evidence based on long-term surveillance operations, or they may send undercover officers to attempt to purchase sexual services. Much like drug houses in some cities, governments may be able to condemn houses of prostitution under local nuisance ordinances.

Prostitution occurs in various settings, and some locations are much more public than others. Prostitutes also fit into several categories of sex workers listed at the beginning of this section, depending on the setting and the fees charged. While we will not attempt an exhaustive list, for our purposes the categories we will consider are: street walkers, call girls, escort services, and the emerging category of virtual prostitutes (see Siegel 2011:357-360).

Prostitutes who are classified as **street walkers** are the primary concern within the context of street crimes. These prostitutes ply their trade in public places, often openly seeking customers. The *MPC* characterizes this as loitering "in or within view of any public place for the purpose of being hired to engage in sexual activity" (American Law Institute 1985:198). In terms of status, street walkers occupy the bottom rung on the prostitution ladder. They work for the lowest wages, are often victimized by their customers or pimps, and they are the most likely to be arrested. Many are poorly educated, and some come from backgrounds of sexual victimization. Increasingly, these individuals are victims of human trafficking and sex slavery (Walker-Rodriguez and Hill 2011). In rural areas and along interstate highways there are also prostitutes in this category that work truck stops and rest areas. The police are likely to observe them making deals at regular locations, and they may use undercover officers to buy-and-bust these prostitutes and their customers.

Street Walkers: prostitutes who ply their trade openly in public places

The next group up the ladder includes call girls/boys or escort services. Since their transactions are often arranged over the phone (or increasingly on the computer) and they meet their clients in hotel rooms, houses, or apartments, these prostitutes are much less likely to come under police scrutiny, making them less likely to be arrested. The police may set up sting operations where they call escort services or individual call girls/boys to arrange meetings at hotels or motels for the purposes of sex. When the prostitutes show up and a deal is struck they are arrested by officers who may be listening in an adjacent room.

Related to escort services are the massage parlors found in many places. Often the women who work in these establishments are foreign nationals, and some may be victims of human trafficking operations. While there are legitimate businesses that offer massages, the massage parlors that the police are interested in have employees who are willing to provide sexual services (often referred to as "full body massages") for an additional fee.

Like many other aspects of life in the United States, prostitution has taken advantage of the boom in computer technology. For a while prostitutes were able to advertise their services in the "erotic services" section of Craigslist.com. However, pressure from a number of states' attorneys general against Craig Newmark, the founder of *Craigslist*, prompted the site to remove this section. As a result prostitutes now often advertise their services on sites such as Backpage .com as well as other locations. They arrange for meetings and even payments over the Internet. Clients are able to look through groups of prostitutes to pick the one they want based upon physical attractiveness, sexual specialization, and price.

In addition to arranging traditional sexual encounters, the Internet has also created an environment for virtual sex. Customers can link to online prostitutes via webcams and can engage in sex simultaneously, although separately, with a person on the other end of the connection. This form of sexual activity may not be entirely illegal, but it is an area that the criminal law may be called upon to address in the future.

In 2011, there were 57,345 arrests in the United States for prostitution and commercialized sex (Federal Bureau of Investigation 2011). While these numbers are substantially smaller than those for drug- and alcohol-related arrests, they do show that the nation's law enforcement officials continue to enforce laws against prostitution, especially when solicitation occurs in public settings. Box 7.5 contains the elements of the crime of prostitution.

Box 7.5 ELEMENTS OF PROSTITUTION

Actus Reus	*Mens Rea*
• Offering sexual favors in return for anything of value • Operating a house of prostitution • Engaging the services of a prostitute	• Intent to offer or to procure sexual services

Concurrence

Linking of *actus reus* and *mens rea*

GAMBLING

Gambling presents a unique set of challenges for law enforcement officials. Prior to the 1970s, most forms of gambling were illegal in every state except Nevada (Barker and Britz 2000). Beginning with the legalization of casino gambling in Atlantic City, New Jersey, legalized gambling in various forms has spread throughout the United States. Currently, every state except Hawaii and Utah has some form of legalized gambling, including horse and dog tracks, "racinos" (race tracks with casinos in states like Florida and New Mexico), high-stakes bingo, state lotteries, American Indian casinos, and non-Indian state-licensed casinos (in states such as Colorado, Louisiana, Mississippi, and South Dakota).

When the wave of legalization began in the 1970s some locations like New York City (with its off-track betting) argued that legalizing and controlling gambling would drive illegal gambling out of business. However, that has proven not to be the case. Illegal gambling still exists in locations with legal gambling, and there are many reasons for this. First, bookmakers will accept bets over the telephone rather than requiring the bettor to appear in person. Second, they will extend credit to bettors (usually with high repayment fees). Third, bookies may give bettors better odds than legalized betting establishments. Whatever the reasons, it is obvious that illegal gambling has continued to flourish alongside legal gambling.

While the topic of cybercrime will be dealt with more in-depth in Chapter 8, at this point it is important to note the existence of online gambling. Beginning in 1994, online "casinos" and poker rooms started to appear. These sites often were operated from Caribbean nations and other locations outside the physical boundaries of the United States, and they allowed players to establish accounts from which they could make bets. By 1997, the number of virtual casinos had increased to over 200, and it was estimated that these sites generated annual revenues of over $830 million (Onlinegambling.com 2013).

Concerned about the spread and relative lack of regulation of online gambling, the U.S. Congress passed the Unlawful Internet Gambling Enforcement Act (UIGEA) in 2006, which "prohibits gambling businesses from knowingly accepting payments in connection with the participation of another person in a bet or wager that involves the use of the Internet and that is unlawful under any federal or state law." As a result, for a time online casinos and poker rooms decided not to accept bets from players in the United States. However, attorneys who carefully studied the UIGEA believed that the wording was such that its enforcement was difficult if not impossible. Therefore, online casinos and poker rooms once again accept

Box 7.6 ELEMENTS OF GAMBLING OFFENSES	
Actus Reus	**Mens Rea**
• Placing or receiving wagers not authorized under law • Operating an unlicensed gambling establishment	• Intent to wager or to receive wagers in an illegal manner

Concurrence
Linking of *actus reus* and *mens rea*

wagers from players in the United States, unless such wagers are specifically prohibited by state law. Interestingly, to date there have been no prosecutions of website owners or operators, or individual players under the UIGEA.

The proliferation of legalized gambling in the United States has caused most local law enforcement agencies to minimize their efforts directed at illegal gambling. Nevertheless, in 2011 there were 8,596 arrests in the United States for gambling law violations (Federal Bureau of Investigation 2011). Box 7.6 contains the elements we normally associate with gambling-related crimes.

WEAPONS OFFENSES

The use of weapons is particularly relevant to any discussion of street crimes. In 2010, weapons of all types "were used in 22% of all violent victimizations and 61% of serious violent victimizations" (Truman 2011:8). Typical crimes included rapes, sexual assaults, other types of assaults, and robberies. There were 852,660 violent victimizations that involved weapons of some sort and 337,960 (about 9% of the total) involved the use of a firearm (Truman 2011:8).

The possession and use of weapons (particularly firearms) may occur in conjunction with other crimes—such as robbery—or they may constitute offenses in and of themselves. A number of states restrict the carrying of firearms, particularly handguns (see Bureau of Alcohol, Tobacco, Firearms, and Explosives 2011). Forty-eight states (the exceptions are Illinois and Wisconsin) allow citizens to carry handguns after complying with licensing, training, and registration requirements. There may be exceptions to the places weapons can be carried, such as establishments that serve alcohol and schools. If a person is found to be in possession of a firearm and is not authorized to have one, this constitutes a crime. The federal Omnibus Crime

Control and Safe Streets Act of 1968 prohibits convicted felons from possessing firearms, and some cities such as Chicago, New York, and Washington, D.C. have passed local ordinances restricting firearms possession. Interestingly, most college campuses in the United States restrict, or outright prohibit, firearms possession on campus by students, faculty, and staff. So how do these restrictions square with the Second Amendment to the Constitution permitting the "right to bear arms?"

The recent U.S. Supreme Court cases of *District of Columbia et al. v. Heller*, 554 U.S. 570 (2008) and *McDonald v. Chicago*, 561 U.S. 3025 (2010) held that such restrictions can be limited by the Second Amendment to the Constitution. In the *Heller* case the Supreme Court, by a 5-4 vote, ruled that the Second Amendment protects the individual right of firearms possession for personal defense in federal enclaves such as the District of Columbia. However, this case did not answer the question of whether this right also extended to the states. Two years after *Heller*, the Supreme Court (again in a 5-4 decision) invalidated Chicago's ban on handgun possession in the *McDonald* case. In *McDonald* the Supreme Court held for the first time that the Second Amendment's "right of the people to keep and bear arms" applied to the states by way of the Fourteenth Amendment's Due Process Clause.

It is important to note, however, that while these two cases provided additional constitutional support to the individual possession of firearms, there are literally hundreds of state and federal statutes dealing with firearms that were unaffected. Therefore, it is somewhat difficult to say what the extent of the Second Amendment's protections are at this point. Still, it is important to note that police officers encounter individuals in a variety of circumstances who have possession of firearms. Some of these will be possessed legally and some will be possessed illegally. Box 7.7 lists the elements associated with weapons offenses.

Box 7.7   ELEMENTS OF WEAPONS OFFENSES

Actus Reus	*Mens Rea*
• Illegal sales or purchases of firearms • Possession of a firearm by a convicted felon • Use of a firearm in the commission of a crime	• Intent to possess and/or use a firearm in a legally unauthorized manner

Concurrence

Linking of *actus reus* and *mens rea*

STRONG-ARM ROBBERY (MUGGING)

Technically, there is no such crime as **mugging**, although this term has long been a part of the English language in reference to physical assaults in conjunction with robberies. The *UCR* defines **robbery** as "the taking or attempting to take anything of value from the care, custody, or control of a person or persons by force or threat of force" (Federal Bureau of Investigation 2011). In 2011, there were 166,674 arrests for robberies around the United States. In all likelihood, as with other street crimes, more robberies were committed than were reported or for which arrests were made.

Therefore, the street crime called mugging is typically an armed robbery or a **strong-arm robbery** (one using force or the threat of force but without a weapon). There are many circumstances under which robberies occur that cause them to be labeled as street crimes. For instance, a woman in her 70s is standing on a street corner waiting for a bus when a teenage boy comes running by and grabs her purse and flees with it. We might call this a purse snatching or a mugging but it is a strong-arm robbery. However, it is important to note that senior adults are not the only victims of such robberies. Thus, if a ten-year-old boy is riding his new bicycle and a group of other children take it away from him, this too would be a strong-arm robbery.

Street-level robberies may be closely associated with the concept of "hot spots" that was discussed at the beginning of the chapter. In fact, recent research in two major cities (Boston and Chicago) found that such robberies tend to cluster in a few locations, often near street corners (Braga et al. 2011; Bernasco and Block 2011).

One of the most unique circumstances under which street robberies occur is during the commission of another crime. For instance, two individuals are involved in a drug deal. One may rob the other and take drugs, cash, and even weapons. This is a situation where although there has been a robbery, it is unlikely to be reported to the police (given the surrounding circumstances). Many of the crimes

Mugging:
strong-arm robbery; taking something of value from a person with force or threat of force

Robbery:
taking anything of value from a person by force or threat of force

Strong-Arm Robbery:
mugging; taking something of value from a person with force or threat of force

---

Box 7.8 ELEMENTS OF STRONG-ARM ROBBERY

Actus Reus	*Mens Rea*
• Taking anything of value from the person by force or threat of force	• Taking anything of value from the person with the intent to permanently deprive the person of the item

Concurrence
Linking of *actus reus* and *mens rea*

involving people who are engaged in another illegal activity may result in informal retaliation (including killings) rather than formally filing charges. For a summary of the elements that constitute strong-arm robbery, see Box 7.8.

POCKET-PICKING

When the crime of pocket-picking is mentioned, most people have images of cities like New York or London in the 1800s. However, American tourists in cities like Rome or Istanbul often find themselves victims of modern-day pick pockets. This is also true in crowded public transportation vehicles in large cities in the United States, and there are signs warning visitors about pick pockets around the sidewalk attractions in Las Vegas, Nevada.

When these offenses occur, they are dealt with in different ways by law enforcement officials. The offenders may be charged with misdemeanors or felonies—depending on the amount stolen—and some cities have started to post pictures of convicted pick pockets to warn unsuspecting potential victims. It is safe to say that in most public places where large crowds gather, pick pockets are nearby practicing their trade as they have for hundreds of years. While it may depend on the jurisdiction, when the police apprehend a pick pocket the offender will most likely be charged with larceny since something of value was taken from another person without the use of force or a threat of force (as is required for robbery charges).

While accurate numbers may be difficult to come by, the Bureau of Justice Statistics reports that in 2008 there were 108,310 cases of pocket-picking reported to authorities. This represents a rate per 1,000 population from 0.3 to 1.2, based on the income of the victim (Rand and Robinson 2011). These numbers do not come close to those of other property and personal crimes committed annually, but they are not insignificant either. Box 7.9 contains the criminal elements that constitute pocket-picking.

Box 7.9   ELEMENTS OF POCKET-PICKING

Actus Reus
- Taking anything of value from a person through the use of stealth or trickery without the person's knowledge

Mens Rea
- Intent to steal and to permanently deprive the owner of the use of the item

Concurrence
Linking of *actus reus* and *mens rea*

SIMPLE ASSAULTS

Assault will be covered more extensively in Chapter 6; nevertheless, it is important to note that many assaults occur as street crimes or in connection with street crimes. To gauge the scope of assault, the 2011 *UCR* disclosed that there were 751,131 aggravated assaults reported in the United States and 397,707 arrests for aggravated assault (Federal Bureau of Investigation 2011). However, because these were aggravated assaults, they involved something more severe than merely instilling fear in the victim. These offenses were accompanied by battery, the use or threatened use of weapons, and other circumstances such as the intent to cause bodily harm. For our purposes, many of the aggravated assaults that occur every year clearly fit into the street crime category. However, there are other common situations in which a person is threatened, but where no physical harm occurs. Any time a person is placed in fear—by explicit or implicit threats—an assault has occurred. When these situations never progress beyond the threat stage, a **simple assault** has taken place. Simple assaults could occur between children playing on a playground or in a park, or they could result from individuals arguing over who got to a parking place first. Many of these types of situations occur between people who are known to each other and who have ongoing relationships. Often there has been alcohol or drug use, and many simple assaults are never reported to the police. Nevertheless, with sufficient provocation, some may escalate into aggravated assaults or even homicides. The important point to remember is that quite a few assaults happen in public places and, therefore, they become part of the total picture of street crime in the United States. To review the elements that constitute simple assault, refer to Box 7.10.

Simple Assault:
the use of threats to place another person in fear of life or safety

---

Box 7.10 ELEMENTS OF SIMPLE ASSAULTS

Actus Reus

- Attempting to cause bodily harm to another; OR
- Negligently causing bodily harm to another with a weapon; OR
- Placing a person in fear by physically menacing serious bodily injury

Mens Rea

- Purposely, knowingly, recklessly, or negligently causing harm or attempting to cause harm to another

Concurrence

Linking of *actus reus* and *mens rea*

GANGS

The gang phenomenon is not new in the United States. In fact, gangs have existed in one form or another since colonial times (Mays and Winfree 2012). However, beginning in the mid-1980s, police agencies around the country became concerned about gangs as a street crime problem. The two elements that intersected around the issue of gangs were the introduction of rock cocaine ("crack") and high levels of violence. The violence typically involved drive-by shootings and intergang warfare (see Sanders 1994), and gang members often died in these violent confrontations. However, innocent bystanders were also shot and killed.

In addition to drugs and violence, street gangs have been associated with various other criminal activities. In some cities, gang members engage in extortion or selling "insurance" to businesses in order to secure protection. They also have been connected to organized burglary and auto-theft rings. The most well-established gangs have moved into territories and activities traditionally associated with organized crime.

As a result of the outcry resulting from very public gang activities, in the 1990s a number of jurisdictions developed legal solutions to the increasingly violent gang problem. For example, some states added "gang enhancement" penalties for any crimes committed by those identified as gang members. Another response was that crafted by the city of Chicago in establishing a "Gang Congregation Ordinance." This ordinance was designed to prevent gang members from congregating in public places, and it gave the police the authority to order the suspected gang members to disperse. If they did not, they could be cited or arrested. Numerous other cities have followed suit by enacting gang congregation ordinances as well. But as Box 7.11 shows, eventually the U.S. Supreme Court struck down the law as being unconstitutionally vague.

Box 7.11   THE CRIMINAL LAW AND GANGS

City of Chicago v. Morales
527 U.S. 41 (1999)

The case of *City of Chicago v. Morales* addresses the legal issues related to gangs and the criminal charge of loitering. It provides an example of the principle of legality discussed in Chapter 1, as well as a ruling on the "void for vagueness" doctrine discussed in that chapter. It also raises the question of status versus action discussed in Chapter 2. The following excerpt is from the Court's 6-3 majority opinion written by Justice John Paul Stevens.

In 1992, the Chicago City Council enacted the Gang Congregation Ordinance, which prohibits "criminal street gang members" from "loitering" with one another or with other persons in any public place. The question presented is whether the Supreme Court of Illinois correctly held that the ordinance violates the Due Process Clause of the Fourteenth Amendment to the Federal Constitution.

Before the ordinance was adopted, the city council's Committee on Police and Fire conducted hearings to explore the problems created by the city's street gangs, and the consequences of public loitering by gang members. The council found that a continuing increase in criminal street gang activity was largely responsible for the city's rising murder rate, as well as an escalation of violent and drug related crimes. Moreover, the council concluded that the city "has an interest in discouraging all persons from loitering in public places with criminal gang members."

Commission of the offense involves four predicates. First, the police officer must reasonably believe that at least one of the two or more persons present in a "public place" is a "criminal street gang member." Second, the persons must be "loitering," which the ordinance defines as "remaining in any one place with no apparent purpose." Third, the officer must then order "all" of the persons to disperse and remove themselves "from the area." Fourth, a person must disobey the officer's order. If any person, whether a gang member or not, disobeys the officer's order, that person is guilty of violating the ordinance.

The Illinois Supreme Court held "that the gang loitering ordinance violates due process of law in that it is impermissibly vague on its face and an arbitrary restriction on personal liberties." In support of its vagueness holding, the court pointed out that the definition of "loitering" in the ordinance drew no distinction between innocent conduct and

conduct calculated to cause harm. "Moreover, the definition of 'loiter' provided by the ordinance does not assist in clearly articulating the proscriptions of the ordinance."

We conclude that the ordinance enacted by the city of Chicago is unconstitutionally vague. Vagueness may invalidate a criminal law for either of two independent reasons. First, it may fail to provide the kind of notice that will enable ordinary people to understand what conduct it prohibits; second, it may authorize and even encourage arbitrary and discriminatory enforcement.

Since the city cannot conceivably have meant to criminalize each instance a citizen stands in public with a gang member, the vagueness that dooms this ordinance is not the product of uncertainty about the normal meaning of "loitering," but rather about what loitering is covered by the ordinance and what is not.

First, the purpose of the fair notice requirement is to enable the ordinary citizen to conform his or her conduct to the law. Although it is true that a loiterer is not subject to criminal sanctions unless he or she disobeys a dispersal order, the loitering is the conduct that the ordinance is designed to prohibit. If the loitering is in fact harmless and innocent, the dispersal order itself is an unjustified impairment of liberty. Because an officer may issue an order only after prohibited conduct has already occurred, it cannot provide the kind of advance notice that will protect the putative loiterer from being ordered to disperse.

Second, the terms of the dispersal order compound the inadequacy of the notice afforded by the ordinance. It provides that the officer "shall order all such persons to disperse and remove themselves from the area." This vague phrasing raises a host of questions. After such an order issues, how long must the loiterers remain apart? How far must they move? If each loiterer walks around the block and they meet again at the same location, are they subject to arrest or merely to being ordered to disperse again?

The Constitution does not permit a legislature to "set a net large enough to catch all possible offenders, and leave it to the courts to step inside and say who could be rightfully detained, and who should be set at large." This ordinance is therefore vague "not in the sense that it requires a person to conform his conduct to an imprecise but comprehensible normative standard, but rather in the sense that no standard of conduct is specified at all."

In our judgment, the Illinois Supreme Court correctly concluded that the ordinance does not provide sufficiently specific limits on the enforcement discretion of the police "to meet constitutional standards for definiteness and clarity." We recognize the serious and difficult problems testified to by the citizens of Chicago that led to the enactment of this ordinance. However, in this instance the city has enacted an ordinance that affords too much discretion to the police and too little notice to citizens who wish to use the public streets.

Accordingly, the judgment of the Supreme Court of Illinois is Affirmed.

***

As a footnote, after the original antiloitering ordinance was held unconstitutional by both the Illinois Supreme Court and the U.S. Supreme Court, the Chicago City Council passed a revised ordinance that was ruled constitutional in a 2002 Illinois state court legal challenge. The new law was more tightly drawn to give specific directions to police officers concerning the targets of the law (gang members) and the prohibited activities. In responding to criticisms of the revised law, an attorney for the city of Chicago said that, in effect, the U.S. Supreme Court decision in the *Morales* case helped draft the law.

1. What is loitering, and when (if ever) should it be a crime?
2. Would an antigang ordinance, such as that of the city of Chicago, give the police too much discretion in deciding when crowds should be dispersed and/or arrests made?
3. What does the U.S. Supreme Court really mean when it applies the "void for vagueness" doctrine?

State and local governments continue to struggle with street gang problems, and a 2008 report by the National Gang Center found that there were approximately 774,000 members in 27,900 gangs around the United States (Egley, Howell, and Moore 2010:1). This means that the criminal law will continue to be used to direct police authorities in combatting street gangs and the various criminal activities associated with them.

LOITERING/VAGRANCY

Throughout much of our nation's history, local governments have had laws that prohibit loitering and vagrancy. Although these two behaviors can constitute different offenses, we will consider them together because of their similarity. In terms of definitions, Sheppard (2012:1660) says that **loitering** is "to linger in one place, or idle, for no apparent purpose" and that **vagrancy** under common law refers to "a person of no known address, who was to give an account of the person's means and purpose or be arrested under the laws for the regulation of the poor" (Sheppard 2012:2921). The *MPC* includes loitering along with prowling and says that the *actus reus* requirement is satisfied if a person "loiters or prowls in a place, at a time, or in a manner not usual for law-abiding individuals under circumstances that warrant alarm for the safety of persons or property in the vicinity" (American Law Institute 1985:193).

In terms of this chapter, all of these activities fit within the street crime category. The problem with both loitering and vagrancy, however, is the purposes of such laws, and the concreteness of the behaviors they are designed to prevent. Technically, homeless people who are living on the streets are violating either one or both of these proscriptions. Realistically, however, it seems that the homeless would not be considered criminal unless their loitering and vagrancy were accompanied by other types of harmful behavior.

As a result of the vagueness of most loitering and vagrancy statutes, appellate courts have struck down most attempts to prohibit these two activities. In response to overturning many local ordinances, local councils frequently have added other stipulations, such as making it illegal to "aggressively panhandle." Even these prohibitions rely on public complaints, and many police departments are passive in their enforcement of these behaviors.

LEGALIZE OR DECRIMINALIZE?

The debate over legalization or decriminalization does not happen with street crimes such as robbery, pocket-picking, and assaults. However, whenever there are discussions about what to do about drugs, alcohol, prostitution, and gambling, some suggest that part or all of these behaviors should be decriminalized, if not fully legalized [see, for example, Inciardi (2007)]. We begin by distinguishing decriminalization from legalization, and then discuss the pros and cons of removing some of the behaviors we have discussed from the realm of criminal law.

Decriminalization

Decriminalization simply means taking an activity that has been prohibited by law and removing the criminal penalties from it (*Black's*

Loitering:
hanging out or standing around certain locations with no apparent purpose

Vagrancy:
existing with no visible means of support; may be applied to homeless people or those otherwise living on the streets

Decriminalization:
taking an activity that has been prohibited by law and removing the criminal penalties from it

Law Dictionary 1991:285). Although criminal penalties may be removed, there still can be a variety of restrictions associated with the activity. As one example, most jurisdictions still prohibit the possession of any amount of marijuana (except when prescribed for medical purposes). People in possession of small amounts might be charged with misdemeanors and they could be subject to jail time and/or fines. Those in possession of larger amounts could be charged with felonies.

Nevertheless, some jurisdictions in the United States have decriminalized the possession of small amounts of marijuana (for example, less than one ounce), and anyone found to be in possession of this amount is given what amounts to a traffic ticket — which the courts have determined is a civil penalty. This means that if possession of small amounts of marijuana is decriminalized the possibility of jail terms would be eliminated. In some ways, the possession and use of alcoholic beverages fits into the realm of decriminalization in that it is legal for adults to use alcohol in most situations. However, cities may restrict the sale of alcoholic beverages to certain times of the day or certain days of the week. They also can limit sales within certain distances of schools or churches. Bars and restaurants also are prohibited from serving customers who appear to be intoxicated.

Legalization

In contrast to decriminalization, **legalization** allows people to engage in certain forms of conduct with virtually no restrictions — although there still might be limits based upon age or the places in which the conduct could be practiced. An example of this is Nevada's approach to legalized prostitution. On a county-by-county basis, Nevada prostitutes can legally offer their services in licensed bordellos. Again, there can be age restrictions (services are not offered to minors), and not all counties have approved legalization. For example, Clark County, the most populous county in the state, does not have legalized prostitution, although illegal prostitution seems to flourish in spite of its prohibition.

Although as a practical matter decriminalization and legalization might be difficult to differentiate, this is an important distinction in the debate over controlling some of the so-called victimless crimes. In the end, the key difference may be the amount of regulation or control that remains.

Drugs

The one area that has seen the greatest debate over decriminalization or legalization involves drugs. In particular, there is a long-standing

Legalization:
allowing people to engage in activities that formerly were prohibited by law with relatively few restrictions

discussion over the legalization of marijuana. As we previously mentioned, some states have decriminalized the possession of small amounts of marijuana. In fact, ten states—Alaska, Arizona, California, Colorado, Massachusetts, Michigan, Nevada, New Hampshire, Oregon, and Washington—have considered provisions for the decriminalization of marijuana. The first state to remove criminal penalties for possession of small amounts of marijuana was Oregon in 1973. To date, only Massachusetts and Michigan have joined Oregon in making simple possession a civil infraction rather than a misdemeanor; however, in 2012 Colorado and Washington legalized private possession of one ounce or less. Otherwise, in terms of legalization, with the major exception of medical marijuana, no other states currently have taken the position that all criminal penalties and regulations should be removed.

Part of the dilemma over state and local laws dealing with drugs like marijuana is that they may come into conflict with federal statutes and enforcement efforts. For example, in the case of *Gonzales v. Raich*, 545 U.S. 1 (2005), the U.S. Supreme Court ruled in a 6-3 vote that the Commerce Clause of the U.S. Constitution gave federal authorities the right to enforce the law against marijuana possession, even for medical purposes as permitted in California. Currently, federal authorities are doing relatively little marijuana enforcement, but with other states considering provisions for decriminalization/legalization and the issue of medical marijuana, this is an area of ongoing legal development.

The other drug about which there has been a decriminalization/legalization debate is heroin. Those who favor removing criminal penalties point to the European experience. In some European countries doctors can prescribe and pharmacies can dispense heroin to addicts to prevent them from buying it on the streets and sharing hypodermic syringes. In these countries, heroin addiction is treated as a public health problem, rather than a crime. While there has been some discussion of this approach in the United States, it has never been seriously considered. The alternative has been to medically dispense the drug Methadone as an alternative treatment for heroin addicts.

Alcohol

For most adults there are few restrictions on alcohol consumption in this country. There are limits on where alcohol is consumed (it is prohibited in some public places), and most jurisdictions still maintain restrictions on being intoxicated in public. Every state prohibits the operation of motor vehicles (including boats) while under the influence of drugs or alcohol, and there are federal and state laws that prohibit the manufacturing of alcohol except within strict limits. Otherwise, adults are free to possess and consume beverage alcohol.

The major restrictions we place on alcohol consumption in this country have to do with a person's age. Once the Twenty-sixth Amendment to the Constitution was ratified in 1971, 18-year-olds gained the right to vote and, in most states, to legally purchase alcohol. After a few years of allowing 18-, 19-, and 20-year-olds to legally buy and consume alcohol, the federal government (and a number of states) became concerned about the number of motor vehicle accidents involving this population. In response, the federal government threatened to withhold highway dollars from the states in order to "persuade" them to prohibit the sale of alcoholic beverages to anyone under the age of 21. To keep from losing much-needed highway funding, states quickly changed their legal drinking age to 21.

Prostitution

For much of our nation's early history prostitution flourished. In some locations it was legal and regulated, and in others it was illegal but tolerated. After World War I, prostitution was outlawed virtually nationwide, often because of the prevalence of venereal diseases among returning American military personnel (Hobson 1990; Rosen 1982). As previously mentioned, except for Nevada no state allows legal prostitution. Even in Nevada, only counties with populations under 400,000 permit legalized brothels. In 2008, there were eight counties with 28 legal brothels in operation (Caron 2008). No other states currently have proposals that would allow for legalized prostitution.

Gambling

Gambling presents an interesting case for the legalization of the so-called victimless crimes. Prior to the 1970s, legalized gambling was confined to Nevada, and a few states that operated lotteries (beginning with New Hampshire in 1964). Today 43 states operate lotteries, either on their own or in multistate operations such as Power Ball or Mega Millions. Only seven states (Alaska, Alabama, Hawaii, Mississippi, Nevada, Utah, and Wyoming) do not have lotteries.

The big change in legalized gambling came in 1976 when New Jersey voted to allow casino gambling in Atlantic City in order to provide an economic revival to the declining seaside tourist destination (Barker and Britz 2000). Resorts International, the first modern casino outside of Nevada, opened in Atlantic City in 1978. Today there are 11 casinos in Atlantic City, and casino gaming has expanded nationwide as a result of passage of the federal Indian Gaming

Regulatory Act of 1988 (Eadington 1998; Mason 2000; Mays and Taggart 2005). In addition to American Indian casinos, states such as Colorado, Louisiana, Mississippi, and South Dakota allow non-Indian casinos in a variety of tourist destinations.

As with the issue of drug legalization, one of the concerns about legalized gambling is the impact it has on other crimes. Authorities particularly worry about the quality of life for citizens who suffer from gambling addiction, or those who might be victims of property crimes perpetrated by compulsive gamblers (Albanese 1985; Stitt, Nichols, and Giacopassi 2003). As a result, gambling establishments in the United States must post signs warning about the dangers of compulsive gambling and provide toll-free numbers for people who think they have gambling problems. While gambling and the other behaviors we have considered in this chapter might be classified as victimless crimes, it is possible that there can be a wider sense of victimization beyond those individuals who engage in these behaviors.

Problems of Legalization or Decriminalization

For all of the calls for legalization or decriminalization of vice-related crimes, there are groups that strongly oppose such movements. The clearest area for this is in the legalization or decriminalization of drugs. Most of the opponents believe that legalizing drugs would appear to sanction use of these substances. This could lead to more widespread use in the United States. While legalizing might allow the government to license and control these activities, there is always the possibility that illegal operations would continue to exist. Opponents to drug legalization point to the example of legalized gambling and the continued vitality of illegal gambling activities as an illustration of the difficulties of moving toward legalization or decriminalization of formerly illegal activities. As we have pointed out in the previous sections, the same types of arguments could be made for legalizing or decriminalizing other types of now-prohibited behaviors.

SUMMARY

The police are routinely called on to deal with petty but troublesome violations that fit within the street crime category. Some of these offenses are property crimes and some are personal crimes, and some bring harm to those who engage in these behaviors while others spill over to the broader public. Whatever their nature, given their prevalence street crimes represent the face of crime to many people. These are minor, public offenses that occur daily in great numbers around this country. Police departments expend a considerable amount of their resources dealing with street crime perpetrators and victims. Victims and offenders often come from similar backgrounds, and they disproportionately represent racial and ethnic minority groups. While the losses associated with each of these crimes is typically small, they are significant because of their sheer volume. They tie up the police and they clog lower-level court dockets in the United States. Therefore, we cannot ignore the prominent role played by street crimes in the criminal law in this country.

KEY TERMS

constructive possession
contraband
decriminalization
drug paraphernalia
exposure
"hot spots"
johns
legalization

loitering
mugging
pimps
robbery
simple assault
street crimes
street walkers
strong-arm robbery
vagrancy

CRITICAL THINKING QUESTIONS

1. What do we mean by "street crimes?" Are street crimes distinct from other types of crimes, or do they share common characteristics?
2. Look again at the list of factors associated with street crimes. Do these elements remind you of certain locations near your college campus or in your hometown? Why?
3. Is it always clear what may constitute drug paraphernalia? If there is some degree of ambiguity, does this open the door to discretionary enforcement?
4. For a brief period in our nation's history (following passage of the Twenty-sixth Amendment to the Constitution in 1971 giving 18-year-olds the right to vote), 18-, 19-, and 20-year-olds could legally buy alcohol in most states. Finally, bowing to pressure from the federal government under the justification of highway safety, states began to increase the legal drinking age to 21 again. Should 18-, 19-, and 20-year-olds be allowed to legally purchase alcohol? Why or why not? What about allowing them to purchase reduced-alcohol-level beverages?
5. Why should prostitution be illegal? If the parties are engaging in a consensual activity (neither is being forced to do something), why should the government be concerned? What do people mean when they say that prostitution is an affront to public decency and human dignity?
6. What forms of gambling are legal in your state? If your state has a state lottery, to what do the proceeds go? Does your state have a lottery scholarship program? Does this make the lottery more acceptable to people? What is the minimum age at which someone can buy a lottery ticket?
7. Take any one of the street crimes we have discussed in this chapter and develop a sheet with two columns on it. On one side list the pros of decriminalization or legalization of this behavior, and on the other side list the cons of decriminalization or legalization. Are the arguments on both sides pretty much the same for all of the areas we discussed in the chapter?

SUGGESTED READINGS

Barker, T. & Britz, M. (2000). *Jokers Wild: Legalized Gambling in the Twenty-First Century*. Westport, CT: Praeger. These authors trace the history of gambling in the United States from colonial times until the beginning of the twenty-first century. They examine the establishment of casino gambling in Nevada and Atlantic City, New Jersey, along with the creation of state lotteries and Indian casinos. They address legalization and control of gambling in the Internet age and also consider the issue of compulsive gamblers.

Inciardi, J.A. (2007). *War on Drugs IV: The Continuing Saga of the Mysteries and Miseries of Intoxication, Addiction, Crime and Public Policy* (4th ed.). Upper Saddle River, NJ: Prentice Hall. Inciardi's conclusion is really the starting place for his book: A war on drugs is not the answer to dealing with the drug problem in the United States. He examines a broad range of legal and illegal drugs and the problems associated with drug use and abuse. He also deals with the failures of drug enforcement policies that have been pursued and are being pursued by governments at all levels in the United States.

Walker, S. (2006). *Sense and Nonsense About Crime and Drugs: A Policy Guide* (6th ed.). Belmont, CA: Wadsworth. Earlier editions of Walker's book focused on crime and crime-control issues. Later editions have included the issue of drugs and what we know about the linkage between drug use and crime. He particularly focuses on the degree to which drug control policy makes a difference (or fails to make a difference) in the crime rate in the United States.

REFERENCES

Albanese, J.S. (1985). "The Effect of Casino Gambling on Crime." *Federal Probation* 49(2):39-44.

American Law Institute (1985). *Model Penal Code: Complete Statutory Text*. Philadelphia, PA.

Barker, T. & Britz, M. (2000). *Jokers Wild: Legalized Gambling in the Twenty-First Century*. Westport, CT: Praeger.

Bernasco, W. & Block, R. (2011). "Robberies in Chicago: A Block-Level Analysis of the Influence of Crime Generators, Crime Attractors, and Offender Anchor Points." *Journal of Research in Crime and Delinquency* 48(1):33-57.

Black's Law Dictionary (1991). St. Paul, MN: West.

Braga, A., Hureau, D.M. & Papachristos, A.V. (2011). "The Relevance of Micro Places to City-wide Robbery Trends: A Longitudinal Analysis of Robbery Incidents at Street Corners and Block Faces in Boston." *Journal of Research in Crime and Delinquency* 48(1):7-32.

Bullcoming v. New Mexico, 564 U.S. ___ (2011).

Bureau of Alcohol, Tobacco, Firearms, and Explosives (2011). "State Laws and Published Ordinances—Firearms, 2010-2011—31st Edition." http://www.atf.gov/publications/firearms/state-laws/31st-edition/index.html.

Caron, C. (2008). "Nevada Brothels Hit Hard by Gas Prices." http://www.abcnews.go.com/Business/PainAtThePump/story?id=5213878.

Centers for Disease Control and Prevention (2013). "Injury Prevention and Control: Motor Vehicle Safety." http://www.cdc.gov/motorvehiclesafety/.

District of Columbia et al. v. Heller, 554 U.S. 570 (2008).

Eadington, W.R., editor (1998). *Indian Gaming and the Law*. Reno, NV: University of Reno Press.

Eck, J.E., Chainey, S., Cameron, J.G., Leitner, M. & Wilson, R.E. (2005). *Mapping Crime: Understanding Hot Spots*. Washington, DC: National Institute of Justice, U.S. Department of Justice.

Egley, A., Jr., Howell, J.C. & Moore, J.P. (2010). "Highlights of the 2008 National Youth Gang Survey." *OJJDP Fact Sheet*. Washington, DC: Office of Juvenile Justice and Delinquency Prevention, U.S. Department of Justice.

Federal Bureau of Investigation (2011). "Crime in the United States, 2011." http://www.fbi.gov/ucr/about-us/cjis/ucr/crime-in-the-u.s./2011/crime-in-the-u.s.-2011.

Ford, M.C. (2005). "Frequent Fliers: The High Demand User in Local Corrections." *Californian Journal of Health Promotion* 3(2):61-71.

Gonzales v. Raich, 545 U.S. 1 (2005).

Gray, J.L. (2010). "Policing Liquor Establishments: A Holistic Approach." *FBI Law Enforcement Bulletin* 79(11):14-19.

Gyimah-Brempong, K. (2001). "Alcohol Availability and Crime: Evidence from Census Tract Data." *Southern Economic Journal* 68(1):2-21.

Hobson, B.M. (1990). *Uneasy Virtue: The Politics of Prostitution and the American Reform Tradition*. Chicago: University of Chicago Press.

Inciardi, J.A. (2007). *War on Drugs IV: The Continuing Saga of the Mysteries and Miseries of Intoxication, Addiction, Crime and Public Policy* (4th ed.). Upper Saddle River, NJ: Prentice Hall.

Legal Information Institute (2013). *Dorsey v. United States* (11-5683); *Hill v. United States* (11-5721). http://www.law.cornell.edu/supct/cert/11-5683.

Mason, W.D. (2000). *Indian Gaming: Tribal Sovereignty and American Politics*. Norman, OK: University of Oklahoma Press.

Mays, G.L. (2012). *American Courts and the Judicial Process*. New York: Oxford University Press.

Mays, G.L. & Taggart, W.A. (2005). "Intergovernmental Relations and Native American Gaming: A Case Study on the Emergence of a New Intergovernmental Relations Participant." *American Review of Public Administration* 35(1):74-93.

Mays, G.L. & Winfree, L.T., Jr. (2012). *Juvenile Justice* (3d ed.). New York: Wolters Kluwer.

McDonald v. Chicago, 561 U.S. 3025 (2010).

Onlinegambling.com (2013). "The History of Online Gambling." http://www.onlinegambling.com/online-gambling-history.htm.

Powell v. Texas, 392 U.S. 514 (1968).

Rand, M.R. & Robinson, J.E. (2011). *Criminal Victimization in the United States, 2008—Statistical Tables*. Washington, DC: Bureau of Justice Statistics, U.S. Department of Justice.

Ratcliffe, J.H., Taniguchi, T.A. & Taylor, R.B. (2011). "Gang Set Space, Drug Markets, and Crime Around Street Corners in Camden." *Journal of Research in Crime and Delinquency* 48(3):327-363.

Robinson v. California, 370 U.S. 660 (1962).

Rosen, R. (1982). *The Lost Sisterhood: Prostitution in America, 1900-1918*. Baltimore, MD: The Johns Hopkins University Press.

Sanders, W.B. (1994). *Gangbangs and Drivebys*. Hawthorne, NY: de Gruyter.

Santos, R. (2011). "Systematic Pattern Response Strategy: Protecting the Beehive." *FBI Law Enforcement Bulletin* 80(2):12-20.

Sheppard, S.M., general editor (2012). *Bouvier Law Dictionary*. New York: Wolters Kluwer Law & Business.

Sherman, L.W. (1995). "Hot Spots of Crime and Criminal Careers of Places." Revised version of paper delivered at the 1989 Gwynne Nettler Lecture, University of Alberta, Edmonton, Alberta, Canada. http://www.popcenter.org/Library/CrimePrevention/Volume_04/02-Sherman.pdf.

Sherman, L.W., Gartin, P. & Buerger, M.E. (1989). "Hot Spots of Predatory Crime: Routine Activities and the Criminology of Place." *Criminology* 27(1):27-55.

Siegel, L.J. (2011). *Criminology: The Core* (4th ed.). Belmont, CA: Wadsworth.

Stitt, B.G., Nichols, M. & Giacopassi, D. (2003). "Does the Presence of Casinos Increase Crime? An Examination of Casino and Control Communities." *Crime and Delinquency* 49(2):253-284.

Taylor, R.B. (1999). "Crime, Grime, Fear, and Decline: A Longitudinal Look." *Research in Brief*. Washington, DC: National Institute of Justice, U.S. Department of Justice.

Truman, J.L. (2011). *Criminal Victimization, 2010*. Washington, DC: Bureau of Justice Statistics, U.S. Department of Justice.

Walker-Rodriguez, A. & Hill, R. (2011). "Human Sex Trafficking." *FBI Law Enforcement Bulletin* 80(3):1-9.

Zhu, L., Gorman, D.M. & Horel, S. (2004). "Alcohol Outlet Density and Violence: A Geospatial Analysis." *Alcohol and Alcoholism* 39(4):369-375.

Crimes Against the State, White Collar Crime, and Cybercrime

LEARNING OBJECTIVES

After reading this chapter you should be able to:

1. Explain the historical evolution of crimes against the state and understand the significance of these crimes in both the formation and maintenance of the U.S. government
2. Define the various crimes against the state and describe the legislation that regulates these crimes
3. Define the various forms of white collar crime
4. Explain the societal implications of white collar crime
5. Define the various types of cybercrime
6. Discuss the consequences for the criminal law system as society conducts increasingly greater amounts of business online

INTRODUCTION

Laws are most often created as a response to a particular event or need within a society. Contemporary events and the development of advanced technology have created new needs for criminal regulation in the United States. In response, many laws regarding crimes against the state, white collar crimes, and cybercrimes have been either developed or updated.

These three crime classifications are addressed together in this chapter because they are criminal enterprises that often go hand in hand and frequently take place in conjunction with one another. There are also many times when one instance of criminal activity may overlap and fit into more than one of these categories. These crimes are part of a complex and constantly evolving area of the law. The list of crimes discussed is by no means exhaustive. There may be others that you can think of or (particularly in the case of cybercrime) new crimes that have developed since this book was written.

CRIMES AGAINST THE STATE

It should be noted that *all* crimes injure a nation and its people in some way. However, **crimes against the state** are criminal acts that are directed at a country's government and citizens. Although laws addressing crimes against the state have evolved significantly as the result of modern events (most notably the 9/11 terrorist attacks), these crimes were among the first addressed by the U.S. government. When the Founding Fathers undertook the formidable task of establishing a new nation, they were aware that there would be significant challenges to the new government. Therefore, it was essential that the government recognize and punish crimes committed against the nation. Crimes against the state are still a very significant part of our modern criminal law.

Crimes against the state are unique for several reasons. First, most crimes have a readily identifiable victim. However, crimes against the state are committed against a nation's government and society at large. While most of the other crimes discussed in this book cause damage to individuals or their property, crimes against the state inflict damage upon the government, its property, and its people. Second, crimes against the state are most often committed with a political or ideological motive. While crimes against individuals or property are primarily committed for personal gain or retaliation,

Crimes Against the State: criminal acts that are directed at a country's government and citizens crimes against the state often occur as a public statement against political or social policies and conditions. Third, because crimes against the state are directed toward the national government, they are primarily governed by **federal law**.

Treason

Treason is considered the most serious crime against the state, and a person who is convicted of treason is eligible for the death penalty (18 U.S.C. § 2381). Treason was such a significant issue during the formation of the U.S. government that it is the only crime specifically defined in the U.S. Constitution. Article III, Section 3 of the Constitution states that treason "shall consist only in levying War against them, or in adhering to their Enemies, giving them Aid and Comfort." The *actus reus* of treason consists of either levying war against the United States or giving aid and comfort to the country's enemies. The *mens rea* of treason is the *intent* to commit these acts in order to damage or destroy the U.S. government. Box 8.1 outlines the elements of treason.

Because treason is such a serious crime with dire consequences, the Founders were careful to require strict proof before an individual could be convicted of treason. Article III, Section 3 of the U.S. Constitution states that "No person shall be convicted of Treason unless on the Testimony of two Witnesses to the same overt Act, or on Confession in open Court." The requirement — known as the **two-witness rule** — that a conviction of treason be supported by either evidence from two witnesses or a confession in open court helps eliminate false charges of treason that are not validated by adequate evidence. The need for concrete evidence to support a treason conviction is further discussed in Box 8.2 through the case of *Cramer v. United States*, 325 U.S. 1 (1945).

Federal Law:
the jurisdiction and legal authority that governs crimes against the United States

Treason:
levying war against the United States or giving aid and comfort to enemies of the United States

Two-Witness Rule:
requirement that a conviction for treason result from either the testimony of two witnesses or a confession in open court

---

Box 8.1   ELEMENTS OF TREASON (*MPC*)

Actus Reus	*Mens Rea*
• Levying war against the U.S. OR • Giving aid to the enemies of the U.S.	• Intent to damage or destroy the U.S. government

Concurrence

Linking of *actus reus* and *mens rea*

Box 8.2 THE REQUIREMENTS FOR A TREASON CONVICTION

Cramer v. United States
325 U.S. 1 (1945)

In *Cramer v. United States*, Anthony Cramer was tried for treason for associating with and giving comfort to the enemies of the United States during World War II. In 1942, when the United States was at war with Germany, German submarines approached the U.S. coast. Several German individuals came ashore on the coasts of New York and Florida. As the United States was heavily entrenched in fighting World War II, any damage that could be done by the German intruders could have been disastrous for the military and the war effort. The U.S. government was well aware of this threat and was on active watch for potential treasonous acts. Two of the German intruders, Werner Thiel and Edward Kerling, were seen having dinner with Anthony Cramer at New York City's Thompson Cafeteria.

Cramer was arrested for and charged with treason on the basis of testimony from FBI agents that he ate dinner and had a long conversation with Thiel and Kerling. Even though Cramer was convicted at the trial court level, the U.S. Supreme Court reversed the conviction on the basis that there was no direct proof of Cramer's treason and that the testimony and observations of the two FBI agents were not substantial enough to support a conviction for treason. The reversal of this conviction during a time in which the United States was at war illustrates the U.S. court system's resolve that treason be treated as an extremely grave offense and that any conviction for treason must be a result of proof from at least two witnesses, and leave nothing to be filled in by the minds of the judge or jurors.

The very minimum function that an overt act must perform in a treason prosecution is that it shows sufficient action by the accused, in its setting, to sustain a finding that the accused actually gave aid and comfort to the enemy. Every act, movement, deed, and word of the defendant charged to constitute treason must be supported by the testimony of two witnesses. The two-witness principle is to interdict imputation of *incriminating acts* to the accused by circumstantial evidence or by the testimony of a single witness. The prosecution cannot rely on evidence which does not meet the constitutional test for overt acts to create any inference that the accused did other acts or did something more than was shown in the overt act, in order to make a giving of aid and comfort to the enemy. The words of the Constitution were chosen, not to make it hard to prove merely routine and everyday acts, but to make the proof of acts that convict of treason as sure as trial processes may. When the prosecution's case is thus established, the Constitution does not prevent presentation of corroborative or cumulative evidence of any admissible character either to strengthen a direct case or to rebut the testimony or inferences on behalf of defendant. The Government is not prevented from making a strong case; it is denied a conviction on a weak one . . . .

It appeared upon the trial that at all times involved in these acts Kerling and Thiel were under surveillance of the Federal Bureau of Investigation. By direct testimony of two or more agents it was established that Cramer met Thiel and Kerling on the occasions and at the places charged and that they drank together and engaged long and earnestly in conversation. This is the sum of the overt acts as established by the testimony of two witnesses. There is no two-witness proof of what they said nor in what language they conversed. There is no showing that Cramer gave them any information whatever of value to their mission or indeed that he had any to give. No effort at secrecy is shown, for they met in public places. Cramer furnished them no shelter, nothing that can be called sustenance or supplies, and there is no evidence that he gave them encouragement or counsel, or even paid for their drinks.

The Government recognizes the weakness of its proof of aid and comfort, but on this score it urges: "Little imagination is required to perceive the advantage such meeting would afford to enemy spies not yet detected. Even apart from the psychological comfort which the meetings furnished Thiel and Kerling by way of social intercourse with one who they were confident would not report them to the authorities, as a loyal citizen should, the meetings gave them a source of information and an avenue for contact. It enabled them to be seen in public with a citizen above suspicion and thereby to be mingling normally with the citizens of the country with which they were at war." The difficulty with this argument is that the whole purpose of the constitutional provision is to make sure that treason conviction shall rest on direct proof of two witnesses and not on even a little imagination. And without the use of some imagination it is difficult to perceive any advantage which this meeting afforded to Thiel and Kerling as enemies or how it strengthened Germany or weakened the United States in any way whatever. It may be true that the saboteurs were cultivating Cramer as a potential "source of information and an avenue for contact." But there is no proof either by two witnesses or by even one witness or by any circumstance that Cramer gave them information or established any "contact" for them with any person other than an attempt to bring about a rendezvous between Thiel and a girl, or that being "seen in public with a citizen above suspicion" was of any assistance to the enemy. Meeting with Cramer in public drinking places to tipple and trifle was no part of the saboteurs' mission and did not advance it. It may well have been a digression which jeopardized its success. . . .

Although nothing in the conduct of Cramer's trial evokes it, a repetition of Chief Justice Marshall's warning can never be untimely:

"As there is no crime which can more excite and agitate the passions of men than treason, no charge demands more from the tribunal before which it is made, a deliberate and temperate inquiry. Whether this inquiry be directed to the fact or to the law, none can be more solemn, none more important to the citizen or to the government; none can more affect the safety of both. . . ."

It is not difficult to find grounds upon which to quarrel with this constitutional provision . . . Certainly the treason rule, whether wisely or not, is severely restrictive. . . . The provision was adopted not merely in spite of the difficulties it put in the way of prosecution but because of them. And it was not by whim or by accident, but because one of the most venerated of that venerated group considered that "prosecutions for treason were generally virulent." Time has not made the accusation of treachery less poisonous, nor the task of judging one charged with betraying the country, including his triers, less susceptible to the influence of suspicion and rancor. The innovations made by the forefathers in the law of treason were conceived in a faith such as Paine put in the maxim that "He that would make his own liberty secure must guard even his enemy from oppression; for if he violates this duty he establishes a precedent that will reach himself." We still put trust in it.

1. Do you agree with the restrictive requirements for a treason conviction? Could there be a time when national security concerns outweigh the rationale for the two-witness rule?
2. Do the requirements for a treason conviction make us more or less secure as a nation?
3. What would be the likely effect(s) of relaxing the requirements to support a treason conviction?

Sedition

The *actus reus* of **sedition** consists of advocating or encouraging another person to overthrow the government. If the person committing sedition took the action himself or herself, he or she would be guilty of treason, but because he or she is encouraging *another* person to take action against the government, he or she is guilty of the lesser crime of sedition. The *mens rea* of sedition is the intent to incite another person to take action against the government. Because sedition involves spurring another person to action, it can be compared to the inchoate crime of solicitation discussed in Chapter 9. Sedition can take place in several forms, including verbal speech or writing. Box 8.3 outlines the elements of sedition.

Even though a person who commits sedition does not actually take any action in attempting to overthrow the government, there are several reasons this activity is criminalized. First, crimes committed by groups are considered to be more dangerous than crimes committed by individuals. Second, people who are moved to action by others will often do things that they would not have done without this provocation from outside parties. Finally, crimes against the state have the potential to inflict more damage than crimes committed against individuals or property. Therefore, law enforcement has a substantial interest in detecting and stopping these crimes while they are in

Sedition: advocating or encouraging another person to overthrow the government

---

Box 8.3   ELEMENTS OF SEDITION (MPC)

Actus Reus	*Mens Rea*
• Advocating or encouraging another person to overthrow the government	• Intent to incite a person to take action against the government

Concurrence

Linking of *actus reus* and *mens rea*

the formation stage (such as sedition), and before real harm occurs (such as treason or terrorism).

In *Yates v. United States*, 354 U.S. 298 (1957), 14 California Communist Party leaders were convicted of "willfully and knowingly conspiring to teach and advocate the overthrow of the government by force" under the **Smith Act**, a statute that criminalized sedition. In the decision that remanded their convictions back to the trial court, the U.S. Supreme Court addressed the difference between discussing governmental overthrow as a conceptual theory and actively inciting this theory into action. Box 8.4 presents a case that illustrates the requirements for a sedition conviction.

Smith Act:
a statute that criminalized sedition

Box 8.4 STANDARDS FOR SEDITION CONVICTIONS

Yates v. United States
354 U.S. 298 (1957)

We are thus faced with the question whether the Smith Act prohibits advocacy and teaching of forcible overthrow as an abstract principle, divorced from any effort to instigate action to that end, so long as such advocacy or teaching is engaged in with evil intent. We hold that it does not.

The distinction between advocacy of abstract doctrine and advocacy directed at promoting unlawful action is one that has been consistently recognized in the opinions of this Court. . . . This distinction was heavily underscored in *Gitlow v. New York*. . . .

"The statute does not penalize the utterance or publication of abstract 'doctrine' or academic discussion having no quality of incitement to any concrete action. . . . It is not the abstract 'doctrine' of overthrowing organized government by unlawful means which is denounced by the statute, but the advocacy of action for the accomplishment of that purpose. . . . This [Manifesto] . . . is [in] the language of direct incitement. . . . That the jury were warranted in finding that the Manifesto advocated not merely the abstract doctrine of overthrowing organized government by force, violence and unlawful means, but action to that end, is clear. . . . That utterances inciting to the overthrow of organized government by unlawful means, present a sufficient danger of substantive evil to bring their punishment within the range of legislative discretion, is clear."

We need not, however, decide the issue before us in terms of constitutional compulsion, for our first duty is to construe this statute. In doing so we should not assume that Congress chose to disregard a constitutional danger zone so clearly marked, or that it used the words "advocate" and "teach" in their ordinary dictionary meanings when they had already been construed as terms of art carrying a special and limited connotation. . . . The legislative history of the Smith Act and related bills shows beyond all question that Congress was aware of the distinction between the advocacy or teaching of abstract doctrine and the advocacy or teaching of action, and that it did not intend to disregard it. The statute was aimed at the advocacy and teaching of concrete action for the forcible overthrow of the Government, and not of principles divorced from action. . . .

"In further construction and interpretation of the statute [the Smith Act] I charge you that it is not the abstract doctrine of overthrowing or destroying organized government by unlawful means which is denounced by this law, but the teaching and advocacy of action for the accomplishment of that purpose, by language reasonably and ordinarily calculated to incite persons to such action. Accordingly, you cannot find the defendants or any of them guilty of the crime charged unless you are satisfied beyond a reasonable doubt that they conspired . . . to advocate and teach the duty and necessity of overthrowing or destroying the Government of the United States by force and violence, with the intent that such teaching and advocacy be of a rule or principle of action and by language reasonably and ordinarily calculated to incite persons to such action, all with the intent to cause the overthrow . . . as speedily as circumstances would permit." (9 F.R.D. 367, 391; and see 341 U.S., at 511-512).

We recognize that distinctions between advocacy or teaching of abstract doctrines, with evil intent, and that which is directed to stirring people to action, are often subtle and difficult to grasp, for in a broad sense, as Mr. Justice Holmes said in his dissenting opinion in Gitlow, "Every idea is an incitement." But the very subtlety of these distinctions required the most clear and explicit instructions with reference to them, for they concerned an issue which went to the very heart of the charges against these petitioners. . . . Instances of speech that could be considered to amount to "advocacy of action" are so few and far between as to be almost completely overshadowed by the hundreds of instances in the record in which overthrow, if mentioned at all, occurs in the course of doctrinal disputation so remote from action as to be almost wholly lacking in probative value. Vague references to "revolutionary" or "militant" action of an unspecified character, which are found in the evidence, might in addition be given too great weight by the jury in the absence of more precise instructions. . . . We cannot allow a conviction to stand on such "an equivocal direction to the jury on a basic issue." (*Bollenbach v. United States*, 326 U.S. 607, 613).

---

1. Should the law make a distinction between teaching a concept as an abstract principle and advocating putting this principle into action? If so, how can such a distinction be made?
2. Is there a societal value in the academic discussion of revolutionary ideas? If so, what productive end(s) can be achieved by such discussion?

Sabotage

Sabotage involves interfering with the use of government property. The *actus reus* of sabotage is the destruction, damage, obstruction, interference with, or contamination of government property. The *mens rea* of sabotage is engaging in these activities to damage the U.S. government's war preparations, or ability to handle national emergencies. The U.S. Code states that people are guilty of sabotage

Sabotage: damaging, destroying, or interfering with the use of government property in order to prevent war preparations or the ability to handle national emergencies

Box 8.5   ELEMENTS OF SABOTAGE (*MPC*)

Actus Reus	*Mens Rea*
• Destroying, damaging, obstructing, interfering with, or contaminating government property	• Intent/purpose to damage preparations for war or national emergencies

Concurrence

Linking of *actus reus* and *mens rea*

if, during a time of national emergency, they "obstruct the U.S. or any associate nation in preparing for or carrying on the war or defense activities" (18 U.S.C. § 2153). Sabotage is a very broad crime and many activities may be included in its scope. Sabotage may be inflicted upon military property, public roads, modes of public transportation, lines of public communication, government buildings, government phones and computers, airways, seaways, and many others. Box 8.5 outlines the elements of sabotage.

Think about all the different people, properties, and functions that are involved in securing the national defense. This list grows substantially during times of war, national emergency, or public crisis. Causing harm or damage to something that might be used or needed by the U.S. government during one of these demanding situations constitutes sabotage. Recall the various agencies that were involved in responding to the terrorist attacks in New York City on September 11, 2001 and at the Boston Marathon on April 15, 2013. If any of the property needed to respond to these emergencies had been sabotaged, the success of the response efforts would have been reduced, and additional lives certainly would have been lost. Situations such as these are the reason that sabotage is strictly regulated by the legal system. Box 8.6 presents a scenario for you determine whether or not an individual is guilty of sabotage.

Espionage

The *actus reus* of **espionage** consists of spying and providing a group or another government with information that might lead to destruction of, or damage to, the U.S. government. The *mens rea* of espionage is the intent to provide this information. The elements of espionage are outlined in Box 8.7. The U.S. government criminalized

Espionage:
intentionally spying and providing a group or government with information that might lead to the destruction of or damage to the U.S. government

---

Box 8.6   YOU DECIDE: IS THIS A CASE OF SABOTAGE?

Doris is an employee of a phone company. In her job training, Doris received instructions that if a national emergency were to occur, all employees would receive a special signal. This would indicate that they were to immediately shut down all telephone communications for the company's customers in order to free the phone lines for government officials to communicate with those needed to help solve the crisis. One day, Doris receives the emergency signal while she is on the phone with her sister discussing a family situation. Doris does not believe that a few minutes will make any difference in shutting down the phone communications, so she spends ten minutes finishing her conversation. Afterward, Doris immediately follows the company's protocol in shutting down the telephone communications. Several months later, investigations reveal that Doris's failure to immediately shut down the phone system prevented first responders from effectively communicating with government officials during a deadly tornado. Five people died as a result. Is Doris guilty of sabotage?

Box 8.7   ELEMENTS OF ESPIONAGE (*MPC*)

Actus Reus

- Spying OR
- Providing information that could damage the U.S. government

Mens Rea

- Intent to provide another country with confidential information

Concurrence

Linking of *actus reus* and *mens rea*

---

espionage through the **Espionage Act of 1917** (18 U.S.C. § 792). Due to fear about what would happen if an enemy country acquired confidential information, this law was passed a short time after the United States entered World War I. Although the Espionage Act was passed due to the potential for information to be transmitted to enemy countries, espionage also includes the transmission of this information to "friendly" countries with which the United States is not currently in conflict. One of the most famous examples of harsh punishment for espionage is seen in the trial of Julius and Ethel Rosenberg, as discussed in Box 8.8.

Espionage Act of 1917: law regulating espionage that was passed shortly after the United States entered World War I

Terrorism

Many modern events, particularly the September 11, 2001 attacks, have shaped and drastically altered the public's ideas of what

Box 8.8   JULIUS AND ETHEL ROSENBERG

In 1953, during the height of the Cold War, U.S. Communist Party members Julius and Ethel Rosenberg were convicted of espionage against the U.S. government. Their conviction was for conspiring or attempting to give the Soviet government information about the American "Manhattan Project" to build an atomic bomb. Both were sentenced to death and were executed for violating the Espionage Act on June 19, 1953.

The execution of the Rosenbergs has been surrounded by controversy. Evidence has shown that Julius Rosenberg most likely gave classified information to the Soviet government. However, there has been doubt about the extent of Ethel's involvement. Two significant points can be noted from the Rosenbergs' executions. First, all crimes against the state are considered grave threats to the nation and the entire population. Second, the interpretation and enforcement of laws, as well as the balance of individual rights, are often different during times of war and times of peace.

---

constitutes **terrorism**. Most people believe that terrorism is an easily identifiable crime, and that the *actus reus* of terrorism consists of a narrow range of activity, such as car bombings, building explosions, or the recent bombings at the Boston Marathon. In reality, terrorism is an extremely broad crime that encompasses a tremendous variety of activities. The *actus reus* of terrorism can be defined as "the unlawful use of force and violence against persons or property to intimidate or coerce a government, the civilian population, or any segment thereof, in furtherance of political or social objectives" (28 C.F.R. § 0.85). The *mens rea* of terrorism is committing these acts with the intent to intimidate or cause fear.

The most important component of terrorism, and what sets it apart from other criminal acts, is the underlying motivation. *Any* crime (murder, assault, robbery, property destruction, etc.) can constitute terrorism, so long as that act is committed as a result of some **political, religious,** or **ideological motivation.** When a person commits a crime with a political or religious motivation, that person may be charged with terrorism *along with* the underlying crime. For example, if an individual who opposes democratic governments sets fire to a building that is hosting a political convention, that person may be charged with terrorism, due to the political motivation of the crime, as well as for arson. Our modern ideas of terrorism tend to focus on things such as building destruction, weapons of mass destruction, biological warfare, and attacking heavily populated areas, all of which certainly constitute terrorist activity. The U.S. Code includes in its definition of terrorism such crimes as using weapons of mass destruction, international terrorist acts, harboring or concealing terrorists, and providing support to terrorists (18 U.S.C. § 2332). However, any crime may constitute terrorism if the perpetrator

Terrorism:
the unlawful use of force and violence against persons or property to intimidate or coerce a government, the civilian population, or any segment thereof, in furtherance of political or social objectives

Political Motivation:
reason for committing acts of terrorism that relates to government or politics

Religious Motivation:
reason for committing acts of terrorism that relates to religion

Ideological Motivation:
motive for committing acts of terrorism that relates to an individual, group, or culture

has the intent to intimidate, wreak havoc, or bring fear to a population for some political, religious, or ideological purpose.

While terrorism is often perceived as something done by foreign groups, a large component of terrorism also takes place from within a nation. In the United States, terrorism includes domestic activity such as the Earth Liberation Front's destruction of real estate developments, vandalism of sports utility vehicles by environmental groups, attacks by animal rights activists on laboratories used for animal experimentation, and the bombing of abortion clinics by pro-life extremists. Box 8.9 outlines the elements of terrorism.

Box 8.9   ELEMENTS OF TERRORISM (MODERN LAW)

Actus Reus

- Use of force and violence against a person or property

Mens Rea

- Intent/purpose to intimidate or cause fear to a government or civilian population

Concurrence

Linking of *actus reus* and *mens rea*

Box 8.10   USA PATRIOT ACT

In response to the terrorist attacks of September 11, 2001, the U.S. Congress passed the Providing Appropriate Tools Required to Interrupt and Obstruct Terrorism Act of 2001, or **USA PATRIOT Act**. This act was signed by President George W. Bush in October 2001 after being passed by Congress within a matter of weeks. The goal of this legislation was to give the government the tools and abilities it needed to detect, seek out, and prevent future terrorist attacks and appropriately punish current acts of terrorism. Provisions of the USA PATRIOT Act include expansion of law enforcement authority to search the homes and businesses of those suspected of terrorist activity. The act also broadened law enforcement's ability to obtain the contents of electronic and telephone communication, as well as

business and personal records. The USA PATRIOT Act raised many questions about its level of intrusiveness. In 2011, President Barack Obama signed a four-year extension to the USA PATRIOT Act provisions that allow for **roving wiretaps**. These are wiretaps that follow a specific person and are not attached to one phone line. The extension also allows for the search of business records and the surveillance of certain suspect individuals.

USA PATRIOT Act:
passed in response to the 9/11 terrorist attacks which attempts to give the government the tools and abilities needed to detect, prevent, and punish terrorist acts

Roving Wiretaps:
wiretaps that follow a specific person and are not attached to one phone line

Although crimes based upon political or social ideologies are hardly new ideas, the terrorist attacks of September 11, 2001 have drastically changed the way terrorism is dealt with in the United States. After these attacks, the U.S. government declared a "War on Terrorism" and has aggressively pursued policies to combat this issue. The primary piece of legislation used to fight terrorism is the USA PATRIOT Act, which is discussed in Box 8.10. Terrorism regulations also have led to discussion about the appropriate balance between individual rights and national security from terrorist activity. As the world has moved into an electronic age, technology has been heavily relied upon to detect and thwart global terroristic efforts. In addition, much terrorism can now be classified as cybercrime because of the significant amount of reliance placed upon computers and technological transactions to carry out terrorist activity.

WHITE COLLAR CRIME

Criminal activity is often viewed as something that is committed by people in lower socioeconomic classes. However, publicity in cases such as WorldCom C.E.O. Bernard Ebbers; Martha Stewart; Bernard Madoff; and Enron executives Kenneth Lay, Jeffrey Skilling, and Andrew Fastow have shown the American public that criminal activity exists in the upper classes as well. These cases and many others have led to public demands for action regarding white collar crimes. **White collar crime** can be defined as crimes "that involve the use of a violator's position of significant power, influence, or trust . . . for personal or organizational gain" (Reiss and Biderman 1980).

White Collar Crime: crimes that involve the use of a violator's position of significant power, influence, or trust for personal or organizational gain

White collar crime also may be called **abuse of trust crime** because it often takes place within the legitimate scope of what people do in the course of their jobs. A company may trust and permit an individual to perform certain activities as part of his or her job function, such as investing money, handling company property, managing employees, and providing documents to accountants. Because they have been entrusted with these responsibilities as part of their employment, performing these tasks is not a law violation. However, laws regulating white collar crime come into play when a person either neglects these duties or performs these duties in an improper manner. As we can see in Reiss and Biderman's definition, white collar crime may be committed for the benefit of an individual, as in the case of a financial planner who keeps his client's money for himself. It also may be committed for the benefit of a group or corporation, as with the Enron accounting fraud. One thing that is certain is that white collar crime is not limited to what we would

Abuse of Trust Crime: crime that takes place when people neglect or improperly perform their job duties

consider "white collar" professions, such as attorneys, medical personnel, accountants, and executives. In any employment scenario, situations may arise in which a person's trust and authority are abused.

Society has a tremendous interest in regulating and punishing white collar crime. When white collar crime takes place, it has a ripple effect that impacts and damages a tremendous number of people. When white collar crime leads to the collapse of huge companies, those companies' employees will likely be unemployed. They may also lose their retirement and investment plans. The company's outside investors may lose significant amounts of money, which may lead to lack of faith in the stock market and damage to the national and world economies. The policing and detection of white collar crime are very expensive endeavors, which raises the overall cost of doing business. This cost is then passed on to consumers.

White collar crime has a devastating price tag attached to it. It was estimated that white collar crime cost U.S. employees $600 billion in 2002 (Center for Corporate Policy 2011). However, because white collar crime is so difficult to detect, it goes unreported in most instances. Because of this, its costs are difficult or impossible to calculate accurately. The purely financial costs of white collar crime are almost certainly greater than any other type of criminal activity. Even more troubling is the fact that white collar crime does not appear to be slowing at any recognizable rate. Most people think of white collar crime taking place exclusively in large corporations, but it is a type of criminal endeavor that occurs throughout the business world. Bank fraud, bribery, embezzlement, forgery, health care fraud, insider trading, insurance fraud, investment schemes, giving or accepting kickbacks, money laundering, racketeering, securities fraud, and tax evasion are just a few of the white collar crimes that exist and abound throughout various occupations.

One of the main challenges associated with white collar crime is that it is incredibly difficult for criminal justice agencies to detect and stop. Another issue is that much white collar crime is committed by people acting as part of a larger corporation or business entity, rather than as individuals. Some white collar crime is classified as **occupational crime**. This is crime committed by individuals *against* company interests, such as employees stealing company money for their own use. However, much white collar crime is classified as **corporate crime**. This involves wrongful acts committed by company employees or representatives in furtherance of the company's interests, such as a company manager who falsely inflates the company's income in order to improve the sale of that company's stock.

When corporate crime takes place, it can be determined that the crime was committed by the business itself as a form of vicarious

Occupational Crime: white collar crime that is committed against company interests

Corporate Crime: wrongful acts committed by company employees or representatives in furtherance of the company's interests

liability. However, it is much more difficult to hold corporations accountable under the criminal law than individuals. The problem is that while a corporation is made up of many different people doing many different jobs, their jobs all revolve around the same activity — the goals and aims of the business. People do various things at work because they are required to — otherwise they will lose their jobs. Since corporations are entities with their own legal identity, it would be illogical to exempt corporations from being punished for wrongful acts. The U.S. Supreme Court has stated that when a criminal act is committed by a person working for or on behalf of a corporation, the corporation can be punished so long as the act was committed within the "scope of the authority and employment" of the corporation's employees or agents [*New York Central & Hudson River Railroad Company v. United States*, 212 U.S. 481 (1909)]. This principle was applied during the 1970s to the Ford Motor Company's criminal trial for negligent homicide as a result of a defective fuel system in the Ford Pinto that led to numerous deaths. Although Ford faced criminal charges as a corporate defendant, the company was acquitted at trial.

Obviously, when a corporation has committed a crime, the corporation itself cannot be sent to prison. Under the *Model Penal Code* (*MPC*), when a corporation or one of its agents is held responsible for a crime "in the conduct of the affairs of the corporation," the court may "institute civil proceedings . . . to forfeit the charter of a corporation" (American Law Institute 1985:88-89). While individual officers may be held responsible, it is very difficult to punish an entire corporation. Below is a discussion of some common forms of white collar crimes that take place in today's business world. Please note that this is not an exhaustive list. Most crimes may become white collar crimes when they are committed within the scope of a person's employment or for the benefit of a corporation or other business entity. Box 8.11 presents a scenario in which you can determine whether or not an employee has committed an abuse of trust crime.

Fraud

Fraud is a form of theft by deception (also discussed in Chapter 4). Under the *MPC*, the *actus reus* of obtaining property by deception is creating or reinforcing a false impression; preventing another from acquiring information that would affect his or her judgment of a transaction; failing to correct a false impression that the deceiver previously created or reinforced, or that the deceiver knows to be influencing another to whom he or she stands in a fiduciary or

Fraud:
obtaining property through deceptive means

Box 8.11   YOU DECIDE: IS THIS AN ABUSE OF TRUST CRIME?

Julie has worked for the Widget Corporation for the past 15 years. She has always been a model employee and has received several awards recognizing her years of loyal service. As part of her job, Julie is given a company laptop computer, and she is permitted to take the computer wherever she pleases and may use it for both business and personal purposes. One Friday, Julie brings the computer home with her to catch up on some work over the weekend. Julie has every intention of bringing the computer back to the office with her on Monday. On Saturday, John, Julie's teenage son, uses the computer with Julie's permission to play games and surf the Internet. John keeps the laptop and continues using it for his own personal purposes. Julie is aware of this, but does nothing to stop him and makes no effort to retrieve the computer to return it to her office. Several months go by, and John continues to keep the laptop and Julie does nothing about this. Has Julie committed an abuse of trust crime?

---

confidential relationship. A **fiduciary relationship** is a special relationship in which one party has a legal responsibility to properly manage the money or property of another person. The *mens rea* of obtaining property by deception is committing any of these acts purposely or knowingly (American Law Institute 1985:150). Fraud is a criminal action that goes to the core of what people think of in regard to white collar crime: lying, deceit, and dishonesty. Box 8.12 outlines the elements of obtaining property by deception.

Fraud occurs in many different ways. In the course of business, people are often entrusted with a significant amount of information. This is normal for day-to-day business operations. As long as human beings continue to operate the functions of the world, people will need to have some level of access to other people's sensitive and confidential information. However, sometimes the people who are

Fiduciary Relationship: a special relationship in which one party has a legal responsibility to properly manage the money or property of another person

---

Box 8.12   ELEMENTS OF OBTAINING PROPERTY BY DECEPTION (*MPC*)

Actus Reus	*Mens Rea*
• Obtaining property be creating or reinforcing a false impression OR • Preventing a person from acquiring information that would affect his or her judgment of a transaction OR • Failing to correct a false impression	• Purposeful or knowingly

Concurrence

Linking of *actus reus* and *mens rea*

entrusted with this information abuse that trust and use this information for fraudulent purposes. For example, it is perfectly normal (and necessary) for medical professionals to have access to their patients' medical records, health histories, and Social Security numbers. This information is usually stored securely, kept confidentially, and used appropriately. However, this information may be used illegally by these professionals to steal personal information for other purposes or to defraud insurance companies.

One common type of fraud takes place through the payment of taxes. Numerous government entities, including the federal government, states, counties, cities, school districts, and hospitals, are dependent upon tax payments to provide services to the communities within their jurisdictions. When people evade paying the taxes that they owe, they may be guilty of **tax fraud**. The *actus reus* of tax fraud is the commission of some affirmative act that constitutes an evasion or attempted evasion of tax liability. The *mens rea* of tax fraud is the intent to defraud authorities in regard to this tax liability. In general, a tax deficiency must be considered substantial before a person will be held liable for tax fraud. For example, a business owner may owe substantial amounts of business-related taxes. If that person takes intentional action to evade that tax liability, such as failing to file a tax return, making false tax deductions, purposely underreporting the amount of property owned by the business, or purposely underreporting that year's business income, that person can be held responsible for tax fraud. Box 8.13 outlines the elements of tax fraud.

Tax Fraud: affirmative act that constitutes an evasion or attempted evasion of tax liability

Another type of fraud that is noteworthy in the context of white collar crime is **securities fraud**, or fraud that is perpetrated through the purchase and sale of stocks and other investments. There are four primary classifications of securities fraud. One type involves either the omission or misrepresentation of material information regarding securities or investments. Examples of this include a stockbroker failing to tell a potential investor about substantial instability within

Securities Fraud: fraud that is perpetrated through the purchase and sale of stocks and other investments

---

Box 8.13 ELEMENTS OF TAX FRAUD (*MPC*)

Actus Reus	*Mens Rea*
• Committing an affirmative act to evade or attempt to evade a tax liability	• Intent to defraud authorities regarding a tax liability

Concurrence

Linking of *actus reus* and *mens rea*

the structure of a company in which the investor is considering purchasing stock or an investment advisor misrepresenting the income and growth potential of a company to a client who is contemplating investing in the company.

The second type is known as **insider trading**, or buying or selling investments illegally based upon confidential and nonpublic information. Examples of insider trading include company employees trading securities based upon confidential restructuring within a corporation, or individuals outside a corporation receiving "tips" about confidential developments that allow them to make investment decisions based upon information that is not publicly available.

Stock parking and broker-dealer fraud are also forms of securities fraud. **Stock parking** takes place when an individual sells or transfers her or his shares of stock to another individual or organization. This is often done in order to conceal the identity of the stock's true owner or to alter the stock's position and worth in the market.

Broker-dealer fraud takes place when a stockbroker or investment advisor sells investments to a client based upon what the broker or dealer may gain from the transaction, rather than based upon what is in the client's best interests. This may take place when a broker convinces a client to purchase a certain security based upon a misrepresentation of the security's potential in a client's investment plan so that the broker will receive a kickback for the securities sale. The *mens rea* of each type of securities fraud is committing these acts intentionally or knowingly. Box 8.14 outlines the elements of securities fraud.

Insider Trading: buying or selling investments based upon confidential and nonpublic information

Stock Parking: takes place when an individual sells or transfers her or his shares of stock to another individual or organization

Broker-Dealer Fraud: takes place when a stockbroker or investment advisor sells investments to a client based upon what the broker or dealer may gain from the transaction, rather than based upon what is in the client's best interests

---

Box 8.14 ELEMENTS OF SECURITIES FRAUD (*MPC*)

Actus Reus	*Mens Rea*
• Omitting or misrepresenting material information about investments OR • Buying or selling securities based upon confidential information OR • Selling or transferring securities to another individual to conceal the owner's identity or alter the investment's value OR • Selling investments based upon factors other than the investor's best interests	• Intentionally or knowingly

Concurrence
Linking of *actus reus* and *mens rea*

Fraud may also take place through the delivery of professional services to consumers. One of the most notable cases of professional fraud occurred in the Enron accounting scheme, which is discussed in Box 8.15. In any business, there is potential for abuse and deceit. An electrician may tell a customer that his or her entire house needs to be rewired when all that really needs to be changed is a circuit breaker. A bank employee may use a customer's identification and personal information to obtain financing or credit for herself. A vacuum cleaner salesman may sell a product to an unsuspecting customer that he knows to be defective. What each of these scenarios has in common is that the fraud was perpetrated by someone who was entrusted with information or who had a professional responsibility, and who failed to fulfill their responsibility or to be truthful in professional dealings.

Investment Schemes

In the normal course of business, professionals are often entrusted with the responsibility of investing other people's money. Just as average Americans have to rely on a doctor's assistance when they

---

Box 8.15   THE ENRON ACCOUNTING FRAUD

There have been numerous cases of business fraud in which one of the most significantly impacted groups of victims was the business's investors and employees. Such was the case in the 2001 Enron accounting fraud. Enron, an energy company based in Houston, Texas, had grown from its initial founding in 1932 into an energy industry giant that employed 22,000 people and claimed $101 billion in revenue in the year 2000.

After investigations uncovered that Enron's revenues were grossly inflated by accounting fraud, the company declared bankruptcy in 2001. Kenneth Lay, who had served as Enron's chief executive officer, was sentenced to 20-30 years in prison, but died before he could be sentenced. Jeffrey Skilling, the company's president, was convicted of conspiracy, insider trading, making false statements to auditors, and securities fraud. For these crimes, he was sentenced to 24 years in federal prison. Andrew Fastow, Enron's chief financial officer, served a six-year prison sentence in exchange for a plea bargain that included pleading guilty to wire and securities fraud, as well as cooperating with the federal government in their investigation of the incident.

The ripple effect of corporate crime was felt sharply from Enron's downfall, as this resulted in job losses for Enron's employees, and, perhaps more significantly, the loss of the employees' 401(k) retirement plans' investments. This financially devastated many families and ruined many retirement plans. The accounting fraud led to the demise of Arthur Andersen, one of the nation's largest and most prominent accounting firms. This scandal of fraud and deceit rocked the business world, and consumers and employees, fearful that they could be victimized in a similar manner, demanded a response from Congress. This response came in the form of the Sarbanes-Oxley Act, which was passed in 2002 (see Box 8.16).

Box 8.16 THE SARBANES-OXLEY ACT OF 2002

The past few decades have seen several accounts of corporate fraud and abuse. Enron investors and employees were the victims of a major accounting fraud, which ended with the company's 2001 bankruptcy. In 2002, the excessive and frivolous spending of Tyco C.E.O. Dennis Kozlowski was made public. This year also saw the bankruptcy of WorldCom after years of reporting false profits through extensive accounting fraud. Unfortunately, these scenarios are not particularly unique and the public is growing more and more accustomed to hearing stories of fraud and deception by business professionals. This lack of trust has shaken consumer confidence in business and corporate governance throughout the world.

As a response to these growing concerns, Congress passed the **Sarbanes-Oxley Act** in 2002. Important provisions of the Sarbanes-Oxley Act include mandatory periodic financial reports and internal financial controls for companies (§ 302), as well as the transparent reporting of transactions that occur off the balance sheet (§ 401). The Sarbanes-Oxley Act requires that all companies give detailed information about their internal financial controls and reporting of financial information to the public (§ 404), and reveal all material financial information in a way that the public can understand (§ 409). Failure to comply with the provisions of the Sarbanes-Oxley Act may result in fines and imprisonment for up to 20 years (§ 802). All companies, regardless of their size, must follow the provisions of this law.

Sarbanes-Oxley Act:
law passed in 2002 in response to instances of corporate fraud; requires financial reporting and controls of all companies

---

get sick or a lawyer's help when they need legal advice, most people do not have the training to undertake aggressive and successful financial investments on their own. To do this, many engage the services of a **financial planner** or **stockbroker**. The client will entrust the planner or broker with his or her money for the purpose of securing strong investments that will hopefully allow the client to make a profit on the investment. Sometimes investments are unsuccessful due to no fault of the broker. There may be weak financial markets, unforeseen changes in business organizations, and sometimes investments just fail to yield a return for a wide variety of other reasons.

However, there have also been instances of financial losses because of **investment schemes** in which the planner or the broker sells false investments, as in the case of Bernard Madoff (see Box 8.17), or gives the client misleading information. Both of these scenarios can lead to devastating financial losses. Other types of investment schemes occur when a broker sells information about his or her client, or when a person illegally uses confidential insider information to make investment decisions. An example of the latter scenario was Martha Stewart's 2004 criminal conviction for her actions surrounding the sale of ImClone Systems stock. Stewart faced nine charges, including securities fraud. It was alleged that she avoided over $45,000 in losses by selling ImClone stock after

Financial Planner/ Stockbroker:
a person who is entrusted with a client's money for investment purposes

Investment Schemes:
when a broker or financial planner sells false investments

> **Box 8.17   BERNARD MADOFF**
>
> One of the most notable examples of an extensive investment scheme was that committed by Bernard Madoff. Madoff was an investment advisor to whom many individuals gave the authority to invest their money in ventures that Madoff advised would be profitable for them. However, Madoff never actually made any of the investments on behalf of his clients. He, and possibly other individuals and companies, took all the money from the investors in what is called a **Ponzi scheme**. A Ponzi scheme is defined as "an investment fraud that involves the payment of purported returns to existing investors from funds contributed by new investors" (U.S. Securities and Exchange Commission 2009).
>
> Madoff's operation has been classified as the largest and most extensive Ponzi scheme in history. Many of the investors in his Ponzi scheme lost millions of dollars' worth of investment money, and the cumulative losses from Madoff's actions have been estimated in excess of $18 billion. In June 2009, Madoff pleaded guilty to 11 charges, including securities fraud, investment advisor fraud, mail fraud, wire fraud, perjury, making false statements, theft from a retirement plan, three counts of money laundering, and filing false documents with the Securities and Exchange Commission. He was sentenced to 150 years in federal prison, the maximum sentence for which he was eligible.
>
> **Ponzi Scheme:**
> an investment fraud that involves the payment of purported returns to existing investors from funds contributed by new investors

obtaining inside information that the company had received an adverse decision from the Food and Drug Administration.

CYBERCRIME

No one can deny the prevalence of the Internet in today's society. Seventy-nine percent of adults and 93 percent of adolescents use the Internet regularly, and 46 percent of people use at least one social networking site (Pew Internet & American Life Project 2010). Computers and the Internet are now used extensively for such tasks as social and business networking, conducting business meetings, and engaging in financial transactions. The Internet allows individuals to engage with other people in many ways, both socially and professionally, that they would never have the ability to interact with otherwise.

However, as society has become more dependent upon technology, cybercrimes have become a significant issue for the criminal justice system. Cybercriminals are able to take advantage of the fact that people now conduct a large amount business over the computer, and use it to commit cybercrimes. A **cybercrime** is a traditional crime that is committed through the use of advanced technology. An act is generally considered a cybercrime when an electronic device (usually a computer) is used to commit a crime, is the target of a crime, or both.

Cybercrime:
use of computers or other electronic devices as a means of committing a crime or as the target of the crime

Most traditional crimes can become cybercrimes when they are committed through the use of electronic devices or other advanced technology. Even when they are not used directly to commit a crime, computers may be used in the facilitation of or preparation for crimes such as drug deals, murders, larceny, burglary, fencing of stolen property, and prostitution. As computers become increasingly necessary for conducting everyday business, the occurrence of accompanying cybercrimes increases as well.

There are several important points to note about cybercrimes. First, the *MPC* was most recently revised in 1985 (before computers were a mainstay in American society), and it does not address cybercrimes. Therefore, this section will approach cybercrimes through existing federal law. Second, the prevalence of cybercrime is almost certainly underestimated due to lack of information about cybercrimes, the tremendous reliance of society on the Internet, and the problems law enforcement agencies encounter in dealing with cybercrime. Third, the Internet is an extremely difficult place for law enforcement to operate effectively. The anonymity of the Internet seems to create an environment that encourages criminal activity. People experience significantly less self-consciousness in online interactions and will often do things online that they would not do in face-to-face encounters. This anonymity and decreased inhibition is called **deindividuation**, and it is a significant factor in the development of many cybercrimes (Rowland 2000).

Deindividuation: the anonymity and decreased social inhibition that people experience in online interactions

Internet access is cheap and readily available to almost anyone. Unlike traditional face-to-face crimes, the Internet allows cybercriminals to reach people who are located anywhere in the world. This gives cybercriminals a vast selection of potential victims. This is compounded by the ever-increasing amount of easily accessible information available online. Personal data are readily available through social networking sites as well as official information sources such as tax rolls, housing departments, and other government records.

The enforcement of cybercrime laws presents many issues for law enforcement and the legal system. Cybercrime is a relatively new area of the law. Therefore, the criminal justice system has less experience with enforcing and prosecuting violations of these laws. As computer technology changes rapidly, so also do the cybercriminals' strategies. Also, because of the Internet's widespread nature, many cybercrimes have a perpetrator and a victim who are located in different legal jurisdictions, which creates prosecution and punishment challenges.

Cybercrime encompasses a wide variety of activities. Almost any "traditional" crime becomes a cybercrime when it is committed by using a computer or electronic device, or when a computer becomes the target of the crime. Box 8.18 outlines the elements of cybercrime

---

Box 8.18 ELEMENTS OF CYBERCRIMES

Actus Reus	*Mens Rea*
• Committing a "traditional" crime through the use of the Internet, computer, or other electronic device	• Required *mens rea* for the traditional (non-cyber) offense

Concurrence

Linking of *actus reus* and *mens rea*

---

and illustrates the large spectrum of activity that its definition encompasses. Cybercrime is closely connected to many other areas of criminal enterprise, including terrorism, white collar crime, and organized crime. For instance, aspects of terrorism may be committed through the use of a computer. Financial crime is frequently perpetrated through the use of a computer. Even more complex, terrorism may be a financial cybercrime when the financing for terrorist activities is conducted by transferring money illegally through computer use. As you can see, these areas of the criminal law are closely interwoven and connected. The following sections provide a discussion of some of the most common and prevalent forms of cybercrime. Again, this is not a comprehensive list, and it is important to remember that our concepts of cybercrime are constantly growing and expanding because (1) almost any crime can become a cybercrime when a computer is used in its commission, and (2) the technology that is used in the commission of cybercrimes is evolving and advancing at a rapid rate.

Hacking

The *actus reus* of **hacking** is the invasion of a computer or computer system without obtaining appropriate permission. The *mens rea* of hacking is committing this action intentionally or willfully. Hacking is more formally known as **cybertrespassing**. Hacking may be committed to complete a wide variety of other crimes. Hacking into computer systems is often done to commit financial crimes by making unauthorized money transfers or purchases. Hacking may also be committed to obtain or alter confidential information that will be used for some criminal purpose. Although it is a crime on its own, hacking is generally committed as a gateway method to perpetrate other crimes. Hacking into individual computers or larger computer systems may assist in the commission of underlying financial crimes,

Hacking/Cybertrespassing: invasion of a computer or computer system without obtaining appropriate permission

data theft, identity theft, cyberterrorism, cyberstalking, and other offenses. Hacking may also take place as a game or contest among computer enthusiasts to see who is able to gain access to the most secure computer systems.

Phishing

Once an initial incident of hacking has been completed, personal or confidential information may be obtained through a form of fraud called **phishing**. Like hacking, phishing often takes place to perpetrate other crimes, such as information theft or financial fraud. Phishing may also involve obtaining secure information through the communication of misleading information to a victim. Often, individuals are sent unsolicited emails stating that information is needed to complete a business transaction, prevent the shutdown of their bank accounts, or some other purpose that appears legitimate (see Figure 8.1). Once the individual sends the requested information, the data are used for a wide variety of purposes, most often unauthorized financial transactions.

Phishing:
obtaining a person's confidential information over the Internet in order to perpetrate other crimes

> From: ***** [mailto:customer service@yourbank.com]
> Sent: September 30, 2011 03:31 PM
> To: 123@abc.net
> Subject: Official information regarding your bank account
>
> ---
>
> Dear Bank Customer!
>
> For security purposes your account needs to be verified. In order to verify your account, please provide us with the necessary data regarding your bank account. If we cannot verify your identity, your bank account will be frozen and your access to your finances will be denied. Please click on the link provided to verify your account information.
>
> Thank you for your attention.

FIGURE 8.1
Example of Phishing Email

Identity Theft

Identity theft is one of the most common crimes committed in the United States. In 2010, 11.1 million people experienced identity theft and that number has increased each year. The financial losses for identity theft exceeded $54 billion in 2010 (Javelin Strategy & Research 2010). Identity theft may take place in many different ways, such as obtaining information through the mail, business databases, financial institutions, government records, and other sources of personal information.

All 50 states have enacted statutes that criminalize identity theft. Most of these state statutes classify identity theft as a felony. At the federal level, identity theft is prohibited by the **Identity Theft and Assumption Deterrence Act of 1998** (18 U.S.C. § 1028). This act defines the *actus reus* of identity theft as the transfer or use of, without lawful authority, a means of identification of another person. The *mens rea* of identity theft is committing this act knowingly, and with the "intent to commit, or to aid or abet, any unlawful activity that constitutes a violation of Federal law, or that constitutes a felony under any State or applicable local law."

Identity theft is particularly devastating for victims because of the many complex issues in regulating this crime. Additionally, there is a lengthy and often frustrating process of correcting the damage caused by identity theft. Victims often face issues in being taken seriously by law enforcement and going through the long process of restoring their identity. Many identity theft victims never completely recover from the damage. Even beyond the $54 billion price tag, there are other indirect costs of identity theft. Identity theft victims face extensive issues, including emotional damage; loss of trust; damage to their business and personal contacts; lost business opportunities; financial devastation; and false criminal accusations.

Identity Theft:
a crime in which a person makes improper use of another person's identity, usually for financial gain

Identity Theft and Assumption Deterrence Act of 1998:
federal law that defines and prohibits identity theft

Denial of Service Attacks

Denial of service (DoS) attacks occur when a cybercriminal prevents a person or a business from making appropriate and productive use of a computer system. This is most commonly performed by either overloading a system's bandwidth or sending a deluge of emails to overload the email inbox, making the computer functions virtually useless. DoS attacks are frequently targeted at businesses such as banks, credit businesses, investment firms, and even government agencies.

The primary purpose of a DoS attack is to stop the normal course of business by disabling vital computer functions. Common types of DoS attacks include teardrop attacks, which cause a system to crash due to vulnerabilities in the system's reassembly codes; ICMP Floods,

Denial of Service (DoS) Attacks:
cybercrime that prevents the appropriate and productive use of a computer system

which send massive amounts of information to a system and overextend the bandwidth; and SYN Floods, which deluge a system with partial but incomplete network connections. Denial of service attacks are regulated by the **Computer Fraud and Abuse Act.** However, this Act only extends to computers that belong to the U.S. government, financial institutions, or those that are used in interstate commerce.

Computer Fraud and Abuse Act:
law that regulates denial of service attacks and applies to computers belonging to the U.S. government, financial institutions, and those used in interstate commerce

Cyberpornography

The Internet has changed the face and operation of the pornography industry. While once dominated by tangible magazines and videos, an abundance of pornographic material is available on the Internet. While much **cyberpornography** is not illegal, the distribution of some materials over the Internet has significant legal ramifications. This is particularly true of child pornography, which is illegal in the United States.

Several legal measures, including the **Child Pornography Prevention Act of 1996**, the **Child Online Protection Act of 1998**, and the **Children's Internet Protection Act of 2000**, have been introduced in an attempt to protect children from online pornography. Two major portions of the Child Pornography Prevention Act of 1996 were struck down as free speech violations in *Ashcroft v. Free Speech Coalition*, 535 U.S. 234 (2002). The Child Online Protection Act of 1998 also encountered challenges based upon First Amendment issues and was deemed unconstitutional in *Ashcroft v. American Civil Liberties Union*, 535 U.S. 564 (2004). Excerpts from this case can be found in Box 8.19. Although the Children's Internet Protection Act of 2000 faced similar First Amendment challenges, the U.S. Supreme Court held it to be constitutional. This law requires that all public elementary, middle, and high schools take appropriate measures to prevent children from viewing online pornography as a condition of receiving federal funding.

Cyberpornography:
the distribution of pornographic material over the Internet

Box 8.19   THE FIRST AMENDMENT IMPLICATIONS OF ONLINE PORNOGRAPHY LEGISLATION

Ashcroft v. American Civil Liberties Union
535 U.S. 564 (2004)

When plaintiffs challenge a content-based speech restriction, the Government has the burden to prove that the proposed alternatives will not be as effective as the challenged statute. The purpose of the test is to ensure that speech is restricted no further than is necessary to accomplish Congress' goal. The District Court's conclusion that respondents were likely to prevail was not an abuse of discretion, because, on the record, the

Government has not met its burden. Most importantly, respondents propose that blocking and filtering software is a less restrictive alternative, and the Government had not shown it would be likely to disprove that contention at trial. Filters impose selective restrictions on speech at the receiving end, not universal restrictions at the source. Under a filtering regime, childless adults may gain access to speech they have a right to see without having to identify themselves or provide their credit card information. Even adults with children may obtain access to the same speech on the same terms simply by turning off the filter on their home computers. Promoting filter use does not condemn as criminal any category of speech, and so the potential chilling effect is eliminated, or at least much diminished. Filters, moreover, may well be more effective than COPA. First, the record demonstrates that a filter can prevent minors from seeing all pornography, not just pornography posted to the Web from America. That COPA does not prevent minors from accessing foreign harmful materials alone makes it possible that filtering software might be more effective in serving Congress' goals. COPA's effectiveness is likely to diminish even further if it is upheld, because providers of the materials covered by the statute simply can move their operations overseas. In addition, the District Court found that verification systems may be subject to evasion and circumvention, e.g., by minors who have their own credit cards. Finally, filters also may be more effective because they can be applied to all forms of Internet communication, including e-mail, not just the World Wide Web. Filtering's superiority to COPA is confirmed by the explicit findings of the Commission on Child Online Protection, which Congress created to evaluate the relative merits of different means of restricting minors' ability to gain access to harmful materials on the Internet. Although filtering software is not a perfect solution because it may block some materials not harmful to minors and fail to catch some that are, the Government has not satisfied its burden to introduce specific evidence proving that filters are less effective. The argument that filtering software is not an available alternative because Congress may not require its use carries little weight, since Congress may act to encourage such use by giving strong incentives to schools and libraries, and by promoting the development of filters by industry and their use by parents . . . absent a showing that a less restrictive technological alternative already available to parents would not be as effective as a blanket speech restriction, the more restrictive option preferred by Congress could not survive strict scrutiny. [This] compel[s] the Court to affirm the preliminary injunction here. To do otherwise would be to do less than the First Amendment commands.

1. Was the Supreme Court correct in deeming the Child Online Protection Act a violation of the First Amendment right to free speech? Should adults be given an unrestricted right to view this type of material?

2. Are filters for online content a reasonable alternative to legislation addressing online pornography? Are filters sufficient to protect minor children from the dangers of online pornography?

3. Is legislation the correct method of attempting to protect certain populations from harmful online content? Is it possible for this type of legislation to be effective?

Internet Gambling

Internet gambling is any wagering activity that takes place over the Internet. Internet gambling is also known as iGambling or online gambling. Internet gambling includes activity in Internet casinos, such as online poker games. It also includes online sports betting, as well as the transfer of money among Internet gambling participants and financial institutions.

Over 12 million people around the world regularly participate in some form of Internet gambling. Approximately 5.3 million of these people are U.S. citizens (Tedeschi 2003). Currently, all U.S. states prohibit online gambling (although the State of Nevada is preparing to legalize online gambling for Nevada residents only). The New Jersey legislature recently passed a law allowing online casinos to accept bets over the Internet for traditional casino games, but it did not allow placing sports bets over the Internet (Bill S490). However, this bill was vetoed by New Jersey Governor Chris Christie, and therefore has yet to take effect.

At the federal level, Internet gambling is prohibited by the **Unlawful Internet Gambling Enforcement Act**, or UIGEA (31 U.S.C. § 5363), which was passed in 2006. This act specifically prohibits all forms of Internet gambling in the United States. However, there have been problems in the interpretation and enforcement of the UIGEA. Despite this law, Internet gambling continues to flourish. Internet gambling businesses made over $12 billion in revenue in 2005, and that number is expected to continue to grown substantially (Shaker 2006).

Internet Gambling: any wagering activity that takes place over the Internet; also known as online gambling

Unlawful Internet Gambling Enforcement Act: federal law passed in 2006 that specifically prohibits all forms of Internet gambling in the United States

Cyberstalking

Of the 3.4 million people who are stalked every year, 26 percent are stalked over the Internet (Baum et al. 2009). Stalking is defined as "a course of conduct that places a person in fear for their safety" (National Center for Victims of Crime 2010). Stalking involves repeated behavior by which the perpetrator intends to cause physical or psychological damage to the victim (Purcell, Pathe, and Mullen 2004; Roberts 2008). The *actus reus* of **cyberstalking** is "the use of the Internet, email, or other electronic communications to create a criminal level of intimidation, harassment, and fear" (Pittaro 2007). The *mens rea* is that perpetrators intend or reasonably know that their actions could cause physical or psychological damage (Purcell, Pathe, and Mullen 2004). Cyberstalking is most commonly conducted through email, instant messaging, message boards, GPS, or technological surveillance (Baum et al. 2009). Cyberstalking often involves communications that contain

Cyberstalking: the use of the Internet, email, or other electronic communications to create a criminal level of intimidation, harassment, and fear

harassing, offensive, or brutal messages. This may include traditional messages, as well as pictures, videos, and even destructive viruses.

Private cyberstalking is unwanted or harassing communication that takes place only between the victim and the perpetrator. By contrast, **public cyberstalking** takes place when the perpetrator posts damaging or embarrassing information about the victim in public electronic forums such as social media sites, blogs, or message boards (Roberts 2008). Cyberstalking encompasses a huge range of activity. Cyberstalkers often make threats or engage in **cyber-smearing**, which is an online effort to damage the victim's reputation. Cyberstalkers may engage in hacking or identity theft to obtain a victim's information (Pittaro 2007). Another noteworthy trend is **third-party cyberstalking**, in which the cyberstalker does not engage in the harassing activity himself or herself, but instead encourages others to stalk the victim over the Internet (Bocij and McFarlane 2003).

Cyberstalking is prohibited by the **Interstate Stalking Punishment and Prevention Act of 1996** (ISPPA). In response to the growing issue of cyberstalking, the ISPPA was amended in 2006, and now prohibits using "any interactive computer service, or any facility of interstate or foreign commerce" to commit any act that would cause a victim to experience "substantial emotional distress to that person or [place] that person in reasonable fear" [Violence Against Women Act, 42 U.S.C. §§ 13925-14045 (1994)]. Box 8.20 presents a scenario for you to decide whether or not cyberstalking has taken place. Cyberstalking is a significant issue for the justice system because of its potential for escalation into further violence, as was the case in Amy Boyer's 1999 murder by Liam Youens (see Box 8.21).

Private Cyberstalking: unwanted or harassing communication that takes place only between the victim and the perpetrator

Public Cyberstalking: unwanted or harassing communication that takes place when the perpetrator posts damaging or embarrassing information about the victim in public electronic forums

Cyber-Smearing: an attempt to damage a victim's reputation through online communications

Third-Party Cyberstalking: cyberstalking activity in which the perpetrator does not engage in the harassing activity, but instead encourages others to stalk the victim over the Internet

Interstate Stalking Punishment and Prevention Act of 1996: cyberstalking legislation that prohibits using a computer in a way that causes another person fear or emotional distress

---

Box 8.20 YOU DECIDE: IS THIS A CASE OF CYBERSTALKING?

Elizabeth and Todd have been acquaintances for some time, but have never really gotten to know one another. Unknown to Todd, Elizabeth is smitten with him and wants to develop a more serious relationship. In order to pursue Todd, Elizabeth starts sending him flirtatious emails, text messages, and postings on his Facebook page, to which she gets no response. Finally, Todd tells Elizabeth that he is not interested in her and to please stop her electronic communications with him. This makes Elizabeth even more determined to make Todd want a relationship with her, so she increases the number and the sexual explicitness of her communications to Todd. After still receiving no positive response from Todd, Elizabeth begins posting derogatory comments about him on his Facebook page, which cause other people to treat Todd badly and to socially shun him. Is Elizabeth guilty of cyberstalking?

Box 8.21 THE DANGERS OF CYBERSTALKING: LIAM YOUENS

One of the most significant problems with cyberstalking is that it is frequently followed by more frequent and destructive occurrences of violence. This can be observed in the 1999 murder of Amy Boyer. Liam Youens had become obsessed with Amy in high school and had stalked her over the Internet for several years. During this time, Youens created a website that described his obsession with her. In addition to pictures and other writings, the website also contained a detailed description of how Youens planned to kill Amy.

Several days before her death, Youens utilized an Internet information service to obtain Amy's Social Security number, date of birth, address, place of employment, and other personal information. On October 15, 1999, Youens went to the office where Amy worked and fatally shot her as she was getting into her car. Youens then killed himself. Amy Boyer's death illustrates the dangers of cyberstalking, particularly the significant possibility that cyberstalking will transition into traditional stalking behavior and lead to violence against the victim.

Cyberbullying

Another Internet-based crime that has received significant attention in recent years is **cyberbullying**. Cyberbullying is defined as "willful and repeated harm inflicted through the use of computers, cell phones, and other electronic devices" (Cyberbullying Research Center 2012). Although cyberbullying takes place among various age groups, it is particularly prevalent among adolescents and teenagers. It is believed that cyberbullying impacts approximately 50 percent of U.S. teenagers (National Crime Prevention Association 2006).

> **Cyberbullying:** willful and repeated harm inflicted through the use of computers, cell phones, and other electronic devices

People who engage in cyberbullying may (1) pretend to be another person while using the Internet or cell phones; (2) spread rumors and untrue information about victims; (3) convince people to reveal personal information about themselves; (4) send malicious messages over the computer or cell phone; or (5) post pictures or other information without the victim's consent (National Crime Prevention Association 2006). Cyberbullying may also include unwanted contact through the Internet or cell phones, or revealing personal and embarrassing information about a victim through an online forum or electronic device. These actions are intended to hurt or embarrass the victim. As of 2012, 14 states had adopted cyberbullying legislation (Cyberbullying Research Center 2012). Box 8.22 describes a high-profile case in which a young girl committed suicide after being cyberbullied by a former friend's mother.

Cyberextortion

People are guilty of extortion if they "obtain property of another by threatening to inflict bodily injury on anyone, accuse anyone of a

---

Box 8.22   CYBERBULLYING IN THE NEWS: LORI DREW

One case that gave cyberbullying national attention was the 2006 suicide of 13-year-old Megan Meier after she was cyberbullied by 49-year-old Lori Drew. The Meiers and the Drews were neighbors, and Drew's daughter had previously been a friend of Megan's. Because Drew was worried that Megan was spreading rumors about her daughter, she set up a fictitious MySpace account under the name "Josh Evans." The profile of Josh Evans stated that he was a 16-year-old boy. For several months, Megan engaged in flirtatious online contact with Josh Evans. Eventually, Drew, posing as Josh Evans, told Megan that the world would be a better place without her. Several other fictional MySpace identities associated with Josh Evans also began to harass Megan. On October 16, 2006, Megan Meier was found dead from hanging herself in her closet. In 2008, Lori Drew was found guilty of violating the Computer Fraud and Abuse Act, but the conviction was overturned. Megan Meier's suicide led several states to enact legislation that specifically prohibited cyberbullying.

---

criminal offense, expose any secret that would subject the person to hatred, contempt or ridicule, or impair his credit or business repute . . . or inflict any other harm that would not benefit the actor" (American Law Institute 1985:§ 223.4). **Cyberextortion** occurs when an individual engages in this behavior through the use of the Internet or other electronic device.

A common cyberextortion scenario is when a cybercriminal illegally obtains a company's electronic files or confidential information, and then demands a large payoff for not destroying or releasing the files. Incidents of cyberextortion are more frequently targeted at businesses than individuals, as businesses generally have the financial means and motivation to comply with a payoff demand to prevent damage to the company, its data, and overall profitability.

Cyberextortion: obtaining someone else's property through threats of future harm that are communicated through the use of the Internet or other electronic device

Cyberterrorism

Terrorist groups now rely heavily on computers and technology to carry out their goals, and this is known as **cyberterrorism**. One type of cyberterrorism takes place when terrorists target government computers and computer systems. This is often done to retrieve classified information or to halt government functions due to an absence of network systems. Attacking or shutting down government computers may significantly damage the population by targeting things such as public services, public transportation, government paychecks and employee benefits, financial institutions, emergency services, telephone, Internet services, and many other public and government functions.

Cyberterrorism: carrying out terroristic objectives by using computers as either a target of or means of facilitating terrorism

Computers may also be used to aid in committing more traditional terrorism. One example is the use of computers or network systems to facilitate financial transactions used to fund terrorist activities. The expanding ability to communicate brought about by computers and electronic devices has also increased terrorists' ability to communicate among themselves regarding their operations, thus allowing them to carry out their activities more effectively.

As with most cybercrimes, there is significant overlap between cyberterrorism and other cybercriminal activity. Cyberterrorism may take place in the form of hacking, DoS attacks, cyberextortion, and other Internet-based crimes. As is the case with traditional terrorism, what sets cyberterrorism apart from other cybercrimes is that the underlying cybercrime (hacking, cyberextortion, DoS attacks, etc.) is committed with a political or ideological motivation for bringing about the resulting harm.

SUMMARY

Crimes against the state, white collar crimes, and cybercrimes are part of an emerging and developing area of the criminal law. Many of these crimes are committed in conjunction with one another, and there are significant areas of overlap among these three classifications. Each encompasses a broad spectrum of criminal activity, much of which is constantly developing and evolving.

Crimes against the state have been heavily regulated since the formation of the United States. These crimes are particularly unique in that they are directed at an entire nation, rather than a distinct victim. Crimes against the state are committed as the result of political, religious, or ideological motives, and they are primarily regulated by federal laws. Crimes against the state include treason, sedition, sabotage, espionage, and terrorism. Statutes regulating crimes against the state have evolved significantly throughout American history, from the first mention of treason in the U.S. Constitution to the USA PATRIOT Act, passed as a response to the terrorist acts of September 11, 2001.

An area of the criminal law that has gained national attention during recent years is white collar crime. Although many people perceive crime as being confined primarily to lower socioeconomic classes, crimes committed by professionals such as Bernard Ebbers, Martha Stewart, Bernard Madoff, Kenneth Lay, and Jeffrey Skilling have shed light on white collar crimes that exist throughout class structures. Since many white collar crimes take place within a person's employment context, they are often referred to as abuse of trust crimes.

White collar crime is particularly significant because of the expanding impact that it has on large numbers of people. When a company executive commits illegal acts, those acts can damage the company's employees, investors, and the larger financial market. The extent of white collar crime is most likely underestimated drastically, and law enforcement officials face significant challenges in detecting the commission of these crimes. Although rarely invoked, corporations may be held criminally liable when someone commits a criminal act in the scope of their employment or for the benefit of the corporation. High-profile cases of white collar crime, and the significant devastation that many people experienced as a result, have led to the passage of white collar crime regulations such as the Sarbanes-Oxley Act of 2002.

As the world has begun using computers and electronic communication at an expanding rate, this technology has been exploited by criminals who use it to commit cybercrimes. Almost any traditional crime can become a cybercrime when it is committed through the use of a computer, or when a computer is the target of the criminal act. Because of the remote nature of cybercrimes, there are many challenges in enforcing laws that regulate and punish this criminal activity. The number of cybercrimes that take place each year is greatly underestimated due to a low rate of victim reporting for crimes that take place online. The number of cybercrimes committed annually is growing, due to the Internet's conducive environment for committing crime, as well as the reduced level of personal inhibition that people experience through the use of computers. Cybercrime includes an almost endless list of activities that grows continuously, and some of the most common and threatening forms of cybercrime include hacking, phishing, identity theft, DoS attacks, cyberpornography, Internet gambling, cyberstalking, cyberextortion, and cyberterrorism.

KEY TERMS

abuse of trust crime
broker-dealer fraud
Child Online Protection Act of 1998
Child Pornography Prevention Act of 1996
Children's Internet Protection Act of 2000
Computer Fraud and Abuse Act
corporate crime
crimes against the state
cyberbullying

cybercrime
cyberextortion
cyberpornography
cyber-smearing
cyberstalking
cyberterrorism
cybertrespassing
deindividuation
denial of service (DoS) attacks
espionage
Espionage Act of 1917

federal law
fiduciary relationship
financial planner
fraud
hacking
identity theft
Identity Theft and Assumption
    Deterrence Act of 1998
ideological motivation
insider trading
Internet gambling
Interstate Stalking Punishment
    and Prevention Act of 1996
investment schemes
occupational crime
phishing
political motivation
Ponzi scheme
private cyberstalking

public cyberstalking
religious motivation
roving wiretaps
sabotage
Sarbanes-Oxley Act of 2002
securities fraud
sedition
Smith Act
stockbroker
stock parking
tax fraud
terrorism
third-party cyberstalking
treason
two-witness rule
Unlawful Internet Gambling
    Enforcement Act
USA PATRIOT Act
white collar crime

CRITICAL THINKING QUESTIONS

1. Discuss some of the historical events and social factors that have influenced and changed laws that govern crimes against the state. What are some of the advantages and disadvantages to allowing these events to heavily impact changes in the law?

2. Explain the requirements that must be met before an individual can be convicted of treason. Since this is a very difficult standard to meet, should the requirements be lessened in order to allow more convictions of those who have been disloyal to the nation? Explain your reasoning.

3. How should the government balance the competing interests of individual privacy and defending the nation against terrorism? What factors should be taken into account when making this type of decision? Explain your reasoning.

4. Discuss the far-reaching impact that white collar crime has on the American public. Suggest at least two ways that would help the government and law enforcement combat this

growing problem, and explain why you believe they would be effective.

5. Because white collar criminals are often members of higher socioeconomic classes, they are frequently in a better position to fight criminal charges due to the ability to hire top attorneys, work with legal consultants, pay large legal fees, and other advantages. Should there be a response to this from the criminal justice system in order to level the playing field? If so, what should the response be? Explain your reasoning.

6. In general, is cybercrime more or less dangerous than "traditional" crime? Which has the ability to inflict the most significant amount of harm upon the victims? Explain your reasoning.

7. As discussed in the chapter, cybercrime is extremely difficult for law enforcement officials to detect and for the legal system to prosecute and punish. Suggest at least three measures that could be taken within the criminal justice system to improve the management of cybercrime. Why do you feel that these measures would be effective? Be specific and explain your reasoning.

SUGGESTED READINGS

Brenner, S.W. (2010). *Cybercrime: Criminal Threats from Cyberspace*. Westport, CT: Praeger. In this book, Brenner gives a comprehensive legal overview of cybercrime that exists around the world. She explores the various challenges associated with regulating cybercrime, and also places cybercrime into the overall pictures of criminal law and procedure.

Chaliand, G. & Blin, A. (2007). *The History of Terrorism: From Antiquity to al Qaeda*. Berkeley: University of California Press. This book gives an outstanding explanation of the historical roots of terrorism and their application to modern-day crimes against the state. The authors discuss how terrorism has shaped warfare since the beginning of time and the ways that various terror strategies have been implemented to achieve a particular objective. The authors explore the various forms of terrorism that were used during the Middle Ages, European revolutions and war movements, the World Wars, and numerous other historical and modern conflicts.

Friedrichs, D.O. (2009). *Trusted Criminals: White Collar Crime in Contemporary Society* (4th ed.). Belmont, CA: Wadsworth. Friedrichs presents a comprehensive overview of white collar crime and its far-reaching effects on contemporary society. This book discusses the problems associated with investigating and prosecuting white collar crime, in addition to the challenges that come from within the legal system. Friedrichs explores the ways that white collar crime can be perpetrated within a wide variety of professional scenarios, not just those that we traditionally think of as "white collar."

McQuade, S.C. (2008). *Encyclopedia of Cybercrime*. Westport, CT: Greenwood Press. As new cybercrimes continue to develop, so too does the jargon that is used to identify and describe these crimes. This book helps keep the terminology organized and provides a concise description of each term. The book also provides a detailed timeline of historical events relevant to cybercrime and its regulation.

Meeropol, M., editor (1994). *The Rosenberg Letters: A Complete Edition of the Correspondence of Julius and Ethel Rosenberg*. Routledge. This book contains all known letters and correspondence from Julius and Ethel Rosenberg during the three years they were in Sing Sing Prison before their executions in 1953. The letters include those that were written to one another, to their children, and to their attorney.

REFERENCES

American Law Institute (1985). *Model Penal Code: Complete Statutory Text*. Philadelphia, PA.

Ashcroft v. American Civil Liberties Union, 535 U.S. 564 (2004).

Ashcroft v. Free Speech Coalition, 535 U.S. 234 (2002).

Baum, K., Catalano, S., Rand, M. & Rose, K. (2009). *Stalking Victimization in the United States*. Washington, DC: U.S. Department of Justice, National Institute of Justice.

Bocij, P. & McFarlane, L. (2003). "Cyberstalking: The Technology of Hate." *Police Journal* 76:204-221.

Center for Corporate Policy (2011). "Corporate Crime and Abuse: Tracking the Problem." http://www.corporatepolicy.org/issues/crime data.htm.

Cramer v. United States, 325 U.S. 1 (1945).

Cyberbullying Research Center (2012). http://www.cyberbullying.us/.

Espionage Act of 1917, 18 U.S.C. § 792 (1917).

Identity Theft and Assumption Deterrence Act of 1998, 18 U.S.C. § 1028 (1998).

Javelin Strategy & Research (2010). "2010 Identity Fraud Survey Report: Consumer Version." February. https://www.javelinstrategy.com/uploads/files/1004.R_2010IdentityFraudSurvey Consumer.pdf.

National Center for Victims of Crime (2010). "Stalking: What Is Stalking?" http://victimsof crime.org/our-programs/stalking-resource-center/stalking-information#what.

National Crime Prevention Association (2006). "Cyber-bullying." http://www.ncpc.org/cyber bullying.

New York Central & Hudson River Railroad Company v. United States, 212 U.S. 481 (1909).

Pew Internet & American Life Project (2010). "Demographic of Internet Users." http:// www. http://pewinternet.org/Trend-Data-(Adults)/Whos-Online.aspx.

Pittaro, M.L. (2007). "Cyber Stalking: An Analysis of Online Harassment and Intimidation." *International Journal of Cyber Criminology* 1(2):180-197.

Purcell, R., Pathe, M. & Mullen, P.E. (2004). "Stalking: Defining and Prosecuting a New Category of Offending." *International Journal of Law and Psychiatry* 27(2):157-169.

Reiss, A. & Biderman, A. (1980). *Data Sources on White Collar Lawbreaking*. Washington, DC: National Institute of Justice.

Roberts, L. (2008). "Jurisdictional and Definitional Concerns with Computer-Mediated Interpersonal Crimes: An Analysis on Cyber Stalking." *International Journal of Cyber Criminology* 2(1):271-285.

Rowland, D. (2000). "Anonymity, Privacy, and Cyberspace." Paper presented at the 15th Annual BILETA Conference: "Electronic Datasets and Access to Legal Information." April 14. http://www.bileta.ac.uk/content/files/conference%20papers/2000/Anonymity,%20Privacy%20and%20Cyberspace.pdf.

Sabotage, 18 U.S.C § 2153 (1948).

Sarbanes-Oxley Act of 2002, 107 P.L. 204 (2002).

Shaker, P. (2007). "America's Bad Bet: How the Unlawful Internet Gambling Enforcement Act of 2006 Will Hurt the House." *Fordham Journal of Corporate and Financial Law* 12(6):1183-1203.

Smith Act, 18 U.S.C. § 2385 (1940).

Spence-Diehl, E. (2003). "Stalking and Technology: The Double-Edged Sword." *Journal of Technology in Human Services* 22(1):5-18.

Tedeschi, B. (2003). "E-Commerce Report: Congress Wants to Put More Restrictions on Online Gambling, and the Sites Look for Ways Around the Rules." *New York Times*, March 31, p. C6.

Terrorism, 28 C.F.R. § 0.85 (1969).

Terrorism, 18 U.S.C. § 2332 (1986).

Unlawful Internet Gambling Enforcement Act, 31 U.S.C. §§ 5361-5367 (2006).

U.S. Securities and Exchange Commission (2009). "Ponzi Schemes." http://www.sec.gov/answers/ponzi.htm.

Violence Against Women Act, 42 U.S.C. §§ 13925-14045 (1994).

Yates v. United States, 354 U.S. 298 (1957).

Inchoate Crimes

LEARNING OBJECTIVES

After reading this chapter you should be able to:

1. Discuss and explain the rationale for punishing inchoate crimes, as well as the debate over this approach
2. Define and explain the acts that constitute a criminal attempt
3. Define and explain the acts that constitute a criminal conspiracy
4. Define and explain the acts that constitute a criminal solicitation
5. Explain and analyze the consequences of the merger doctrine
6. Characterize and describe the various defenses that may be available to those accused of inchoate offenses

INTRODUCTION

Now that you have a more complete understanding of the elements of a number of crimes, it is time to discuss another classification of criminal activity—inchoate crimes. "Inchoate" is a word that describes something still in its beginning or formation stage. Thus, **inchoate offenses** are crimes that have begun to be committed but have not yet been fully completed. Inchoate crimes are often referred to as **anticipatory offenses** because they take place with the expectation of fully completing a larger or more significant criminal act. The inchoate crimes that will be addressed in this chapter are attempt, conspiracy, and solicitation. When any of these crimes are committed, the perpetrator has the intent that his or her criminal conduct will conclude with the completion of the intended or underlying crime. However, for one reason or another, the intended crime is never fully completed. Thus, the perpetrator can instead be charged with the commission of one of the inchoate offenses, rather than with the commission of the crime that he or she intended to complete.

Inchoate Offenses / Anticipatory Offenses: crimes that have begun to be committed but have not yet been fully completed

AN OVERVIEW OF INCHOATE CRIMES

All inchoate crimes are associated with an intended but incomplete criminal act, which is called the **underlying offense** (or sometimes the target offense). For instance, recall the elements required for the completion of the crimes that have been discussed in previous chapters. A person may intend to complete a robbery and take action to rob someone, but ultimately fail to fully complete the robbery due to external circumstances. A group of individuals may conspire with one another to commit arson but fail to complete the arson because they are interrupted by something or someone in the process. Someone may solicit another person to commit a murder, but the person who is solicited does not actually follow through with the planned killing. When the commission of the underlying crime fails and is not actually completed, the person who has taken some action in furtherance of that crime may be charged with the inchoate crime (attempt, solicitation, or conspiracy) of the underlying offense. In these examples, the individuals involved in each scenario could be charged with attempted robbery, conspiracy to commit arson, and solicitation of murder, respectively. Think about the scenarios in Boxes 9.1, 9.2, and 9.3.

Underlying Offense: intended but incomplete criminal act that is associated with inchoate crimes

Box 9.1 YOU DECIDE: IS THIS A CRIME?

A woman decides that she wants to kill her husband in order to collect the proceeds of his life insurance. She develops a plan to kill him by putting strychnine (a lethal poison) in his food. She makes intricate decisions about the murder, such as what day is best to carry out the plan, as well as what she will say to medical personnel in order to exonerate herself. On the day that she has decided to carry out her plan, she makes her husband's favorite lasagna and puts a lethal amount of strychnine powder in the tomato sauce. She serves her husband his dinner with the intent that he will ingest enough of the poison to kill him shortly thereafter. However, before he begins eating, the husband receives an emergency phone call and has to leave their house. At that particular point in time, what is the wife's level of criminal liability? She certainly cannot be charged with her husband's murder because he is still alive. However, it seems reasonable that she should be held to some level of criminal accountability. Is she guilty of attempted homicide?

Box 9.2 YOU DECIDE: HAS A CRIME BEEN COMMITTED? IF SO, WHICH ONE?

A group of friends determine that the government is no longer meeting the needs of its citizens. They decide that it is necessary to remedy these issues, so they reach an agreement that they will work together to burn several government buildings. They begin gathering the materials needed to set fire to the buildings, and they spend time planning the specifics of the crime. However, before the group is able to complete the destruction of the government buildings, their criminal enterprise is discovered and they are apprehended by law enforcement. At this point in time, they cannot be charged with arson because no burning was actually carried out. Should these individuals be held criminally responsible for a criminal objective that was never actually completed? If they are criminally responsible, exactly what crime should they be held accountable for committing?

Box 9.3 YOU DECIDE: IS THIS PERSON GUILTY WHEN THE CRIME WAS NOT COMPLETED?

In a final illustration, an individual is involved in the cross-border drug trade due to its potential as a money-generating business. However, because of the complex nature of conducting a drug-trafficking operation, he must recruit other people to help with his criminal endeavor by offering some incentive for their participation. The drug trafficker approaches another man and asks for his help in smuggling the drugs through international airports. In exchange, the drug trafficker promises the man a significant cash payment. However, before the plot can proceed and before any drugs have been smuggled, the man who was approached is intercepted by law enforcement officials. At this point in time, what is the drug trafficker's level of criminal responsibility? Although the ultimate goal of the criminal endeavor (moving the drugs across international borders) never actually took place, it seems logical that the drug trafficker should have some level of criminal responsibility.

INCHOATE CRIMES PUNISHMENT DEBATE

Each of these scenarios raises a number of important and complicated questions that are associated with inchoate crimes. Should people be held criminally responsible for offenses that are never actually committed? After all, the criminal objective that they intended to carry out was never fully completed. Nevertheless, these people clearly had the intent to complete some type of crime, but failed to do so because of some external factor beyond their control. Should these individuals simply be released back into society without facing criminal punishment for what they intended to do? If people should be punished for inchoate crimes, how severe should the punishment be?

There has been a significant amount of debate about whether and how inchoate crimes should be punished when the crime that the person intends to commit or facilitate is never fully completed. One argument against punishing inchoate offenses is that people should not receive a criminal sanction when no actual harm has taken place. Another argument against punishment for inchoate offenses is that one of the most important tenets of the American legal system is that it is better for a guilty person to go free than for an innocent person to be punished for a crime that they did not commit. This is an issue closely associated with inchoate crimes because law enforcement has a considerable interest in exercising diligence in tracking and stopping criminal activity at the inchoate stages, before the actual crime is completed. This makes it more likely that a person could be punished for innocent activity that merely appears suspicious and resembles some type of criminal activity in the formation stages.

By contrast, one of the most significant reasons for allowing criminal punishment for inchoate offenses is because penalizing this activity has the potential to create a **deterrent effect** for the commission of other crimes. The idea of a deterrent effect is that if people see other individuals being punished for crimes that were not fully completed, they will have reason to abstain from engaging in similar criminal activity themselves. Another reason for punishing inchoate offenses is that while the intended offense was not fully completed, the person being punished is far from blameless. In fact, many argue that they are just as mentally culpable as those who fully complete criminal offenses since the reason that the underlying offense was not completed was due to circumstances beyond their own control. Had these outside conditions not prevailed, the underlying crime would have been completed as was intended by the culprit. Indeed, the rationale for punishing uncompleted crimes focuses on two primary areas of danger: those individuals who commit dangerous or criminal acts (*actus reus*) and those people who have a criminal mindset (*mens rea*). Although these may not result in the

Deterrent Effect:
idea that if people see others being punished for crimes that were not completed, they will have reason to abstain from engaging in similar criminal activity

full completion of any particular crime, these concerns are both legitimate threats to society that the criminal law has a strong interest in regulating and stopping.

Another issue that arises with inchoate crimes is that it is necessary for the law to make a distinction between someone who merely thinks about committing a crime and a person who actually takes an affirmative step toward completing that crime. Obviously, people cannot be punished for their thoughts alone, even thoughts of committing a crime. If people could be punished for fleeting thoughts of criminal activity, it is likely that a very significant portion of the world's population would be imprisoned. After all, many people probably imagine either committing a crime or the positive results that might arise from that criminal endeavor. However, very few of these people ever act upon these thoughts.

Some distinction has to be made between people's thoughts and any actions they actually take to make these thoughts a reality. It is the job of the legal system to determine exactly where that line is drawn and at what point people may be subjected to criminal punishment. It has been suggested that there are six steps that an individual goes through in the completion of a crime (Dressler 2009:379). During the first three steps of the process, a potential criminal (1) forms the idea of committing a crime, (2) assesses the potential crime, and (3) develops the objective of moving forward with the criminal endeavor. Many people abandon all notions of committing a crime during one of these initial steps. As long as no additional action is taken beyond these steps, the person has not committed a crime and cannot be criminally punished. However, during the final three steps, that person proceeds to (4) organize the commission of the crime, (5) begins the necessary steps of moving forward with the crime, and finally (6) commits the crime. It is during these last three steps that an individual can be punished to varying degrees for the action that he or she has taken in furtherance of committing a crime.

The reason that a person cannot be punished during the first three stages of the criminal process is that while there has been some amount of criminal thought, there has been no criminal action. Recall that the principle of **concurrence** requires a person to have a criminal *mens rea* at the same time as performing a criminal *actus reus*. This means that people can be punished for what they actually do, but not for what they merely think about doing. There has to be some amount of criminal action before a crime has been committed. For a person to be guilty of the crimes that were addressed in previous chapters, all six steps of criminal activity must have been completed. Once a person has taken these steps, he or she has completed the underlying offense and may be criminally punished accordingly. However, if a

Concurrence:
principle of criminal liability that a person must have a criminal *mens rea* at the same time that they perform a criminal *actus reus*

person has moved beyond the first three stages and is at stage four or five (having taken some action, but not yet completing the underlying offense), he or she may have completed a sufficient amount of activity to be held responsible for an inchoate crime. This raises the question of what quantity and quality of activity is necessary for a person to be punished for an inchoate offense.

ATTEMPT

Think for a moment about the elements that are required for the crimes we have discussed in previous chapters. There are a significant number of scenarios in which someone might complete several elements of a crime, but be forced to cease his or her actions before all elements of the crime were completed due to some external circumstance. A robbery is stopped short due to a third party's interference. A murder plot is foiled because the victim escapes. A drug sale is not completed due to law enforcement interception. The possibilities for crimes that are attempted but never completed are as numerous as the circumstances under which the crimes themselves may take place.

The *Model Penal Code* (*MPC*) states that an individual may be held responsible for an **attempt** when

> acting with the kind of culpability otherwise required for commission of the crime, he: (a) purposely engages in conduct that would constitute the crime if the attendant circumstances were as he believes them to be; or (b) when causing a particular result is an element of the crime, does or omits to do anything with the purpose of causing or with the belief that it will cause such result without further conduct on his part; or (c) purposely does or omits to do anything that, under the circumstances as he believes them to be, is an act or omission constituting a substantial step in a course of conduct planned to culminate in his commission of the crime. (American Law Institute 1985:74)

Attempt: when a person takes action to perform a criminal act but is stopped before the crime can be fully completed

Within this definition, the *MPC* classifies three different types of activity that may constitute a criminal attempt. The first is when people believe that what they are doing is a crime, but some external circumstance of which they are not aware prevents their action from being the crime they intended to commit. This type of attempt would take place when Bob is invited to Ann's house as a dinner guest. As Bob is getting ready to leave for the evening, he notices a lovely crystal vase on Ann's entry table. Bob tries to place the vase inside his jacket in order to take it for himself. Bob's attempt at stealing the vase is foiled when he is interrupted by another party guest. However, unbeknownst to Bob, Ann had placed the vase on the entry table in order to give it to Bob as a gift. In Bob's mind, he has attempted to commit the crime of theft. Although Bob has not really committed a theft because Ann intended to give him the vase, the circumstances were not what he believed. Because Bob has taken a substantial step toward completing what he believes to be a crime, and what would be a crime if the circumstances were as he thought, Bob can still be held accountable for attempted theft.

Another type of attempt takes place when "the actor has completed conduct that he expects to cause a proscribed result." For example, in order for a person to be guilty of murder, they must cause the death of another person. A man wishes to murder his wife and makes plans to shoot her when she enters their house one evening. On the night that he has planned to kill her, the wife enters their home, and the husband shoots her with the intent to cause her death (a proscribed result). However, the next-door neighbor hears the shot and immediately calls the paramedics. The paramedics arrive and are able to rush the wife to the hospital in time to save her life. Clearly, the husband expected that by shooting his wife, his actions would result in her death. However, since his actions did not actually cause his wife to die, he will instead be held responsible for attempted murder.

Another type of attempt takes place where the perpetrator has taken **substantial steps** toward the completion of a particular crime. One of the most significant aspects of applying the substantial steps test is being able to make a distinction between merely preparing for the commission of a crime and taking active steps

Substantial Steps: an affirmative act toward committing a crime that goes beyond merely preparing for the crime to be committed

---

Box 9.4   ELEMENTS OF ATTEMPT (*MPC*)

Actus Reus	*Mens Rea*
• Engaging in conduct that would constitute the crime if the circumstances were as the actor believes them to be OR • Completing conduct that the actor expects to cause a proscribed result OR • Taking substantial steps toward the completion of a crime	• Purpose to commit and fully complete the crime that was attempted

Concurrence

Linking of *actus reus* and *mens rea*

toward the completion of that crime. Box 9.4 outlines the elements of attempt.

Substantial Steps

The *MPC*'s substantial steps test leads to the question of just *how extensive* a step needs to be in order to hold someone criminally liable for an attempted crime. Is just thinking about the crime or developing a plan to commit the crime enough? Or does a person need to have completed all the necessary steps except for one final act? Does a person need to have pointed the gun and be just shy of pulling the trigger, or could he or she be guilty of attempted murder at some point prior to this final moment?

A substantial step requires some type of affirmative act that goes beyond merely preparing for the crime to be committed. An act is not considered a substantial step unless it is "strongly corroborative of the actor's criminal purpose." The action in question should clearly demonstrate that the person was acting to commit a specific crime. The following actions may be considered substantial steps if they support a criminal purpose:

(a) lying in wait, searching for, or following the contemplated victim of a crime;
(b) enticing or seeking to entice the contemplated victim of the crime to go to the place contemplated for its commission;
(c) reconnoitering the place contemplated for the commission of the crime;
(d) unlawful entry of a structure, vehicle, or enclosure in which it is contemplated that the crime will be committed;
(e) possession of materials to be employed in the commission of the crime, that are specially designed for such unlawful use or that can serve no lawful purpose of the actor under the circumstances;
(f) possession, collection or fabrication of materials to be employed in the commission of the crime, at or near the place contemplated for its commission, if such possession, collection or fabrication serves no lawful purpose of the actor under the circumstances;
(g) soliciting an innocent agent to engage in conduct constituting an element of the crime. (American Law Institute 1985:74-75)

It is important to note that there is no exact formula for identifying a substantial step toward the commission of a crime. None of these acts, on their own, is enough to hold a person responsible for an attempted crime. Rather, these actions must be examined within the context of the situation and in light of the totality of the circumstances. At that point, if any of these acts support a criminal objective, they "shall not be held insufficient as a matter of law" and should be taken into consideration by the trial court (American Law Institute 1985:74). In the case of *United States v. Gladish*, 536 F.3d 646 (2008), the Seventh Circuit Court of Appeals examined what constitutes a substantial step in the context of an attempt to persuade a minor to engage in sexual activity. This case also analyzes the logic for punishing attempts to commit crimes (see Box 9.5).

Box 9.5   WHAT CONSTITUTES A "SUBSTANTIAL STEP"?

United States v. Gladish
536 F.3d 646 (2008)

The defendant, a 35-year-old man, was caught in a sting operation in which a government agent impersonated a 14-year-old girl in an Internet chat room called "Indiana regional romance." The defendant visited the chat room and solicited "Abagail" (as the agent called herself) to have sex with him. The defendant lived in southern Indiana; "Abagail" purported to live in the northern part of the state. She agreed to have sex with the defendant and in a subsequent chat he discussed the possibility of traveling to meet her in a couple of weeks, but no arrangements were made. He was then arrested.

The defendant of course did not succeed in getting "Abagail" to have sex with him, and if he had, he would not have been guilty of a completed violation . . . because the agent who called herself "Abagail" was not a minor. The question (the only one we need answer to resolve the appeal) is whether the defendant is guilty of having *attempted* to get an underage girl to have sex with him. To be guilty of an attempt you must intend the completed crime and take a "substantial step" toward its completion.

In tort law, unsuccessful attempts do not give rise to liability. If you plan to shoot a person but at the last minute change your mind . . . you have not committed a tort.

The criminal law, because it aims at taking dangerous people out of circulation before they do harm, takes a different approach. A person who demonstrates by his conduct that he has the intention and capability of committing a crime is punishable even if his plan was thwarted.

In the usual prosecution based on a sting operation for attempting to have sex with an underage girl, the defendant after obtaining the pretend girl's consent goes to meet her and is arrested upon arrival. It is always possible that had the intended victim been a real girl the defendant would have gotten cold feet at the last minute and not completed the crime even though he was in position to do so. But there is a sufficient likelihood that he would have completed it to allow a jury to deem the visit to meet the pretend girl a substantial step toward completion, and so the visit is conduct enough to make him guilty of an attempt and not merely an intent.

But we disagree with the government's suggestion that the line runs between "harmless banter" and a conversation in which the defendant unmistakably proposes sex. In all the cases cited to us by the government or found by our independent research there was more than the explicit sex talk that the government quotes from the defendant's chats with "Abagail."

But the fact that the defendant in the present case said to a stranger whom he thought a young girl things like "ill suck your titties" and "ill kiss your inner thighs" and "ill let ya suck me and learn about how to do that," while not "harmless banter," did not indicate that he would travel to northern Indiana to do these things to her in person; nor did he invite her to meet him in southern Indiana or elsewhere. His talk and his sending her a video of himself masturbating . . . are equally consistent with his having intended to obtain sexual satisfaction vicariously. There is no indication that he has ever had sex with an underage girl. Indeed, since she furnished no proof of her age, he could not have been sure and may indeed have doubted that she was a girl, or even a woman. He may have thought (this is common in Internet relationships) that they were both enacting a fantasy.

The requirement of proving a substantial step serves to distinguish people who pose real threats from those who are all hot air; in the case of Gladish, hot air is all the record shows. So he is entitled to an acquittal.

1. Did the court decide correctly that Mr. Gladish's actions were not substantial enough to constitute attempting to convince a minor to have sex with him? Why or why not?
2. What factors should courts consider in determining whether a person is responsible for an attempted crime?
3. How should courts strike a balance between punishing dangerous people who have the intent to commit crimes and the idea that it is better for a guilty person to go free than for an innocent person to be punished? Explain.

The *mens rea* of attempt is having the purpose to commit and fully complete the crime that was attempted. This means that the person must not intend to only *attempt* to complete the crime, but must have the criminal purpose to wholly complete and carry out each element of that particular crime. Furthermore, attempt is a specific intent crime, so the person must have the intent to commit the exact crime of which he or she is liable for attempting to commit.

Complicity

It is also important to note that a person may also be held responsible for attempt under the concept of **complicity** that was discussed in Chapter 3. Under the notion of complicity, "a person who engages in conduct designed to aid another to commit a crime that would establish his complicity . . . if the crime were committed by such other person, is guilty of an attempt to commit the crime, although the crime is not committed or attempted by such other person"

Complicity:
to be associated with or to be an accomplice in a criminal act

(American Law Institute 1985:75). In this situation, when a person is guilty of assisting or being involved with a principal criminal actor, the secondary criminal actor who is complicit in the commission of a crime may still be held responsible for the attempt of that crime even when the principal actor does not actually complete the underlying crime.

Defenses to Attempt

Although defenses to crimes will be addressed more extensively in Chapters 10 and 11, it is appropriate to note here that there are some special defenses that may be used to relieve a person of criminal liability for the commission of inchoate offenses. Box 9.6 presents a scenario for you to decide whether a person has a valid defense for an attempted crime.

Abandonment

The *MPC* states that when a person's actions constitute a valid attempt at the commission of a crime, "it is an affirmative defense that he abandoned his effort to commit the crime or otherwise prevented its commission, under circumstances manifesting a complete and voluntary renunciation of his criminal purpose" (American Law Institute 1985:75). The most important aspect of the defense of **abandonment** is determining whether a person has abandoned a criminal endeavor voluntarily and of his or her own free will. If the abandonment is not entirely voluntary, or if it is the result of some other external compelling force or inducement, it will not constitute a valid defense to an attempted crime.

Abandonment: a defense to attempt when a person gives up a criminal endeavor voluntarily

The *MPC* provides that "renunciation of a criminal purpose is not voluntary if it is motivated, in whole or in part, by circumstances, not present or apparent at the inception of the actor's course of conduct, that increase the probability of detection or apprehension or that make more difficult the accomplishment of the criminal purpose."

Box 9.6   YOU DECIDE: IS SHE GUILTY OF ATTEMPTED MURDER?

Consider the example in Box 9.1 of the woman who attempted to kill her husband in order to collect his life insurance. What would happen if she pondered the idea of killing him and then reconsidered? What if she prepared the lasagna with the strychnine and then changed her mind before serving it? What if she served the poisoned lasagna to her husband and just as he was about to take a bite, she pulled it away from him and threw it in the trash? Are any or all of these actions a valid defense to her attempt to murder her husband?

Furthermore, "renunciation is not complete if it is motivated by a decision to postpone the criminal conduct until a more advantageous time or to transfer the criminal effort to another but similar objective or victim" (American Law Institute 1985:75). This means that for abandonment to be a legitimate defense, it cannot be the result of a factor that the perpetrator did not know about when he or she began taking steps toward the completion of the crime.

For instance, the wife who attempted to murder her husband in the previous example could not claim abandonment of her murder plan if the abandonment resulted from her finding out that she was not the beneficiary of her husband's life insurance. People cannot claim abandonment as a defense if they abandon a drug deal because they learn that they are under police surveillance and will be inevitably caught in the act. Abandonment is not a defense to an attempted burglary when the perpetrator discovers that a home will be more difficult to break into than was originally anticipated. Abandonment cannot take place due to some external factor that makes the commission of the crime under those particular circumstances less appealing, such as searching for items with a higher resale value to steal or a more opportune time, place, or person against whom to commit a crime. The logic for this is that the defense of abandonment is reserved for times when a person who is in the process of committing a crime has a legitimate change of heart and decides independently to abandon the criminal endeavor.

Impossibility

Another potential defense to an attempted crime is **impossibility**. Here, it is important to make a distinction between factual and legal impossibility. **Factual impossibility** exists when a person takes all the steps necessary to complete a particular crime, but some circumstance outside the perpetrator's control makes it impossible for him or her to actually complete that crime. An example of factual impossibility exists in the previous example of Bob attempting to steal a vase from Ann when, unbeknownst to Bob, Ann had already decided to give him the vase as a gift. Bob took all the steps necessary to attempt a theft offense. However, it was impossible for him to steal the vase because Ann intended it to be given to him as a gift. Because a person cannot steal something that has been given to them, it would be impossible for Bob to be guilty of theft in this case.

Another example of factual impossibility involves a person who takes all the steps necessary to complete a murder. A man develops an elaborate plan to poison a woman and put a slow-acting poison in her drink with the intent that it will kill her several hours later. However, before the poison has a chance to work, the woman is killed in a

Impossibility:
defense to attempt in which a fact or a law makes the commission of a crime unattainable

Factual Impossibility:
when a person takes all the steps necessary to complete a crime, but some circumstance outside their control makes the commission of the crime impossible

car accident. In both of these situations, some outside intervening *fact* or circumstance prevented the intended offense from being completed. Classic examples of factual impossibility include trying to murder someone who is already dead due to another cause; firing a defective or unloaded gun at someone with the intent to kill them; or attempting to rob someone who has no money in their wallet. In each of these situations, if some fact that was unknown to perpetrator were different, then that person would have been able to fully complete the intended crime. Instead, some external factor or circumstance makes it impossible for the person to commit the underlying crime.

In contrast, **legal impossibility** exists when a person intends to commit a specific crime and takes action to complete that crime, but the act that the person commits is not prohibited by the law. For instance, a person may have the intent to solicit sex with a minor and may believe that the jurisdiction's laws have placed the age of majority at 18. The person then solicits sex with a 17-year-old, believing that this is a crime. However, the jurisdiction in which they reside has placed the age of majority at 17. Since there is no law that prohibits soliciting sex with a 17-year-old, this is an example of a legal impossibility. If there were a law prohibiting what the person tried to do, then that person would be guilty of an attempted crime. However, because there is no law prohibiting his or her actions, it is legally impossible for that person to have attempted a crime.

> **Legal Impossibility:** when a person takes all the steps necessary to complete a crime, but the act is not prohibited by the law

While legal impossibility can be used as a valid defense for attempt, factual impossibility is not a legitimate defense to a criminal attempt. The reason for this is that in a situation where factual impossibility exists, the perpetrator has developed the requisite mental state to commit a crime and has taken affirmative steps to ensure that the intended crime is completed. The only thing that stops the crime from being committed is that there is some external factor about which the perpetrator has no knowledge or control that makes the crime impossible. It would be contrary to public policy to let this person go unpunished since but-for the outside circumstance, the crime would have been completed in accordance with the actor's criminal *mens rea*.

Unlike factual impossibility, legal impossibility *is* a valid defense to attempt. The reason for this is the **principle of legality** that was discussed in Chapter 1. To review, the principle of legality provides that no one can be sanctioned with a criminal punishment unless there is a law that prohibits the conduct at the time that the actions took place. People cannot be punished when no law exists, despite their intent to commit a crime. Even though this person does indeed have a criminal *mens rea*, constitutional protections outweigh these concerns.

> **Principle of Legality:** provides that no one can be sanctioned with a criminal punishment unless there is a law that prohibits the conduct at the time that the actions took place

Therefore, legal impossibility can be used as a valid defense to a criminal attempt, while factual impossibility cannot.

CONSPIRACY

A criminal **conspiracy** is essentially two or more people agreeing to commit a crime. Under the *MPC*, a person is guilty of a conspiracy to commit a crime:

> if with the purpose of promoting or facilitating its commission he:
>
> (a) agrees with such other person or persons that they or one or more of them will engage in conduct that constitutes such crime or an attempt or solicitation to commit such crime; or
> (b) agrees to aid such other person or persons in the planning or commission of such crime or of an attempt or solicitation to commit such crime. (American Law Institute 1985:77)

Conspiracy:
two or more people agreeing to commit a crime

In addition to the requirement that an agreement be formed among two or more people, the *MPC* states that "no person may be convicted of a conspiracy to commit a crime, other than a felony of the first or second degree, unless an overt act in pursuance of such conspiracy is alleged and proved to have been done by him or by a person with whom he conspired" (American Law Institute 1985:78). The requirement that there be an act in furtherance of the conspiracy helps the legal system differentiate between relatively harmless people who merely talk with other people about engaging in criminal activity and those who are truly dangerous and have a real intention to band together with others to commit a crime.

The *mens rea* of conspiracy is purpose to promote or facilitate a crime's commission. Neither the agreement nor the intent to promote or facilitate a crime has to be in writing, nor do they have to be explicitly stated by those involved in the conspiracy. As you can imagine, requiring the agreement to be either in writing or explicitly stated would leave a significant portion of criminal conspiracies outside the scope of criminal punishment. Particularly in highly complex criminal enterprises, a written or explicit criminal agreement would be very difficult to acquire and prove. Instead, the intent that the commission of a crime be facilitated can be inferred from the totality of the circumstances and the behavior of the parties. Similar to attempt, conspiracy is also a specific intent crime, which requires that the parties intend to carry out the crime of which they are responsible for conspiring. Box 9.7 outlines the elements of a criminal conspiracy.

Box 9.7   ELEMENTS OF CONSPIRACY (*MPC*)

Actus Reus	*Mens Rea*
• Agreeing with another person(s) to commit a crime OR • Agreeing to aid another person(s) in the planning or commission of a crime	• Purpose to promote or facilitate a crime's commission

Concurrence

Linking of *actus reus* and *mens rea*

In many criminal endeavors that involve a significant number of participants, such as organized crime, cybercrime, and financial crime rings, it is quite likely that all the parties do not have an explicit agreement with one another and probably do not even know everyone's true identity. One such arrangement is known as a **wheel conspiracy**. This is a conspiracy in which a primary leader of a criminal enterprise engages in all of the separate and distinct dealings with each party to the conspiracy. However, each of these separate transactions has the common goal or purpose of furthering a central criminal objective. The primary leader serves as the wheel's hub and the more peripheral actors, each of whom has an independent relationship with the hub, serve as the wheel's spokes.

Wheel Conspiracy: conspiracy in which a primary leader acts as a hub and engages in all of the separate dealings with each party to the conspiracy, who act as spokes

Another arrangement is called a **chain conspiracy**. In a chain conspiracy, each actor has a distinct role to fill in the chronological execution of a criminal plan. In this arrangement, each actor works independently of his or her co-conspirators. Each actor fulfills a role in sequence to bring about the common end goal of the conspiracy. Unlike a wheel conspiracy, a chain conspiracy has each person involved working in succession, rather than revolving around a central hub. Figure 9.1 gives a visual representation of both wheel and chain conspiracies.

Chain Conspiracy: a conspiracy in which each actor works independently to fulfill his or her role in the chronological execution of a criminal plan

There is a particularly strong motivation for courts to regulate the formation of conspiracies because this activity enters into the area of group crime that poses a particularly realistic threat, as people have a significantly lesser likelihood of abandoning criminal ambitions when they have someone else to work with and hold them accountable for their responsibilities in a criminal enterprise [*Callanan v. United States*, 364 U.S. 587 (1961)]. Because of this, there are significant public policy motivations for detecting and stopping conspiratorial activity before it moves beyond the inchoate stage and real harm takes place. Conspiracies encompass a wide range of underlying offenses, including personal crimes, property crimes, and, more

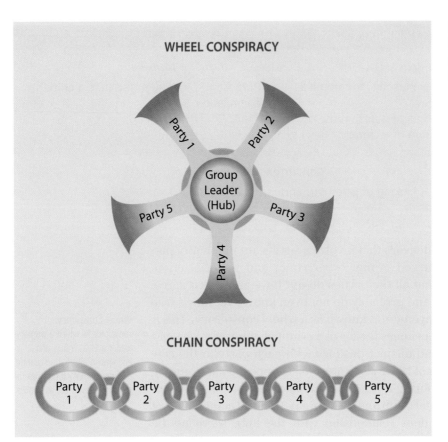

FIGURE 9.1
Illustration of Wheel and Chain Conspiracies

recently, criminal activity such as terrorism, financial crimes, drug trafficking and selling, and human smuggling.

One issue that arises is whether a valid conspiracy exists when not all parties actually intend to follow through with the criminal act. Although jurisdictions differ in their approach to this issue, the *MPC* handles this situation based upon the perspective of the actors in the conspiracy. All individuals who form an agreement, or believe that they are forming an agreement, to commit a crime can be held responsible for a criminal conspiracy (American Law Institute 1985:79). Furthermore, the *MPC* states that "it is immaterial to the liability of a person who solicits or conspires with another to commit a crime that (a) he or the person whom he solicits or with whom he conspires does not occupy a particular position or have a particular characteristic that is an element of such crime, if he believes that one of them does; or (b) the person whom he solicits or with whom he conspires is irresponsible or has an immunity to prosecution or conviction for the commission of the crime" (American Law Institute 1985: 80).

As an example of subsection (a), one of the requirements for embezzlement is that a person who unlawfully keeps someone else's property has been entrusted with the rightful possession of that property. Nathan may conspire with Ted to embezzle money with which Nathan believes Ted has been rightfully entrusted. However, Ted was never entrusted with the money. The fact that Ted does not occupy a position or have a characteristic (being rightfully entrusted with the money) necessary for embezzlement does not affect Nathan's liability for conspiring with him to commit embezzlement.

As an example of subsection (b), a person may conspire with another to commit a crime, not knowing that the co-conspirator is an undercover federal agent carrying out a sting operation. The federal agent's immunity to prosecution and conviction will not affect the co-conspirator's liability for the formation of that conspiracy.

Distinctive Features of Conspiracy

Conspiracy is a unique crime because it cannot be completed individually, thus placing it in the realm of group crime. It is widely believed that group crime is more dangerous than crimes committed by individuals. This is because individuals acting alone are more likely to abandon criminal aspirations than people who are being held accountable by others involved in the commission of a common crime.

Because of the threat posed by group crime, there is a significant incentive for conspiracies to be detected in their formative stages and to be dealt with harshly by the legal system. One way that the legal system has accomplished this is through the implementation of the *Pinkerton* rule. The *Pinkerton* rule states that all people involved in a conspiracy may be held responsible for all the actions that result from that conspiracy, even if a person did not participate directly. So long as the results brought about by the conspiracy are reasonably foreseeable, all the people who were involved in the conspiracy may be held legally accountable for the actions of their co-conspirators. This is based upon the idea that all of the people involved in a conspiracy are agents of one another and, therefore, may be held accountable for the acts of others [*Pinkerton v. United States*, 328 U.S. 640 (1946)]. In Box 9.8, the Pennsylvania Superior Court addressed an individual's liability for the acts of his co-conspirators in *Commonwealth v. Azim*, 313 Pa. Super. 310, 459 A.2d 1244 (Pa. Super. 1983).

Pinkerton Rule:
states that all people involved in a conspiracy may be held responsible for all the actions that result from that conspiracy, even if a person did not participate directly

Box 9.8   LIABILITY FOR THE ACTS OF CO-CONSPIRATORS

Commonwealth v. Azim

313 Pa. Super. 310, 459 A.2d 1244 (Pa. Super. 1983)

Appellant was arrested, along with Mylice James and Thomas Robinson, on September 18, 1977 for simple assault, robbery, and conspiracy. The victim of the robbery was Jerry Tennenbaum, a Temple University student. Appellant drove a car in which the other two men were passengers. Appellant stopped the car, Robinson called Tennenbaum over to the curb, the two passengers got out of the car, inflicted bodily injury on Tennenbaum, took his wallet which had fallen to the ground, and immediately left the scene in the same car driven by appellant. Robinson and appellant were tried [by] a jury and convicted as co-defendants in April 1978. After denial of post-trial motions, appellant was sentenced to five to ten years for robbery and five to ten years for conspiracy, the sentences to run concurrently. . . . He argues that because his conspiracy conviction was not supported by sufficient evidence against him, the charges of assault and robbery must also fail.

Criminal conspiracy is defined as:

(a) Definition of conspiracy—A person is guilty of conspiracy with another person or persons to commit a crime if with the intent of promoting or facilitating its commission he:

(1) agrees with such other person or persons that they or one or more of them will engage in conduct which constitutes such crime or an attempt or solicitation to commit such crime; or

(2) agrees to aid such other person or persons in the planning or commission of such crime or of an attempt or solicitation to commit such crime. 18 Pa.C.S.A. § 903 (1973)

The essence of criminal conspiracy is a common understanding, no matter how it came into being, that a particular criminal objective be accomplished. . . . And although a conspiracy cannot be based upon mere suspicion or conjecture, a conspiracy "may be inferentially established by showing the relationship, conduct or circumstances of the parties, and the overt acts on the part of the co-conspirators have uniformly been held competent to prove that a corrupt confederation has in fact been formed."

At trial, the prosecution presented evidence that established that appellant was the driver of the car in which James and Robinson (the men who demanded money from Tennenbaum and beat and choked him) rode. Robinson was seated on the front seat, next to appellant. Robinson rolled down the car window, twice beckoned to the victim to come close to the car, and when Tennenbaum refused, the two passengers got out, assaulted Tennenbaum, and took his wallet. Appellant sat at the wheel, with the engine running and lights on, and the car doors open, while the acts were committed in the vicinity of the car. He then drove James and Robinson from the scene.

Among those circumstances relevant to proving conspiracy are association with alleged conspirators, knowledge of the commission of the crime, presence at the scene of the crime, and, at times, participation in the object of the conspiracy. Conspiracy to commit burglary has been found where the defendant drove codefendants to the scene of a crime and then later picked them up. "Thus, the driver of a 'get away' car can be found guilty as an accomplice if it is reasonable to infer that he was aware of the actual perpetrator's intention. His agreement to effectuate the escape aids the perpetrator in the planning and commission of the actual crime." We find no merit in appellant's claim that he was merely a hired driver, with no knowledge of his passengers' criminal activity.

We hold that a rational factfinder could find, beyond a reasonable doubt, that appellant conspired with James and Robinson to commit assault and robbery.

1. Does driving a getaway car meet the test for being involved in a criminal conspiracy? Why or why not?
2. How much involvement in a criminal enterprise should be required before a person can be held accountable for being involved in a conspiracy?

Another unusual aspect of criminal conspiracy is the ability to use certain **hearsay statements** at trial in order to prove the existence of a conspiracy. Hearsay statements are secondhand statements that may be used in order to prove the truth of a matter at trial. The **hearsay rule** generally excludes the use of these statements at trial. However, conspiracy trials provide an exception to this rule and hearsay statements made "in furtherance of the conspiracy" may be admitted at trial and heard by the jury [*Commonwealth v. Thomas*, 189 A.2d 255 (Pa. 1963)], so long as there is other substantial evidence from outside sources that can be used to demonstrate the existence of the conspiracy. Because of these unique advantages that the state is given in proving the existence of a conspiracy and holding people accountable through the criminal law, conspiracy is often called the "darling" of prosecutors and is one of the most frequently charged criminal offenses at both the state and federal levels.

It is also important to note that conspiracy is the one inchoate crime that does not fall within the merger doctrine, which is discussed later in the chapter. The merger doctrine is the idea that once the underlying offense actually takes place, a person will not be held accountable for either the solicitation or attempt of that crime. Conversely, when a criminal conspiracy leads to the completion of a crime, the individuals involved may be charged and convicted of both conspiracy to commit the crime *and* the underlying criminal offense.

> **Hearsay Statements:** secondhand statements that may be used in order to prove the truth of a matter at trial
>
> **Hearsay Rule:** excludes the use of hearsay statements at trial

SOLICITATION

A person is guilty of the **solicitation** of a crime "if with the purpose of promoting or facilitating its commission he commands, encourages or

> **Solicitation:** when one person tries to convince another person to commit a specific crime

requests another person to engage in specific conduct that would constitute such crime or an attempt to commit such crime or would establish his complicity in its commission or attempted commission" (American Law Institute 1985:76). In its most basic form, solicitation takes place when one person tries to convince another person to commit a specific crime. An example of this would be a husband hiring another person to kill his wife. The *actus reus* of solicitation is commanding, encouraging, or requesting that another person commit a crime. The *mens rea* of solicitation is the purpose to promote or facilitate the commission of that crime. Box 9.9 outlines the elements of solicitation.

One aspect that differentiates solicitation from the other inchoate crimes is that there is no requirement that an act in furtherance of the crime take place. Also, the *MPC* does not require direct communication of the solicitation to the person who is being asked to commit the crime. The *MPC* states that "it is immaterial . . . that the actor fails to communicate with the person he solicits to commit a crime if his conduct was designed to effect such communication" (American Law Institute 1985:76-77). Instead, solicitation may be inferred from an individual's conduct that clearly demonstrates the request that a crime be committed. In other words, a person can still be held responsible for solicitation even if he or she does not expressly utter words that attempt to convince another person to commit a certain crime. For instance, rather than directly asking another person to kill his wife, a man might mention repeatedly the financial gain that someone could obtain if he or she happened to kill his wife. Because the husband's action was intended to effect the communication to another person that he would like his wife to be killed and that there would be a reward for doing this, the husband could be held responsible for the solicitation of his wife's murder.

The person who has solicited the commission of a crime can only be held responsible for solicitation if the person that he or she has

---

Box 9.9   ELEMENTS OF SOLICITATION (*MPC*)

Actus Reus	*Mens Rea*
• Commanding, encouraging, or requesting another person to commit a crime	• Purpose to promote or facilitate the commission of a crime

Concurrence

Linking of *actus reus* and *mens rea*

asked to commit the crime has not yet agreed to do so. Once the person agrees to commit the crime, then both individuals involved can be held accountable for a conspiracy to commit the underlying offense.

Solicitation of crime is taken very seriously by the legal system. In the excerpted case *State v. Mann*, 317 N.C. 164, 345 S.E.2d 365 (1986), the North Carolina Supreme Court addressed the actions that may constitute solicitation to commit a robbery, as well as whether solicitation of a robbery is an infamous crime (see Box 9.10). **Infamous crime** is a term used under the common law, and includes capital crimes, serious felonies, and crimes involving the use of deceit.

Infamous Crime:
a common law term that includes capital crimes, serious felonies, and crimes involving the use of deceit

---

Box 9.10   IS THE SOLICITATION OF ROBBERY AN INFAMOUS CRIME?

State v. Mann
317 N.C. 164, 345 S.E.2d 365 (1986)

At trial, the state's evidence showed that Penelope Dawkins, the fiancée of Richard Lockamy, lived with Lockamy in a Mebane trailer park which was managed by codefendant Keith Barts. In September 1983, while visiting Lockamy's sister, Penelope and Lockamy met defendant, Charlie Mann. Thereafter, Penelope and Lockamy would, about two to three times a week, help Mann with his sawmill, straighten up his yard, and clean his house. At some point, Mann told Lockamy that he knew Lockamy had a criminal record and that Lockamy and Penelope needed money. Penelope testified that Mann told them that he knew an elderly man in Snow Camp who carried large sums of money in his bib overalls and that "[h]e would be an easy man to rob. It would take two men to rob the man. The best thing to do would be to go to a shed and wait for him to come home and after he got out of his truck, rob him from there." Lockamy told Mann he would think about it. Penelope testified that thereafter the subject came up three or four times a week. . . . "Mr. Mann kept telling him that if he didn't do it himself, . . . that he would find somebody else to do it or he

would do it." About a week later, Mann picked up Lockamy at his trailer one morning in order to show him where the intended victim, Richard Braxton, lived.

On 20 November 1983, Barts arrived at Penelope's trailer. He told Lockamy, "I did that job last night. . . . The job in the country, but I think I killed the man." Barts went on to say that he had gone to the old man's house, hidden in the shed, and waited for him to come home. When the old man arrived home, Barts jumped him and began beating him. Barts said, "I beat the old . . . until I got plumb tired of beating him. . . . I beat him until he quit moving."

In exchange for his testimony for the state, as well as for his guilty pleas to conspiracy to commit robbery and armed robbery, all other charges against Richard Lockamy were dismissed. Lockamy substantially corroborated Penelope's testimony, saying that Mann had told him he probably could tie Braxton up with a rope and wouldn't have to use any weapons to get the money. Mann also told Lockamy what he considered to be "the best way to do the job." Lockamy testified that Mann "was very persistent about someone doing the job."

A crime is "infamous" within the meaning of the statute if it is an act of depravity, involves moral turpitude, and reveals a heart devoid of social duties and a mind fatally bent on mischief. . . . Our courts in prior cases have followed this analysis and concluded that solicitation to murder is an infamous crime, and that solicitation to commit perjury is an infamous offense. The Court of Appeals has held, at the other end of the spectrum, that solicitation to commit crime against nature is not infamous. Solicitation to commit common law robbery lies somewhere between these opposite poles.

Solicitation involves the asking, enticing, inducing, or counseling of another to commit a crime. The solicitor conceives the criminal idea and furthers its commission via another person by suggesting to, inducing, or manipulating that person. As noted by Wechsler, Jones, and Korn . . . "the solicitor, working his will through one or more agents, manifests an approach to crime more intelligent and masterful than the efforts of his hireling," and a solicitation, "an attempt to conspire," may well be more dangerous than an attempt. Indeed, a solicitor may be more

dangerous than a conspirator; a conspirator may merely passively agree to a criminal scheme, while the solicitor plans, schemes, suggests, encourages, and incites the solicitation. Further, the solicitor is morally more culpable than a conspirator; he keeps himself from being at risk, hiding behind the actor, as occurred in this case.

Common law robbery, the solicitation of which defendant here was convicted, is the felonious taking of money or goods of any value from the person of another, or in his presence, against his will, by violence or putting him in fear. It is a crime against the person, effectuated by violence or intimidation. Where a defendant has counseled, enticed, or induced another to commit as degrading an offense as theft from the person or presence of a victim by force or violence by putting him in fear, he has committed an act of depravity and a crime involving moral turpitude and has demonstrated that he has a mind fatally bent on mischief and a heart devoid of social duties. It is an infamous crime within the meaning of N.C.G.S. § 14-3 and defendant should be subject to punishment as a felon instead of as a misdemeanant.

1. What factors should the court look at to determine whether a person has solicited the commission of a crime?
2. Do you agree that a person who solicits a crime is more culpable than a person who conspires to commit a crime? Why do you feel that this is the case?

Defenses to Solicitation

Similar to the use of abandonment, the *MPC* states that "it is an affirmative defense that the actor, after soliciting another person to commit a crime, persuaded him not to do so or otherwise prevented the commission of the crime, under circumstances manifesting a complete and voluntary renunciation of his criminal purpose" (American Law Institute 1985:77). However, because solicitation necessarily involves at least two people engaged in a criminal endeavor, it is not enough that the person guilty of solicitation merely abandon the plan to commit a crime. Because that person has solicited and enticed another person to commit a crime, the person who solicited the crime must either convince the other person to abandon the crime or must prevent the crime from being committed.

MERGER DOCTRINE

Another issue with inchoate crimes is what an individual will be charged with if the underlying crime is actually committed. For instance, it does not make sense to punish someone for an attempted murder if the murder has actually been committed, or of solicitation of terrorist activity when the terrorist activity is actually carried out. Based upon the merger doctrine, a person will not be punished for both an inchoate offense and the underlying offense. The idea is that once someone successfully completes a crime, the inchoate offense has then *merged* into the underlying offense. Because the underlying offense is more severe and has certainly caused considerably more harm than the inchoate offense would have, it makes sense to hold the person accountable and punish her or him for the commission of the underlying offense rather than the inchoate offense. The merger doctrine applies to both attempt and solicitation, but it does not apply to conspiracy. Therefore, a person can be held accountable for both conspiracy and the underlying offense.

SUMMARY

Inchoate crimes are criminal offenses that have not actually been completed. The primary inchoate crimes are attempt, conspiracy, and solicitation. Inchoate crimes raise many issues such as whether people should be held criminally responsible for crimes that they did not complete, and, if so, how these offenses should be punished.

The three types of attempt under the *MPC* are when an individual commits acts that would be a crime in the absence of some unknown circumstance; when an individual takes purposeful action in order to cause a particular result; and when an individual takes a substantial step toward the completion of a crime. A substantial step is one that strongly corroborates that individual's criminal purpose. Defenses to attempted crimes include abandonment and legal impossibility. Factual impossibility is not a valid defense to an attempted crime.

A conspiracy is two or more people agreeing to commit a crime. The *MPC* also requires that some overt act in furtherance of the conspiracy take place. Individuals in a conspiracy act as agents of one another so people may be held liable for the acts of others in a conspiracy. Conspiracies pose a significant threat because they are classified as group crimes. Conspiracy is a unique offense because it does not fall within the merger doctrine and because hearsay statements may be used to prove the existence of a conspiracy.

Solicitation takes place when one person attempts to convince another to commit a crime. Solicitation can take place through any form of communication that is intended to transmit the message. Abandonment may be used as a defense to solicitation if the person responsible for the solicitation either convinces the other person to abandon the criminal objective or prevents the criminal act from taking place.

Attempt and solicitation fall within the merger doctrine, which means that if the underlying offense is committed, the criminal actor will be punished only for the commission of the underlying offense. Within the merger doctrine, actors will not be punished for the inchoate offense as well. Conspiracy does not fall within the merger doctrine, so an individual may be punished for both a conspiracy and the underlying offense.

KEY TERMS

abandonment
anticipatory offenses
attempt
chain conspiracy
complicity
concurrence
conspiracy
deterrent effect
factual impossibility
hearsay rule

hearsay statements
impossibility
inchoate offenses
infamous crime
legal impossibility
Pinkerton rule
principle of legality
solicitation
substantial steps
underlying offense
wheel conspiracy

CRITICAL THINKING QUESTIONS

1. Should inchoate crimes be punished at all? Is it fair to hold someone accountable when no resulting harm has occurred? If so, in what way should inchoate crimes be punished (as harshly as or less harshly than the underlying offense)? How did you reach your decision and what factors did you take into account? Be specific and explain your reasoning.

2. Should abandonment be considered a legitimate defense to inchoate crimes? If so, under what circumstances should the defense of abandonment be available? Discuss the public policy implications of your response and how you arrived at that decision.

3. Should the legal system have the ability to punish people for their thoughts? Might a person's thoughts to be a legitimate threat to public safety that warrants criminal punishment? Explain your reasoning.

4. Is the substantial steps test the most appropriate way to determine whether someone is guilty of an attempted crime? Does this test encompass too much behavior that may be innocent? Be specific and explain your reasoning.

5. Do you agree with the merger doctrine, or should people be held accountable for both inchoate crimes and the underlying offense?

Think about the public policy considerations of your response. Explain your reasoning.

6. Discuss the rationale for punishing an attempted crime that was used by the circuit court in *United States v. Gladish*. Do you agree with this rationale? Is taking a substantial step truly an indication of a person's dangerousness?

7. Discuss the special policy considerations that must be taken into account in the regulation and punishment of conspiracies. Are these significant enough for conspiracy to be excluded from the merger doctrine? Explain your reasoning.

SUGGESTED READINGS

Alexander, L. & Kessler, K.D. (1997). "Mens Rea and Inchoate Crimes." *Journal of Criminal Law and Criminology* 87(4):1138-1193. This paper discusses the mental state required for the completion of inchoate crimes and the differences of the *mens rea* requirements for inchoate crimes and underlying criminal offenses. The authors discuss areas of uncertainty in the required mental state of purpose and the issues that this creates for the appropriate administration of justice and the prosecution of inchoate crimes.

Bittner, T. (2008). "Punishment for Criminal Attempts: A Legal Perspective on the Problem of Moral Luck." *Canadian Journal of Philosophy* 38(1):51-83. In this paper, the author discusses the various issues associated with punishing an individual for the crime of attempt. The author addresses the arguments of sentencing reformers who advocate that attempted crimes should be punished equivalently to the underlying offense, and discusses reasons why an attempted crime should have a sentencing scheme separate from completed offenses.

LaFave, W.R. (2010). *Criminal Law* (Hornbook Series Student Edition, 5th ed.). St. Paul, MN: West. This book explains critical concepts in criminal law at a level appropriate for graduate students or those wishing to examine various aspects of criminal law in more detail. The author includes a thorough and in-depth examination of concepts relevant to inchoate offenses, including attempt, conspiracy, solicitation, accomplice liability, and defenses to inchoate crimes. This book also explores many of the differences between liability under the *MPC* and various state and federal statutes.

Ohlin, J.D. (2007). "Group Think: The Law of Conspiracy and Collective Reason." *Journal of Criminal Law and Criminology* 98(1):147-206. In this paper, the author explores in detail the Pinkerton Rule, which allows conspirators to be held criminally liable for the actions of their co-conspirators. The author discusses the problems with this rule, particularly when the person being held accountable has no knowledge of the actions of his or her co-conspirators. The author makes recommendations for when collective liability should be utilized and when it should be eliminated in conspiracy cases.

Stenson, T. (2006-2007). "Inchoate Crimes and Criminal Responsibility under International Law." *Journal of International Law and Policy* 5:1-24. In this paper, the author explores inchoate crimes from an international perspective. This paper discusses the manner in which inchoate crimes are handled in various U.S. jurisdictions, as well as by international tribunals.

The author explores the reasons that this is important to effectively handle inchoate crimes internationally as the need grows to deal with inchoate crimes that may lead to international threats such as terrorism and international genocide.

REFERENCES

American Law Institute (1985). *Model Penal Code: Complete Statutory Text*. Philadelphia, PA.

Callanan v. United States, 364 U.S. 587 (1961).

Commonwealth v. Azim, 313 Pa. Super. 310, 459 A.2d 1244 (Pa. Super. 1983).

Commonwealth v. Thomas, 189 A.2d 255 (Pa. 1963).

Dressler, J. (2009). *Understanding Criminal Law* (5th ed.). Newark, NJ: Matthew Bender/LexisNexis.

Pinkerton v. United States, 328 U.S. 640 (1946).

State v. Mann, 317 N.C. 164, 345 S.E.2d 365 (1986).

United States v. Gladish, 536 F.3d 646 (2008).

Justification Defenses

LEARNING OBJECTIVES

After reading this chapter you should be able to:

1. Define and explain the distinctions between excuse and justification defenses, and between perfect and imperfect defenses
2. Discuss and analyze the implications and outcomes of successfully raising a legal defense to a criminal act
3. Describe the requirements for the use of self-defense and apply this concept to a fact scenario
4. Characterize situations in which third parties and property may and may not be protected under the self-defense doctrine
5. Describe the requirements for the use of choice-of-evils/necessity as a valid defense and apply this concept to a fact scenario
6. Describe the requirements for the use of consent as a valid defense and apply this concept to a fact scenario

INTRODUCTION

The *Model Penal Code* (*MPC*) states that a person is criminally liable, or responsible for committing a crime, when that individual commits a criminal act without a valid justification or excuse for their actions (American Law Institute 1985:2). We have explored the actions and circumstances that may constitute a criminal law violation in the previous chapters where various crimes and their specific elements were examined in detail. However, there is a very important second part to the criminal liability equation. In order for someone to be held responsible for the commission of a crime, he or she must first commit a criminal act by completing all the necessary elements of a specific crime (such as those discussed in previous chapters). However, that person must also complete each of the elements of the crime without a valid justification or excuse for the actions taken.

This is the point at which a criminal **defense** becomes important for determining whether an individual can be held responsible for committing a criminal act. If a person has a legally recognized justification or excuse for his or her actions, then that person has a valid criminal defense. Having a defense to a crime may allow a person to avoid all criminal responsibility or to have the responsibility mitigated, even if that person has taken the necessary steps to fully complete all elements of a crime.

> **Defense:**
> a legally recognized justification or excuse for a criminal act

It is important to note that there are two types of defenses to crimes: justification defenses and excuse defenses. In both situations, the defendant concedes that he or she committed the *actus reus* that constitutes a criminal act. However, one of two situations exists that relieves the defendant from full or partial criminal liability for that act because he or she lacks the appropriate criminal *mens rea*, or criminal mindset.

A **justification defense** exists when a person has fully completed a course of criminal conduct, but some circumstance exists that makes the criminal action right or justified. Using force as a form of self-defense is an example of a justification defense. By contrast, an **excuse defense** exists when a person has fully completed a course of criminal conduct that was *not* justified, yet some circumstance exists that gives that person a valid excuse for her or his wrongful behavior. An example of an excuse defense is when a person commits a crime at a time that he or she is legally insane. The sets of potential circumstances that allow for justification and excuse defenses are quite different, but each type of defense may serve to either eliminate or lessen a person's criminal liability. Justification defenses are addressed in this chapter, and excuse defenses are discussed in Chapter 11.

> **Justification Defense:**
> exists when a person has fully completed a course of criminal conduct, but some circumstance exists that makes the criminal action right or justified
>
> **Excuse Defense:**
> exists when a person has fully completed a course of criminal conduct that was not justified but where some circumstance exists that gives that person a valid reason for the criminal act

It is important to note that some defenses will relieve a defendant of all criminal liability, while other defenses only lessen the liability associated with a crime. On the one hand, a **perfect defense** demonstrates that a person has no criminal culpability for the actions that have been taken and this entitles that person to a full acquittal from the crime with which he or she has been charged. On the other hand, an **imperfect defense** does not eliminate the full amount of a person's criminal culpability, and only mitigates or lessens the charge or the punishment given for a criminal action. For instance, an imperfect defense might serve to show that a person should be charged with manslaughter instead of first degree murder in a homicide case. Whether a defense is perfect or imperfect varies significantly based upon the criminal law jurisdiction, the type of crime with which the defendant is charged, and the facts and circumstances surrounding the commission of that crime.

Perfect Defense: demonstrates that a person has no criminal culpability for the criminal act and entitles a person to a full acquittal from the crime with which he or she has been charged

Imperfect Defense: defense that does not eliminate the full amount of a person's criminal culpability, and only mitigates or lessens the charge or the punishment given for a criminal action

AFFIRMATIVE DEFENSES

You will remember from previous chapters and the discussion of criminal trials that it is the state or the prosecution that bears the **burden of proof** or the responsibility of demonstrating to the fact finder (a judge or jury) that a defendant committed all the necessary elements of a specific crime. Although the defense is certainly permitted to offer evidence to the contrary, the defendant does not have any legal responsibility to offer proof of his or her innocence to the judge or jury. Rather than offering affirmative evidence of his or her innocence, the defendant could rely upon demonstrating to the judge or jury that there are inherent flaws in the prosecution's theory of the case, or that the prosecution's evidence is flawed. One manner by which the defendant may demonstrate that the prosecution's evidence is faulty is through **impeachment**, or showing that the prosecution's witnesses are inherently unreliable and should not be believed by the judge or jury.

Burden of Proof: responsibility of demonstrating to the finder of fact that a defendant committed all the necessary elements of a specific crime

However, the burden of proof changes if the defendant wishes to assert that a valid defense exists that should either eliminate or mitigate his or her responsibility for a criminal act. If the defendant wishes to offer a defense, it is the defendant's responsibility to prove to the judge or jury that the circumstances were such that he or she has a valid defense to the criminal act charged. At this point, the prosecution has no burden in regard to disproving a defense.

Impeachment: demonstrating that a witness is inherently unreliable and should not be believed by the finder of fact

The *MPC* states that "justification is an affirmative defense" (American Law Institute 1985:42). An **affirmative defense** is one in which the defendant demonstrates the existence of facts or circumstances that, even if all the evidence offered by the prosecution were

Affirmative Defense: a defense in which the defendant demonstrates the existence of facts or circumstances that, even if all the evidence offered by the prosecution were true, would eliminate or mitigate the criminal charges

true, would eliminate or mitigate the charge made against the defendant. Essentially, the defendant concedes that he or she committed the acts that technically constitute a crime, but that there are also extenuating circumstances that must be taken into account because these factors exonerate him or her of criminal responsibility. Affirmative defenses do not challenge the quality of the government's case, but instead present separate pieces of evidence that demonstrate the validity of a criminal defense in the case at hand, thereby relieving the defendant of some or all criminal liability. For example, the prosecution may assert that a criminal defendant committed a murder when he or she caused the death of a homicide victim. The defendant may concede that he or she did cause the person's death in the manner suggested by the prosecution. However, the defendant may offer as an affirmative defense evidence proving that he or she acted in self-defense in killing the deceased, and that the defendant's conduct is therefore not subject to criminal punishment.

Self-Defense

When we think of justification defenses, the first one that comes to mind is most likely self-defense. The premise behind **self-defense** is that a person uses force against another person in a way that would normally constitute a criminal act, but that person is justified in the use of this force because it was necessary for self-protection. Necessity forms the basis of all justification defenses. People who successfully raise justification defenses are able to do so because there was no viable and reasonable alternative to their actions. Because of this inherent need, the force used against another person in self-defense is considered to be legally justified by the criminal law.

It is important to have a clear understanding of exactly when and under what circumstances this use of force in self-defense is justified. There are four (4) elements that must be present before the use of self-defense is considered legally valid. These required elements are:

1. an unprovoked attack,
2. immediate danger,
3. necessity for force, and
4. reasonable use of force.

The first requirement for self-defense is an unprovoked attack. This means that the person who used self-defense was assaulted or violently confronted without any fault or instigation on their part. The purpose of legitimizing self-defense is to allow truly innocent parties to defend themselves from having harm inflicted upon them without fear

Self-Defense:
a defense in which a person uses force against another person in a way that would normally constitute a criminal act, but the actor is justified in the use of this force because it was necessary for self-protection

of legal ramifications. However, it would be contrary to public policy to allow people to inflict harm upon others and then claim self-defense for their actions when the victim of the first attack reacts by using force against the person who instigated the attack.

This means that self-defense is not available as a defense to a person who is the **initial aggressor** or the person who first attacked or used force against another person in an altercation. The *MPC* states that self-defense cannot be claimed when "the actor, with the purpose of causing death or serious bodily injury, provoked the use of force against himself" (American Law Institute 1985:45). However, there is a **withdrawal exception** that may be available to initial aggressors under certain circumstances. Under the withdrawal exception, self-defense may be used by initial aggressors who completely remove or extract themselves from an incident involving physical force. Box 10.1 illustrates the issues that may arise when an initial aggressor makes a claim of self-defense.

The second requirement for the use of self-defense is that the need for such force must be immediate. The *MPC* states that "the use of force upon or toward another person is justifiable when the actor believes that such force is immediately necessary for the purpose of protecting himself against the use of unlawful force by such other person on the present occasion" (American Law Institute 1985:44). This means that in order to use force as a valid form of self-defense, the person must have a need to use force at that very moment in order to protect himself or herself from harm or injury. The *MPC* requires that the danger of harm be here and now, not some time even in the very near future. This requirement means that preemptive strikes are not permitted as a form of self-defense. A **preemptive strike** is an attack or use of force against a person to prevent that person from inflicting harm at some later time. Box 10.2

Initial Aggressor: the person who first uses force against another person in an altercation

Withdrawal Exception: allows for the use of self-defense by an initial aggressor if that person has completely removed or extracted themselves from an incident involving physical force

Preemptive Strike: an attack or use of force against a person to prevent that person from inflicting harm at some later time

---

Box 10.1   YOU DECIDE: CAN ELIZABETH CLAIM SELF-DEFENSE?

One afternoon, Elizabeth and Amy get into a verbal argument. All of a sudden, Elizabeth violently attacks Amy, making Amy fear for her personal safety. In response, Amy pushes Elizabeth to the ground in order to prevent harm to herself. At this point, would Elizabeth be justified in using self-defense if she uses force in order to thwart Amy's use of force against her? Why or why not?

What if Elizabeth initially attacked Amy, then backed away saying "I am so sorry, I don't want to fight. Let's call a truce." Then, as Elizabeth turned to leave without inflicting any further harm, Amy wanted to get revenge for the attack and so swung at Elizabeth with a baseball bat. Has Elizabeth had completely withdrawn herself from the altercation? Is she justified in using self-defense to thwart Amy's attack and protect herself under the withdrawal exception?

Box 10.2   YOU DECIDE: IS NICK ABLE TO USE SELF-DEFENSE?

While Nick is on his lunch break, he overhears some coworkers talking about beating him up after work that day. Instead of alerting law enforcement, Nick gathers a group of his friends. They all wait in the bushes outside Nick's office building until his coworkers emerge at the end of the day. Nick and his friends then attack his coworkers and violently assault them. At that point, is Nick justified in using physical force against his coworkers? What if Nick heard his coworkers talk about killing him after work that day? What is the appropriate course of action for Nick to take?

gives an example in which you can decide whether or not a person has used a preemptive strike in order to defend himself or herself.

In the previous example, while there is certainly a threat of future harm to Nick, that threat is not immediate. If Nick were to use force against his coworkers to prevent them from attacking him later that day, this would be a preemptive strike and would not be a legitimate form of self-defense. The logic for the rule against preemptive strikes is that self-defense should be used as a last resort. In this particular example, Nick has adequate time to alert law enforcement authorities to the threat and make arrangements to protect himself, such as having someone escort him to his car after work. In this way, the criminal law recognizes that law enforcement officers should handle this type of situation in most instances, and that ordinary citizens should only be permitted to take the law into their own hands when there are no other viable alternatives available.

Although preemptive strikes are not permitted, a person does not need to wait until being physically assaulted or attacked in order to validly use self-defense. A person is entitled to use self-defense not only after the blow has been struck and injury has occurred, but also to prevent an imminent blow. For example, Bryce is angry and wants to hurt Tony, so he raises his fist in order to punch Tony in the mouth. At that point, Tony is entitled to use self-defense in order protect himself as soon as it becomes clear to him that Bryce has threatened him with imminent harm. Tony does not have to wait until Bryce actually hits him to protect himself in self-defense. Allowing a person to use force in order to thwart an imminent attack seems to be more fully in line with policy considerations that value the proactive prevention of harm above the reactive use of force once harm has already been inflicted upon a person.

Because self-defense requires imminent harm, retaliation is not a legal use of self-defense. **Retaliation** is when a defendant uses force against someone who has used unlawful force against them, but after some amount of time has passed since the initial use of unlawful force.

Retaliation: when a defendant uses force against someone who has used unlawful force against them, but after some amount of time has passed since the initial use of unlawful force

For instance, Michael is angry at Don and hits him with a baseball bat. Don leaves the argument, but wishes to seek revenge against Michael for the harm he caused. The following day, Don sneaks up on Michael and hits him in the back with a hammer. While Don probably would have been justified in using force against Michael at the time that Michael was attacking him, too much time had passed for Don's use of force to be valid. Because the harm was no longer immediate, Don cannot legitimately claim self-defense in this situation. Self-defense is intended to give people the ability to protect themselves when no other means of protection are available; therefore, self-defense can be used only at the very point in time when harm is threatened. It is clear that in this particular situation, Don should call the police and make a report about Michael's actions rather than taking matters into his own hands.

The third element for a valid use of self-defense is that there must be **necessity** for the use of force. Self-defense can only be used when no alternative means are available for protecting oneself from harm. Public policy considerations dictate that when some alternative method of resolving a situation other than the use of force would be effective, those means should be used. However, self-defense *can* be used when other means of resolution (such as discussing the situation or alerting law enforcement) would not be effective, leaving the defendant with self-defense as the only viable means of preventing harm to himself or herself. In order to demonstrate that the use of self-defense was necessary, the defendant will need to show the judge or the jury that a reasonable person in the same situation would believe that the use of force was the only means available to prevent the initial harm (or further harm) from occurring.

Necessity:
a defense in which the defendant commits the *actus reus* of a crime due to being forced to make a choice between two situations, either of which would result in some type of injury or damage

Finally, when a person uses force as a form of self-defense, the level and amount of force used must be **reasonable** relative to the threat posed. This raises the issue of *what type* and *how much* force is considered reasonable for the use of self-defense in various situations. Obviously, this can vary greatly based upon the specific circumstances of the force being used or threatened. A general answer is that the person using self-defense is permitted to utilize the minimum amount of force necessary to thwart the attacker and prevent the infliction of harm. The *MPC* states that "a person employing protective force may estimate the necessity thereof under the circumstances as he believes them to be when the force is used" (American Law Institute 1985:45-46). In other words, when a person is attacked or threatened, he or she may permissibly defend himself or herself by using the amount of force that is demanded by the imminent danger presented in order to be effectively protected from harm.

Reasonable:
the minimum amount of force necessary to thwart an attacker and prevent the infliction of harm

A very special situation arises when self-defense is utilized in the form of deadly force. Like any valid use of self-defense, the use of

---

Box 10.3   ELEMENTS OF SELF-DEFENSE

- Unprovoked attack AND
- Immediate danger AND
- Necessity for force AND
- Reasonable use of force

---

deadly force must be reasonable under the circumstances. The *MPC* states that deadly force is permitted only when "the actor believes that such force is necessary to protect himself against death, serious bodily injury, kidnapping or sexual intercourse compelled by force or threat" (American Law Institute 1985:45). Deadly force cannot be used by an initial aggressor or if the actor has the opportunity of avoiding harm by "retreating, . . . surrendering possession . . . , or by complying with a demand" (45). However, an actor is under no duty to retreat, surrender possession of property, or comply with a demand when he or she is attacked in his or her own home or place of work, unless that person was the initial aggressor, or unless the attack takes place in the workplace and the aggressor is someone who is also employed in that workplace. In determining whether the use of deadly force was appropriate, the actions will be judged by the actor's perception of the circumstances at the time that the force was used. However, there may be legal repercussions if the belief that deadly force was necessary resulted from the actor's negligent or reckless actions (American Law Institute 1985:46-47). Box 10.3 outlines the elements that must be present for the valid use of self-defense. The case *Young v. State of Indiana*, 451 N.E.2d 91 (Ind. App. 1983) addresses the circumstances in which deadly force can be used as a form of self-defense (see Box 10.4).

Box 10.4   WHEN CAN DEADLY FORCE BE USED?

Young v. State of Indiana
451 N.E.2d 91 (Ind. App. 1983)

Appellant Ernest Robert Young was distributing religious literature on a street corner in Gary on December 20, 1980. At one point in the day George Coleman approached Young, began to harass and swear at him, and then left. Later that day Young gave Danita Chin a ride to work while he was driving home.

Chin worked at Charlie's Carry Out, an establishment which provides hot dogs and hamburgers for its patrons. Young and Chin were discussing some of Young's emotional problems over a bag of french fries when Coleman walked in the shop. Upon seeing Young, Coleman approached him, began swearing at him, and grabbed Young's arm. At this point Young pulled out a gun and administered three fatal shots to Coleman.

Young was charged with and tried for murder. At trial Young presented evidence in support of his claim that he acted in self-defense. However, the jury chose not to believe his story and returned a verdict of guilty of voluntary manslaughter.

On appeal Young raises three issues [including] whether the evidence was sufficient to support his conviction. Appellant also attacks the sufficiency of the evidence in support of his conviction. It is appellant's contention that the State failed to disprove beyond a reasonable doubt that he acted in self-defense as the State is required to. Appellant seems to believe that because he is a 72-year-old man the jury must believe that he was justified in killing a 39-year-old man, who was six feet tall and weighed two hundred pounds and was harassing him.

When reviewing a challenge to the sufficiency of the evidence, this Court does not reweigh the evidence or rejudge the credibility of witnesses. Only the evidence most favorable to the verdict will be reviewed, and if substantial evidence supports that verdict, it will be upheld.

The issue of whether the State has disproved an accused's claim of self-defense is a question of fact to be determined by the jury. The jury must view the incident from the accused's point of view but need not believe his story. Further, threats alone are not sufficient to warrant the use of deadly force.

In the case at bar there is no evidence that decedent did anything more than threaten appellant on two occasions. Further, there is no evidence that decedent had a weapon or used it to threaten appellant. The mere fact that decedent outweighed appellant and was younger than him is not sufficient by itself to justify the use of deadly force.

The jury heard appellant's story and it determined that he acted in the heat of the moment rather than in self-defense. There is ample evidence to support its verdict. For the reasons stated above the conviction is affirmed.

1. Do you think that the appellate court was correct in deciding that Young's use of self-defense was not valid? Why or why not?
2. Should the size and age of the parties be taken into consideration in a self-defense case?
3. What factors should be considered in determining whether the use of force was reasonable?

Who Can Be Protected?

Self-defense also raises the issue of who a person is legally entitled to protect from harm through the use of force. As has been discussed, people are certainly entitled to protect themselves from death or serious bodily injury. But what about third parties? Can one person legitimately use force against another person to protect someone else from harm? The *MPC* states that the use of force is permissible to protect a third party when: "(a) the actor would be justified . . . in using such force to protect himself against the injury he believes to be threatened to the person whom he seeks to protect; and (b) under the circumstances as the actor believes them to be, the person whom he seeks to protect would be justified in using such protective force; and (c) the actor believes that his intervention is necessary for the protection of the other person" (American Law Institute 1985:47). In other words, a person may use force to protect third parties if the third parties would be entitled to use the force themselves based upon the requirements for self-defense. Also, the person protecting the third party must reasonably believe that the third party is unable to act on his or her own behalf, thereby making the use of force necessary to ensure the protection of the third party who is in danger.

Protection of Property

The rationale for the use of self-defense is to protect people from harm. There are significant public policy considerations in the law's recognition that a person's right to life is superior to a person's right to property. But are people ever entitled to use self-defense to protect their property? After all, a significant number of people are hurt or killed during the commission of crimes against property, such as burglary, arson, and other property offenses. People's right to protect their own property from an unlawful intruder is referred to as the **Castle Doctrine**. The *MPC* tells us that force can be used to defend property when a person believes that such force is necessary

Castle Doctrine:
a person's right to protect his or her own property from an unlawful intruder

> (a) to prevent or terminate an unlawful entry or other trespass upon land . . . or (b) to effect an entry or re-entry upon land or to retake tangible movable property, provided that the actor believes that he . . . was unlawfully dispossessed of such land or movable property and is entitled to possession, and provided, further that (i) the force is used immediately or on fresh pursuit after such dispossession; or (ii) the actor believes that the person against whom he uses force has no claim of right to the possession of the property and, in the case of land, the circumstances, as the actor believes them to be, are of such urgency that it would be an exceptional hardship to postpone the entry or re-entry until a court order is obtained. (American Law Institute 1985:49)

In addition to permitting the use of force against someone who has entered or is attempting to enter a home, this means that when the person who has used self-defense has lawful possession of real or personal property and someone tries to interfere with that possession, the actor may use self-defense if he or she reasonably believes that this force is essential to the protection of the property. However, due to the requirement that the threat be immediate, self-defense may only be used immediately after property is unlawfully taken or occupied. The *MPC* takes a very expansive approach to the use of self-defense for the protection of property in that its protection extends to both real and personal property.

Many states have adopted Castle Doctrines, which may either allow people to use deadly force against someone attempting to break into their home, or may eliminate a duty to retreat when people are inside their homes. Currently, at least 30 states have enacted statutes that either eliminate the duty to retreat if an attack takes place in the home, or eliminate the duty to retreat regardless of where the attack takes place (Clark 2012). However, there are several significant limitations to the use of force in the defense of property.

For example, because the primary objective of the criminal law is to protect people from harm, the defense of a person's home or habitation is given much more expansive protection than personal property. Additionally, force cannot be used automatically against any person who comes near a home or other piece of property. The *MPC* states that "the use of force is justifiable . . . only if the actor first requests the person . . . to desist from his interference with the property, unless the actor believes that: (i) such request would be useless; or (ii) it would be dangerous to himself or another person to make the request; or (iii) substantial harm will be done to the physical condition of the property that is sought to be protected before the request can effectively be made" (American Law Institute 1985:49-50).

The defense of property is particularly problematic when it involves the use of deadly force. Under the *MPC*, deadly force can be used to defend property only when the actor believes that

> (i) the person against whom the force is used is attempting to dispossess him of his dwelling otherwise than under a claim of right to its possession; or (ii) the person against whom the force is used is attempting to commit or consummate arson, burglary, robbery or other felonious theft or property destruction and either: (A) has employed or threatened deadly force against or in the presence of the actor; or (B) the use of force other than deadly force to prevent the commission or the consummation of the crime would expose the actor or another in his presence to substantial danger of serious bodily injury. (American Law Institute 1985:50)

The extreme situations to which the use of deadly force to defend property are limited reflects the idea that human life is significantly more valuable than property, and that the use of deadly force to protect property should be limited to situations in which a person's life is in danger.

In addition to force inflicted upon an intruder by a person, there have been a number of instances in which devices, such as spring-guns or traps, have been set by property owners to defend against intruders. Under certain circumstances, these devices may be used to protect property. The *MPC* states that devices can be used to protect property only if "(a) the device is not designed to cause or known to create a substantial risk of causing death or serious bodily injury; and (b) the use of the particular device to protect the property from entry or trespass is reasonable under the circumstances, as the actor believes them to be; and (c) the device is one customarily used for such a purpose or reasonable care is taken to make known to probable intruders the fact that it is used" (American Law Institute 1985:50-51). The *MPC* makes it clear that that the use of devices as a form of self-defense is valid only in very limited circumstances. In the case *People v. Ceballos*, 526 P.2d 241 (Cal. 1974), the court addresses when such devices may be used to defend property (see Box 10.5).

Box 10.5   WHEN CAN A DEVICE BE USED TO DEFEND PROPERTY?

People v. Ceballos
526 P.2d 241 (Cal. 1974)

In March 1970 some tools were stolen from defendant's home. On May 12, 1970, he noticed the lock on his garage doors was bent and pry marks were on one of the doors. The next day he mounted a loaded .22 caliber pistol in the garage. The pistol was aimed at the center of the garage doors and was connected by a wire to one of the doors so that the pistol would discharge if the door was opened several inches.

The damage to defendant's lock had been done by a 16-year-old boy named Stephen and a 15-year-old boy named Robert. On the afternoon of May 15, 1970, the boys returned to defendant's house while he was away. Neither boy was armed with a gun or knife. After looking in the windows and seeing no one, Stephen succeeded in removing the lock on the garage doors with a crowbar, and, as he pulled the door outward, he was hit in the face with a bullet from the pistol.

Defendant, testifying in his own behalf, admitted having set up the trap gun. He stated that after noticing the pry marks on his garage door on May 12, he felt he should "set up some kind of a trap, something to keep the burglar out of my home." When asked why he was trying to keep the burglar out, he replied, "Because somebody was trying to steal my property and I don't want to come home some night and have the thief in there, usually a thief is pretty desperate and they just pick up a weapon if they don't have one and do the best they can."

Defendant contends that had he been present he would have been justified in shooting Stephen since Stephen was attempting to commit burglary, that under [precedent] cases . . . defendant had a right to do indirectly what he could have done directly, and that therefore any attempt by him to commit a violent injury upon Stephen was not "unlawful" and hence not an assault. The People argue that the rule in *Gilliam* is unsound, that as a matter of law a trap gun constitutes excessive force, and that in any event the circumstances were not in fact such as to warrant the use of deadly force.

Allowing persons, at their own risk, to employ deadly mechanical devices imperils the lives of children, firemen and policemen acting within the scope of their employment, and others. Where the actor is present, there is always the possibility he will realize that deadly force is not necessary, but deadly mechanical devices are without mercy or discretion. Such devices "are silent instrumentalities of death. They deal death and destruction to the innocent as well as the criminal intruder without the slightest warning. The taking of human life [or infliction of great bodily injury] by such means is brutally savage and inhuman."

It seems clear that the use of such devices should not be encouraged.

Moreover, whatever may be thought in torts, the foregoing rule setting forth an exception to liability for death or injuries inflicted by such devices "is inappropriate in penal law for it is obvious that it does not prescribe a workable standard of conduct; liability depends upon fortuitous results." We therefore decline to adopt that rule in criminal cases.

In the instant case the asserted burglary did not threaten death or serious bodily harm, since no one but Stephen and Robert was then on the premises. A defendant is not protected from liability merely by the fact that the intruder's conduct is such as would justify the defendant, were he present, in believing that the intrusion threatened death or serious bodily injury. There is ordinarily the possibility that the defendant, were he present, would realize the true state of affairs and recognize the intruder as one whom he would not be justified in killing or wounding.

---

1. In applying the elements of self-defense, do you believe that the defendant would have been justified in the use of self-defense if he had been on the property at the time of the intrusion?
2. Should people be permitted to take steps to protect their property from intrusions in their absence? If so, how extensive should these steps be?

Retreat

Another issue that arises in the context of self-defense is whether people are required to **retreat**, or escape from their attackers, before using self-defense. There are two primary approaches to this issue, which have been utilized by various criminal law jurisdictions.

Retreat:
an attempt to escape from an attacker before using self-defense

In jurisdictions that have adopted the **stand your ground approach**, a person is under no legal duty to attempt to retreat before utilizing force as a form of self-defense so long as he or she was not the initial aggressor. Under the stand your ground rule, a person does not have an obligation to retreat when attacked in any location where he or she has a lawful right to be. This is the rule that has been adopted by the majority of U.S. criminal law jurisdictions. Conversely, jurisdictions that have adopted the **retreat rule** require a person to attempt to flee or escape before utilizing self-defense, so long as that person could do so reasonably and safely. However, even states that have adopted the retreat rule generally utilize the **castle exception**, which allows people to use deadly force without a duty to retreat if they (1) reasonably believe that they are in danger of death or serious bodily injury, and (2) the attack takes place while they are in their home.

The *MPC* also addresses this issue and adopts the retreat rule with a castle exception. The *Code* states that self-defense is not justifiable when "the actor knows that he can avoid the necessity of using such force with complete safety by retreating or by surrendering possession of a thing to a person asserting a claim of right thereto or by complying with a demand that he abstain from any action that he has no duty to take." However, "the actor is not obliged to retreat from his dwelling or place of work, unless he was the initial aggressor" (American Law Institute 1985:45).

Battered Spouse Syndrome

One of the significant developments in the law of self-defense is that of **battered spouse syndrome**. For many years, people who killed an abusive spouse at times when the abuse was not taking place were unable to use self-defense as a valid justification for their use of force. The reason for this was that while the abusive spouse generally posed some danger, the danger was not imminent since they were not acting in an abusive manner at the time force was used by the victim. The growing body of knowledge of domestic violence has recognized that those in abusive relationships are generally unable to leave the abusive situation. Cycles of abuse often involve severe psychological manipulation of the victim that makes it unreasonable to expect them to simply depart the situation. The presence of the battered spouse syndrome must usually be established through the use of expert testimony at trial. As is seen in *Commonwealth v. Rodriquez*, 418 Mass. 1; 633 N.E.2d 1039 (Mass. 1994), courts are obligated to allow expert testimony to help guide the jury in deciding whether battered spouse syndrome was present and the presence of battered spouse syndrome may mitigate the criminal behavior of a victim of abuse (Box 10.6).

Stand Your Ground Approach: approach under which a person is under no legal duty to retreat before utilizing force as a form of self-defense

Retreat Rule: approach under which a person must attempt to flee or escape before utilizing force as self-defense so long as they can do so safely

Castle Exception: allows a person to use deadly force without a duty to retreat if they reasonably believe that they are in danger or death or serious bodily injury and the attack takes place in their home

Battered Spouse Syndrome: a limited defense that is recognized in some jurisdictions in which an abuse victim uses force against the abuser at a time when there is no imminent threat

Box 10.6   SHOULD JURIES CONSIDER EVIDENCE OF ABUSE?

Commonwealth v. Rodriquez
418 Mass. 1; 633 N.E.2d 1039 (Mass. 1994)

LIACOS, C.J. delivered the opinion of the court.

The defendant fatally stabbed her boyfriend during an argument. She was indicted on a charge of manslaughter. At trial, she claimed self-defense. A jury found her guilty. She was sentenced to from sixteen to twenty years in prison. In this appeal she asserts that the judge erred in excluding certain evidence that the defendant had suffered a long history of physical abuse by the victim.

For most of the night on March 26, 1989, the defendant was at home, in her apartment, with her four children. At approximately 9 P.M., the victim, Julio Montalban, who was living with the defendant, left to go to work. The victim returned shortly before midnight.

Some time after midnight, a friend and neighbor of the defendant, Maria Perez, came to the apartment . . . the defendant began to put on her coat and shoes, planning to go to Perez's house. The victim told the defendant that "she wasn't going anywhere." The defendant countered that she was.

After the defendant had been at Perez's house for about five minutes, the victim arrived. He and the defendant argued. The defendant testified that the victim called her a "whore," slapped her in the face, and pulled her hair. She also testified that the victim told her that they were "going to solve some problems" when they got back to her apartment.

When they were back at the defendant's apartment the defendant and the victim yelled at each other, and pushed one another . . . the victim pushed the defendant into the kitchen, grabbed a knife from a drawer, and held the knife close to the

defendant's face. The defendant then pushed the victim into the dining room. The victim placed the knife on the dining room table.

The defendant testified that, when she told her daughter to telephone the police, the victim threw the telephone and other household objects at her. The defendant then picked up the knife and told the victim to get out of the apartment. She opened the door, and told him to leave. The victim slammed the door shut and told her that he would not go. The defendant opened the door again and again, the victim slammed it shut. He slapped the defendant's face. The defendant then stabbed and fatally wounded the victim.

The defendant attempted to introduce evidence of prior beatings by the victim, which the judge excluded . . . witnesses would have testified that, among other things, during their relationship, the victim verbally abused the defendant; hit and punched her on many occasions; tried to strangle her with an extension cord; raped her; punched her in the abdomen while she was pregnant with their son, in an attempt to induce an abortion; threw bleach in her face; and held a baseball bat to her head and threatened to kill her with it.

We believe that the judge took an overly restrictive view of this evidence. It is well established that a defendant asserting self-defense is allowed to introduce evidence showing "that at the time of the killing [she] knew of specific violent acts recently committed by the victim." Such evidence is admissible to assist the jury in "assessing the reasonableness of the defendant's reaction to the events leading to the homicide." Here, the claimed acts of violence were directed at the defendant herself and, thus, were even more relevant. We believe that the jury would have been aided considerably in determining the reasonableness of the defendant's use of deadly force if they had heard evidence of other violent acts recently committed by the victim against the defendant.

The critical issue at trial was whether the defendant acted in self-defense. The excluded testimony would have enhanced the defendant's assertion of that defense so significantly that its exclusion constitutes reversible error. A new trial is required.

1. Should an individual who uses self-defense be given to ability to present to the jury past instances of violence, rather than just those that occurred in the case at hand?
2. Is the introduction of this type of evidence likely to prejudice the jury against the victim? If so, how could this be remedied?
3. Are there ever circumstances where a person should be permitted to use self-defense when there is not an immediate threat of harm? If so, when might this be justified?

However, the battered spouse syndrome defense is quite limited in its scope. While the threat does not necessarily have to be imminent, there must be some type of threat present at the time that the force is used. For example, an abused spouse cannot stab her abuser in the back as he is walking away or attack him while he is sleeping. While the battered spouse syndrome is not recognized as a legal defense in and of itself, it is admissible to allow the jury to help determine whether the behavior of the battered spouse was reasonable, and whether the battered spouse perceived herself to be in imminent danger in a self-defense case [*United States v. Brown*, 891 F. Supp. 1501 (D. Kan. 1995)].

Choice of Evils

The choice of evils justification defense is also referred to as the defense of necessity. This defense is available in a situation where the defendant commits the *actus reus* of a crime due to being forced to make a choice between two situations, either of which would result in some type of injury or damage. It is logical that when a person must choose between two wrongs, a valid defense should be available to the person who makes a logical choice to embark on the course of action that would produce the lesser amount of harm of the two choices. This is the case even if that person has to commit a criminal act in order to avoid the greater amount of harm that would be brought about by the alternative action.

In order to utilize this defense, it is necessary that the defendant have no viable and reasonable alternative to committing a criminal act. The *MPC* states that

> conduct that the actor believes to be necessary to avoid a harm or evil to himself or to another is justifiable, provided that: (a) the harm or evil sought to be avoided by such conduct is greater than that sought to be prevented by the law defining the offense charged; and (b) neither the Code nor other law defining the offense provides exceptions or defenses dealing with the specific situation involved; and (c) a legislative purpose to exclude the justification claimed does not otherwise plainly appear. (American Law Institute 1985:42)

Box 10.7 presents a scenario for you to decide whether or not a person can utilize the choice of evils defense for the actions taken.

In the previous example, Jim could probably utilize the choice of evils defense for breaking into a structure belonging to someone else when he was forced to seek shelter from a deadly blizzard. Had he not committed a crime (breaking into another person's structure), he would have died as a result of the severe weather. The criminal law certainly recognizes that human life is more significant and afforded greater protections than property interests, so if he had no reasonable alternative to escape from the blizzard, the choice of evils defense would be available to him. However, if Jim had a reasonable opportunity to seek shelter in a location available to the public, then the choice of evils defense could not be used for the unlawful entry into a privately owned structure.

However, a defendant cannot use the choice of evils defense if his or her own recklessness or negligence resulted in the situation that required him or her to make a choice among criminal acts. The *MPC*

Box 10.7 YOU DECIDE: IS THIS AN APPROPRIATE CHOICE OF EVILS?

Jim has spent the day hiking near his mountain cabin. He is enjoying the scenery and being outside in the fresh air. Before he realizes what time it is, he notices that it is getting dark and a snowstorm is approaching. Jim is heading back toward his own cabin when he loses his way in the blizzard. Fearful for his life, Jim stumbles upon an unoccupied cabin with a "No Trespassing" sign posted. Jim breaks into the cabin and spends the night there. He leaves the next morning once the blizzard has passed and he is able to see where he is going. Is Jim criminally liable for breaking into a structure that belongs to someone else? What if the owners of the cabin are outraged that Jim entered their home without permission and demand that charges be filed against him?

Box 10.8 ELEMENTS OF CHOICE OF EVILS

- Action is necessary to prevent harm to oneself or another AND
- The evil committed was lesser than the harm avoided AND
- No reasonable alternative was available AND
- The actor's negligence or recklessness did not create the situation requiring a choice of evils

---

states that "when the actor was reckless or negligent in bringing about the situation requiring a choice of harms or evils or in appraising the necessity for his conduct, the justification afforded . . . is unavailable in a prosecution for any offense for which recklessness or negligence . . . suffices to establish culpability" (American Law Institute 1985:42-43).

Also, there are situations in which the legislature has taken all discretion out of the hands of the citizens and has made a decision through a statute about what decision must be made when a choice among evils presents itself. In these situations, the person must follow the legislative mandate in determining an appropriate course of action. It is also important to note that once an imminent threat no longer exists, the availability of the choice of evils defense ceases. In the previous example, Jim would lose his ability to utilize the choice of evils defense if he unlawfully remained in the private structure after the danger from the blizzard had passed and he was able to safely go on his way.

The trier of fact will make a determination about whether an appropriate choice of evils was made based upon the actor's perception at the time that the events took place. In other words, the actor may use the choice of evils defense so long as he or she reasonably believed that a certain course of conduct was necessary to avoid harm, whether or not that actually turns out to be the case. Box 10.8 outlines the elements of the choice of evils defense.

Consent

It is an important tenet of the legal system to recognize individual autonomy and that within reason people should be able to determine what is done to themselves and their own property. It is from this notion that **consent** is available as a justification defense to certain crimes. The consent defense allows a person to say that while she did commit a criminal act, the person against whom the crime was committed voluntarily gave his or her permission for the crime to take

Consent:
a defense that is available when a person did commit a criminal act, but the person against whom the crime was committed voluntarily gave his or her permission for the crime to take place

place. As such, the performance of the criminal act was justified. There are four primary situations in which consent can be used as valid defense:

(1) Criminal acts that cause no significant harm or damage to a person or property
(2) Injuries that take place during sporting events
(3) When the conduct is of benefit to the person who gave the consent
(4) The consent is given to sexual conduct. (Fletcher 1978:770)

The first type of consent might result when a person gives permission for someone to touch him or her (battery) or to take an object that rightfully belongs to the consenting person. In the second instance, a concept known as **implied consent** is present when a person participates in a sporting event. This is because sporting events inherently and unavoidably involve physical contact that may result in some type of injury. There is essentially no way to avoid this if a person wishes to be involved in a sporting event. Because there is no way for a sporting event participant to eliminate all risk of injury, a person effectively gives his or her consent to injuries that are reasonably foreseeable to that sport when he or she voluntarily participates in a particular sporting event. For example, a football player could not be held criminally liable for a battery when tackling a player from the opposing team. This is because the players gave their implied consent to such contact when they chose to participate as part of the football team.

> **Implied Consent:**
> when a person effectively gives consent to injuries that are reasonably foreseeable to the activity in which they are participating

Consent also exists when the act performed benefits the consenting person. For example, if a person is gravely injured in a car accident and is brought to the hospital in an unconscious state, a physician will not be charged with a battery for performing an operation to save that person's life. The operation provided a benefit to the injured person that greatly outweighs any detriment that was caused by the doctor's actions.

Finally, consent is often used as a defense to sexual conduct. The emphasis placed on individual autonomy is particularly important in the context of a person's sexual decisions. However, consent cannot be used as a defense to sexual conduct with an individual who has not yet reached the legal age. In this case, the legislature has given guidelines about when a person has reached an age to be able to consent to sexual activity. Individuals who have not yet reached that age are unable to give consent, and so any consent asserted would not be valid. This is the case for the crime of statutory rape (discussed in Chapter 2).

In order to use consent as a defense to a crime, it is necessary for the defendant to prove that the consent was voluntary,

Box 10.9   ELEMENTS OF CONSENT
• Consent was to an action for which consent can be given AND
• Consent was voluntary, knowing, and authorized

knowing, and authorized. Voluntary consent means that the consent was given as a product of the consenting individual's free will and that the person was not forced or tricked into giving consent. Knowing consent means that consenting persons have a strong and solid understanding of exactly to what they are consenting. Knowing consent requires, at a minimum, that people be aware of their actions, mentally competent, and legally sane. Authorized consent means that someone who is giving consent had the legal authority to do so. Unless a relationship fits into a few very narrow categories (parent and minor child, guardian and conservator, etc.), one person generally cannot give consent on behalf of another. It is also important to note that consent can be withdrawn. Once consent is withdrawn, it is no longer effective and cannot be used as a defense from that point forward. Box 10.9 outlines the elements of a consent defense.

SUMMARY

In order to be held criminally liable, a person must commit a criminal act without a valid excuse or justification for his or her actions. These excuses or justifications for criminal acts are known as defenses. A valid defense may result in a person's criminal liability being either lessened or eliminated completely. Justification defenses assert that a defendant's criminal behavior was correct or justified. Excuse defenses assert that while a defendant's criminal behavior was not justified, they have a reason for the actions taken that excuses the criminal liability. These are affirmative defenses, which means that the defendant will introduce evidence of facts or circumstances that do not challenge the quality of the state's case, but that serve to eliminate or mitigate the charge made against the defendant. The primary justification defenses are self-defense, choice of evils, and consent.

A person may use self-defense in order to protect himself or herself from the infliction of force. The elements for a valid use of self-defense are: (1) an unprovoked attack; (2) immediate danger; (3) necessity for force; and (4) reasonable use of force. Self-defense cannot be used by an initial aggressor, unless it falls within the withdrawal exception. Self-defense also cannot be used as a preemptive strike or as a means of retaliation. Self-defense may be used to protect third parties so long as those parties would be entitled to use force to protect themselves.

Under certain circumstances, force may also be used to protect property. In furtherance of this right, some states have adopted Castle Doctrines, which may either entitle people to use deadly force when someone is attempting to unlawfully enter their home or eliminate a person's duty to retreat from an intruder when they are in their own home. Some jurisdictions have adopted a stand your ground approach, which means that a person has no legal duty to attempt to retreat, or escape, before using self-defense. Other jurisdictions utilize a retreat rule, which imposes the duty for a person to attempt to retreat before using force, so long as the person can do so reasonably. One recent advance in the law is the consideration of the presence of the battered spouse syndrome in use of force cases against abusive spouses by their victims.

Another justification defense is choice of evils, also referred to as necessity. This defense may be utilized when a person commits a crime because they are forced to choose between two actions, either of which will cause some degree of harm. To legitimately use this defense, individuals must have no reasonable alternative to committing a crime, and they must choose the course of action that will minimize harm.

Consent may also be used as a justification defense to criminal actions. The situations in which consent may be a viable defense include: (1) criminal acts that cause no significant harm or damage to a person or property; (2) injuries that take place during sporting events; (3) when the conduct is of benefit to the person who gave their consent; and (4) when the consent is given to sexual conduct. Consent must be voluntary, knowing, and authorized.

KEY TERMS

affirmative defense
battered spouse syndrome
burden of proof
castle doctrine
castle exception
consent
defense
excuse defense
impeachment
imperfect defense
implied consent

initial aggressor
justification defense
necessity
perfect defense
preemptive strike
reasonable
retaliation
retreat
retreat rule
self-defense
stand your ground approach
withdrawal exception

CRITICAL THINKING QUESTIONS

1. Discuss the public policy considerations of the Castle Doctrine. Should people be able to use deadly force to protect their homes? What considerations should be weighed in making this decision? Be specific and explain your reasoning.

2. Should people be able to use self-defense to prevent harm from occurring, or should it be a requirement that self-defense be used only in response to the actual infliction of force? What are the advantages and disadvantages to each approach? Explain your reasoning.

3. Is the battered spouse syndrome a legitimate justification for the use of force? Should victims of domestic abuse be given special treatment with regard to the requirement that imminent harm be present before self-defense can be used? Discuss the public policy implications of your response and how you arrived at that decision.

4. Should the consent defense be expanded to give people the ability to consent to more offenses? Should the acts to which people are allowed to consent be determined by individual autonomy or by the criminal law? Consider the balance that must be struck between allowing individuals to make decisions concerning their own welfare and the need to protect vulnerable populations. Explain your reasoning.

5. Discuss the advantages and disadvantages of the stand your ground rule and the retreat approach. Which is more consistent with the goal of preventing the most significant amount of harm? Which approach provides the greatest amount of protection for society at large? Explain your reasoning.

6. Are there situations other than the ones discussed in this chapter in which a person might be justified in committing a criminal act? Be specific and give examples.

7. Are there any situations in which self-defense should be available to an initial aggressor, or in which preemptive strikes should be permitted? Discuss the public policy implications of your response and give specific examples.

SUGGESTED READINGS

Bedi, M. (2011). "Excusing Behavior: Reclassifying the Federal Common Law Defenses of Duress and Necessity Relying on the Victim's Role." *Journal of Criminal Law and Criminology* 101 (2):575-632. In this paper, the author explores the difficulty that is often faced in classifying a criminal defense as a justification or an excuse. Bedi addresses the idea that a defense could potentially fit into both categories depending upon theoretical framework and the role and activities of the crime victim. While this article focuses on the defenses of duress and necessity, the issues addressed have broad implications throughout the study of criminal defenses. The author presents the idea that whether a defense is properly categorized as an excuse or justification is not a one-size-fits-all approach, and depends primarily upon the victim's role in the crime, rather than the actions of the defendant. This paper discusses the manner in which federal courts have handled duress and necessity, and suggests a new method of defense classification, said to be more comprehensive, that focuses on the role of the victim. Bedi proposes that a defense should be considered an excuse when the victim had no role in the commission of a crime, and a justification when the victim played some role in the crime.

Levin, B. (2010). "A Defensible Defense? Reexamining Castle Doctrine Statutes." *Harvard Journal on Legislation* 47(2):523-553. In this paper, Levin explores the history of the defense of property and the duty to retreat, and various modern-day Castle Doctrines that have been legislatively created in various jurisdictions, as well as the use of these statutes as justification for self-defense. The paper addresses the moral implication of the Castle Doctrine, whether the Castle Doctrine should be used as a form of self-defense, and the societal implications that result from Castle Doctrines. Levin utilizes a case study in which a man was killed for threatening another individual outside his home. This homicide resulted in a manslaughter conviction.

Schopp, R.F. (2008). *Justification Defenses and Just Convictions*. Cambridge: Cambridge University Press. In this book, Schopp examines the full spectrum of justification defenses and discusses their use from both a practical and philosophical perspective. Topics covered include the numerous issues associated with self-defense and necessity, the use of battered spouse syndrome, and the distinctions between conduct that is excused by the law and that which is truly justified. Schopp also addresses numerous ethical and philosophical perspectives and their relationships to justification defenses, as well as the distinction between justified conduct and moral conduct, and role that society's perception of morality plays in making this distinction.

Walker, L. (2009). *The Battered Woman Syndrome* (3d ed.). New York: Springer. Lenore Walker is a forensic psychologist who specializes in interpersonal violence. In this book, she presents the theoretical aspects of battered woman syndrome and integrates field research cases on the subject. Topics addressed in this book include risk factors, post-traumatic stress disorder, qualitative results for battered woman syndrome, and the cycle of violence. Walker also discusses male victims of domestic violence, forensic psychology, and abuse victims who kill in self-defense. The first edition of this book was one of the first to address battered woman syndrome, and was significant in its establishment as a credible legal defense.

REFERENCES

American Law Institute (1985). *Model Penal Code: Complete Statutory Text*. Philadelphia, PA.

Clark, M. (2012). "'Castle Doctrine' Laws Provoke Heated Debate." January 10. Pew Center on the States. http://stateline.org/live/details/story?contentId=623723.

Commonwealth v. Rodriquez, 418 Mass. 1; 633 N.E.2d 1039 (Mass. 1994).

Fletcher, G. (1978). *Rethinking Criminal Law*. Boston: Little, Brown.

People v. Ceballos, 526 P.2d 241 (Cal. 1974).

United States v. Brown, 891 F. Supp. 1501 (D. Kan. 1995).

Young v. State of Indiana, 451 N.E.2d 91 (1983 Ind. App.).

Excuse Defenses

LEARNING OBJECTIVES

After reading this chapter, you should be able to:

1. Identify the competing principles of the criminal justice system within excuse defenses
2. Explain the differences between a mistake of fact defense and the exceptions to a mistake of law not being a defense
3. Analyze the circumstances surrounding the superior orders defense
4. Compare and contrast the circumstances when intoxication is a defense and when it is not
5. Identify the different types of presumptions found in an infancy defense
6. Apply the requirements of the entrapment defense to a set of facts
7. Analyze and apply the requirements of the different tests for the insanity defense

INTRODUCTION

In Chapter 2 we outlined the requirements for criminal liability. A person is criminally liable if the state can prove the elements of a particular crime have been fulfilled *and* the person does not have a valid justification or excuse—that is, he or she does not have a valid defense. These defenses can be categorized into two main types: justification defenses and excuse defenses. Chapter 10 addressed justification defenses; this chapter addresses excuse defenses. While justification defenses are applicable to the *actus reus* element of criminal liability ("my actions were not wrong"), excuse defenses are applicable to the *mens rea* element ("my actions were wrong, but I am not blameworthy").

As we have noted, a crime is one in which the defendant has an evil mind coupled with a wrongful act. Excuse defenses address the "evil mind" portion of the offense—or one's mental state. These defenses can be as simple as the accused party's age or as complex as legal insanity. Regardless of the specific defense involved, they all have the common thread of addressing the accused's mental state.

Excuse defenses allow the criminal law to be consistent regarding the principles it supports. One of the criminal law's principles is to punish those who are blameworthy and deserving of punishment. Defendants who can attribute their actions to some valid excuse outlined in this chapter are not blameworthy and, therefore, are not deserving of punishment (see Robinson 2009). If they are considered dangerous (e.g., legally insane) then the criminal law provides a process by which these defendants are given treatment to reduce that danger. Additionally, as we noted in Chapter 1 (and further in Chapter 12), one punishment goal is to prevent future wrongdoing through deterrence. However, deterrence requires the person to be rational, weighing costs and benefits. With a valid excuse defense, rational decision making is not necessarily present and, therefore, the punishment will not be effective in preventing future wrongdoing via deterrence. The most prominent excuse defenses, therefore, will be discussed in this chapter.

MISTAKE

People may make mistakes that might cause them to commit a crime. Sometimes, these mistakes can excuse their behavior as a defense, while others do not. Generally speaking, a **mistake of law** is not a defense—a concept illustrated by the adage "ignorance of the law is not a defense." For example, not knowing that dumping chemicals in a public water source is against the law does not eliminate one's criminal responsibility. Or, believing that borrowing a neighbor's car

Mistake of Law:
due to an honest and/or reasonable mistake of a law, the defendant may still be criminally liable for committing the crime

against his will for a quick trip is not against the law (joyriding). Ignorance of the law does not excuse this behavior; therefore, the person can be found guilty of joyriding. We say that citizens have the duty to know and understand the law that governs their actions, which harkens back to what we learned about Thomas Hobbes, who believed in the social contract. The social contract suggests that in exchange for safety provided by the state, citizens adhere to the limitations placed by the state. Since citizens are aware that limitations exist in exchange for their safety, then they also should understand the limits to their own behavior. Additionally, it would be difficult to oversee citizens' behavior if they could merely "excuse" their actions claiming ignorance of the law.

Although generally a mistake of law is not a defense, there are two circumstances where it might be a defense: (1) the authorized reliance exception and (2) the "different law" exception. When their requirements are fulfilled, these exceptions dictate that the accused can avoid criminal liability given a mistake of law.

The first exception (called **authorized reliance**) can be found in Section 2.04(3)(b) of the *Model Penal Code* (*MPC*).

> (3) A belief that conduct does not legally constitute an offense is a defense to a prosecution for that offense base upon such conduct when:
>
> > (b) he acts in reasonable reliance upon an official statement of the law, afterward determined to be invalid or erroneous, contained in . . . an official interpretation of the public officer or body charged by law with responsibility for the interpretation, administration or enforcement of the law defining the offense. (American Law Institute 1985:27)

Authorized Reliance: an exception to the rule that a mistake of law is not a defense where the defendant trusted an official's misinterpretation of a criminal law

Authorized reliance allows the accused to avoid liability by relying on a third party who has the authority to give the best interpretation of the law. In order for this exception to be valid as a defense the accused must believe that the law did not apply to his or her conduct *and* his or her belief was based on an official erroneous interpretation of the law. The first part of the exception is the actual mistake of the law. The second part of the exception is that the accused seeks professional advice from someone who has the authority to interpret the law and that this interpretation is incorrect. Finally, Section 2.04(4) suggests that this mistake of law defense is an affirmative defense requiring the defendant to prove the requirements of the defense by a preponderance of the evidence. Box 11.1 raises questions about whether Sam has a mistake of law defense or not.

Sam Van Winkleman just bought a franchise of Ray's Point, an ice cream shop specializing in soft-serve gourmet ice cream. He went to business school at Graves State University where he studied accounting. His father recently passed away, and Sam wanted to pay tribute to his father, who loved ice cream, by being a successful ice cream shop owner. Even though his accounting degree was helpful in balancing his books and understanding expenses and budgets, Sam's degree did not help him understand business models, regulations, and human resource policies.

Sam decided to put his personal spin on his market and included sundaes with their own French Fry Scoops. He understood that many people like to mix salty with sweet, and he feels this technique will be the source of great revenue for his shop. However, he needs to purchase a fryer. Once he purchases and uses the fryer, he does not know what to do with the old, used oil. Sam wants to dispose of it down the drain that runs directly into the city's sewage system. Sam believes he is okay, but he wants to make sure. He contacts an old friend who used to own a Happy Burger Palace franchise. His friend informs him that he is not doing anything unlawful or unethical because that is what he used to do.

Unknown to both Sam and his friend, using the city sewage drains violates a recent environmental ordinance. Has Sam broken any laws? Explain.

A second exception has no particular phrase associated with it; so, we will use our own term and call it the "different law" exception. Here, if the accused misunderstands the meaning or application of a non-criminal law that causes him or her to violate the criminal law, then his or her mistake of the non-criminal law would eliminate his or her liability for violating the criminal law. In other words, the mistake of the "different law" (non-criminal law) removes his or her blameworthiness of committing the criminal law. Box 11.2 also provides a scenario about whether Elgin has a mistake of law defense.

Elgin Roberts has been estranged from his wife, Nora, for two years. They have not attempted to secure a divorce because, according to Nora, "it's way too messy." The problem is that Elgin has fallen in love with Tameka Smith, his neighbor. Their relationship has developed to the extent that they believe they are life partners and want to get married. But, to avoid drama from Nora, Elgin travels to Tomsk Oblast in Russia to file his paperwork. Elgin found out that the cost of divorce in Tomsk Oblast is very inexpensive and speedy and would give him opportunities to expand his shoehorn company in Slavic areas; so, he decided to travel to Tomsk Oblast to complete his divorce from Nora. When he arrived back in the States, he and Tameka get married. Unknown to Elgin, the state in which he resides does not recognize divorce rulings from the federal subject of Tomsk Oblast. The state charged Elgin with polygamy — being married to multiple partners at once. Is he guilty of polygamy? Explain.

We understand that ignorance (or mistake) of the law, generally, is not an excuse for violating the law. There are the two exceptions to this general rule where a mistake of law *can* be a defense to a criminal violation. However, what if an individual mistakes a *fact* rather than a law? Is that mistake a defense? Yes, it can be and is known as the **mistake of fact** defense. For example, if Bob is hunting with his brother Larry who advances too far up the field, and Bob believes Larry is a deer and shoots and kills him, is Bob guilty of homicide? Or, does Bob's mistake in believing Larry is a deer eliminate his guilt?

The *MPC* is not necessarily instructive on ignorance or mistake of fact as a defense. Section 2.04 states:

> (1) Ignorance or mistake as to a matter of fact . . . is a defense if:
> (a) The ignorance or mistake negatives the purpose, knowledge, belief, recklessness or negligence required to establish a material element of the offense; or
> (b) The law provides that the state of mind established by such ignorance or mistake constitutes a defense. (American Law Institute 1985:26-27)

A mistake of fact *can* be an excuse defense; however, a defendant would have to apply a given line of logical questions as proof of a mistake of fact defense. The first question is whether the crime is a specific intent crime, general intent crime, or strict liability crime. The answer to this first question relates to the next phase of questions. If the crime is a specific intent crime (the desire for the criminal result is required), then the next question is whether the mistake addresses the specific intent portion of the offense much like Section 2.04 of the *MPC* addresses. Homicide is a specific intent offense where the defendant must have purpose in causing the victim's death — the criminal result. If the defendant believed he or she was throwing knives at a target but did not know that his or her friend was crouching behind the target, this mistake negates the specific intent portion of that homicide. Therefore, this person is not guilty of homicide if one of the knives hits and kills the friend. Box 11.3 outlines the required questions for the mistake of fact defense.

If the crime is a general intent crime (the desire to do the general action but not necessarily the desire for a particular criminal result is required), the next question is whether the mistake was reasonable or not. If the mistake was reasonable, then the mistake can be an excuse defense to the illegal act. For example, a person might set his briefcase on the park bench while eating his lunch. At the same time another person sits on the same park bench and sets a similar briefcase next to the first one. When the first person gets an urgent call, he hurriedly picks up the wrong briefcase and starts to walk away. Because the "intent to take" in a larceny is general intent, we

Mistake of Fact:
due to an honest and reasonable mistake of an underlying fact, the defendant is not criminally liable for committing the crime

---

Box 11.3   REQUIREMENTS FOR MISTAKE OF FACT DEFENSE

Was the crime

Specific intent crime?
- Does the mistake address the specific intent portion of the offense?

Strict liability crime?
- No defense allowed

General intent crime?
- Was the mistake reasonable?

---

must ask if the mistake of the briefcase is reasonable or not. If the briefcases were similar, you could argue that the taking (hence, the intent to take) was reasonable. If the briefcases were vastly different in size, color, and weight, you might argue that the mistake was *not* reasonable, and, therefore, the mistake would not be a valid defense.

Finally, if the crime is a strict liability crime, mistake of fact cannot be a defense. For example, speeding violations are strict liability offenses, requiring no proof of an evil mind. If the defendant's speedometer is broken, and the defendant did not realize she was going over the speed limit, she is still liable for speeding even if she has no knowledge that her speedometer is broken. Remember, mistake of fact is an excuse defense that eliminates one's blameworthiness or malicious mental state. Since strict liability crimes do not require proof of an evil mind, there is no evil mind to eliminate based on this defense.

DURESS

Much like the mistake of fact defense, **duress** addresses the crime's mental element. Even though the act is wrongful, the person using the defense is not blameworthy for the actions. Generally, duress is used in situations where the individual feels he or she does not have the will to choose not to commit the crime. The coercive nature of the threats by another person forces the one using the defense to commit a criminal act.

The defense of duress has changed from the common law definition. At common law, you had to show that you were in immediate risk of death or great bodily harm in order to avoid criminal liability. Additionally, the defendant must show that he or she reasonably believed that there was no reasonable alternative to avoid the harm threatened other than to commit the crime. Finally, the

Duress:
defendant's feeling of being coerced to commit a crime eliminating his guilt

defendant cannot be at fault for being placed in the coercive situation. At common law, the threat must be of death or great bodily harm but not a threat of harm to one's reputation or property. The threat of great bodily harm can also be directed at someone else but only with whom the defendant had a special relationship. Finally, "immediate," at common law, meant that the harm threatened was going to occur soon after the threat as opposed to a continued threat or a "present danger."

The *MPC* describes different requirements to prove duress as a valid excuse defense. Section 2.09 states:

> (1) It is an affirmative defense that the actor engaged in the conduct charged to constitute an offense because he was coerced to do so by the use of, or a threat to use, unlawful force against his person or the person of another, that a person of reasonable firmness in his situation would have been unable to resist. (American Law Institute 1985:37)

The requirements suggest an objective perspective. In other words, it is "a person of reasonable firmness" in the defendant's circumstances who can use the duress defense. However, it is not valid to use the duress defense merely because the defendant himself or herself felt threatened when that belief was not reasonable. There is also a subjective component to the requirements because the defendant must feel coerced to engage in criminal activity. Unlike the common law definition of duress, there is no mention of the immediacy of the threat or that the threat must be death or great bodily harm; it simply needs to be "unlawful force," which might be something less than death or great bodily harm. Box 11.4 summarizes the requirements for the duress defense.

In addition to the base requirements for duress, Section 2.09 also provides some limitations to the duress defense. Section 2.09(2) states:

> The defense provided by this Section is unavailable if the actor recklessly placed himself in a situation in which it was probable that he would be subjected to duress. The defense is also unavailable if he was negligent in placing himself in such a situation, whenever negligence suffices to establish culpability for the offense charged. (American Law Institute 1985:37)

Box 11.4 REQUIREMENTS FOR DURESS DEFENSE

- Coerced to commit crime
  - By use or threatened use of unlawful force AND
  - A person of reasonable firmness in defendant's situation could not have resisted the coercion

This rule suggests that a person cannot use duress as a defense if he or she places himself or herself in the coercive situation in a reckless or negligent way.

A special case under the duress defense is the *military orders defense* (sometimes called *superior orders defense*). Here, military personnel may feel coerced by their superiors' order to do something that may or may not be legal. Section 2.10 of the *MPC* states:

> It is an affirmative defense that the actor, in engaging in the conduct charged to constitute an offense, does no more than execute an order of his superior in the armed services that he does not know to be unlawful. (American Law Institute 1985:38)

Under this standard, there are only two requirements for a valid defense. First, the person claiming the defense must execute an order of a superior officer. Second, the defendant must not have any knowledge that the act is unlawful; this implies a subjective standard. That is, the defendant must be aware of the circumstances surrounding the physical act. However, the question comes when, under the circumstances, the defendant who was given a superior order *should* have known it was unlawful. The U.S. Court of Military Appeals addressed this issue and declined to recognize the defense in *United States v. Calley*, 22 U.S.C.M.A. 534 (1973) (see Box 11.5).

Box 11.5   DO ORDERS FROM SUPERIORS EXCUSE CRIMINAL LIABILITY?

United States v. Calley
22 U.S.C.M.A. 534 (1973)

First Lieutenant Calley stands convicted of the premeditated murder of 22 infants, children, women, and old men, and of assault with intent to murder a child of about 2 years of age. All the killings and the assault took place on March 16, 1968 in the village of My Lai in the Republic of South Vietnam. The Army Court of Military Review affirmed the findings of guilty and the sentence, which, as reduced by the convening authority, includes dismissal and confinement at hard labor for 20 years. The accused petitioned this Court for further review, alleging 30 assignments of error. We granted three of these assignments.

In the third assignment of error, appellate defense counsel asserts gross deficiencies in the military judge's instructions to the court members. Only two assertions merit discussion. One contention is that the judge should have, but did not, advised the court members of the necessity to find the existence of "malice aforethought" in connection with the murder charges; the second allegation is that the defense of compliance with superior orders was not properly submitted to the court members.

We turn to the contention that the judge erred in his submission of the defense of superior orders to the court. After fairly summarizing the evidence, the judge gave the following instructions pertinent to the issue:

> Both combatants captured by and non-combatants detained by the opposing force, regardless of their loyalties, political views, or prior acts, have the right to be treated as prisoners until released, confined, or executed, in accordance with law and established procedures, by competent authority sitting in judgment of such detained or captured individuals. Summary execution of detainees or prisoners is forbidden by law. Further, it's clear under the evidence presented in this case, that hostile acts or support of the enemy North Vietnamese or Viet Cong forces by inhabitants of My Lai at some time prior to 16 March 1968, would not justify the summary execution of all or a part of the occupants of My Lai on 16 March. I therefore instruct you, as a matter of law, that if unresisting human beings were killed at My Lai while within the effective custody and control of our military forces, their deaths cannot be considered justified, and any order to kill such people would be, as a matter of law, an illegal order. Thus, if you find that Lieutenant Calley received an order directing him to kill unresisting Vietnamese within his control or within the control of his troops, that order would be an illegal order.
>
> A determination that an order is illegal does not, of itself, assign criminal responsibility to the person following the order for acts done in compliance with it. Soldiers are taught to follow orders, and special attention is given to obedience of orders on the battlefield. Military effectiveness depends upon obedience to orders. On the other hand, the obedience of a soldier is not the obedience of an automaton. A soldier is a reasoning agent, obliged to respond, not as a machine, but as a person.
>
> The acts of a subordinate done in compliance with an unlawful order given him by his superior are excused and impose no criminal liability upon him unless the superior's order is one which a man of ordinary sense and understanding would, under the circumstances, know to be unlawful, or if the order in question is actually known to the accused to be unlawful.
>
> If you find beyond a reasonable doubt, on the basis of all the evidence, that Lieutenant Calley actually knew the order under which he asserts he operated was unlawful, the fact that the order was given operates as no defense.

Appellate defense counsel contend that these instructions are prejudicially erroneous in that they require the court members to determine that Lieutenant Calley knew that an order to kill human beings in the circumstances under which he killed was illegal by the standard of whether "a man of ordinary sense and understanding" would know the order was illegal.

In the stress of combat, a member of the armed forces cannot reasonably be expected to make a refined legal judgment and be held criminally responsible if he guesses wrong on a question as to which there may be considerable disagreement. But there is no disagreement as to the illegality of the order to kill in this case. For 100 years, it has been a settled rule of American law that even in war the summary killing of an enemy, who has submitted to, and is under, effective physical control, is murder. Appellate defense counsel acknowledge that rule of law and its continued viability, but they say that Lieutenant Calley should not be held accountable for the men, women and children he killed because the court-martial could have found that he was a person of "commonest understanding" and such a person might not know what our law provides.

Whether Lieutenant Calley was the most ignorant person in the United States Army in Vietnam, or the most intelligent, he must be presumed to know that he could not kill the people involved here. The United States Supreme Court has pointed out that "[t]he rule that 'ignorance of the law will not excuse' [a positive act that constitutes a crime] is deep in our law." An order to kill infants and unarmed civilians who were so demonstrably incapable of resistance to the armed might of a military force as were those killed by Lieutenant Calley is, in my opinion, so palpably illegal that whatever conceptional difference there may be between a person of "commonest understanding" and a person of "common understanding," that difference could not have had any "impact on a court of lay members receiving the respective wordings in instructions," as appellate defense counsel contend.

Consequently, the decision of the Court of Military Review is affirmed.

1. Is there a danger in military personnel questioning orders? Does this danger supersede the superior orders defense for less serious offenses?
2. How do military personnel decide whether or not an order is to be followed? What factors determine if an order is unlawful?
3. If the circumstances were merely to detain the women and children for two to three days, would the Court have ruled differently? Why or why not?

Following military orders under the notion of duress still remains today. For example, Private First Class Lynndie England claimed that she was following orders when evidence came out that she participated in torturing and humiliating Iraqi inmates and detainees at Abu Ghraib prison in Iraq. Photographs appeared with Pfc. England and other military personnel humiliating naked Iraqi detainees, forcing them to perform humiliating acts, and suffering torture at the hands of military personnel (Restivo 2006). According to England's defense, there was a larger plan within the armed forces to prepare witnesses for interrogation by "softening them up" through humiliation, sleep deprivation, and similar acts (Restivo 2006). However, the defense proved to be unsuccessful. Rule 916 of the Manual for Court Martial disallows the defense of superior orders when the orders are unlawful (Restivo 2006). According to Restivo (2006) and others, England should have known that the orders were unlawful.

The duress defense suggests that a person is not blameworthy because he or she did not have the required mental state to commit the underlying crime due to coercion. According to the *MPC*, duress requires both the coercion and the use of, or threatened use of, unlawful force, which is something less than serious bodily injury or death. It also requires that a person of "reasonable firmness" could not resist the coercion to commit the underlying act. Specifically, with superior orders, you can use the defense to eliminate blameworthiness for wrongful acts as long as you do not know or have reason to know that the act ordered was unlawful.

INTOXICATION

With most of these defenses, there are conflicting principles at work. On the one hand, the law holds citizens accountable for their actions because any violation is a violation against society. The state acts on behalf of its citizens by prosecuting wrongdoers (Johns 2010). On the other hand, the law only punishes those who are blameworthy. Our purpose here is to outline the circumstances under which someone can avoid criminal liability based on a lack of culpability. If a citizen is not blameworthy, then the law suggests that he or she should not be punished.

Intoxication is a defense that illustrates the dilemma posed by these competing principles. We want to hold citizens accountable for their actions; however, we cannot hold citizens responsible when their mental faculties are impaired to the point that they may not be blameworthy. Most of the time, citizens choose to ingest intoxicants and likely know the impairment they cause. These understood effects make them blameworthy for acts that are derived from that behavior.

Intoxication is "a disturbance of mental or physical capacities resulting from the introduction of substances into the body" (American Law Institute 1985:36). Generally, intoxication is not a defense because it is usually voluntary. Section 2.08(1) of the *MPC* states: "Except as provided in Subsection (4) of this Section, intoxication of the actor is not a defense" (American Law Institute 1985:35).

Thus, **voluntary intoxication** is not a defense because the act is voluntary, and this does not negate the evil intent of the underlying crime or voluntary status of the physical element. You cannot claim you did not have the mental state to complete the crime (e.g., vandalism or theft) because you willingly placed yourself in that position with knowledge of the effects of the intoxicants. Additionally, Section 2.08(3) adds that "(i)ntoxication does not, in itself, constitute mental disease within the meaning of Section 4.01" (American Law Institute 1985:35). Given these circumstances, therefore, we can say that voluntary intoxication—a willingness to and knowledge of becoming intoxicated—is not a defense to any crime that might result from an intoxicated state.

Voluntary Intoxication: the defendant cannot use the intoxication defense if he or she becomes intoxicated within his or her control

Another type of intoxication that *can* be a defense is called **involuntary intoxication**. This is where the party is not willingly intoxicated and does not have knowledge of the intoxicants' effects. The circumstances under which the involuntary intoxication can be a defense are provided in Box 11.6.

Involuntary Intoxication: the defendant can use the intoxication defense if he or she becomes intoxicated beyond his or her control

The *MPC* outlines a few circumstances that constitute involuntary intoxication. First, it is involuntary if it is coerced or due to extreme duress. This type of intoxication sounds familiar given the earlier discussion regarding the duress defense. The difference here is that the activity coerced was not a crime itself (intoxication) but caused the intoxicated person to commit an underlying crime. Since the intoxication is involuntary, the underlying crime is not intended and, therefore, is excused. Section 2.08(4) states:

> Intoxication that (a) is not self-induced or (b) is pathological is an affirmative defense if by reason of such intoxication the actor at the time of his conduct lacks substantial capacity either to appreciate its criminality [wrongfulness] or to conform his conduct to the requirements of law. (American Law Institute 1985:35)

The section claims that the intoxication cannot be self-induced.

> Intoxication caused by substances that the actor knowingly introduces into his body, the tendency of which to cause intoxication he knows or ought to know, unless he introduces them pursuant to medical advice or under such circumstances as would afford a defense to a charge of crime. (American Law Institute 1985:36).

Section 2.08(4) states that it is a defense where the intoxication is not self-induced and when it is caused by a lack of mental state much like the defense of insanity.

Similar to the circumstance of duress, a second situation — unexpected intoxication due to medically prescribed drugs — can also be an affirmative defense. The definition of self-induced intoxication requires the party to have knowledge (or "ought to know") of the intoxicating effects "unless he introduces them pursuant to medical advice" (American Law Institute 1985:36). Therefore, ingesting prescribed medication with the result that someone becomes intoxicated unexpectedly (or without knowledge) allows involuntary intoxication to be used as a defense.

Box 11.6 CIRCUMSTANCES OF INVOLUNTARY INTOXICATION

- Intoxication under duress
- Unexpected intoxication from medically prescribed drugs
- Pathological intoxication
- Innocent mistake intoxication

A third circumstance is called pathological intoxication. **Pathological intoxication**, according to *MPC* Section 2.08(5)(c) is "Intoxication grossly excessive in degree, given the amount of the intoxicant, to which the actor does not know he is susceptible" (American Law Institute 1985:36).

There are a few conditions for this particular defense. First, the effect of the intoxicant must be grossly excessive — that is, beyond merely excessive — and does not excuse behavior for someone who can become easily intoxicated (some might say a "lightweight"). To put it into perspective, consider this illustration. Sally has two beers and is already intoxicated; the defense for pathological intoxication is likely not going to be available since it is very possible for a person to be intoxicated after only two beers given differences of tolerance, size, and chemical makeup. However, if Steve — a 200-pound linebacker for State University — drinks two ounces of light beer and is extremely intoxicated to the point that he is blacked out, then the pathological intoxication defense might be used. Some, though, question the validity of such a defense unless the intoxication involves certain medications — not alcohol — simply based on the chemical makeup of alcohol and its biological effects on human behavior (Johns 2010).

The second condition for use of pathological intoxication is that the actor must not know of the potential effect. Similar to unexpected intoxication to prescribed medications, if a person is either aware of the intoxicating effect or suspects there is an intoxicating effect and purposely chooses not to find out if his or her suspicions are true ("willful blindness" as discussed in Chapter 2), then pathological intoxication is not present. If Toni has previously blacked out after one alcoholic drink, then she cannot use pathological intoxication as an involuntary intoxication.

A final circumstance in which involuntary intoxication can be a defense is when the intoxication is due to an **innocent mistake**. As described above, a mistake of fact defense can be used if the mistake causes one to commit an underlying crime ("I thought my friend was a deer, and I shot him by mistake"). The mistake under this form of involuntary intoxication is the mistake of ingesting an intoxicant which, in itself, is not a crime. For example, Tommy goes to the school dance and drinks from the punch bowl. As he drinks, he starts feeling "funny." It is Tommy's first dance, and he comes from a fairly sheltered family environment. He did not know that the punch bowl was spiked with alcohol, which causes his erratic behavior, including vandalizing several cars in the school's parking lot. Tommy might be able to use involuntary intoxication — innocent mistake — as a defense.

The involuntary intoxication defense, though, can only be asserted when a few conditions are met. First, the one asserting the defense

Pathological Intoxication: an involuntary intoxication where one is abnormally disoriented to the ingestion of ordinary intoxicants

Innocent Mistake: an involuntary intoxication where one makes an honest and reasonable mistake of the intoxicating effect of a particular material ingested must, in fact, be intoxicated in an involuntary way. Second, due to the involuntary intoxication, it must be shown that the one using the defense no longer engages in the required mental state for the underlying crime. The state of intoxication eliminates the mental state required for the underlying crime. Finally, for some of these situations (duress and pathological intoxication), the defense is required to show that, due to these circumstances, the individual "lacks the substantial capacity either to appreciate its criminality [wrongfulness] or to conform his conduct to the requirements of law" (American Law Institute 1985:35).

AGE

Sometimes, one's biological (and mental) age can be a defense to criminality. The law recognizes a connection between age and the development of criminal intent (see Carter 2006). Studies have linked age, mental and physical development, and criminal activity with behavior learned over time (Akers 2006). For example, the Supreme Court in *Roper v. Simmons*, 543 U.S. 551 (2005) suggested that the death penalty was unconstitutional for offenders under the age of 18 because they lacked the mental maturity for those select defendants who faced the death penalty (see Fabian 2011). The true understanding of the impact of the imposition of capital punishment is lost on offenders less than 18 years old. Similarly, young people are likely to be less blameworthy for criminal activity due to their lack of ability to form the necessary mental state for the underlying crime. The defense of age—also called the **infancy defense**—acknowledges this mental development dilemma.

At common law, there were clear age distinctions in assessing one's ability to fulfill the required mental element of the crime. There are two components for these distinctions: (1) presumption of ability to form the required mental state and (2) whether that presumption is rebuttable (or reversible). A **rebuttable presumption** that a person has the mental capacity to commit the crime means the individual is understood to have the required mental state for the underlying crime, but the defense could convince the trier of fact otherwise. An **irrebuttable presumption** that a person *lacks* the mental capacity to commit the crime means that the individual does *not* have the required mental state for the underlying crime, and no one is allowed to convince the trier of fact otherwise. At common law, there are three age categories that characterize these presumptions.

First, for defendants under seven years old at the time of the crime, there is an irrebuttable presumption not to have the mental

Infancy Defense: depending on the defendant's age, one is not criminally liable for the crime because he or she cannot form the mental element of the underlying crime

Rebuttable Presumption: an assumption that can be refuted

Irrebuttable Presumption: an assumption that cannot be refuted

capacity to complete the crime. A prosecutor could not overcome the presumption that the defendant did not possess the necessary mental element for the underlying crime (Sobie 2012). For defendants between the ages of 7 and 14 at the time of the crime, there is a rebuttable presumption not to have the mental capacity to complete the crime (Sobie 2012). A prosecutor would have to overcome the presumption that a defendant of this age can have the mental ability to complete the crime. Unlike the presumption for defendants under 7 years old, the presumption for defendants who were 7-14 years old can be overcome — the burden, though, to prove this is with the prosecutor. Finally, for defendants over the age of 14 at the time of the crime, there is a rebuttable presumption to have the mental capacity to commit the crime. Here, the presumption is rebuttable where the burden is with the defense to prove that the defendant did not have the mental capacity to commit the crime. Box 11.7 outlines the common law distinctions for the infancy defense.

Although we use the *MPC* as a common guide for criminal law in this book, it cannot help us since it does not speak to the infancy defense. The *MPC* contemplates criminal law from an adult perspective without consideration of youthful offending, leaving this offending to the juvenile justice system. Therefore, the *MPC* does not consider infancy as a specific defense. The only consideration regarding age and offending in the *MPC* is in Section 4.10, distinguishing juvenile justice jurisdiction independent from the adult criminal justice jurisdiction:

> (1) A person shall not be tried for or convicted of an offense if:
> a. At the time of the conduct charged to constitute the offense he was less than sixteen years of age [, in which case the Juvenile Court shall have exclusive jurisdiction]; or
> b. At the time of the conduct charged to constitute the offense he was sixteen or seventeen years of age, unless:
> i. The Juvenile Court has no jurisdiction over him, or
> ii. The Juvenile Court has entered an order waiving jurisdiction and consenting to the institution of criminal proceedings against him.

Box 11.7 COMMON LAW AGE DISTINCTIONS FOR THE INFANCY DEFENSE

- Under 7 years old
  - Irrebuttable presumption of *no* mental capacity
- 7-14 years old
  - Rebuttable presumption of *no* mental capacity
- Over 14 years old
  - Rebuttable presumption of mental capacity

ENTRAPMENT

Most of the defenses outlined in this chapter consider the specific behavior of the defendant. Entrapment is a defense where the defendant's criminal behavior is excused and is the result of pressure and encouragement by government officials. Given the actions of these government officials, the defendant's wrongful behavior may not be blameworthy.

One of the primary purposes of law enforcement is to collect evidence of wrongful behavior. Sometimes, during investigative work, officers might encourage a person to commit a crime that he or she would not otherwise commit. During these times, the **entrapment** defense acts as a check against the government's authority over its citizens; however, this defense is limited to governmental but not private action.

Entrapment: government creates the intent in the defendant to commit the crime that he or she would not ordinarily commit

Traditionally, there were objective and subjective standards used for the entrapment defense. The objective standard suggests that if the government encourages criminal behavior by an otherwise law-abiding citizen, then this citizen can use the entrapment defense to avoid criminal liability. In other words, a reasonable person, given the individual's circumstances, would not have committed this crime. The behavior is excused because the person did not possess the mental state required for the underlying crime.

The subjective standard has more complex components. In this approach, the defense must prove that the government creates the necessary mental element to commit the crime. This could be proved by the actions of state agents and the gravity of their attempts to induce criminal conduct. Second, the defense must prove that the defendant is not predisposed to commit the crime. If the defendant is found to have participated in the crime based on his or her predisposition, then the court will find that the government's actions were *not* coercive but merely provided the opportunity for the crime. Taken as a whole (known as **totality of the circumstances**), these factors can prove an individual's predisposition to commit the crime:

Totality of the Circumstances: an approach that takes everything into consideration in the assessment

- Defendant has prior arrests or convictions for similar offenses
- Defendant has a willingness to commit the offense or other similar offenses
- Defendant displays criminal expertise in the offense or other similar offenses
- Defendant has the ready ability to commit the offense.

Given the totality of circumstances, if the court rules that the defendant is predisposed to commit the underlying crime, entrapment is not an available defense. The difficulty is proving who is blameworthy for the crime—the defendant or the government—which is addressed in *Jacobson v. United States*, 503 U.S. 540 (1992) (see Box 11.8).

Box 11.8   IS SENDING CHILD PORNOGRAPHY TO A CITIZEN ENTRAPMENT?

Jacobson v. United States
503 U.S. 540 (1992)

In February 1984, petitioner, a 56-year-old veteran-turned-farmer who supported his elderly father in Nebraska, ordered two magazines and a brochure from a California adult bookstore. The magazines, entitled Bare Boys I and Bare Boys II, contained photographs of nude preteen and teenage boys. The contents of the magazines startled petitioner, who testified that he had expected to receive photographs of "young men 18 years or older." On cross-examination, he explained his response to the magazines:

> [PROSECUTOR]: [Y]ou were shocked and surprised that there were pictures of very young boys without clothes on, is that correct?
> [JACOBSON]: Yes, I was.
> [PROSECUTOR]: Were you offended?
> [JACOBSON]: I was not offended because I thought these were a nudist type publication. Many of the pictures were out in a rural or outdoor setting. There was—I didn't draw any sexual connotation or connection with that.

The young men depicted in the magazines were not engaged in sexual activity, and petitioner's receipt of the magazines was legal under both federal and Nebraska law. Within three months, the law with respect to child pornography changed; Congress passed the Act illegalizing the receipt through the mails of sexually explicit depictions of children. In the very month that the new provision became law, postal inspectors found petitioner's name on the mailing list of the California bookstore that had mailed him Bare Boys I

and II. There followed over the next 2 1/2 years repeated efforts by two Government agencies, through five fictitious organizations and a bogus pen pal, to explore petitioner's willingness to break the new law by ordering sexually explicit photographs of children through the mail.

By March 1987, 34 months had passed since the Government obtained petitioner's name from the mailing list of the California bookstore, and 26 months had passed since the Postal Service had commenced its mailings to petitioner. Although petitioner had responded to surveys and letters, the Government had no evidence that petitioner had ever intentionally possessed or been exposed to child pornography. The Postal Service had not checked petitioner's mail to determine whether he was receiving questionable mailings from persons—other than the Government—involved in the child pornography industry.

The Postal Service also continued its efforts in the Jacobson case, writing to petitioner as the "Far Eastern Trading Company Ltd." The letter began:

> As many of you know, much hysterical nonsense has appeared in the American media concerning 'pornography' and what must be done to stop it from coming across your borders. . . . [W]hy is your government spending millions of dollars to exercise international censorship while tons of drugs, which makes yours the world's most crime ridden country are passed through easily.

The letter went on to say:

> [W]e have devised a method of getting these to you without prying eyes of U.S. Customs seizing your mail. . . . After consultations with American solicitors, we have been advised that once we have posted our material through your system, it cannot be opened for any inspection without authorization of a judge.

The letter invited petitioner to send for more information. Petitioner responded. A catalog was sent, and petitioner ordered *Boys Who Love Boys*, a pornographic magazine depicting young boys engaged in various sexual activities. Petitioner was arrested after a controlled delivery of a photocopy of the magazine.

When petitioner was asked at trial why he placed such an order, he explained that the Government had succeeded in piquing his curiosity:

> In petitioner's home, the Government found the Bare Boys magazines and materials that the Government had sent to him in the course of its protracted investigation, but no other materials that would indicate that petitioner collected, or was actively interested in, child pornography. Petitioner was indicted for violating 18 U.S.C. § 2252(a)(2)(A). (P)etitioner was convicted.

There can be no dispute about the evils of child pornography or the difficulties that laws and law enforcement have encountered in eliminating it. Likewise, there can be no dispute that the Government may use undercover agents to enforce the law. "It is well settled that the fact that officers or employees of the Government merely afford opportunities or facilities for the commission of the offense does not defeat the prosecution." *Sorrells v. United States*, 287 U.S. 435 (1932).

In their zeal to enforce the law, however, Government agents may not originate a criminal design, implant in an innocent person's mind the disposition to commit a criminal act, and then induce commission of the crime so that the Government may prosecute. Where the Government has induced an individual to break the law and the defense of entrapment is at issue, as it was in this case, the prosecution must prove beyond reasonable doubt that the defendant was disposed to commit the criminal act prior to first being approached by Government agents.

But that is not what happened here. By the time petitioner finally placed his order, he had already been the target of 26 months of repeated mailings and communications from Government agents and fictitious organizations. Therefore, although he had become predisposed to break the law by May 1987, it is our view that the Government did not prove that this predisposition was independent and not the product of the attention that the Government had directed at petitioner since January 1985.

---

1. Should the predisposition be based on whether the activity was criminal or whether the activity occurred regardless of its criminality?
2. Should entrapment only require inducement of the behavior without the need for proof of predisposition?

The *MPC* offers slightly different requirements for the proof of entrapment. Predisposition is not a significant component except as intimated in Section 2.13(1)(b). Section 2.13 of the *MPC* outlines the requirements for the entrapment defense (emphasis added).

(1) A public law enforcement official or a person acting in cooperation with such an official perpetrates an entrapment if for the
purpose of obtaining evidence of the commission of an offense, he
induces or encourages another person to engage in conduct constituting such offense by either:

a. Making knowingly false representation designed to
induce the belief that such conduct is not prohibited; or

b. Employing methods of persuasion or inducement that
create a substantial risk that such an offense will be committed
by persons *other than those who are ready to commit it.*
(American Law Institute 1985:41)

The requirements from this *MPC* section are similar to the
subjective standard above. First, the defense is limited to the state's
actions. The section says "A public law enforcement official or a
person acting in cooperation with such an official" (American Law
Institute 1985:41). Thus, if a state agent or his or her informant or
one who assists at the request of the state agent induces criminal conduct, then the entrapment defense might be available. In *Jacobson,*
the government worked with U.S. Postal Service and other agencies
to encourage illegal activity. Box 11.9 references the requirements for
the entrapment defense.

The second requirement is that the state agent must induce or
encourage the defendant to commit the crime. Similar to the
subjective standard noted above, the defense must provide evidence
of the government's inducement to commit the crime. In *Jacobson,*
the government fabricated organizations and offers on multiple occasions, which created the intent.

The third requirement addresses the method by which the inducement occurs. The first method is "making knowingly false representation designed to induce the belief that such conduct is not
prohibited" (American Law Institute 1985:41). Here, the defense
will have to prove that the state made false representations with
knowledge that it is encouraging the defendant to believe that his
or her conduct was not criminal when, in fact, it *was* criminal.

Box 11.9   REQUIREMENTS FOR THE ENTRAPMENT DEFENSE

- The acting agent must be a state agent and/or informant
- State agent induces or encourages the defendant to commit the crime by:
  - Making false presentation with knowledge to encourage to believe that his or her act is not criminal when it is criminal OR
  - Creating a substantial risk of committing a criminal act when otherwise not ready to commit

In the case outlined above, the government sent multiple materials from fictitious organizations enticing the defendant to engage in the illegal activity—the purchase and possession of child pornography.

The second method by which the unlawful encouragement takes place is akin to the subjective standard outlined above—"employing methods of persuasion or inducement that create a substantial risk that such an offense will be committed by persons *other than those who are ready to commit it*" (American Law Institute 1985:41, emphasis added). This requirement suggests that the defendant was not a person who was ready to commit the underlying criminal act. Criminal law is intended to hold citizens accountable for their unlawful conduct. If conduct is created out of the desire generated by the state, then it is difficult to hold a person accountable for an act that he or she did not first desire or create. The Court in *Jacobson* found that previous activity in viewing pornographic material of children—when it was legal to do so—does not, by itself, suggest readiness of such illegal activity. Also, the repeated denial of such materials *after* it was illegal to do so suggests the *lack* of readiness of such illegal activity. The defense of entrapment, therefore, excuses behavior by eliminating the evil intent.

INSANITY

One of the most well-known, and potentially controversial, excuse defenses is insanity. Research indicates that there is a relationship between mental illness and criminal activity (Silver, Felson, and Vaneseltine 2008). Although this relationship is moderate, it is consistent across multiple factors. In fact, specialty courts have been developed in the last decade to address the needs of mentally ill offenders. Mental health courts are similar to drug courts, both having similar components: mental health screening, voluntary participation, community-based intervention strategies, and periodic review of the offender's treatment plan (Mann 2011). While mental health courts are designed to divert defendants from the traditional court system, the insanity defense completely removes criminal liability.

The casual observer may not realize that insanity is a legal term and not a medical term. According to the mission statement of the American Psychiatric Association, the association is an "organization of psychiatrists working together to ensure humane care and effective treatment for all persons with mental disorders, including intellectual developmental disorders and substance use disorders" (American Psychiatric Association 2012). The American Psychiatric Association publishes the *Diagnostic and Statistical Manual of Mental Disorders*—the most recent is the DSM-IV-TR—to assist the medical field in diagnosing mental illness (see American Psychiatric Association 2012). In this manual and the mission statement of the American Psychiatric Association, there is no mention of insanity.

Before going further, it is important to understand that different jurisdictions treat insanity differently. States that apply a version of the insanity defense are likely to allow for two types of pleas at arraignment. The first type of plea is the traditional **not guilty by reason of insanity**. The effect of this plea is that the defendant avoids further prosecution in exchange for treatment in a mental health facility until "he or she is better," at which time the defendant is released into the community. There has been quite a transformation in the insanity plea over the years—especially since John Hinkley, Jr.'s assassination attempt on President Ronald Reagan (see Steadman et al. 1993). A greater restriction on insanity pleas has created a second plea option called **guilty but mentally ill**. The effect of this plea is that the defendant will receive treatment but is still held accountable for wrongful actions. The defendant is similarly sent to a mental health facility for treatment until "he or she is better," and, once "better," the state will transfer the defendant to a correctional facility to carry out the rest of the sentence.

It is also important to distinguish between the insanity defense and incompetency to stand trial since these concepts are often confusing. Both involve a distorted mental capacity, whether it is through a developmental disability or a mental disease or defect. The distinction lies with the timing of the mental incapacity. For both concepts, a psychiatric evaluation is ordered at the time of the trial (Haun, Gallagher, and Milz 2010). The distinction is that the insanity defense is about the lack of mental capacity to form the required mental state for the underlying crime *at the time of the crime*, whereas competency is the lack of mental capacity to assist in one's case *at the time of the trial*.

An additional distinction is that competency usually allows for less severe mental disabilities than the insanity defense. For example, developmental disability or anxiety disorders can result in a mental incompetency assessment but usually do not raise the mental incapacity to an insanity defense. An insanity defense usually implies some sort of severe mental defect such as a psychosis (e.g., schizophrenia) (see Haun, Gallagher, and Milz 2010).

There has been an evolution in the insanity defense over the years where multiple tests were used to prove that a person was legally insane to avoid criminal liability. The first test is called the **M'Naghten Rule**. This test requires that the defendant had a mental disease or defect at the time of the crime and that defect or disease caused the defendant not to:

Not Guilty by Reason of Insanity:
a type of insanity plea where the defendant serves time in a mental health facility until he or she is better and then is released

Guilty but Mentally Ill:
a type of insanity plea where the defendant serves time in a mental health facility until he or she is better and then serves the remaining time in a correctional facility

M'Naghten Rule:
a test of insanity where, due to a mental disease or defect at the time of the crime, a person does not know the nature and quality of his or her actions or know what he or she did was wrong and, therefore, is not criminally liable for the crime

- Know the nature and quality of his or her criminal act OR
- Know what he or she was doing was wrong

Oftentimes, this is termed the "right/wrong test" based on the second part of this test. This particular test for insanity assesses whether a mental disease or defect caused a person not to know right from wrong, and it is used by the majority of states (Rolf 2006). Box 11.10 summarizes the requirements for the M'Naghten Rule for the insanity defense.

Generally, this test has multiple points that inform other tests and are important to outline here. First, all tests of insanity require a mental disease or defect at the time of the crime. These tests typically articulate "mental disease or defect" as either a psychosis or some sort of massive brain injury. Simple anxiety disorders or depressive disorders cannot be used for insanity defenses that eliminate one's criminal liability. Second, the test uses the legal phrase "know." On the one hand, it can be pure intellectual awareness, which implies an intellectual understanding of how the world operates. On the other hand, knowledge can be one's appreciation of the circumstances, which implies a more emotional response. Most states hold that "know" is cognition or an intellectual awareness of the facts and not an appreciation of the circumstances. Additionally, the test requires that the person may not have known the "nature and quality of the criminal act." This requirement implies that the defendant does not have true insight into the consequences of his or her actions. It is more than a simple cognition of right versus wrong—which is visible in the second part of the test; it is a true insight into his or her actions and their consequences. Therefore, due to mental disease or defect, the defendant must either lack the knowledge of the true insight of his or her actions or lack the knowledge that his or her actions were wrong.

A second but rarely used test of insanity is the **irresistible impulse test**. Here, it is less about the defendant's ability to determine right from wrong and more about the ability to control one's actions. The irresistible impulse test requires (1) the defendant to have a mental

Irresistible Impulse Test: a test of insanity where, due to a mental disease or defect at the time of the crime, one cannot control one's behavior from committing the crime

---

Box 11.10 REQUIREMENTS FOR THE M'NAGHTEN RULE FOR THE INSANITY DEFENSE

- The defendant has a mental disease or defect at the time of the crime AND
- The mental disease or defect caused the defendant not to:
  - Know the nature and quality of his or her conduct OR
  - Know what he or she was doing was wrong

disease or defect at the time of the crime, and (2) this mental disease or defect solely caused the defendant not to control his or her behavior. This test does not require proof that the defendant failed to know right from wrong but only proof of lack of control of one's behavior. The problem in using this defense is that it is difficult to prove or disprove lack of control or impulsive behavior. Box 11.11 outlines the requirements for the irresistible impulse test for the insanity defense.

Another less popular — and virtually overruled[1] — test is called the **product test** or the ***Durham*** **test**, named after the case from which it was generated. In 1972, the United States Court of Appeals, District of Columbia Circuit overruled the use of the product test in *United States v. Brawner*, 471 F.2d 969 (1972). However, to understand the development of the insanity plea, it is important to outline its requirements here.

Much like the other insanity tests, this test requires the defendant to have a mental disease or defect at the time of the crime. It also requires proof that, without the mental disease or defect, the defendant would not have committed the crime. Much like using the "but for" test to prove actual cause for a result crime (see Chapter 2), one can ask the question "but for the mental disease or defect, would the defendant have committed the crime?" Was the criminal act a *product* of the mental disease or defect? However, few jurisdictions adopted this test because there is no showing of an altered mental state. The proof of the mental disease and the physical act in question is a self-fulfilling prophecy, where proof of the mental disease is proof of the insanity defense. Box 11.12 articulates the requirements for the product test for the insanity defense.

Finally, the *MPC* has its own test identified as the *MPC* **test** (or **substantial capacity test**). Section 4.01 of the *MPC* outlines this test for the insanity defense:

> **Product Test /** *Durham* **Test:** a test of insanity where the outcome of a mental disease or defect at the time of the crime was the defendant's behavior

> **MPC Test / Substantial Capacity Test:** a test of insanity where, due to a mental disease or defect at the time of the crime, a person does not have the substantial capacity to appreciate the criminality of his or her act or to conform his or her conduct to the law and, therefore, is not criminally liable for the crime

---

Box 11.11 REQUIREMENTS FOR THE IRRESISTIBLE IMPULSE TEST FOR THE INSANITY DEFENSE

- The defendant has a mental disease or defect at the time of the crime AND
- The mental disease or defect solely caused the defendant not to control his or her behavior

---

1. New Hampshire — the state that initiated the product test — is the only state remaining to use this test.

Box 11.12 REQUIREMENTS FOR THE PRODUCT (OR *DURHAM*) TEST FOR THE INSANITY DEFENSE

- The defendant has a mental disease or defect at the time of the crime AND
- But for the mental disease or defect, the defendant would not have committed the crime

---

    (1) A person is not responsible for criminal conduct if at the time of such conduct as a result of mental disease or defect he lacks substantial capacity either to appreciate the criminality [wrongfulness] of his conduct or to conform his conduct to the requirements of the law. (American Law Institute 1985:61)

Like the other insanity tests, the defendant must prove that he or she has a mental disease or defect at the time of the crime. The defendant must also prove that this mental disease or defect causes him or her to lack "substantial capacity" either (1) to appreciate the wrongfulness of his or her act, or (2) to follow the law correctly. Box 11.13 summarizes the *MPC* test for the insanity defense.

    In this section, the drafters of the *MPC* outlined that the person lacks "substantial capacity." This is distinct from most of the other tests where mere incapacity was enough—except for the M'Naghten Rule, which requires complete incapacity. The *MPC*, therefore, requires the defense to show not only a lack of capacity but a lack of *substantial* capacity. This distinction produces a more restrictive test than the product and irresistible impulse tests but less restrictive than the M'Naghten Rule.

    Additionally, the object of the lack of capacity is a lack of appreciation of the wrongful act. As we have discussed earlier, an appreciation is true insight into one's actions. Therefore, this appreciation is not a cognitive, intellectual awareness but true, emotional insight into

---

Box 11.13 REQUIREMENTS FOR THE *MPC* (OR SUBSTANTIAL CAPACITY) TEST FOR THE INSANITY DEFENSE

- The defendant has a mental disease or defect at the time of the crime AND
- The mental disease or defect caused the defendant to lack a substantial capacity to:
  - Appreciate the criminality (or wrongfulness) of his or her act OR
  - Conform his or her conduct to the law

recognizing wrongfulness. The commentary suggests that this section of the *MPC* offers the alternative to criminality with "wrongfulness" because there are some cases where a wrongful act could lead to a criminal one (American Law Institute 1985).

The second object of the defendant's lack of capacity is inability "to conform his conduct to the requirements of the law" (American Law Institute 1985:61). The commentary for this section of the *MPC* relates to "volitional incapacities." If the mental disease or defect creates a lack of capacity where the defendant does not have voluntary control over the abilities to follow the law, then it is a defense. The *Cone v. Bell* case is used in Box 11.14 to answer the question whether the insanity defense should be considered at sentencing or not.

Box 11.14   SHOULD THE INSANITY DEFENSE BE CONSIDERED AT SENTENCING?

Cone v. Bell

556 U.S. 449 (2009)

This case outlines if and when evidence should be considered as a mitigating circumstance in sentencing even though the evidence does not secure a not guilty finding during the guilt phase of the trial. We have discussed insanity in this chapter as it is applied during the guilt phase. The purpose of including this case is to outline the specific facts as they are applied to the *MPC* test of insanity even though the major purpose of the case is to acknowledge mitigation in the criminal trial's sentencing phase. Students should focus on the Court's application of the facts to the *MPC* test.

STEVENS, J., delivered the opinion of the Court.

On the afternoon of Saturday, August 10, 1980, Cone robbed a jewelry store in Memphis, Tennessee. Fleeing the scene by car, he led police on a high-speed chase into a residential neighborhood. Once there, he abandoned his vehicle and shot a police officer. When a bystander tried to impede his escape, Cone shot him, too, before escaping on foot.

(The next) afternoon, Cone gained entry to the home of 93-year-old Shipley Todd and his wife, 79-year-old Cleopatra Todd. Cone beat the couple to death with a blunt instrument and ransacked their home. Later, he shaved his beard and escaped to the airport without being caught. Cone was arrested several days later after robbing a drugstore in Pompano Beach [, Florida].

A Tennessee grand jury charged Cone with two counts of first-degree murder, two counts of murder in the perpetration of a burglary, three counts of assault with intent to murder, and one count of robbery by use of deadly force. At his jury trial in 1982, Cone did not challenge the overwhelming physical and testimonial evidence supporting the charges against him. His sole defense was that he was not guilty by reason of insanity.

Cone's counsel portrayed his client as suffering from severe drug addiction attributable to trauma Cone had experienced in Vietnam. Counsel argued that Cone had committed his crimes while suffering from chronic amphetamine psychosis, a disorder brought about by his drug abuse. That defense was supported by three witnesses. First was Cone's mother, who described her son as an honorably discharged Vietnam veteran who had changed following his return from service. She recalled Cone describing "how terrible" it had been to handle the bodies of dead soldiers, and she explained that Cone slept restlessly and sometimes "holler[ed]" in his sleep.

Two expert witnesses testified on Cone's behalf. Matthew Jaremko, a clinical psychologist, testified that Cone suffered from substance abuse and posttraumatic stress disorders related to his military service in Vietnam. Jaremko testified that Cone's mental disorder rendered him substantially incapable of conforming his conduct to the law. Jonathan Lipman, a neuropharmacologist (testified that) Cone's drug abuse had led to chronic amphetamine psychosis, a disorder manifested through hallucinations and ongoing paranoia that prevented Cone from obeying the law and appreciating the wrongfulness of his actions.

In rebutting Cone's insanity defense the State's strategy throughout trial was to present Cone as a calculating, intelligent criminal who was fully in control of his decisions and actions at the time of the crimes. The prosecution also adduced expert and lay testimony to establish that Cone was not addicted to drugs and had acted rationally and intentionally before, during, and after the Todd murders.

Particularly damaging to Cone's defense was the testimony of rebuttal witness Ilene Blankman (a user herself who lived with Cone), who testified that she had never seen Cone use drugs, had never observed track marks on his body, and had never seen him exhibit signs of paranoia.

The jury rejected Cone's insanity defense and found him guilty on all counts. At the penalty hearing Cone's counsel called no witnesses but rested on the evidence adduced during the guilt phase proceedings. Acknowledging that the prosecution's experts had disputed the existence of Cone's alleged mental disorder, counsel nevertheless urged the jury to consider Cone's drug addiction when weighing the aggravating and mitigating factors in the case. The jury found all four aggravating factors and unanimously returned a sentence of death.

The documents suppressed by the State vary in kind, but they share a common feature: Each strengthens the inference that Cone was impaired by his use of drugs around the time his crimes were committed. In sum, both the quantity and the quality of the suppressed evidence lends support to Cone's position at trial that he habitually used excessive amounts of drugs, that his addiction affected his behavior during his crime spree, and that the State's arguments to the contrary were false and misleading.

During the guilt phase of Cone's trial, the only dispute was whether Cone was "sane under the law," as his counsel described the issue, or "criminally responsible" for his conduct, as the prosecutor argued. Under Tennessee law, Cone could not be held criminally responsible for the murders if, "at the time of [his] conduct as a result of mental disease or defect he lack[ed] substantial capacity either to appreciate the wrongfulness of his conduct or to conform his conduct to the requirements of law." Although we take exception to the Court of Appeals' failure to assess the effect of the suppressed evidence "collectively" rather than "item by item," we nevertheless agree that even when viewed in the light most favorable to Cone, the evidence falls short of being sufficient to sustain his insanity defense.

The same cannot be said of the Court of Appeals' summary treatment of Cone's claim that the suppressed evidence influenced the jury's sentencing recommendation. There is a critical difference between the high standard Cone was required to satisfy to establish insanity as a matter of Tennessee law and the far lesser standard that a defendant must satisfy to qualify evidence as mitigating in a penalty hearing in a capital case. As defense counsel emphasized in his brief opening statement during penalty phase proceedings, the jury was statutorily required to consider whether Cone's "capacity to appreciate the wrongfulness of his conduct or to conform his conduct to the requirements of the law was substantially impaired as a result of mental disease or defect or intoxication which was insufficient to establish a defense to the crime but which substantially affected his judgment." It is possible that the suppressed evidence may have persuaded the jury that Cone had a far more serious drug problem than the prosecution was prepared to acknowledge, and that Cone's drug use played a mitigating, though not exculpating, role in the crimes he committed.

Although we conclude that the suppressed evidence was not material to Cone's conviction for first-degree murder, the lower courts erred in failing to assess the cumulative effect of the suppressed evidence with respect to Cone's capital sentence. Accordingly, the judgment of the Court of Appeals is vacated, and the case is remanded to the District Court with instructions to give full consideration to the merits of Cone's *Brady* claim.

1. Should this case discuss the intoxication defense? Is there a potential claim here? Why or why not?
2. Is post-traumatic stress disorder enough for a defendant to claim insanity?
3. If the timing of the crime spree was closer to the return from Vietnam, would the Court have ruled differently? If not, what different facts would need to be present for the insanity defense to succeed?

There are misconceptions regarding the insanity defense. First, the insanity defense is rarely used successfully. Scholars note that the use of the insanity plea rate is less than 1 percent; approximately one-fourth of those who use the defense are successful even though the media, television, and movies depict something entirely different (Daftary-Kapur et al. 2011). Relatedly, those using the defense must demonstrate that they had a mental disease or defect at the time of the crime, which is a difficult component to prove let alone proving the connection between this disease or defect and their understanding of the reality of the situation. The use (successful use or otherwise) of the insanity defense is directly tied to the difficulty in proving the link between the defendant's mental disease and his or her behavior. Contrary to popular belief, defendants using the insanity defense do not typically "fake it" but, rather, have some of the more serious mental disorders (see Daftary-Kapur et al. 2011).

SUMMARY

This chapter outlined excuse defenses, suggesting that a person's behavior is wrongful but that he or she is not blameworthy because he or she could not form the appropriate mental state for the underlying crime. There are competing criminal law principles at the heart of each of these defenses. For example, the criminal law is intended to hold citizens accountable for their law-violating actions. Additionally, the criminal law is intended to punish those offenders who are blameworthy. Since actions that are excused are not blameworthy, they should not be punished given this principle. These competing principles—holding citizens accountable to the law but only punishing them if they are blameworthy—create a need for excuse defenses.

The first excuse defense we discussed was mistake of fact. The adage "ignorance of the law is not a defense" is true in the criminal law. Therefore, there is no "mistake of *law* defense." There are two exceptions to this general rule, though: authorized reliance and different law exception. By contrast, a mistake of *fact* can be a defense as long as the mistake is related to the mental element of the crime.

A second excuse defense is duress, which is applied in coercive situations in which some people might find themselves. As long as the one using the defense is not at fault for being in the coercive situation, the duress defense may be available. Given the fear of serious bodily injury from a coercive situation, one no longer has the required mental capability to complete the underlying crime, thereby eliminating one's deservedness of punishment.

Another excuse defense is involuntary intoxication—by duress, pathological intoxication, unexpected intoxication from medications, and by honest mistake—which eliminates one's blameworthiness. Voluntary intoxication, by contrast, is generally not a defense because of the defendant's willingness to administer intoxicants that he or she knows might distort his or her thinking. Voluntary intoxication, therefore, goes against the principle of not punishing those who are not blameworthy because having the willingness to engage in activity that might impair a person's abilities to do what is right maintains his or her blameworthiness.

A fourth excuse defense is infancy. Human development experts note that age can influence the determination and realization of the difference between right and wrong. Therefore, at common law, for those who were under the age of seven, it was presumed that they could not form the required mental state for criminal behavior, and this presumption was not reversible. For those who were 7 to 14 years old, it was presumed that they, too, could not form the required mental state for criminal behavior, but this presumption *was* reversible with a burden on the prosecutor to prove capacity. Finally, for those over the age of 14, it was presumed that they *could* form the required mental state for criminal behavior, but this presumption was also reversible with a burden on the defense to prove incapacity.

Entrapment is another excuse defense that generally restricts the government from creating the desire to commit a crime in a citizen who would ordinarily not commit the crime. The two standards used are the objective and subjective standards. The objective standard states that if a reasonable person would not have committed the crime, then it is entrapment. For the subjective standard, the defendant must show that the state created the circumstances that caused the intent or desire to do the crime and that the defendant was not predisposed to do the crime in the first place. Again, the entrapment defense can absolve criminal liability since the defendant does not have the required mental state—other than that induced by the state—for the underlying crime.

Finally, the insanity defense is given the most attention of the excuse defenses. Generally, a defendant with a mental disease or defect that might cause him or her not to appreciate the wrongfulness of his or her act can avoid criminal liability by using the insanity defense. As we have noted, insanity is not a medical term but is a legal term. There are multiple tests that could be used to determine insanity. The *MPC* requires that the defendant have a mental disease or defect—usually a psychosis—at the time of the crime, where the disease or defect causes the defendant to lack a substantial capacity to appreciate the wrongfulness of his or her act or to be able to conform his or her action to the law.

All excuse defenses eliminate criminal liability for a lack of fulfilling the required mental state for the underlying crime. The purpose of the criminal law is to punish those who are blameworthy and deserving of punishment. However, for one to have committed a crime, that person must fulfill all the required elements of the crime. Other than strict liability crimes—where excuse defenses usually do not apply—all crimes require a mental element. If circumstances are as such that one cannot fulfill the mental element because of duress or age or insanity, then the person is not blameworthy and, therefore, will avoid criminal liability.

KEY TERMS

authorized reliance
duress
entrapment
guilty but mentally ill
infancy defense
innocent mistake
involuntary intoxication
irrebuttable presumption
irresistible impulse test

mistake of fact
mistake of law
M'Naghten Rule
MPC (or substantial capacity) test
not guilty by reason of insanity
pathological intoxication
product (or *Durham*) test
rebuttable presumption
totality of the circumstances
voluntary intoxication

CRITICAL THINKING QUESTIONS

1. Why is a mistake of law not a defense? What are the guiding principles?
2. A principle of the duress defense is not to require citizens to act contrary to self-interest. Since some Good Samaritan laws require citizens to come to the aid of others, could one argue that the state is violating this principle?
3. Is brainwashing a form of duress, or is brainwashing another form of superior orders defense?
4. Why is voluntary intoxication not a defense? Shouldn't you have the opportunity to indulge in legal intoxicants without the fear that your actions might lead to criminal behavior? Shouldn't voluntary intoxication be a defense? Is there any potential byproduct for doing so? Is this byproduct safe?
5. The infancy defense says that being too young can be a defense. What about being too old?
6. Should entrapment be a defense at all? Should the state eliminate this as a defense? If citizens don't want to commit crimes, then they should not commit crimes regardless of what the state does, right? What is the major assumption in this argument? Explain.
7. How does one prove whether a person, due to the mental illness, could not appreciate the wrongfulness of their act according to the insanity defense?
8. Should we eliminate all excuse defenses? For example, Idaho does not have the insanity plea because the defendant can assert evidence of mental illness as a rebuttal to the state's proof of the mental element. Should all excuse defenses operate in the same way?

SUGGESTED READINGS

Graebner, W. (2008). *Patty's Got a Gun: Patricia Hearst in 1970s America*. Chicago: University of Chicago Press. This is the most recent retelling of one of the most infamous criminal trials to use brainwashing as a failed duress-type defense. The account discusses the greater sociopolitical environments in which this case rested. Patty Hearst was kidnapped and brainwashed into the ideological society of Symbionese Liberation Army in the 1970s.

Poore, N.W. (2005). *Deadly Confidante*. Bothell, WA: Book Publishers Network. This book outlines a true crime murder investigation of Robin Lee, who is sitting on death row in the state of Idaho for setting fire to her house and killing her husband and two children. It is a story of a woman who was obsessed and a true manipulator. The story outlines a defendant's attempt at an insanity case in a state that does not allow insanity pleas.

Restivo, N.M. (2006). "Defense of Superior Orders in International Criminal Law as Portrayed in Three Trials: Eichmann, Calley and

England." *Cornell Law School Graduate Student Papers.* Paper 18. http://scholarship.law.cornell.edu/lps_papers/18. This article outlines the superior orders defense. It is an accounting of when the defense can be used and the circumstances on which it relies. It outlines recent uses of the defense, including the humiliation of detainees at Abu Ghraib.

Steadman, H.J., McGreevy, M.A., Morrissey, J.P., Callahan, L.A., Robbins, P.C. & Cirincione, C. (1993). *Before and After Hinckley: Evaluating Insanity Defense Reform.* New York: Guilford Press. This book outlines key reforms to the insanity defense before and after the assassination attempt on former President Ronald Reagan. John Hinkley, Jr. pled not guilty by reason of insanity for shooting the President and several others, including James Brady, the President's press secretary.

REFERENCES

Akers, R. (2006). "Social Learning and Life Course Criminology." *Conference Papers—American Society of Criminology* 1.

American Law Institute (1985). *Model Penal Code: Complete Statutory Text.* Philadelphia, PA.

American Psychiatric Association (2012). http://www.psych.org/.

Carter, A.M. (2006). "Age Matters: The Case for a Constitutionalized Infancy Defense." *University of Kansas Law Review* 54:687-746.

Cone v. Bell, 556 U.S. 449 (2009).

Daftary-Kapur, T., Groscup, J.L., O'Connor, M., Coffaro, F. & Galietta, M. (2011). "Measuring Knowledge of the Insanity Defense: Scale Construction and Validation." *Behavioral Sciences and the Law* 29:40-63.

Fabian, J.M. (2011). "Applying *Roper v. Simmons* in Juvenile Transfer and Waiver Proceedings: A Legal and Neuroscientific Inquiry." *International Journal of Offender Therapy and Comparative Criminology* 55:732-755.

Haun, J.J., Gallagher, J.A. & Milz, A.A. (2010). "The Influence of Time and Treatment on Recall of Mental State at the Time of Offense: Incompetent Defendants and Evaluation of Insanity." *Journal of Forensic Psychology Practice* 10:464-475.

Jacobson v. United States, 503 U.S. 540 (1992).

Johns, A. (2010). "Serious Violent Offending and Medico-Legal Responses." *Medico-Legal Journal* 78:2-10.

Mann, J. (2011). "Delivering Justice to the Mentally Ill: Characteristics of Mental Health Courts." *Southwest Journal of Criminal Justice* 8(1):44-58.

Restivo, N.M. (2006). "Defense of Superior Orders in International Criminal Law as Portrayed in Three Trials: Eichmann, Calley and England." *Cornell Law School Graduate Student Papers.* Paper 18. http://scholarship.law.cornell.edu/lps_papers/18.

Robinson, P.H. (2009). "A System of Excuses: How Criminal Law's Excuse Defenses Do, and Don't, Work Together to Exculpate Blameless (and Only Blameless) Offenders." *Texas Tech Law Review* 42:259-272.

Rolf, C.A. (2006). "From M'Naghten to Yates—Transformation of the Insanity Defense in the United States—Is It Still Viable?" *River College Online Academic Journal* 2:1-18.

Roper v. Simmons, 543 U.S. 551 (2005).

Silver, E., Felson, R.B. & Vaneseltine, M. (2008). "The Relationship Between Mental Health Problems and Violence Among Criminal Offenders." *Criminal Justice and Behavior* 35:405-426.

Sobie, M. (2012). "The Delinquent 'Toddler.'" *Criminal Justice* 26(4):36-42.

Steadman, H.J., McGreevy, M.A., Morrissey, J.P., Callahan, L.A., Robbins, P.C. & Cirincione, C. (1993). *Before and After Hinckley: Evaluating Insanity Defense Reform.* New York: Guilford Press.

United States v. Calley, 22 U.S.C.M.A. 534 (1973).

United States v. Brawner, 471 F.2d 969 (1972).

Punishment and Sentencing

LEARNING OBJECTIVES

After reading this chapter, you should be able to:

1. Analyze and apply the theories of punishment
2. Identify the different types of punishment
3. Describe and analyze the effects of sentencing guidelines
   as a sentence reform
4. Identify the problem areas of mandatory penalties and
   truth-in-sentencing policies
5. Identify and analyze the arguments of constitutional attacks on
   the death penalty
6. Apply the right to jury on sentencing practices at the state and
   federal levels

INTRODUCTION

Punishment and sentencing are often minimally addressed in criminal law textbooks. Criminal trials are known to be bifurcated—split into two parts. The first part involves the determination of guilt. The previous chapters summarize rules about the burden the state has to prove the defendant's guilt known as the "guilt phase" of the trial. The second part of a criminal trial is known as the "sentencing phase," which only takes place after the defendant is found guilty. This phase includes testimony and evidence to assist in determining the appropriate sentence for the guilty. Since criminal law not only addresses the definition of crimes and defenses but also punishment and sentencing, we intentionally devote an entire chapter to punishment and sentencing. As we discussed in Chapter 1, the criminal law is set apart from other law systems—namely, civil law—because the state has the authority to punish wrongdoers. Therefore, the coverage of punishment and sentencing is a necessary topic in a criminal law textbook.

There are many reasons why criminal punishment is delivered, and it depends on your perspective to understand why certain punishments are imposed over others. For example, you might want to deliver a particular punishment to hold the defendant accountable for his or her actions. Another reason might be to deliver a different sentence as a preventive measurement. The purpose of punishment (often identified as "theories" of punishment) typically follows ideological lines that we will address in this chapter.

In the last few decades, there have been significant reforms to sentencing policies and practices. Prior to the 1980s, sentencing in most states was only limited by the ranges mandated by criminal statutes; these ranges were expansive and this offered great opportunities for judges to use their own discretion in sentencing. With vast discretional authority, many suspected there was a great amount of unwarranted disparity in sentencing practices. Therefore, the system enacted a variety of reforms to limit judicial discretion and, therefore, limit opportunities for unwarranted disparity. Reforms such as sentencing guidelines, mandatory penalties, and truth in sentencing significantly reduce judicial discretion (and parole board discretion) in hopes that unwarranted disparity will also be limited; sentences become more certain and more severe. Discretion still remains a potential avenue for unwarranted disparity through discretion displacement to the legislature and prosecutors. Additionally, judges may not comply with these new sentencing policies and, therefore, this might lead to a continuation of unwarranted disparity for certain groups of defendants.

In addition to sentencing reforms, sentencing and punishment in the United States have also undergone constitutional scrutiny. We will discuss constitutional limitations to punishment and sentencing in this chapter, which are similar to the restrictions on criminal definitions in Chapter 1. Since the defendant has already been found guilty of a crime, though, different constitutional limitations apply. Specifically, protection against cruel and unusual punishment is discussed with respect to both the death penalty and imposition of life in prison; the protection of the right to a jury trial is also discussed regarding sentencing. In this chapter, we will explore the balance between legal and social science perspectives to the sentencing and punishment of criminal defendants.

THEORIES OF PUNISHMENT

In Chapter 1 we briefly covered several reasons why the state punishes law violators. There are three categories of reasons—or theories—that punishment is utilized: (1) retributive theory, (2) utilitarian theory, and (3) restorative theory. Practically, sentences are handed down for many reasons, and they are differentially applied among these theories depending on the circumstances and the political environment surrounding the case. Given a judge's approach to punishment, sentences can be applied differently. For example, one judge may be most interested in holding violators responsible for their actions based on the perceived or real blameworthiness; this is a retributive ideal. Another judge might be most interested in the utilitarian theory of punishment, where prevention of future wrongdoing is key. Finally, a judge may insist on restoring those affected by the criminal incident—both the victim and the community. In other words, victims and communities might need repair and, therefore, the judge might impose a sentence where multiple parties are involved, following a restorative justice ideal. Each of these theories has a place in the criminal justice system, and sentences might reflect multiple theories of punishment. It is important, though, to understand each of these theories independently.

Prior to the discussion of these theories, we need to make a few general comments about the structure of the discussions. First, each theory is addressed as if in a vacuum; practical concerns are not considered in discussing these punishment theories. Therefore, the first part of the discussion of each theory addresses the structure of the theory and does not consider concerns such as funding or prison overcrowding. Also, each theory is treated independently even though the reality is that each sentence can be handed down for multiple reasons. The second part of the discussion addresses, as a singular theory, the practical necessities of applying each theory in a real-life sentencing scenario. For example, a theory may call for treatment in order to prevent future wrongdoing, but the application of this theory may require certain components that are unconventional compared to current practice. In this chapter, each theory and its components will be addressed as a theory unto itself and then followed with the practical considerations of applying the theory to a sentencing scenario.

The first theory of punishment that most attribute to our system of justice is retribution. Retributive punishment theory is likely to be the most direct and most easily understood of the theories. Given the era of "tough on crime," **retribution** is a sanctioning theory that is often used as a reason for particular punishments. In this theory of punishment, the state attempts to assess the defendant's blameworthiness as a factor to determine the degree of punishment deserved. The saying "do the crime; do the time" is most applicable to this theory. As a theory, you must examine the seriousness of the current criminal incident and the seriousness of the defendant's prior criminal history to determine blameworthiness and what punishment the defendant deserves. In other words, it is a theory that is backward-looking. The defendant's punishment will be harsher if the current offense and/or prior criminal history are more serious than another defendant's.

Retribution: punishment that addresses the blameworthiness of the defendant

The practical considerations that must be applied for this theory, therefore, are straightforward. Given that the assessment under this theory is based on seriousness in order to determine the punishment severity, it is relevant that the application of the theory is proportioned sentencing, which means that the sentence is determined by making the punishment proportionate to someone's level of blameworthiness. Under retribution, a defendant who committed a serious personal crime and had multiple prior convictions is likely to receive a harsher punishment than another defendant who committed a minor property crime with no prior convictions. In this sense, the punishment should fit the crime (and prior criminal history) as applied. As we will discuss later, sentencing reforms such as mandatory minimum sentencing and sentencing guidelines are developed based on this theory of punishment.

The second theory is the **utilitarian theory** of punishment. This theory applies utilitarian ideology, which says that the greatest good is to be sought for the greatest number of people. Unlike retribution, where a punishment is applied only considering the one who committed the crime, utilitarian theory addresses the "greater good." This theory, therefore, is forward-looking, where the prevention of wrongdoing is the key for the greater good. However, there are multiple mechanisms provided to achieve this ultimate goal, including incapacitation, deterrence, and rehabilitation. Each of these mechanisms will be treated similarly, where the theory will be discussed first

Utilitarian Theory: punishment theory that addresses the greater good for the greater amount of people through preventing of future criminal wrongdoing

and then the practical application of the theory will be addressed. Keep in mind, though, that these theories all have the same goal—the prevention of future crime.

The **incapacitation** mechanism is designed to prevent wrongdoing by limiting the freedom to perform the act in the future. For example, a defendant cannot commit another homicide on the street if he or she is in prison. The theory is intended to limit freedom in order to prevent future crime. The practical application, though, is that due to limited resources, the criminal justice system cannot imprison or restrain every individual who violates the criminal law. Therefore, the state must engage in **selective incapacitation**, which involves restraining those who are the most dangerous and most likely to reoffend. Low-level offenders or those who do not repeat their law-violating behavior are not candidates for incapacitation as applied based on the limited resources available. Finally, incapacitation can be carried out in multiple ways in order to restrain a person's freedom. For obvious reasons, incarceration is a way to restrain freedom; however, other types of punishments can also be used. For example, a suspended license is intended to prevent someone from driving while intoxicated. Another example is medical castration for sex offenders; one, theoretically, cannot perform a sexual penetration in the traditional sense after being medically castrated. *Can you think of other examples?*

Deterrence is the second mechanism to uphold the ideals of prevention of future wrongdoing. Deterrence is the ultimate prevention model, where the state attempts to inflict more pain than the pleasure the defendant receives from committing the crime. There are two categories of deterrence: **specific deterrence** and **general deterrence**. Specific deterrence focuses on the individual who violated the law, where the punishment is handed down to prevent that person from committing future crimes. General deterrence focuses on individuals who are aware of the punishment for that individual and not necessarily for the benefit of that person; the focus is on preventing others in the community from committing future crimes.

The theory of deterrence, though, requires the defendant (or the community) to be able to weigh the pleasure or benefits of the crime and the pain or costs of the punishment. In other words, the theory assumes that the defendant (or the community) is knowledgeable and rational. What do we know about most individuals who commit most of the crimes? Are most criminals rational? Most of these individuals are not cognitively weighing the cost and benefits of committing the crime in a rational way. In fact, one could argue that the most serious crimes—probably excluding a premeditated, cold-blooded murder— are the least rational. From a strictly deterrence point of view—at least specific deterrence—does it make much sense to punish people if they are not rational in the first place?

Incapacitation: punishment that restricts a defendant's freedom to prevent future criminal wrongdoing

Selective Incapacitation: restraining of freedom based on particular criteria such as level of crime seriousness or prison space availability

Specific Deterrence: punishment that prevents defendants from committing future criminal wrongdoing

General Deterrence: punishment that prevents other non-defendants from committing future criminal wrongdoing

The practical consideration of deterrence is that the punishment must be of the type and severity to overcome the benefit of the crime. Thus, the state only needs to apply as much punishment as is necessary to prevent the defendant (or others) from committing future crimes. For deterrence to be successful the punishment must be *swift*, *certain*, and *severe*. There are several limitations to this application, though. First, our system is designed to be a slow, careful system of justice due to one's right to appeal as a matter of justice and fairness. Second, sentencing in the American criminal justice system lacks the kind of certainty needed for effective deterrence. Even though sentencing is more determinate today—that is, more formal and certain—judges can still employ discretion. Finally, one component of deterrence that the criminal justice system does utilize is severity; however, even though severe sentences are important, the severity used, according to deterrence, should be for the purpose of prevention and not more extensive than is necessary. Additionally, a person must be rational for severe punishment to be effective in preventing future wrongdoing. For example, you might argue that harsh sentences for drug crimes might not be the type of severity that is most effective in terms of deterrence since those possessing illicit drugs, arguably, are not rational.

The final mechanism of the utilitarian theory of punishment is rehabilitation. Again, the goal is to prevent future wrongdoing for the greater good, and rehabilitation prevents future wrongdoing by treating individuals who are sick, following a medical model. Treatment is made to "heal" defendants so they will not commit future crimes; however, this treatment should be individualized in order to be effective. Rehabilitation is the only mechanism that looks back in order to look forward because you must know what has been effective and in what areas the defendant will need assistance. In other words, there might be some activities and circumstances in someone's past to inform how treatment should be applied to prevent future wrongdoing. For example, if the defendant was abused as a child, then counseling might be an appropriate treatment to handle aggressive tendencies. Or, if the defendant has had substance abuse difficulties in the past, then substance abuse treatment might assist in correcting the problems that cause that person to break the law.

The practical consideration for rehabilitation is in the length of treatment. Ordinarily, when you cut your hand, you treat it with a bandage to help stop the bleeding and start the healing process. The question, though, is for how long do you keep the bandage on? You keep it on until the wound is better, right? So, if we follow the medical model to suggest that offenders are sick and need treatment, then for how long do we treat them? According to theory, we should treat them until they are better. However, there are a few problems with this rationale. First, our system does not treat until offenders are better because it is costly and it is likely politically dangerous. If we rely on the rehabilitative model to determine punishment, then a serious offender might be "better" after one week of treatment, which would be politically unwise. Second, the criminal justice system is ineffective in predicting who commits crime in the future and who does not. Forecasting models are difficult to manage and provide relatively weak predictive power compared to the natural science world. For example, a research team found only a moderate effect in predicting a decrease in robbery rates from proactive policing (Kubrin et al. 2007). Predicting that a defendant is "better" is likely to have similar difficulties. We are ineffective not only in predicting the type of treatment that is successful for certain people but also in assessing whether someone is better or not [see *Tarasoff v. Regents of the University of California*, 551 P.2d 334 (1976)]. Much like the other mechanisms under the utilitarian punishment theory, rehabilitation seeks to prevent future wrongdoing. The next scenario provides you the opportunity to put these theories in practice to assess what you have learned so far. Box 12.1 provides a scenario by which you can use the theories to determine Jermaine's punishment.

Box 12.1 YOU DECIDE: SHOULD THE DEFENDANT BE PUNISHED? IF SO, WHAT TYPE OF PUNISHMENT AND FOR HOW MUCH OR LONG?

Jermaine and Shavonda had been dating for six months. After work on Friday, Jermaine was going to meet Shavonda at the Boom Boom Saloon to have drinks. When Jermaine arrived, he saw Javon whispering in Shavonda's ear with her laughing. Jermaine is very jealous and protective and became upset seeing them. Jermaine came up and pushed Javon away from Shavonda and asked what his problem was. Javon said, "Hey, your girl is hot and I don't see a ring on her finger!" Jermaine became enraged and started hitting Javon with head shots and body blows, catching Javon off guard. Jermaine and Javon were separated but not before Javon suffered several injuries including a split lip, several bruises and gashes, and a concussion. In the melee, Jermaine also shoved Shavonda to the ground and called her a "two-timing bitch" after she tried to pull him off of Javon. She sustained a bruised hip from the fall.

Jermaine was charged with and found guilty of one count of misdemeanor assault and one count of felony assault causing major injury. Jermaine has been convicted three times before: (1) minor in possession of alcohol when he was 19 years old, (2) public intoxication on his twenty-first birthday, and (3) misdemeanor assault when he was 22. He is from an abusive childhood, where he was beaten every weekend when his father got intoxicated. He left the house when he was 16 years old and never graduated high school. You are both the legislator creating the law and the judge imposing the sentence. Applying each theory (retribution, incapacitation, deterrence, and rehabilitation), should Jermaine be punished for his actions? If so, what should the punishment be and for how much or for how long?

The last approach to punishment is restorative theory. This theory applies the notion that crime involves three major parties: the offender, victim, and community. Crime is understood to injure all three parties in different ways. The victim is injured directly and the community is injured either directly or indirectly since crime is a violation against the community. Finally, the offender may also be hurting and need repair or treatment—much like rehabilitation above. **Restorative justice** seeks to repair or restore each of these parties after a crime has occurred, where restoration is to a better place or, at the very least, the same place prior to the commission of the crime. For example, a vandalism of someone's store might result in the compensation for all repairs for the victim as well as a victim-offender mediation—for the benefit of both the victim and the offender. The community can be restored by community service hours that are visible so that their fear may be minimized knowing that the system is enforcing the law. Finally, in addition to the victim-offender mediation, the defendant could receive counseling or work therapy to improve the offender's ability to work through emotional problems that he or she might be having. In the end, all three parties can be restored to the same (or better) position before the crime occurred.

> **Restorative Justice:** punishment that places the three parties — the defendant, the victim, and the community — involved in any crime to the place or a better place prior to the crime

Each of these theories of punishment gives purpose and meaning to sentences the judges decide. These theories have different components and structures and require different approaches to applying them to a particular case. Each of the theories serves different purposes even though the types of sentences (prison, counseling, etc.) might be similar. The next section addresses the different types of punishments.

TYPES OF PUNISHMENT

Briefly, there are several options for punishment in criminal law. These options usually are prescribed by statute. The most severe punishment—not found in all states—is capital punishment or the death penalty (see Spohn and Hemmens 2012). The state becomes justified in ending the defendant's life for the defendant's egregious actions (Gillers 1980). Capital punishment law requires the state to prove aggravating circumstances [see *Ring v. Arizona*, 536 U.S. 584 (2002)]. That is, the state must prove that either the killing was especially heinous or severe or that the victim is a high-ranking official. The next most serious punishment type is incarceration—jail or prison. This punishment normally is reserved for the most dangerous and the most likely to reoffend (Spohn 2009).

Probation is used in many cases, and it allows the defendant to avoid incarceration without granting complete freedom. Those on probation must check in with a probation officer and meet certain conditions, such as counseling or job training (Spohn and Hemmens 2012). If the defendant does not meet these conditions, then incarceration is likely. The least serious punishment in criminal law is a fine and/or citation. Typically, these are reserved for traffic violations, but they can be used for other less serious criminal offenses.

Finally, an increasing number of jurisdictions are enacting **intermediate sanctions**, where there is more supervision and state involvement than probation or fines but less intrusion than incarceration. These sanctions include intensive supervised probation, day reporting centers, community service, and shock incarceration. They are designed as alternatives to traditional incarceration where prison space is saved, and they allow the system to supervise closer than traditional probation (Spohn 2009). However, some argue that prison provides documented evidence of reducing criminal behavior whereas intermediate sanctions simply widen the net of offenders who are in the system (Byrne and Miofsky 2009).

> **Intermediate Sanctions:** punishment that resides somewhere between probation and incarceration, where more restriction is applied than probation but less restrictive than incarceration

SENTENCING REFORM

In the last 40 years, there have been substantial state and federal reforms to sentencing practices in the United States. Prior to these reforms, sentencing was only limited by what was enumerated in the statute, often including a wide range within which the judge had great discretion. Therefore, sentencing prior to these reforms was mainly indeterminate. **Indeterminate sentencing** practices are characterized by high levels of judicial discretion, leaving the range of sentencing open, where it is virtually unpredictable to the casual observer or the seasoned courtroom veteran. Scholars feared that indeterminate sentencing would likely lead to disparate treatment of certain groups — mainly racial and ethnic minorities (Spohn 2009). Thus, the solution to reducing disparate treatment — whether from individual judges or from the system as a whole — was to reform sentencing practices through **determinate sentencing** policies, where the sentences are formally and consistently applied.

> **Indeterminate Sentencing:** sentencing policies that are more discretionary than mandatory

> **Determinate Sentencing:** sentencing policies that are more mandatory than discretionary

Sentencing Guidelines

The use of sentencing guidelines is one of the most notable sentencing reforms to date. It provides a structure, formality, and predictability to sentencing. In 1980, Minnesota was the first state to legislate sentencing guidelines to instruct judges in their sentencing decisions (Moore and Miethe 1986). In 1984, the U.S. Congress passed the Sentencing Reform Act, which mandated sentencing guidelines for federal courts (Stith and Cabranes 1998). Sentencing guidelines direct judges to impose prison sentences considering only two factors: the number of prior convictions and the severity of the current offense. Some states have legislated **presumptive sentencing guidelines**, which require judges to adhere their sentencing practices to the guidelines, whereas other states have **advisory sentencing guidelines**, which make judicial adherence voluntary. Box 12.2 includes the sentencing guideline grid from the State of Washington. The inclusion of the sentencing guideline matrices here are merely illustrative.

The federal sentencing guidelines are much more complex. The federal sentencing guideline matrix was noted as a 43-level "sentencing machine" (Tonry 1996). In fact, Tonry (1996) went so far to suggest that "one of the (federal sentencing) commission's worst blunders was the promulgation of the forty-three-level sentencing grid" (98). Criticisms about the confusing and complex interpretation of this massive sentencing grid may have foreshadowed the Supreme Court's ruling in *United States v. Booker* and *United States v. Fanfan* in 2005 to make the guidelines merely advisory and not presumptive (see discussion on *United States v. Booker* and *United States v. Fanfan* later in this chapter). Box 12.3 includes the federal sentencing guidelines grid.

Even though sentencing guidelines restrict judicial discretion in making most sentencing decisions, judges still retain some discretionary authority in making upward and downward departures. **Upward departures** are decisions to increase the sentence above the guideline range maximum, whereas **downward departures** are decisions to decrease the sentence below the guideline range minimum. Most states require judges to provide explanations for such departures—especially for upward departures since they increase the defendant's sentence. For example, a judge might rely on substantial assistance for other cases that might decrease the sentence or behavior that is relevant to the criminal act in question that may not have been proven at trial (i.e., "relevant conduct") that might justify an increase to the sentence (see Spohn 2009). However, upward departure decisions have come under constitutional scrutiny in both state and federal sentencing guideline systems (see "right to jury trial" later in this chapter).

Presumptive Sentencing Guidelines: mandatory system of sentencing based on one's prior criminal record and severity of the current offense(s) to direct judges in making their sentencing decision

Advisory Sentencing Guidelines: voluntary system of sentencing based on one's prior criminal record and severity of the current offense(s) to direct judges in making their sentencing decision

Upward Departure: decision to sentence the defendant with a higher sentence than that suggested by the sentencing guidelines

Downward Departure: decision to sentence the defendant with a lower sentence than that suggested by the sentencing guidelines

Box 12.2   Washington Sentencing Guideline Grid

SERIOUSNESS LEVEL	OFFENDER SCORE									
	0	1	2	3	4	5	6	7	8	9 or more
XVI	Life Sentence Without Parole/Death Penalty									
XV	240-320	250-333	261-347	271-361	281-374	291-388	312-416	338-450	370-493	411-548
XIV	123-220	134-234	144-244	154-254	165-265	175-275	195-295	216-316	257-357	298-397
XIII	123-164	134-178	144-192	154-205	165-219	175-233	195-260	216-288	257-342	298-397
XII	93-123	102-136	111-147	120-160	129-171	138-184	162-216	178-236	209-277	240-318
XI	78-102	86-114	95-125	102-136	111-147	120-158	146-194	159-211	185-245	210-280
X	51-68	57-75	62-82	67-89	72-96	77-102	98-130	108-144	129-171	149-198
IX	31-41	36-48	41-54	46-61	51-68	57-75	77-102	87-116	108-144	129-171
VIII	21-27	26-34	31-41	36-48	41-54	46-61	67-89	77-102	87-116	108-144
VII	15-20	21-27	26-34	31-41	36-48	41-54	57-75	67-89	77-102	87-116
VI	12+-14	15-20	21-27	26-34	31-41	36-48	46-61	57-75	67-89	77-102
V	6-12	12+-14	13-17	15-20	22-29	33-43	41-54	51-68	62-82	72-96
IV	3-9	6-12	12+-14	13-17	15-20	22-29	33-43	43-57	53-70	63-84
III	1-3	3-8	4-12	9-12	12+-16	17-22	22-29	33-43	43-57	51-68
II	0-90 days	2-6	3-9	4-12	12+-14	14-18	17-22	22-29	33-43	43-57
I	0-60 days	0-90 days	2-5	2-6	3-8	4-12	12+-14	14-18	17-22	22-29

*Unless otherwise noted, numbers represent months.
Adapted from the following website (accessed May 10, 2012): http://apps.leg.wa.gov/rcw/default.aspx?cite=9.94A.510.

Mandatory Minimum Penalties and Truth in Sentencing

Other sentencing reforms reduced the potential for judicial discretion and, therefore, unwarranted disparity in the punishment system. In an attempt to accomplish this end, states created legislation that had both front-end and back-end effects. In other words, laws were created that impacted the punishment's length and certainty at the

Box 12.3   Federal Sentencing Guidelines Grid

SENTENCING TABLE (in months of imprisonment)

Offense Level	Criminal History Category (Criminal History Points)					
	I (0 or 1)	II (2 or 3)	III (4, 5, 6)	IV (7, 8, 9)	V (10, 11, 12)	VI (13 or more)
1	0–6	0–6	0–6	0–6	0–6	0–6
2	0–6	0–6	0–6	0–6	0–6	1–7
3	0–6	0–6	0–6	0–6	2–8	3–9
4	0–6	0–6	0–6	2–8	4–10	6–12
5	0–6	0–6	1–7	4–10	6–12	9–15
6	0–6	1–7	2–8	6–12	9–15	12–18
7	0–6	2–8	4–10	8–14	12–18	15–21
8	0–6	4–10	6–12	10–16	15–21	18–24
9	4–10	6–12	8–14	12–18	18–24	21–27
10	6–12	8–14	10–16	15–21	21–27	24–30
11	8–14	10–16	12–18	18–24	24–30	27–33
12	10–16	12–18	15–21	21–27	27–33	30–37
13	12–18	15–21	18–24	24–30	30–37	33–41
14	15–21	18–24	21–27	27–33	33–41	37–46
15	18–24	21–27	24–30	30–37	37–46	41–51
16	21–27	24–30	27–33	33–41	41–51	46–57
17	24–30	27–33	30–37	37–46	46–57	51–63
18	27–33	30–37	33–41	41–51	51–63	57–71
19	30–37	33–41	37–46	46–57	57–71	63–78
20	33–41	37–46	41–51	51–63	63–78	70–87
21	37–46	41–51	46–57	57–71	70–87	77–96
22	41–51	46–57	51–63	63–78	77–96	84–105
23	46–57	51–63	57–71	70–87	84–105	92–115
24	51–63	57–71	63–78	77–96	92–115	100–125
25	57–71	63–78	70–87	84–105	100–125	110–137
26	63–78	70–87	78–97	92–115	110–137	120–150
27	70–87	78–97	87–108	100–125	120–150	130–162
28	78–97	87–108	97–121	110–137	130–162	140–175
29	87–108	97–121	108–135	121–151	140–175	151–188
30	97–121	108–135	121–151	135–168	151–188	168–210
31	108–135	121–151	135–168	151–188	168–210	188–235
32	121–151	135–168	151–188	168–210	188–235	210–262
33	135–168	151–188	168–210	188–235	210–262	235–293
34	151–188	168–210	188–235	210–262	235–293	262–327
35	168–210	188–235	210–262	235–293	262–327	292–365
36	188–235	210–262	235–293	262–327	292–365	324–405
37	210–262	235–293	262–327	292–365	324–405	360–life
38	235–293	262–327	292–365	324–405	360–life	360–life
39	262–327	292–365	324–405	360–life	360–life	360–life
40	292–365	324–405	360–life	360–life	360–life	360–life
41	324–405	360–life	360–life	360–life	360–life	360–life
42	360–life	360–life	360–life	360–life	360–life	360–life
43	life	life	life	life	life	life

Zones: Zone A, Zone B, Zone C, Zone D

*Unless otherwise noted, numbers represent months.
Adapted from the following website (accessed May 10, 2012): http://dc.fd.org/sentencing/sentencing_grid.pdf.

sentencing stage (front-end) as well as at the parole release stage (back-end). Mandatory minimum penalties are examples of front-end reforms and truth-in-sentencing policies are examples of back-end reforms. Each of these reforms addressed the severity and certainty of punishment that we described earlier in this chapter as tenets of deterrence.

Mandatory minimum penalties are the result of a more punitive philosophy of justice. Spohn (2009) suggests that mandatory minimum penalties are a direct result of the "war on crime" and "war on drugs" rationales of the late 1970s and early 1980s. Depending on the particular offense, a defendant might receive a **mandatory minimum penalty** (e.g., ten years in prison) regardless of the circumstances surrounding the crime. Again, the judge's discretion is significantly limited. One of the most well-known mandatory penalties is "three strikes you're out" laws. Generally, these laws mandate a certain sentence length after the defendant is found guilty of a third felony, for example.[1]

Mandatory Minimum Penalty: minimum punishment that is required for a particular conviction according to statute

Mandatory penalties have recently come under criticism. First, they often result in the imposition of unduly harsh sentences (Tonry 1996). Some mandatory penalties imposed harsh sanctions on offenders who had committed relatively non-serious offenses, and opponents to mandatory penalties call for these sanctions only to be applied to serious crimes (Spohn 2009; Tonry 1996). For example, some jurisdictions require automatic incarceration for certain, non-serious drug crimes. A second criticism addresses the **hydraulic displacement hypothesis**. That is, discretionary power has shifted from the judge to the prosecutor through charging and plea bargaining practices (Frenzel and Ball 2007; Spohn 2009; Tonry 1996). Given all of the restrictions on judges now, the discretionary authority is given to a virtually unrestricted prosecutor. "Discretionary power . . . places the prosecutor in a position of influence perhaps unmatched in the entire system of criminal justice" (Gottfredson and Gottfredson 1988:113). Third, court officials who are disgruntled by these restrictions can often circumvent them—especially mandatory minimum penalties. Their ill feelings to these sentencing reforms are created by the perceived (or real) high costs to the public with increased trial and case processing time (Tonry 1996). Finally, some have suggested that mandatory penalties—especially three-strikes laws—are not effective in reducing and/or preventing crime (Loftin, Heumann, and McDowall 1983; McDowall, Loftin, and Wiersema 1992; Marvell and Moody 1995).

Hydraulic Displacement Hypothesis: hypothesis that suggests that when discretion is restricted in one jurisdictional area or with one actor, the discretion is simply transferred to another jurisdictional area or to another actor

---

1. Under California's three-strikes law, certain misdemeanors (called "wobblers") also qualify for strikes in addition to felonies.

Truth-in-sentencing policies address discretion at the back end of the system. Prior to introduction of truth in sentencing, parole boards were the sole determining agency of whether the offender was released or not. In states with truth-in-sentencing laws, sentences are much more certain with offenders serving a minimum of 85 percent of their sentences. The 1994 Crime Act provided monetary incentives to states if they required offenders to serve at least 85 percent of their prison sentences (Spohn 2009). States responded by abolishing release by parole boards for certain types of offenders (Ditton and Wilson 1999). Unlike sentencing guidelines and mandatory penalties, this reform limited discretion of parole boards in their early release practices (Ditton and Wilson 1999). Stith and Cabranes (1998) found that prison terms in the federal system were served for longer periods of times during the post-reform era—increasing from 47 percent to 85 percent of the imposed sentence served in the federal system.

Truth in Sentencing: defendants serve most (75-85%) of their sentence per state statute

LEGAL RESTRICTIONS ON SENTENCING

There are several constitutional constraints on sentencing practices. Two areas of constitutional interest are: (1) the protection against cruel and unusual punishment and (2) the right to a jury trial. Most of the sentencing practices under question with regard to cruel and unusual punishment are death penalty sentences; however, life prison sentences can also come under cruel and unusual scrutiny. There are essentially two basic areas of challenge under the protection against cruel and unusual punishment: (1) whether the punishment is torturous or abnormally brutal and (2) whether the punishment is unreasonably disproportionate to the crime committed. With regard to the right to jury trial, sentencing guidelines have come under significant scrutiny. We will address each of these areas.

Protection Against Cruel and Unusual Punishment

The Eighth Amendment of the U.S. Constitution protects citizens against cruel and unusual punishment. Most of the time this right is questioned as it pertains to the death penalty. The first general area of challenge is whether the punishment imposed is unconstitutionally heinous. The Supreme Court has identified several distinct areas of scrutiny for the death penalty. One area is that some heinous punishments, such as drawing and quartering, disembowelment, and being burned alive, are seen as cruel and unusual punishments [see *Wilkerson v. Utah*, 99 U.S. 130 (1878)].

A second area is whether the method of execution (e.g., lethal injection, electrocution, firing squad) violates the protection against cruel and unusual punishment. The only Supreme Court case to approach this question is *Baze v. Rees*, 553 U.S. 35 (2008). In this case, the Court questioned whether lethal injection violated the Eighth Amendment's protection against cruel and unusual punishment on the basis of whether the pain inflicted was heinous (see Box 12.4).

Box 12.4 DOES LETHAL INJECTION — AS A METHOD OF EXECUTION — VIOLATE THE RIGHT AGAINST CRUEL AND UNUSUAL PUNISHMENT?

Baze v. Rees
553 U.S. 35 (2008)

Justice ROBERTS delivered the opinion of the Court.

Petitioners in this case — each convicted of double homicide — acknowledge that the lethal injection procedure, if applied as intended, will result in a humane death. They nevertheless contend that the lethal injection protocol is unconstitutional under the Eighth Amendment's ban on "cruel and unusual punishments," because of the risk that the protocol's terms might not be properly followed, resulting in significant pain.

By the middle of the 19th century, "hanging was the 'nearly universal form of execution' in the United States." In 1888, following the recommendation of a commission empaneled by the Governor to find "the most humane and practical method known to modern science of carrying into effect the sentence of death" (*Campbell v. Wood*, 511 U.S. 1119). New York became the first State to authorize electrocution as a form of capital punishment. By 1915, 11 other States had followed suit, motivated by the "well-grounded belief that electrocution is less painful and more humane than hanging" (*Malloy v. South Carolina*, 237 U.S. 180).

Electrocution remained the predominant mode of execution for nearly a century, although several methods, including hanging, firing squad, and lethal gas were in use at one time. Following the 9-year hiatus in executions (see *Gregg v. Georgia*), state legislatures began responding to public calls to reexamine electrocution as a means of ensuring a humane death. In 1977, legislators in Oklahoma, after consulting with the head of the anesthesiology department at the University of Oklahoma College of Medicine, introduced the first bill proposing lethal injection as the State's method of execution. A total of 36 States have now adopted lethal injection as the exclusive or primary means of implementing the death penalty, making it by far the most prevalent method of execution in the United States. It is also the method used by the Federal Government.

Of these 36 States, at least 30 (including Kentucky) use the same combination of three drugs in their lethal injection protocols. The first drug, sodium thiopental (also known as Pentothol), is a fast-acting barbiturate sedative that induces a deep, coma-like unconsciousness when given in the amounts used for lethal injection. The second drug, pancuronium bromide (also known as Pavulon), is a paralytic agent that inhibits all muscular-skeletal movements and, by paralyzing the diaphragm, stops respiration. Potassium chloride, the third drug, interferes with the electrical signals that stimulate the contractions of the heart, inducing cardiac arrest. The proper administration of the first drug ensures that the prisoner does not experience any pain associated with the paralysis and cardiac arrest caused by the second and third drugs.

We begin with the principle, settled by *Gregg*, that capital punishment is constitutional. It necessarily follows that there must be a means of carrying it out. Some risk of pain is inherent in any method of execution—no matter how humane—if only from the prospect of error in following the required procedure. It is clear, then, that the Constitution does not demand the avoidance of all risk of pain in carrying out executions.

Simply because an execution method may result in pain, either by accident or as an inescapable consequence of death, does not establish the sort of "objectively intolerable risk of harm" that qualifies as cruel and unusual. Throughout our history, whenever a method of execution has been challenged in this Court as cruel and unusual, the Court has rejected the challenge. Our society has nonetheless steadily moved to more humane methods of carrying out capital punishment. The firing squad, hanging, the electric chair, and the gas chamber have each in turn given way to more humane methods, culminating in today's consensus on lethal injection. The broad framework of the Eighth Amendment has accommodated this progress toward more humane methods of execution, and our approval of a particular method in the past has not precluded legislatures from taking the steps they deem appropriate, in light of new developments, to ensure humane capital punishment. There is no reason to suppose that today's decision will be any different.

The judgment below concluding that Kentucky's procedure is consistent with the Eighth Amendment is, accordingly, affirmed.

---

1. What is the "heinous" rule about? The petitioners argue (unsuccessfully) the risk of pain is heinous. What change of circumstances about lethal injection would make it heinous and in violation of the Eighth Amendment protection against cruel and unusual punishment?
2. Is there a better solution to the death penalty than lethal injection?
3. Would any method ever ensure that the individual being executed suffered no pain whatsoever?

Another area where capital punishment has been challenged for violating the Eighth Amendment's protection against cruel and unusual punishment is based on the proportionality of the sentence compared to the severity of the offense. This area of scrutiny examines whether the punishment should be proportionate to the crime committed—a retributive theory ideal. The Supreme Court in *Coker v. Georgia* (1977) ruled that a death penalty sentence for an offender who committed a rape of an adult victim is grossly disproportionate and, therefore, violates the Eighth Amendment's protection against cruel and unusual punishment. "Rape is without doubt deserving of serious punishment; but in terms of moral depravity and of the injury to the person and to the public, it does not compare with murder, which does involve the unjustified taking of human life" [*Coker v. Georgia*, 433 U.S. (1977) at 598].

In 2008, the Supreme Court revisited the issue of disproportionate sentencing with regard to the death penalty for the rape of a *child* in *Kennedy v. Louisiana*, 554 U.S. 407 (2008). Although the Court in *Coker v. Georgia* suggested that a death sentence for an offender convicted of raping an adult woman was grossly disproportionate and, therefore, violated his right against cruel and unusual punishment, the question for the Court in *Kennedy v. Louisiana* was whether this rule is similarly applied to an offense of raping a child (see Box 12.5).

Box 12.5 DOES A DEATH SENTENCE FOR RAPING A CHILD VICTIM VIOLATE THE EIGHTH AMENDMENT'S RIGHT AGAINST CRUEL AND UNUSUAL PUNISHMENT?

Kennedy v. Louisiana
554 U.S. 407 (2008)

Justice KENNEDY delivered the opinion of the Court.

Patrick Kennedy was charged with the aggravated rape of his then-8-year-old step-daughter. After a jury trial petitioner was convicted and sentenced to death under a state statute authorizing capital punishment for the rape of a child under 12 years of age. This case presents the question whether the Constitution bars respondent from imposing the death penalty for the rape of a child where the crime did not result, and was not intended to result, in death of the victim.

When police arrived at petitioner's home between 9:20 and 9:30 a.m., they found L.H. on her bed, wearing a T-shirt and wrapped in a bloody blanket. She was bleeding profusely from the vaginal area.

L.H. was transported to the Children's Hospital. An expert in pediatric forensic medicine testified that L.H.'s injuries were the most severe he had seen from a sexual assault in his four years of practice. The injuries required emergency surgery.

L.H. was interviewed several days after the rape by a psychologist. The interview was videotaped, lasted three hours over two days, and was introduced into evidence at trial. On the tape one can see that L.H. had difficulty discussing the subject of the rape. And on December 16, 1999, about 21 months after the rape, L.H. recorded her accusation in a videotaped interview with the Child Advocacy Center. The State charged petitioner with aggravated rape of a child under 12 and sought the death penalty.

The jury unanimously determined that petitioner should be sentenced to death. The Supreme Court of Louisiana affirmed. The court rejected petitioner's reliance on *Coker v. Georgia*, noting that, while *Coker* bars the use of the death penalty as punishment for the rape of an adult woman, it left open the question which, if any, other nonhomicide crimes can be punished by death consistent with the Eighth Amendment.

The (Eighth) Amendment "draw[s] its meaning from the evolving standards of decency that mark the progress of a maturing society" (*Trop v. Dulles*, 356 U.S. at 101, 1958). Evolving standards of decency must embrace and express respect for the dignity of the person, and the punishment of criminals must conform to that rule. As we shall discuss, punishment is justified under one or more of three principal rationales: rehabilitation, deterrence, and retribution. It is the last of these, retribution, that most often can contradict the law's own ends. For these reasons we have explained that capital punishment must "be limited to those offenders who commit 'a narrow category of the most serious crimes' and whose extreme culpability makes them 'the most deserving of execution.'"

In these cases the Court has been guided by "objective indicia of society's standards, as expressed in legislative enactments and state practice with respect to executions." Whether the death penalty is disproportionate to the crime committed depends as well upon the standards elaborated by controlling precedents and by the Court's own understanding and interpretation of the Eighth Amendment's text, history, meaning, and purpose.

Based both on consensus and our own independent judgment, our holding is that a death sentence for one who raped but did not kill a child, and who did not intend to assist another in killing the child, is unconstitutional under the Eighth and Fourteenth Amendments.

Respondent insists that the six States where child rape is a capital offense reflect a consistent direction of change in support of the death penalty for child rape. Consistent change might counterbalance an otherwise weak demonstration of consensus. But whatever the significance of consistent change where it is cited to show emerging support for expanding the scope of the death penalty, no showing of consistent change has been made in this case. (A showing of support) is evidenced by six new death penalty statutes, three enacted in the last two years. Here, the total number of States to have made child rape a capital offense after *Furman* is six. This is not an indication of a trend or change in direction.

It must be acknowledged that there are moral grounds to question a rule barring capital punishment for a crime against an individual that did not result in death. These facts illustrate the point. Here the victim's fright, the sense of betrayal, and the nature of her injuries caused more prolonged physical and mental suffering than, say, a sudden killing by an unseen assassin. The attack was not just on her but on her childhood. We cannot dismiss the years of long anguish that must be endured by the victim of child rape.

It does not follow, though, that capital punishment is a proportionate penalty for the crime. The constitutional prohibition against excessive or cruel and unusual punishments mandates that the State's power to punish "be exercised within the limits of civilized standards." *Trop*, 356 U.S., at 99.

Evolving standards of decency that mark the progress of a maturing society counsel us to be most hesitant before interpreting the Eighth Amendment to allow the extension of the death penalty, a hesitation that has special force where no life was taken in the commission of the crime.

Consistent with evolving standards of decency and the teachings of our precedents we conclude that, in determining whether the death penalty is excessive, there is a distinction between intentional first-degree murder on the one hand and non-homicide crimes against individual persons, even including child rape, on the other. The latter crimes may be devastating in their harm, as here, but "in terms of moral depravity and of the injury to the person and to the public," they cannot be compared to murder in their "severity and irrevocability" (*Coker*, 433 U.S., at 598).

It is not at all evident that the child rape victim's hurt is lessened when the law permits the death of the perpetrator. Capital cases require a long-term commitment by those who testify for the prosecution. L.H. was required to discuss the case at length with law enforcement personnel. In a public trial she was required to recount once more all the details of the crime to a jury as the State pursued the death of her stepfather.

In addition, by in effect making the punishment for child rape and murder equivalent, a State that punishes child rape by death may remove a strong incentive for the rapist not to kill the victim. Assuming the offender behaves in a rational way, as one must to justify the penalty on grounds of deterrence, the penalty in some respects gives less protection, not more, to the victim, who is often the sole witness to the crime.

These concerns overlook the meaning and full substance of the established proposition that the Eighth Amendment is defined by "the evolving standards of decency that mark the progress of a maturing society" (*Trop*, 356 U.S., at 101). Confirmed by repeated, consistent rulings of this Court, this principle requires that use of the death penalty be restrained. In most cases justice is not better served by terminating the life of the perpetrator rather than confining him and preserving the possibility that he and the system will find ways to allow him to understand the enormity of his offense.

The judgment of the Supreme Court of Louisiana upholding the capital sentence is reversed. This case is remanded for further proceedings not inconsistent with this opinion.

---

1. Do you agree with the ruling? In other words, do you agree with the Supreme Court that the death penalty is grossly disproportionate to the crime of child rape? What if you knew that defendant lied (and had the victim lie) about the circumstances of the rape? The child initially suggested that neighborhood boys had raped her. What if you knew that the defendant had called a professional cleaner to get blood stains out of the carpet?

2. Is legal precedent or legislation the best measures of the consensus of "evolving standards of decency?" What if there is a pattern of executions for child rapes in states that have death penalty legislation for this type of non-homicide offense?

3. Should fear of wrongful convictions persuade the state not to invoke capital punishment? If so, to what percentage of certainty should the state be required to establish in these cases?

There are other cases where the protection against cruel and unusual punishment is put into question. The difference in these cases, compared to *Coker* and *Kennedy*, is that the focus is not only the type of victim (adult versus child) or type of crime (homicide versus non-homicide) but on the type of offender. The Supreme Court in *Atkins v. Virginia* (2002) addressed whether capital punishment is a violation of the Eighth Amendment for defendants with a mental disability. Much like the *Kennedy* case, The Supreme Court in *Atkins* examined the general consensus regarding the execution of the developmentally disabled. "(Most) states (prohibit) the execution of mentally retarded persons . . . (which) provides powerful evidence that today our society views mentally retarded offenders as categorically less culpable than the average criminal" [*Atkins v. Virginia*, 536 U.S. (2002) at 315-316]. The Supreme Court also noted that for those states that allowed executions of the developmentally disabled, executions were rare. Therefore, the Court concluded that capital punishment for developmentally disabled defendants violates the Eighth Amendment's protection against cruel and unusual punishment.

In 2005, the Supreme Court also addressed the death penalty for youthful defendants. Similar to *Kennedy* and *Atkins*, the Court questioned the constitutionality of the death penalty for youthful defendants—those under 18 years old—by examining the national consensus in the justification of executing youthful defendants. [*Roper v. Simmons*, 543 U.S. 551 (2005)]. Much like the rationale in *Atkins*, the Court noted that the majority of states either have a general prohibition on the use of the death penalty or a prohibition on the use of the death penalty for youthful offenders. The Court in *Roper* also noted that even with the states that have no explicit prohibition on the use of the death penalty for youthful defendants, death sentences for youthful offenders are rare.

The majority of cases regarding the Eighth Amendment right against cruel and unusual punishment address the death penalty with regard to grossly disproportionate sentencing compared to the crime. What about other non-capital sentencing—namely life in prison penalties? Can defendants claim that life sentences are grossly disproportionate to the crimes they committed and, therefore, violate their right against cruel and unusual punishment?

In *Rummel v. Estelle* (1980), the Supreme Court addressed these questions. In this case, a defendant was convicted for two previous felonies (fraudulent use of a credit card for $80 worth of goods or services and passing a forged check for $28.36). For his third felony conviction (receiving $120.75 under false pretenses), he was given a mandatory life sentence under the mandatory sentencing policy in Texas—a version of the "three strikes and you're out" law. The question in this case was whether a life sentence violated the Eighth

Amendment right against cruel and unusual punishment given that the sentence—life in prison—was disproportionate to the crime involved—false pretenses involving less than $150. The Supreme Court ruled that each state has its own perspective on which offenses deserve harsh punishments. "Texas is entitled to make its own judgment as to where such lines lie, subject only to those strictures of the Eighth Amendment that can be informed by objective factors." *Rummel v. Estelle*, 445 U.S. (1980) at 284. In other words, unless there are objective criteria that were violated, a court is not likely to determine that a life sentence is grossly disproportionate and, thereby, in violation of the right against cruel and unusual punishment.

Right to a Jury Trial

A second area of constitutional interest concerns the right to a jury trial in making sentencing decisions. In 1989, the Supreme Court upheld the constitutionality of the federal sentencing guidelines in *Mistretta v. United States*, 488 U.S. 361 (1989). The issue in this case, though, addressed Congress' power to delegate law-making authority to the Federal Sentencing Commission in creating the federal sentencing guidelines. The Supreme Court supported their delegation power in transferring their law-making authority to the Commission, legitimizing the federal sentencing guidelines as a viable mechanism to determine sentencing for those found guilty in a criminal court.

Since 2000, judicial sentencing has come under significant constitutional scrutiny. The Supreme Court addressed the right to a jury trial in sentencing practices in *Apprendi v. New Jersey*, 530 U.S. 466 (2000). Charles Apprendi, Jr. pled guilty to second degree possession of a firearm for an unlawful purpose (maximum of ten years in prison) for shooting into the home of an African-American family. Additionally, he pled guilty to third degree possession of an antipersonnel bomb (maximum of five years in prison). After the plea was accepted by the court, the prosecutor filed a sentence enhancement for a hate crime. During the sentencing phase of the trial, the judge heard evidence to support the hate crime sentence enhancement and, therefore, imposed a 12-year prison sentence.

Apprendi appealed this decision to the Supreme Court claiming that his Sixth Amendment right to a jury trial had been violated because the facts that supported a sentence enhancement had only been heard by a judge and not by a jury. The Supreme Court agreed and held that any facts that raise the sentence above the statutory maximum must be submitted to a jury and proved beyond a reasonable doubt. The only exception to this rule is there is no requirement that a jury must hear and decide the facts of prior convictions that might increase one's sentence.

Following *Apprendi,* the Supreme Court similarly addressed the right to a jury trial in death penalty sentencing in *Ring v. Arizona,* 536 U.S. 584 (2002). Among other charges, Timothy Ring was convicted of armed robbery and felony murder of a bank employee during a pickup of cash and checks from a department store. Before a death sentence could be imposed, Arizona required the court to find proof of at least one aggravating circumstance and no mitigating circumstances. Even though felony murder in Arizona could not carry a death penalty, the judge could impose a death sentence if he or she found that the defendant was a "major participant" in the armed robbery. During the sentencing phase, the judge heard evidence and found that Ring was a major participant and sentenced him to death. Based on the precedent set in *Apprendi,* Ring claimed that he had a right to a jury trial to determine the facts upon which this finding was made. The Supreme Court in *Ring v. Arizona* agreed and required that death penalty cases use a jury to decide the facts upon which aggravating circumstances are decided and that instruct the imposition of the death penalty.

In 2004, the Supreme Court continued its constitutional assessment of sentencing practices and the right to jury trial in *Blakely v. Washington,* 124 S. Ct. 2531 (2004). Based again on the precedent of *Apprendi, Blakley* addressed judicial decisions in making an upward departure in a sentencing guideline state (see Box 12.6).

Box 12.6 DO UPWARD DEPARTURES IN STATE SENTENCING GUIDELINES VIOLATE THE RIGHT TO JURY TRIAL?

Blakely v. Washington
124 S. Ct. 2531 (2004)

Justice SCALIA delivered the opinion of the Court.

Ralph Howard Blakely, Jr. pleaded guilty to the kidnapping of his estranged wife. In 1998, he abducted her from their orchard home in Grant County, Washington, binding her with duct tape and forcing her at knifepoint into a wooden box in the bed of his pickup truck. In the process, he implored her to dismiss the divorce suit and related trust proceedings.

The State charged petitioner with first-degree kidnaping. Upon reaching a plea agreement, however, it reduced the charge to second-degree kidnaping involving domestic violence and use of a firearm. Petitioner entered a guilty plea admitting the elements of second-degree kidnaping and the domestic violence and firearm allegations, but no other relevant facts.

The case then proceeded to sentencing. In Washington, second-degree kidnaping is a class B felony. State law provides that "[n]o person convicted of a [class B] felony shall be punished by confinement . . . exceeding . . . a term of ten years." § 9A.20.021(1)(b). Other provisions of state law, however, further limit the range of sentences a judge may impose. Washington's Sentencing Reform Act specifies, for petitioner's offense of second-degree kidnaping with a firearm, a "standard range" of 49 to 53 months.

A judge may impose a sentence above the standard range if he finds "substantial and compelling reasons justifying an exceptional sentence." § 9.94A.120(2). . . . "[A] reason offered to justify an exceptional sentence can be considered only if it takes into account factors other than those which are used in computing the standard range sentence for the offense." *State* v. *Gore*, 21 P. 3d at 277 (2001).

Pursuant to the plea agreement, the State recommended a sentence within the standard range of 49 to 53 months. After hearing Yolanda's description of the kidnaping, however, the judge rejected the State's recommendation and imposed an exceptional sentence of 90 months—37 months beyond the standard maximum.

He justified the sentence on the ground that petitioner had acted with "deliberate cruelty," a statutorily enumerated ground for departure in domestic-violence cases. Petitioner appealed, arguing that this sentencing procedure deprived him of his federal constitutional right to have a jury determine beyond a reasonable doubt all facts legally essential to his sentence.

This case requires us to apply the rule we expressed in *Apprendi* v. *New Jersey*, 530 U.S. 466, 490 (2000): "Other than the fact of a prior conviction, any fact that increases the penalty for a crime beyond the prescribed statutory maximum must be submitted to a jury, and proved beyond a reasonable doubt." In this case, petitioner was sentenced to more than three years above the 53-month statutory maximum of the standard range because he had acted with "deliberate cruelty." The facts supporting that finding were neither admitted by petitioner nor found by a jury. The State nevertheless contends that there was no *Apprendi* violation because the relevant "statutory maximum" is not 53 months, but the 10-year maximum for class B felonies in § 9A.20.021(1)(b). It observes that no exceptional sentence may exceed that limit. Our precedents make clear, however, that the "statutory maximum" for *Apprendi* purposes is the maximum sentence a judge may impose *solely on the basis of the facts reflected in the jury verdict or admitted by the defendant.* In other words, the relevant "statutory maximum" is not the maximum sentence a judge may impose after finding additional facts, but the maximum he may impose *without* any additional findings.

By reversing the judgment below, we are not, as the State would have it, "find[ing] determinate sentencing schemes unconstitutional." This case is not about whether determinate sentencing is constitutional, only about how it can be implemented in a way that respects the Sixth Amendment. Justice O'CONNOR argues that, because determinate sentencing schemes involving judicial fact-finding entail less judicial discretion than indeterminate schemes, the constitutionality of the latter implies the constitutionality of the former. This argument is flawed. (T)he Sixth Amendment by its terms is not a limitation on judicial power, but a reservation of jury power. It limits judicial power only to the extent that the claimed judicial power infringes on the province of the jury.

Petitioner was sentenced to prison for more than three years beyond what the law allowed for the crime to which he confessed, on the basis of a disputed finding that he had acted with "deliberate cruelty." The Framers would not have thought it too much to demand that, before depriving a man of three more years of his liberty, the State should suffer the modest inconvenience of submitting its accusation to "the unanimous suffrage of twelve of his equals and neighbours," 4 Blackstone, *Commentaries*, at 343, rather than a lone employee of the State.

The judgment of the Washington Court of Appeals is reversed, and the case is remanded for further proceedings not inconsistent with this opinion.

1. You might argue that the judge is better suited to determine the fate of someone's freedom than a jury of 12 citizens and that the holding of this case is wrong. Do you agree or disagree?
2. Does this ruling apply to downward departures? Why or why not?
3. What is the practical effect of this ruling on presumptive sentencing guidelines? Does it have the same effect for states with presumptive sentencing guidelines as it does for the federal sentencing guidelines given the rulings in *United States v. Booker* and *United States v. Fanfan* (discussed next)?

Following very closely, the Supreme Court confronted the same issue for the federal sentencing guidelines. In 2005, the Supreme Court addressed the right to jury trial in cases that experience upward departures from the federal sentencing guidelines in two cases: *United States v. Booker* and *United States v. Fanfan*. These cases were consolidated [125 S. Ct. 738 (2005)], as *Booker* addressed the constitutional issue of the right to jury trial in upward departure decisions in the federal system and *Fanfan* addressed the practical effect of the holding from *Booker*.

Freddie Booker was found guilty in a federal court for the possession with the intent to distribute at least 50 grams of crack cocaine. The federal sentencing guidelines mandated a "base" sentence range of no more than 262 months. During sentencing, the judge found that Booker had possessed an additional 566 grams of crack. The judge imposed a mandatory minimum sentence of 360 months with the maximum of life imprisonment. Similar to *Blakely*, the Supreme Court found that this upward departure violated the defendant's Sixth Amendment right to jury trial.

The notable difference between *Blakely* and *Booker* is the case that is consolidated with *Booker*. *United States v. Fanfan* addressed the effect on the federal sentencing guidelines given the ruling in *Booker*. The Supreme Court in *Fanfan* had several options:

- do nothing
- make the presumptive federal sentencing guidelines merely advisory
- invalidate the federal guidelines altogether, which would, essentially, overrule the *Mistretta* case

The Court decided to make the federal sentencing guidelines advisory rather than presumptive.

We have seen a progression from the Supreme Court's overwhelming support of the presumptive sentencing guidelines in *Mistretta* in the late 1980s to now mandating that sentencing guidelines—at the federal level—are to be merely advisory in *Booker* and *Fanfan*. Some suggest that the line of cases, starting with *Apprendi*, merely displaces discretion from the judge to the legislature in its law-making authority (see Bibas 2001) or to the prosecutor in its charging authority (see Iannachione and Ball 2008).

SUMMARY

In each criminal trial where the defendant is found guilty there are two phases: (1) the guilt phase, where the state has a burden to prove the defendant is guilty of the crime; and (2) the sentencing phase, where testimony is heard and evidence reviewed to determine the appropriate sentence. Previous chapters addressed specific rules regarding the guilt phase of a criminal trial. This chapter contains information regarding sentencing and punishment that is integral for consideration in the sentencing phase of a criminal trial.

One of the most unique features of the criminal law is that the state punishes wrongdoers in ways that can include a loss of liberty. There are three basic approaches to punishment in the American criminal justice system: retributive theory, utilitarian theory, and restorative theory. Retributive punishment theory suggests that punishment is to be imposed on those that are blameworthy or deserving of punishment. The punishment should be proportionate to the crime—or, "do the crime, do the time." Punishment under this theory should address current and past criminal behavior to determine the level of punishment. It is a backward-looking theory.

Utilitarian theory, by contrast, is forward-looking in an attempt to prevent future wrongdoing. There are three mechanisms by which the state can accomplish this preventive goal: incapacitation, deterrence, and rehabilitation. The way incapacitation prevents future offenses is to restrict the offender's freedom so that he or she is unable to commit any wrongdoing. However, since the system is not able to do that for every citizen who violates the law, it must choose which defendants' freedom to restrict; this is called selective incapacitation. The second mechanism is deterrence, and it is characterized as the ultimate "scare tactic," where the fear of the punishment outweighs the benefit inherent in committing the crime. Therefore, this mechanism of the utilitarian theory presumes that the defendant is a rational thinker weighing the benefits and costs of committing the crime prior to completing it. There are two types of deterrence: specific deterrence assesses punishment on an individual to prevent that individual from wrongdoing in the future, whereas general deterrence assesses punishment on an individual to prevent others from future wrongdoing. The final mechanism of the utilitarian theory of punishment is rehabilitation. Rehabilitation presumes that the defendant is sick and needs treatment to prevent future wrongdoing. Unlike other theories or mechanisms, rehabilitation punishes in order to treat offenders until they are better. Theoretically, there is no time limit for this process.

The final punishment theory addressed in this chapter is the restorative theory of punishment, or restorative justice. In most—if not all—crimes, there are three parties involved: the offender, the victim, and the community. The goal of restorative justice is to restore the parties to a similar or better place in comparison to before the crime occurred. Therefore, if property was taken from the victim, then the property would either be returned or replaced with equal or greater value. The community would be restored through community service or greater safety measures. Defendants would likely be treated through education, emotional therapy, and/or work training so that they can be restored to a better place prior to the crime.

The chapter described specific types of sentences ranging from fines and probation to incarceration. Intermediate sanctions were developed to provide an alternative to incarceration that was more restrictive than probation and was more individualized. Examples of intermediate sanctions are day reporting centers, electronic monitoring, and intensive probation supervision.

In the last few decades, sentencing practices and policies in American jurisprudence have been reformed to provide more formal, uniform sentencing to avoid unwarranted disparities. The three most apparent sentencing reforms in the past few decades are sentencing guidelines, mandatory minimum penalties, and truth-in-sentencing policies. Sentencing guidelines—a grid of presumptive sentencing ranges based on prior record and severity of current conviction—appear in several states and the federal government. Some states have presumptive or mandatory guidelines and some states have advisory or voluntary guidelines. However, in all jurisdictions with sentencing guidelines, there are opportunities for judges to make downward departures—decreasing the length and/or severity of a sentence below the sentencing guideline range recommended—or upward departures—increasing the length and/or severity of a sentence above the sentencing guideline range recommended. However, the practice of upward departures has come under recent legal scrutiny.

Sentencing and punishment in American jurisprudence has experienced certain levels of constitutional scrutiny, such as protection against cruel and unusual punishment and right to a jury trial. More specifically, protection against cruel and unusual punishment has addressed proportionate sentencing with respect to the death penalty, life sentences, and punishing certain groups of individuals. Although courts shy away from striking life sentences down as violating the protection against cruel and unusual punishment, they have addressed the constitutionality of capital punishment insomuch as striking down death sentences for rape of an adult or of a child. Also, the death penalty has been struck down for youthful and developmentally disabled defendants. The death penalty has also come under constitutional scrutiny for violating the right to a jury trial in a judicial determination of facts that would support a death sentence. Judges have also been scrutinized for violating a defendant's right to a jury trial because they determined facts, without jury consultation, that raised the sentence above the sentencing guideline range maximum.

Punishment and sentencing in the United States have gone through recent transformation in hopes to maintain uniformity and consistency. Until recently, these sentence reforms have gone unquestioned. Based upon the decision in *United States v. Booker* and *United States v. Fanfan*, some might argue that the sentencing guidelines, at least at the federal level, have virtually been overruled since the Supreme Court proclaimed the federal guidelines are now advisory. Although punishment will always be a unique feature of the criminal law, the form and application of this punishment are constantly evolving.

KEY TERMS

advisory sentencing guidelines
determinate sentencing
downward departure
general deterrence
hydraulic displacement hypothesis
incapacitation
indeterminate sentencing
intermediate sanctions

mandatory minimum penalty
presumptive sentencing guidelines
restorative justice
retribution
selective incapacitation
specific deterrence
truth in sentencing
upward departure
utilitarian theory

CRITICAL THINKING QUESTIONS

1. Which theory or mechanism of sentencing is most effective? In your answer address what "effective" means.
2. If you were a judge and could create any punishment you wanted to (keeping it ethical), what would you choose for each of the following offenses: sexual assault of a child, robbery, and marijuana possession?
3. Do mandatory minimums create more problems than solutions? Explain.
4. What principle does "truth in sentencing" serve?
5. Given that those convicted of crimes are eligible for the death penalty, should we even have a protection against cruel and unusual punishment? Why should there even be the question?
6. Why isn't the right to jury trial only for the guilt phase of the criminal court?

SUGGESTED READINGS

Hanks, G.C. (1997). *Against the Death Penalty: Christian and Secular Arguments Against Capital Punishment.* Scottsdale, PA: Herald Press. This book gives food for thought regarding the argument against the death penalty from both a faith-based perspective and a secular perspective. The author(s) may or may not agree with the arguments laid out in this text, but it gives good sources of discussion around the morality of the death penalty.

Tonry, M. (1996). *Sentencing Matters.* New York: Oxford University Press. This text is one of the leading readings in understanding the full picture of sentencing decision making and sentence reform. Tonry lays out the structure and research in an understandable way that addresses the heart of the issues of sentencing in American jurisprudence.

Ulmer, J. (1997). *Social Worlds of Sentencing: Court Communities Under Sentencing Guidelines.* New York: SUNY Press. This book discusses the courtroom workgroup and its influence on sentencing decisions in a sentencing guideline system. Even though sentencing guidelines are intended to formalize and create uniformity in sentencing decisions, Ulmer finds that the courtroom workgroup and other social facts still maintain their influence.

REFERENCES

Apprendi v. New Jersey, 530 U.S. 466 (2000).

Atkins v. Virginia, 536 U.S. 304 (2002).

Baze v. Rees, 553 U.S. 35 (2008).

Bibas, S. (2001). "Judicial Fact-Finding and Sentence Enhancements in a World of Guilty Pleas." *Yale Law Journal* 110:1097-1185.

Blakely v. Washington, 124 S. Ct. 2531 (2004).

Byrne, J.M. & Miofsky, K.T. (2009). "From Preentry to Reentry: An Examination of the Effectiveness of Institutional and Community-Based Sanctions." *Victims and Offenders* 4:348-356.

Coker v. Georgia, 433 U.S. 584 (1977).

Ditton, P.M. & Wilson, D.J. (1999). "Truth in Sentencing in State Prisons." Washington, DC: U.S. Bureau of Justice Statistics.

Frenzel, E.D. & Ball, J.D. (2007). "Effects of Individual Characteristics on Plea Negotiations Under Sentencing Guidelines." *Journal of Ethnicity in Criminal Justice* 5:59-82.

Gillers, S. (1980). "Deciding Who Dies." *University of Pennsylvania Law Review* 129: 1-124.

Gottfredson, M.R. & Gottfredson, D.M. (1988). *Decision Making in Criminal Justice* (2d ed.). New York: Plenum.

Iannacchione, B. & Ball, J.D. (2008). "The Effect of *Blakely v. Washington* on Upward Departures in a Sentencing Guideline

State." *Journal of Contemporary Criminal Justice* 24:419-436.

Kennedy v. Louisiana, 554 U.S. 407 (2008).

Kubrin, C.E., Messner, S.F., Deane, G., McGeever, K. & Stucky, T.D. (2010). "Proactive Policing and Robbery Rates Across U.S. Cities." *Criminology* 48:57-97.

Loftin, C., Heumann, M. & McDowall, D. (1983). "Mandatory Sentencing and Firearms Violence." *Law and Society Review* 17:287-318.

Marvell, T.B. & Moody, C.E. (1995). "The Impact of Enhanced Prison Terms for Felonies Committed with Guns." *Criminology* 33:247-281.

McDowall, D.C., Loftin, C. & Wiersema, B. (1992). "A Comparative Study of the Preventive Effects of Mandatory Sentencing Laws for Gun Crimes." *Journal of Criminal Law and Criminology* 83:378-394.

Mistretta v. United States, 488 U.S. 361 (1989).

Moore, C.A. & Miethe, T.D. (1986). "Regulated and Unregulated Sentencing Decisions: An Analysis of First-Year Practices Under Minnesota's Felony Sentencing Guidelines." *Law and Society Review* 20:253-278.

Ring v. Arizona, 536 U.S. 584 (2002).

Roper v. Simmons, 543 U.S. 551 (2005).

Rummel v. Estelle, 445 U.S. 263 (1980).

Spohn, C. (2009). *How Do Judges Decide? The Search for Fairness and Justice in Punishment* (2d ed.). Thousand Oaks, CA: Pine Forge Press.

Spohn, C. & Hemmens, C. (2012). *Courts: A Text/Reader* (2d ed.). Los Angeles: Sage.

Stith, K. & Cabranes, J.A. (1998). *Fear of Judging: Sentencing Guidelines in the Federal Courts*. Chicago: University of Chicago Press.

Tarasoff v. Regents of the University of California, 551 P.2d 334 (1976).

Tonry, M. (1996). *Sentencing Matters*. New York: Oxford University Press.

United States v. Booker, 125 S. Ct. 738 (2005).

United States v. Fanfan, 125 S. Ct. 738 (2005).

Wilkerson v. Utah, 99 U.S. 130 (1878).

abandonment (9): a defense to attempt when a person gives up a criminal endeavor voluntarily

absolute liability (2): a rule of criminal responsibility that allows for the conviction of an otherwise innocent person without proof of *mens rea*

abuse of trust crime (4, 8): crime that takes place when people neglect or improperly perform their job duties; see also *white collar crime*

accessories (3): people who assist in the commission of a crime in some material way

accessories after the fact (3): people who assist those who have committed a crime after the crime has been completed

accessories before the fact (3): people who assist those who are in the process of committing a crime before the actual crime has been completed

accomplice liability (3): criminal responsibility for individuals who assist in the commission of a crime in some material way

accomplices (3): individuals who assist those who actually carry out a crime; also may be known as accessories or aiders and abettors

actual breaking (4): actions taken to break into a home or other structure that involve the use of force, such as breaking a window or kicking in a locked door; see also *constructive breaking*

actual cause (2): the conduct that created a result that was prohibited by law; also known as *factual cause*

actual possession (2): to be in physical possession of some item; to have something on one's person

actus reus (2): Latin phrase meaning the wrongful act that is part of a crime

advisory sentencing guidelines (12): voluntary system of sentencing based on one's prior criminal record and severity of the current offense(s) to direct judges in making their sentencing decision

affirmative defense (10): a defense in which the defendant demonstrates the existence of facts or circumstances which, even if all the evidence offered by the prosecution were true, would eliminate or mitigate the criminal charges

age of consent (2): the statutory age at which a person can legally consent to engage in sexual behavior; see also *statutory rape*

aider or abettor (3): any person who knowingly assists another person in the commission of a crime

anticipatory offenses (9): take place with the expectation of completing a larger criminal act; see also *inchoate offenses*

arson (4): starting a fire or causing an explosion with the purpose of damaging or destroying a building or property

asportation (6): the carrying away or moving requirement for kidnapping

attempt (9): when a person takes action to perform a criminal act but is stopped before the crime can be fully completed

attendant circumstances (2): statutory language that provides further elaboration of a prohibited criminal act (for example, the crime was committed at night or with possession of a weapon)

authorized reliance (11): an exception to the rule that a mistake of law is not a defense where the defendant trusted an official's misinterpretation of a criminal law

battered spouse syndrome (10): a limited defense that is recognized in some jurisdictions in which an abuse victim uses force against the abuser at a time when there is no imminent threat

blackmail (4): obtaining the property of another through threats of future harm; see also *extortion*

broker-dealer fraud (8): takes place when a stockbroker or investment advisor sells investments to a client based upon what the broker or dealer may gain from the transaction, rather than based upon what is in the client's best interests

burden of proof (10): responsibility of demonstrating to the finder of fact that a defendant committed all the necessary elements of a specific crime

burglary (4): breaking and entering a building or structure with the intent to commit a crime

bystander rule (2): no duty to act or rescue a person in peril unless such a duty is recognized by law

carnal knowledge (6): penile to vaginal sexual penetration

castle doctrine (10): a person's right to protect his or her own property from an unlawful intruder

castle exception (10): allows a person to use deadly force without a duty to retreat if they reasonably believe that they are in danger of death or serious bodily injury and the attack takes place in their home

chain conspiracy (9): a conspiracy in which each actor works independently to fulfill his or her role in the chronological execution of a criminal plan; see also *conspiracy, wheel conspiracy*

Child Online Protection Act of 1998 (8): law designed to protect children from online pornography; has been struck down as a First Amendment violation

Child Pornography Prevention Act of 1996 (8): law designed to protect children from online pornography; portions have been struck down as free speech violations

Children's Internet Protection Act of 2000 (8): law requiring schools to take measures to prevent children from viewing online pornography as a condition of receiving federal funding

circumstantial evidence (2): indirect factors that point to an individual's involvement in a crime

common law (1): a source of law initiated in England to support principles governing behavior that was consistently applied across the country

common law assault (6): attempted or threatened common law battery

common law battery (6): offensive, unlawful touching of another

complicity (3, 9): to be associated with or to be an accomplice in a criminal act; see also *accomplice liability*

Computer Fraud and Abuse Act (8): law that regulates denial of service attacks and applies to computers belonging to the U.S. government, financial institutions, and those used in interstate commerce

concurrence (2, 9): principle of criminal liability that a person must have a criminal *mens rea* at the same time that they perform a criminal *actus reus*

concurring opinion (1): the legal opinion by appellate court justices who agree with the majority opinion but disagree with the legal reasoning used

conduct (2): the wrongful act associated with a crime

consent (10): a defense that is available when a person did commit a criminal act, but the person against whom the crime was committed voluntarily gave his or her permission for the crime to take place; see also *implied consent*

consolidated theft statutes (4): statutes that combine larceny, embezzlement, obtaining property by false pretenses, receiving stolen property, and extortion into a single crime of theft; see also *theft*

conspiracy (9): two or more people agreeing to commit a crime

constructive breaking (4): actions taken to break into a home or other structure that do not involve the use of force, such as opening an unlocked door or window; see also *actual breaking*

constructive possession (2, 7): to not have an item on one's person, but have dominion or control over the item; see also *actual possession*

contraband (7): any item or device that is illegal to possess in and of itself

conversion (4): civil law violation of unlawfully obtaining another person's property

convert (4): keeping another person's property by an unlawful possessor for his or her own use and enjoyment

corporate crime (8): wrongful acts committed by company employees or representatives in furtherance of the company's interests; see also *white collar crime*

crimes against the state (8): criminal acts that are directed at a country's government and citizens

criminal homicide (5): the *Model Penal Code*'s classification for the unlawful killing of another person; see also *manslaughter, murder,* and *negligent homicide*

criminal trespass (4): unlawfully entering or remaining on another person's property

culpability (2): to possess the *mens rea* for a criminal act; blameworthiness

curtilage (4): the area surrounding a person's home, such as residential yards and structures on residential premises

cyberbullying (8): willful and repeated harm inflicted through the use of computers, cell phones, and other electronic devices

cybercrime (8): use of computers or other electronic devices as a means of committing a crime or as the target of the crime

cyberextortion (8): obtaining someone else's property through threats of future harm that are communicated through the use of the Internet or other electronic device

cyberpornography (8): the distribution of pornographic material over the Internet

cyber-smearing (8): an attempt to damage a victim's reputation through online communications; see also *cyberstalking*

cyberstalking (8): the use of the Internet, email, or other electronic communications to create a criminal level of intimidation, harassment, and fear

cyberterrorism (8): carrying out terroristic objectives by using computers as either a target of or means of facilitating terrorism

cybertrespassing (8): invasion of a computer or computer system without obtaining appropriate permission; see also *hacking*

decriminalization (7): taking an activity that has been prohibited by law and removing the criminal penalties from it

defense (10): a legally recognized justification or excuse for a criminal act; see also *excuse defense, justification defense*

deindividuation (8): the anonymity and decreased social inhibition that people experience in online interactions

denial of service (DoS) attacks (8): cybercrime that prevents the appropriate and productive use of a computer system

derivative liability (3): to be held criminally liable for the acts of another as a result of acting as an accomplice

determinate sentencing (12): sentencing policies that are more mandatory than discretionary

deterrent effect (9): idea that if people see others being punished for crimes that were not completed, they will have reason to abstain from engaging in similar criminal activity

diffusion of responsibility (3): when different actors play a role in the criminal conduct

dissenting opinion (1): the legal opinion of the justices who disagree with the holding of the majority opinion

domestic violence (6): aggressive physical, emotional, and/or sexual behavior that is either provoking and/or threatening to another family or household member

downward departure (12): decision to sentence the defendant with a lower sentence than that suggested by the sentencing guidelines

drug paraphernalia (7): any implement or device that can be used to smoke, ingest, or inject illegal drugs

due process (1): individual liberty that gives citizens the process that is due to them

duress (11): defendant's feeling of being coerced to commit a crime eliminating his or her guilt

elements (1): points that must be proven in order to establish that a person has committed a crime

entrapment (11): government creates the intent in the defendant to commit the crime that he or she would not ordinarily commit

espionage (8): intentionally spying and providing a group or government with information that might lead to the destruction of or damage to the U.S. government

Espionage Act of 1917 (8): law regulating espionage that was passed shortly after the United States entered World War I

excuse defense (10): exists when a person has fully completed a course of criminal conduct that was not justified but where some circumstance exists that gives that person a valid reason for the criminal act; see also *defense*

***ex post facto* law (1):** principle governing behavior that is enforced retroactively

exposure (7): to come into close contact; with street crimes, the people in closest contact are most likely to be both victims and victimizers

extortion (4): obtaining the property of another through threats of future harm; see also *blackmail*

extrinsic force (6): force required beyond the force necessary to sexually penetrate

factual cause (2): see *actual cause*

factual impossibility (9): when a person takes all the steps necessary to complete a crime, but some circumstance outside their control makes the commission of the crime impossible

false imprisonment (6): intentional unlawful restraint of freedom of another

false pretenses (4): obtaining the property of another by the use of deception; see also *theft by deception*

federal law (8): the jurisdiction and legal authority that governs crimes against the United States

felonious restraint (6): the *Model Penal Code*'s version of false imprisonment that also includes involuntary servitude

felony murder (5): the incidental killing of another person during the commission of one of the statutorily specified felonies; see also *inherently dangerous felonies*

fencing (4): knowingly purchasing stolen goods in order to resell them for a profit; see also *receiving stolen property*

fetal death statutes (5): laws that make it a form of criminal homicide to cause the death of an unborn fetus

fiduciary relationship (8): a special relationship in which one party has a legal responsibility to properly manage the money or property of another person

financial planner (8): a person who is entrusted with a client's money for investment purposes; see also *stockbroker*

first degree murder (5): under common law the unlawful killing of another person as a result of malice aforethought; the deliberate or premeditated killing of another person

fraud (8): obtaining property through deceptive means

general deterrence (12): punishment that prevents other non-defendants from committing future criminal wrongdoing

general intent (2): the intent to commit an act that results in some degree of harm

Good Samaritan statutes (2): laws that require a person to aid another person in need or distress; these statutes often protect citizens from civil liability from actions that may cause injury during their assistance

guilty but mentally ill (11): a type of insanity plea where the defendant serves time in a mental health facility until he or she is better and then serves the remaining time in a correctional facility

hacking (8): invasion of a computer or computer system without obtaining appropriate permission; see also *cybertrespassing*

hearsay rule (9): excludes the use of hearsay statements at trial

hearsay statements (9): secondhand statements that may be used in order to prove the truth of a matter at trial

"hot spots" (7): locations that have disproportionately high levels of criminal and other disorderly behavior

human trafficking (6): the recruitment or transport of persons through some form of fraud, force, or coercion for an exploitative end purpose

hydraulic displacement hypothesis (12): hypothesis that suggests that when discretion is restricted in one jurisdictional area or with one actor, the discretion is simply transferred to another jurisdictional area or to another actor

identity theft (8): a crime in which a person makes improper use of another person's identity, usually for financial gain

Identity Theft and Assumption Deterrence Act of 1998 (8): federal law that defines and prohibits identity theft

ideological motivation (8): motive for committing acts of terrorism that relates to an individual, group, or culture; see also *terrorism*

imminent harm (4): harm that will be inflicted immediately

immovable property (4): property that is fixed or attached to land in such a way that it cannot be easily moved, such as land, buildings, or other structures

impeachment (10): demonstrating that a witness is inherently unreliable and should not be believed by the finder of fact

imperfect defense (10): defense that does not eliminate the full amount of a person's criminal culpability, and only mitigates or lessens the charge or the punishment given for a criminal action; see also *perfect defense*

implied consent (10): when a person effectively gives consent to injuries that are reasonably foreseeable to the activity in which they are participating; see also *consent*

impossibility (9): defense to attempt in which a fact or a law makes the commission of a crime unattainable; see also *factual impossibility*, *legal impossibility*

incapacitation (12): punishment that restricts a defendant's freedom to prevent future criminal wrongdoing

inchoate offenses (9): crimes that have begun to be committed but have not yet been fully completed; see also *anticipatory offenses*

independent causes (2): any factors that break the chain between the initial cause and the result

indeterminate sentencing (12): sentencing policies that are more discretionary than mandatory

infamous crime (9): a common law term that includes capital crimes, serious felonies, and crimes involving the use of deceit

infancy defense (11): depending on the defendant's age, one is not criminally liable for the crime because he or she cannot form the mental element of the underlying crime

inferences (2): a method of reasoning in which a fact that is to be established is deduced as a logical consequence from other facts that might have been proven or admitted

inherently dangerous felonies (5): any one of a group of statutorily defined crimes (such as rape, robbery, or home invasion) that are designed to cause, or that may cause, death or great bodily harm

initial aggressor (10): the person who first uses force against another person in an altercation

innocent instrumentality rule (2, 3): the use by one person of another person who is otherwise not blameworthy to commit a wrongful act

innocent mistake (11): an involuntary intoxication where one makes an honest and reasonable mistake of the intoxicating effect of a particular material ingested

innocent possession (2): possession without knowledge of origin

insider trading (8): buying or selling investments based upon confidential and nonpublic information

intangible property (4): property, such as stock certificates and property deeds, that has no value in and of itself, but which signifies something of value

intermediate sanctions (12): punishment that resides somewhere between probation and incarceration, where more restriction is applied than probation but less restrictive than incarceration

intermediate scrutiny (1): the second highest level of scrutiny under an equal protection claim that is applied to those laws that address quasi-suspect class

Internet gambling (8): any wagering activity that takes place over the Internet; also known as online gambling

Interstate Stalking Punishment and Prevention Act of 1996 (8): cyberstalking legislation that prohibits using a computer in a way that causes another person fear or emotional distress

intervening causes (2): see *independent causes*

intrinsic force (6): force required for sexual penetration itself

investment schemes (8): when a broker or financial planner sells false investments

involuntary intoxication (11): the defendant can use the intoxication defense if he or she becomes intoxicated beyond his or her control

involuntary manslaughter (5): the unintentional killing of another person as a result of recklessness or criminal negligence

irrebuttable presumption (11): an assumption that cannot be refuted

irresistible impulse test (11): a test of insanity where, due to a mental disease or defect at the time of the crime, one cannot control one's behavior from committing the crime

johns (7): the people who procure the services of prostitutes

joint possession (2): exists when several people maintain access and control over common spaces

justification defense (10): exists when a person has fully completed a course of criminal conduct, but some circumstance exists that makes the criminal action right or justified; see also *defense*

kidnapping (6): taking and carrying away of another against their will

larceny (4): taking and sneaking away with someone else's property

legal cause (2): see *proximate cause*

legal impossibility (9): when a person takes all the steps necessary to complete a crime, but the act is not prohibited by the law

legalization (7): allowing people to engage in activities that formerly were prohibited by law with relatively few restrictions

loitering (7): hanging out or standing around certain locations with no apparent purpose

majority opinion (1): an appellate court legal opinion based on the ruling of the majority members

mala in se (1): evil in itself or inherently evil/wrongdoing

mala prohibita (1): prohibited evil/wrongdoing as defined by the community

malice aforethought (5): hatred or ill feelings that result in one person killing another after deliberation

mandatory minimum penalty (12): minimum punishment that is required for a particular conviction according to statute

manslaughter (5): under both the common law and the *Model Penal Code* the killing another person without the presence of malice aforethought

marital rape allowance (6): charging a husband with a lesser degree of rape for the unwanted sexual penetration of his wife; the mitigated charge is the result of their marital status

marital rape exception (6): a husband cannot be charged with a rape for the unwanted sexual penetration of his wife

material fact (4): information that is the reason a person is willing to part with his or her property; see also *false pretenses*

mercy killings (5): to take the life of another person as a result of that individual being in an advanced state of mental or physical decline

mistake of fact (11): due to an honest and reasonable mistake of an underlying fact, the defendant is not criminally liable for committing the crime

mistake of law (11): due to an honest and/or reasonable mistake of a law, the defendant may still be criminally liable for committing the crime

M'Naghten Rule (11): a test of insanity where, due to a mental disease or defect at the time of the crime, a person does not know the nature and quality of his or her actions or know what he or she did was wrong and, therefore, is not criminally liable for the crime

motive (5): the reason someone commits a crime

movable property (4): property that can be transported, such as books, furniture, and other personal property

MPC (or substantial capacity) test (11): a test of insanity where, due to a mental disease or defect at the time of the crime, a person does not have the substantial capacity to appreciate the criminality of his or her act or to conform his or her conduct to the law and, therefore, is not criminally liable for the crime

mugging (7): strong-arm robbery; taking something of value from a person with force or threat of force (it may or may not involve the use of a weapon)

murder (5): the most serious form of criminal homicide; taking the life of another human being intentionally, deliberately, and with malice aforethought

natural law (1): principle governing behavior generated from an external force (e.g., Supreme Being or innate sense)

necessity (10): a defense in which the defendant commits the *actus reus* of a crime due to being forced to make a choice between two situations, either of which would result in some type of injury or damage

negligence (5): acting in a way that deviates from the standard of care that would be exercised by a reasonable or reasonably prudent person; contrast with *recklessness*

negligent homicide (5): to cause the death of another human being as a result of a negligent act or actions

not guilty by reason of insanity (11): a type of insanity plea where the defendant serves time in a mental facility until he or she is better and then is released

occupational crime (8): white collar crime that is committed against company interests; see also *white collar crime*

pathological intoxication (11): an involuntary intoxication where one is abnormally disoriented to the ingestion of ordinary intoxicants

perfect defense (10): demonstrates that a person has no criminal culpability for the criminal act and entitles a person to a full acquittal from the crime with which he or she has been charged; see also *imperfect defense*

perpetrators (3): a general term for people who commit crimes

phishing (8): obtaining a person's confidential information over the Internet in order to perpetrate other crimes

pimps (7): individuals who control one or more prostitutes by arranging for their clients (johns) and taking a percentage of their earnings

Pinkerton **rule (9):** states that all people involved in a conspiracy may be held responsible for all the actions that result from that conspiracy, even if a person did not participate directly

political motivation (8): reason for committing acts of terrorism that relates to government or politics; see also *terrorism*

Ponzi scheme (8): an investment fraud that involves the payment of purported returns to existing investors from funds contributed by new investors

positive law (1): principle governing behavior that is defined by society rather than an external force

possession (2): to have some item on one's person or to have it under one's custody or control; see also *actual possession* and *constructive possession*

precedent (1): rulings of past decisions governing decisions on current cases

preemptive strikes (10): an attack or use of force against a person to prevent that person from inflicting harm at some later time

presumptions (2): an assumption that a fact exists as a result of other known or proven facts

presumptive sentencing guidelines (12): mandatory system of sentencing based on one's prior criminal record and severity of the current offense(s) to direct judges in making their sentencing decision

principal in the first degree (3): an individual primarily responsible for the commission of a crime

principal in the second degree (3): anyone who assists in the commission of the crime and who is actually or constructively present when the crime is committed

principals (3): the individuals who are primarily responsible for the commission of a crime; see also *perpetrators*

principle of legality (1, 9): provides that no one can be sanctioned with a criminal punishment unless there is a law that prohibits the conduct at the time that the actions took place

private cyberstalking (8): unwanted or harassing communication that takes place only between the victim and the perpetrator; see also *cyberstalking*

product (or *Durham*) test (11): a test of insanity where the outcome of a mental disease or defect at the time of the crime was the defendant's behavior

property (4): things that people own and accumulate, and which are protected by property crimes statutes

property crimes (4): punish people for depriving others of their rightful possession of property

proximate cause (2): adding the element of actual cause to the necessary *mens rea* to establish that a crime has been committed and that we have a specific suspect; proximate cause asks (1) whether it is fair to hold an actor responsible for resulting harm, and (2) whether the harm was reasonably foreseeable from their actions

public cyberstalking (8): unwanted or harassing communication that takes place when the perpetrator posts damaging or embarrassing information about the victim in public electronic forums; see also *cyberstalking*

quasi-suspect class (1): group of individuals (i.e., gender and legitimacy) upon which a law distinguishes where intermediate scrutiny is used to test whether the right of equal protection of the law is applied

rape (6): unwanted sexual penetration of another

rational basis (1): the lowest level of scrutiny under an equal protection claim that is applied to any law that does not address fundamental rights, suspect class, or quasi-suspect class

reasonable (10): the minimum amount of force necessary to thwart an attacker and prevent the infliction of harm

reasonable resistance (6): the victim used a reasonable amount of his or her physical faculties to defend against an attack

rebuttable presumption (11): an assumption that can be refuted

receiving stolen property (4): receiving, retaining, or disposing of property that has been stolen

recklessness (5): to undertake a substantial and unjustified risk about which a person has knowledge

religious motivation (8): reason for committing acts of terrorism that relates to religion; see also *terrorism*

restitution (4): restoring the rightful owner of property to his or her original position before being wrongfully deprived of the property

restorative justice (12): punishment that places the three parties—the defendant, the victim, and the community—involved in any crime to the place or a better place prior to the crime

results (2): in criminal law, the social harm that is caused by someone's conduct

retaliation (10): when a defendant uses force against someone who has used unlawful force against them, but after some amount of time has passed since the initial use of unlawful force

retreat (10): an attempt to escape from an attacker before using self-defense

retreat rule (10): approach under which a person must attempt to flee or escape before utilizing force as self-defense so long as they can do so safely; see also *stand your ground approach*

retribution (12): punishment that addresses the blameworthiness of the defendant

robbery (7): taking anything of value from a person by force or threat of force; see also *mugging*

roving wiretaps (8): wiretaps that follow a specific person and are not attached to one phone line

sabotage (8): damaging, destroying, or interfering with the use of government property in order to prevent war preparations or the ability to handle national emergencies

Sarbanes-Oxley Act of 2002 (8): law passed in 2002 in response to instances of corporate fraud; requires financial reporting and controls of all companies

second degree murder (5): deliberately taking a human life without malice aforethought; malice is implied rather than express; in common law a crime that exists in terms of seriousness between first degree murder and manslaughter

securities fraud (8): fraud that is perpetrated through the purchase and sale of stocks and other investments

sedition (8): advocating or encouraging another person to overthrow the government

selective incapacitation (12): restraining of freedom based on particular criteria such as level of crime seriousness or prison space availability

self-defense (10): a defense in which a person uses force against another person in a way that would normally constitute a criminal act, but the actor is justified in the use of this force because it was necessary for self-protection

sexual assault (6): a more expansive term than rape and involves both unwanted sexual penetration but also includes uninvited sexual touching and lewd behavior

sexual contact (6): a criminal charge of touching sexual areas of a person's body

simple assault (7): the use of threats to place another person in fear of life or safety

sine qua non (2): Latin meaning "but for"; a concept in criminal law that says that one action could not have occurred but for the occurrence of another action

Smith Act (8): a statute that criminalized sedition

social contract (1): an agreement between citizens and the state where citizens give up some freedom in exchange for the state protecting them

social solidarity (1): sense of belonging to the community

solicitation (9): when one person tries to convince another person to commit a specific crime

specific deterrence (12): punishment that prevents defendants from committing future criminal wrongdoing

specific intent (2): the purpose to perform a particular prohibited act that is concerned with the outcome or result

standard of review (1): process by which the courts rule whether a law violates the equal protection clause of the Fourteenth Amendment of the United States Constitution

stand your ground approach (10): approach under which a person is under no legal duty to retreat before utilizing force as a form of self-defense; see also *retreat rule*

stare decisis (1): binding principle that requires a judge to rule a current case based on precedent

statutory rape (2, 6): the sexual penetration—whether wanted or unwanted—of a person who is under a specified legal age; see also *age of consent*

stockbroker (8): a person who is entrusted with a client's money for investment purposes; see also *financial planner*

stock parking (8): takes place when an individual sells or transfers his or her shares of stock to another individual or organization

street crimes (7): any type of criminal activity that occurs in open, public spaces; some of these offenses are felonies, but many are misdemeanors or petty misdemeanors (violations or infractions)

street walkers (7): prostitutes who ply their trade openly in public places

strict liability (2): see *absolute liability*

strict scrutiny (1): the highest level of scrutiny under an equal protection claim that is applied to those laws that address fundamental rights and/or suspect class

strong-arm robbery (7): see *mugging*

substantial factor test (2): in situations where there may be two or more potential causes of some harm the courts will employ this test to determine which of the causes was more likely to have contributed to the result

substantial steps (9): an affirmative act toward committing a crime that goes beyond merely preparing for the crime to be committed

surreptitious remaining (4): continuing to stay on property once the privilege to be on that property has expired

suspect class (1): group of individuals (i.e., race/ethnicity, national origin, and religion) upon which a law distinguishes where strict scrutiny is used to test whether the right of equal protection of the law is applied

tangible property (4): property, such as currency and household goods, that can be seen and touched and which has value in itself

tax fraud (8): affirmative act that constitutes an evasion or attempted evasion of tax liability

terrorism (8): the unlawful use of force and violence against persons or property to intimidate or coerce a government, the civilian population, or any segment thereof, in furtherance of political or social objectives

theft (4): the taking of someone else's property; see also *consolidated theft statutes*

theft by deception (4): obtaining the property of another by the use of dishonesty; see also *false pretenses*

theory of forms (1): immaterial essences that bring forth senses of right from wrong

third-party cyberstalking (8): cyberstalking activity in which the perpetrator does not engage in the harassing activity, but instead encourages others to stalk the victim over the Internet; see also *cyberstalking*

totality of the circumstances (11): an approach that takes everything into consideration in the assessment

transferred intent (2): applied in situations where the harm that was anticipated was not the harm that ultimately was achieved

treason (8): levying war against the United States or giving aid and comfort to enemies of the United States

truth in sentencing (12): defendants serve most (75-85%) of their sentence per state statute

two-witness rule (8): requirement that a conviction for treason result from either the testimony of two witnesses or a confession in open court; see also *treason*

underlying offense (9): intended but incomplete criminal act that is associated with inchoate crimes; also called the target offense

Unlawful Internet Gambling Enforcement Act (8): federal law passed in 2006 that specifically prohibits all forms of Internet gambling in the United States

upward departure (12): decision to sentence the defendant with a higher sentence than that suggested by the sentencing guidelines

USA PATRIOT Act (8): passed in response to the 9/11 terrorist attacks which attempts to give the government the tools and abilities needed to detect, prevent, and punish terrorist acts

utilitarian theory (12): punishment theory that addresses the greater good for the greater amount of people through preventing future criminal wrongdoing

utmost resistance (6): the victim used all of his or her physical faculties to defend against an attack

vagrancy (7): existing with no visible means of support; may be applied to homeless people or those otherwise living on the streets

vandalism (4): damaging or injuring someone's personal property

vicarious criminal liability (3): to be held responsible or blameworthy for the criminal acts of another; see also *complicity* and *derivative liability*

void for vagueness doctrine (1): principle that voids a law that violates due process because it is so loosely defined that "a person of ordinary intelligence" does not know what behaviors violate the law

voluntary act (2): action that is a conscious choice

voluntary intoxication (11): the defendant cannot use the intoxication defense if he or she becomes intoxicated within his or her control

voluntary manslaughter (5): intentional killings absent malice aforethought; deaths resulting from "heat of passion" actions, or in response to adequate provocation

wheel conspiracy (9): conspiracy in which a primary leader acts as a hub and engages in all of the separate dealings with each party to the conspiracy, who act as spokes; see also *conspiracy, chain conspiracy*

white collar crime (8): crimes that involve the use of a violator's position of significant power, influence, or trust for personal or organizational gain; see also *abuse of trust crime*

willful blindness (2): an attempt to make oneself unaware of some fact or to deliberately avoid confirming a fact

withdrawal exception (10): allows for the use of self-defense by an initial aggressor if that person has completely removed or extracted themselves from an incident involving physical force

INDEX